CHARLES E. KANY

American-Spanish Euphemisms

UNIVERSITY OF CALIFORNIA PRESS

1960 BERKELEY AND LOS ANGELES

University of California Press
Berkeley and Los Angeles, California
Cambridge University Press
London, England
© 1960 by The Regents of the University of California
Library of Congress Catalog Card Number: 60-11847
Printed in the United States of America

PREFACE

The purpose of this book is to offer a workable body of classified linguistic material exemplifying euphemistic tendencies on various levels of American Spanish, with special reference to popular speech, where most changes have taken place. Some of the euphemisms coincide with those of peninsular Spanish, but the majority of them are new formations that have arisen on American soil and are unfamiliar to the average Spaniard. The speech of any typical Spanish American or a page of typical Spanish-American literature bears witness to a new spirit, new connotations, new gradations of meaning and feeling that may differ not only from normal peninsular usage but also from region to region according to shifting environment and modes of life in the eighteen Spanish-speaking republics.

A euphemism is the means by which a disagreeable, offensive, or fear-instilling matter is designated with an indirect or softer term. Euphemisms satisfy a linguistic need. For his own sake as well as that of his hearers, a speaker constantly resorts to euphemisms in order to disguise an unpleasant truth, veil an offense, or palliate indecency. Hence the frequency of euphemisms on nearly all levels of communication, from lofty literary style to slang and cant. To be sure, usage varies, as in other aspects of language, not only with time and place but also with social class. The populace may resort to euphemisms more generally for reasons of superstition; the cultured are inclined to do so for reasons of delicacy, urbanity, decency, or even hypocrisy. Furthermore, if a euphemism falls from careful and decorous speech into a lower style of expression, it easily loses its euphemistic quality and will then be avoided by careful speakers. However, no speaker can avoid euphemisms completely. They accompany him from the cradle to the grave.

Not a little of the linguistic importance of euphemisms lies in their incessant creation and renewal when they become contaminated by a too direct relation with the unpleasant referent. Hence, too, any study of euphemisms can never be complete.

Often the taboo is rendered inoffensive with a humorous twist of speech. Such substitutions are surely euphemistic even though a pure euphemism may be said to differ from a humorous locution in that its intent is primarily not jocose.

The utility of euphemisms is occasionally questioned. While they help to overcome some difficulties, they may create others. A moralist might aver that euphemisms undermine morality by veiling the truth, by concealing ugliness, by palliating vice and crime. However, such thinkers have found few followers. In modern times speakers do not generally protest against euphemisms of decency, though they may frown upon some euphemisms of superstition and of delicacy. Normally, euphemisms are not thought of as a necessary evil but rather as a legitimate means of gracious communication with our fellow men.

Euphemisms may bring about changes in meaning and may alternately enrich and impoverish vocabulary. If the old sense remains beside the new, then the semantic domain has been increased. However, if the original meaning disappears completely, then the euphemism will soon cease to function as such and will have to be replaced, with a consequent loss to vocabulary. The latter is true rather of primitive euphemisms of superstition than of more modern euphemisms of delicacy or decency.

Euphemisms are achieved in various ways. They may completely omit the offensive term, alter its form, substitute for it some general term, or translate it into a foreign tongue. The listener must usually supply something to clarify the referent: he comes half way and therefore can hardly take offense.

Euphemisms may be classified either according to the various linguistic processes involved or according to the motive that induced the change. This second method of classification will be followed in the present discussion. The examples will be grouped under euphemisms of superstition (chap. i), of delicacy (chaps. ii, iii, iv, v), and of decency (chaps. vi and vii).

The illustrative material presented in this book derives from several sources: (*a*) many hundreds of informants whom I consulted on my numerous field trips to Spanish-American countries over a period of twenty-five years, (*b*) scores of native consultants among students and instructors at the University of California, (*c*) the lexicographical works and authoritative monographs which I mention in my text, and (*d*) regional literature that confirms observed oral usage of the terms I discuss.

The social level and the geographical limits of each expression are indicated as far as our present knowledge permits. The term *standard* (or its abbreviation *std.*) is used here to mean the general Spanish norm of today (formerly often inaccurately referred to as *Castilian*); that is, Spanish of a high and rather uniform level as found in literary style and as used by cultured speakers in formal or careful discourse, without reference to geographical background. The *familiar standard* (*fam. std.*) applies to a freer, quite informal level of speech, still rather homogeneous, used by educated speakers in unconstrained daily conversation, particularly in Spain (peninsular Spanish). Below these two levels are the substandard modes known as *popular, vulgar, rustic,* and *cant* (convicts' and thieves' jargon).

The so-called *standard* is often associated with peninsular academic usage. However, forms so indicated may be current not only in Spain but also in much of America. Difficulties in classification and nomenclature arise from the fact that each Spanish-American country may in many cases have its own high-level norms used by the local cultured. However, above such regional norms native speakers generally recognize an *ideal norm* valid for all Spanish America as well as for all Spain. This ideal norm (for the most part the peninsular academic standard) is regarded by most Spanish Americans as a unifying force, a model of common reference for all Spanish speakers, although for most purposes they may prefer their local norm. The influence of the ideal norm is felt in varying degrees, depending on place, time, and social level. Spanish-American writers in particular favor the ideal norm when they aim at a wider circle of readers. Popular local terms should be studied in relationship to local norms rather than to the academic or general norm. Nevertheless, the ideal norm (the so-called *standard*) is often indicated in the text beside the local word not necessarily as a reference to a linguistic process or as a measuring rod but merely to remind the student what the corresponding ideal norm is considered to be.

As for geographical limits, a word that is known to be current in more

than four or five countries may for our purposes be called "rather general."
The important aspect of the present work is not a record of minutely exact
socioeconomic levels or geographical limits, but rather a workable classification of a large body of examples of euphemistic change. As will be seen,
many of the words are used only in a single country or by a certain class
within that country or subdivision of it, but many of them cross a
political boundary and may be current in some region of Spain. Words
discussed are not *ipso facto* to be regarded as local standard usage. Many
of them are alternates, or merely the least common of such alternates.
They find a place here because they embody some euphemistic change.

Being the first comprehensive volume of its kind dealing with American-
Spanish usage, the present work will no doubt be found lacking in many
details that must await years of further study. Meanwhile it should prove
helpful to students and teachers of Spanish language and literature, to
translators and travelers, to folklorists and anthropologists, as a reference
book for linguistic phenomena not readily available elsewhere.

CONTENTS

ABBREVIATIONS OF
GEOGRAPHICAL NAMES

Ant	Antilles	Pan	Panama
Arg	Argentina	Para	Paraguay
Bol	Bolivia	PR	Puerto Rico
CA	Central America	RP	River Plate region
Col	Colombia		(Arg, Para, Urug)
CR	Costa Rica	SA	South America
Ec	Ecuador	Salv	El Salvador
Guat	Guatemala	SD	Santo Domingo
Hond	Honduras	Tab	Tabasco
Mex	Mexico	Tex	Texas
New Mex	New Mexico	Urug	Uruguay
Nic	Nicaragua	Ven	Venezuela

I SUPERSTITION

A euphemism of superstition is closely allied to the primitive sense of taboo. Because of the supposedly magic relationship between a word and its referent, the person who uttered a word, or merely knew it, was thought to have a degree of power over its referent. The spoken word, containing the essence of the referent, could attract and irritate the thing or being designated, with possibly fatal results to the speaker. Such beliefs led speakers to avoid the names of gods, demons, tribal chiefs, priests, and supposedly perilous things and beings (including all harmful animals, dangerous diseases, death, and the like) through modification of their form or through substitution. Some of these attitudes have continued to the present day among many peoples who designate as superstition any belief or usage not consistent with their particular concept of reality. Such superstitions are the number 13: the fear of having thirteen guests at table, Friday the thirteenth (Spanish peoples consider Tuesday ominous: "el martes, no te cases ni te embarques"); the wearing of charms and amulets: a buckeye or horse chestnut, a lead or silver ring, a horseshoe, and red flannels; knocking on wood or keeping one's fingers crossed to avert evil and insure success.

WORDS FOR 'DEVIL'

From time immemorial many Spanish speakers have avoided the words *diablo* and *demonio* for reasons of superstition. This is attested by the proverb "en nombrando al *ruin de Roma,* luego asoma" 'speak of the *devil* and he soon appears.' The Spanish euphemism *ruin de Roma* 'rascal of Rome' has been further softened in Spanish America to *rey de Roma* 'king of Rome' ("nombrando al *rey de Roma,* pronto asoma"), thus elevating the rank of the disturbing referent and retaining the alliteration, which helps to explain the original *ruin de Roma.*

Sometimes the word is omitted completely, as in standard *poseso* 'possessed' for *poseído por el demonio,* and in *ayudado* (Col) 'assisted' for *hechicero* or *endemoniado.* Sometimes a slight change in sound suffices for it to escape the taboo. Thus, peninsular *diacho, dianche, diantre,* and *diantres* (with final *-s* frequent in exclamations and oaths [*BDH,* II, 214; see also Spitzer and Gamillscheg, p. 107], as in "A ese muchacho se le ha metido el *diantres,"* CR: Gagini), *diájoles* and *diájule* (*BDH,* II, 211), *demontre(s), demonche(s), demónchico(s), demongris,* etc., have additional euphemistic forms in America. Among these are *diache,* which is general, as in "*¡Diache* con las muchachas!" (PR), "más que el *diache"* (SD: *BDH,* V, 186); *diajo, diaño* (Ven: Rosenblat, 373); *diango* (Cuba), with the popular and widespread *-ango* suffix; *diasque* (Chile, Hond, Mex); *diastre* (influence of *desastre?*) and *diastres* (Col, where *diablura* may become *diastrura*), as in "Ese muchacho es un *diastre"* and "*¡Qué diastres!"* (Tobón); *demónchiros* (Col), and probably others.

A euphemistic combination of *Dios* and *diablo* we find in the New Mexican oath forms *pordioble(s)* and *pordiobligo(s)* (*BDH,* II, 52, 214; Old Spanish *¡pardiobre!* was used with the value of *¡rediez!*). The ending *-igo* in *pordiobligo(s)* may well be a new euphemistic deformation, a masking with the verbal form *obligo* (*ibid.,* p. 214).

Sometimes taboo *diablo* is replaced by another word of vague or general import, such as *malo, enemigo, feo,* or by a word related to certain qualities of the referent, such as familiar standard *patas* (*pata* 'foot or leg of an animal'), *pateta, patillas.* These three epithets stem from the general belief that the devil when appearing in human form was somewhat lame and sometimes showed the foot of a horse or goat, as well as horns and tail, etc. Other forms based on *pata* are general el *patudo,* with the suffix *-udo* expressing an exaggerated and deprecatory sense of the primitive word; el *patica* (Ec: Toscano), in which the diminutive suffix *-illas* has been replaced by the diminutive *-ica.* The form *catete* (Chile) seems to be a slightly altered *pateta,* as in the expressions "saber uno más que *catete,*" "ser más astuto o hábil que *catete,*" and "ser más feo que *catete*" (std. "más feo que *Picio*"). Popular Chilean *chambeco* (as in "Compaire, mire el *chambeco,* la cola lo bien relarga," ap. Román) is possibly influenced by *chambón* 'awkward.' Popular Mexican *chamuco* ("se lo llevó *chamuco*"), however, is probably related to *chamuscar* 'to scorch,' although Duarte postulates an Aztec *chamoco* 'evil spirit.'

References to other qualities of the devil are seen in the popular euphemisms *el chucuto* (Ven) 'bobtailed'; *el coludo* or *el rabudo* 'longtailed'; *el cachudo* (std. *cornudo*) 'the horned one,' from American-Spanish *cacho* (std. *cuerno*) 'horn'; *el matoco* or *matucho* (Chile, especially in certain convents) from *matar* 'to kill,' since the devil was the first *matón* 'manslayer'; *el quemado* (Mex) 'the black one' (lit. 'burned'; cf. *chamuco,* above) and *el colorado* 'the red one' (Ec), since the devil may be pictured black (cf. *mandinga,* below) or red, as in "Tiene trato con er Colorao ... El Colorao era el diablo" (Cuadra, p. 194); *tapatarro(s)* (Chile) 'garbage-can lid'(?) because of his filthy undercover activities, as in "se lo llevó *tapatarro,*" or as an adjective in "gringo *tapatarro*" (Román); from older standard *cabrón* 'he-goat' > 'devil' (and from *cachudo*) derives a long list of euphemisms, such as *Cachica, Cabica, Cachafaz, Caplán, Capracio,* and *Carramplán* (Rosenblat, p. 374).

In Colombia (Cuervo, § 672) the exclamation *con quinientos diablos* is softened by saying *con quinientos dia ... caballo* (= *de a caballo*); that is, after pronouncing the first syllable of *diablos,* the speaker bethinks himself of the taboo and suddenly changes the word.

Often a foreign word is substituted for the taboo term. Since for the speaker a foreign word normally bears few associations with the unpleasant referent, he can use it with relative impunity. In Spanish America such borrowings are frequent from the local Indian languages, or from African tongues brought in by the early slaves. Often the foreign word has a more general sense and thus avoids the taboo. For instance, *mandinga* (reduced form *mingas* in Colombia), originally meaning a Negro from western Sudan, has in many regions acquired the sense of *demonio* (as well as *tonto*) and also of 'elf, goblin, witchery,' as in "Parece *mandinga* que no puedo dar con las llaves; tienes *mandinga* en el cuerpo, muchacho— todo lo rompes y desarreglas; me lleva *mandinga* cuando tal veo u oigo" (Arg: Granada); "tiene quien le ayude: el mismo *Mandinga*" (Ven: Gallegos, p. 80). In Colombia, *maldita sea* 'cursed be' often becomes *maldinga sea* (Uribe), then *maldingo sea* replaces *maldito sea* (Restrepo). In *mandinga sea* the euphemistic process is more radical and efficient: *maldita* is replaced by a foreign word related to it both semantically and phonetically (it contains the same assonance *a - í - a*).

Another term, probably of African origin, *candanga* (*candinga,* CA, Mex), in addition to its sense of *tonto,* now means *diablo* in expressions like "se lo llevó *candanga*" (CA, Cuba). Further euphemization is apparent in the use of *chandenguis* (Mex), as in "¡Era el mesmísimo *Chandenguis,* el Enemigo Malo que me llevaba por haber faltao al juramento!" (Anda, p. 103).

In general, heathen deities and gods of subjected tribes were considered to be evil spirits or demons, and various diseases were ascribed to their agency as living but imperceptible beings (modern microbes). One of the gods of the Antilles Indians was *Mabuya,* possibly meaning 'serpent' (Ortiz), whom the conquistadores, not understanding the new culture, identified with the devil or evil spirits. Today *mabuya* may be heard in Cuba in the sense of *diablo.* In Chile, *pillán,* of Mapuche origin (Lenz), meant a devil or a deity or some superior being who, the Araucanians claimed, caused thunder, lightning, and volcanic eruptions. In the interior of Peru, Quechua *supay* is used for *diablo.* In some regions it is believed that the *supay* may violate a woman, and the child born of that union is called *supaypaguagua* 'devil's son,' a word which is a grave insult. In northern Argentina *supay* or *zopay* or *zupay* appears as the name of the devil in folk tales and legends. In parts of Colombia, Chibcha *piranchico* is used for *demonio;* in Venezuela the word for the evil one may be *tijuy;* in the River Plate region it may be the Guaraní *añangá* or *anacuá.* Among other words registered for *diablo* are *cadejo* (CA) 'fantastic horned animal' especially in phrases like "me llevó el *cadejo,*" "le va a salir el *cadejo,*" or "más negro que el *cadejo*" (Correa, p. 62); *cuijen,* meaning specifically a person disguised as a devil who frightens children at public festivals, from Aztec *cuixin* meaning a dark-colored and spotted 'hawk' and a 'rogue'; *pericana* (Arg), *viruñas* (Valle del Cauca, Col: Tobón), *mañoco* (Riohacha, Col: Revollo), *piscuicas* (CR), *gualicho* (Arg), and *pingo* (Mex). Mexican *nagual,* from Nahuatl *nahualli* 'witch,' means a sorcerer who, with the aid of evil spirits can transform himself into a dog or a pig to roam the countryside doing mischief. Derivative *nagualizar* (or *nagualear*) means 'to steal, rob.'

The preceding words for 'evil spirits' express analogous but not identical ideas. Often in different regions of Spanish America one finds a great abundance of words to express the same fundamental idea with some slight variation of mode. In many cases it was this modal variation, rather than euphemistic considerations, that induced the multifarious local usage. So, in matters of witchcraft and the devil—in the River Plate region, for instance—the idea can be expressed either by standard *diablo* or by the Hispanized Pampa *gualicho,* or by the Guaraní *añangá,* or by African *mandinga* or Quechua *zopay.* In literary style and cultured speech the purely Spanish term is the norm; in familiar style, and especially in rural areas, one generally hears the terms of Indian or African origin. Thus, traditional Spanish superstition has in many regions received abundant accretions from Indian and Negro magic and enchantment.

NAMES OF ANIMALS

Many speakers avoid the names of certain animals, particularly such as are harmful or were thought originally to possess supernatural qualities. In Spain, especially in Andalusia, the word *culebra* (in some areas also *víbora*) 'snake' is by many still considered ominous (as attested by the saying "nombrar la *culebra* es traer desdichas") and is often replaced by a general term like *animal* or *bicha.* In Lima some persons substitute *serpiente* to avoid the evil effects of *culebra;* in Huánuco (Peru) Indians use Quechua *curu* or *curo* 'worm' lest the *culebra* if mentioned by name devour their chickens and eggs (Benvenutto, p. 81). Plath (p. 11) reports that in parts of Chile *culebra* is replaced by euphemistic Quechua *huacho* or *guacho* 'orphan,' which, particularly in the diminutive form *guachito,* is frequently applied as a term of endearment to motherless lambs and kids brought up in the home. Other terms of Indian origin are frequent, some of them indicating varying modes: *ampalagua* or *lampalagua* (RP) 'boa,' *birrí* (Col), *bocaracá* (CA), *boyé* (RP), *cantil* (Guat), *cencuate* or *zincuate* (Mex, Aztec *coatl* 'snake'), *cuaima* (Ven), *curigú* (Arg) 'boa,' *guata* (Col, Ven), *guayacana* (Ven), *güío* (Col), *istacuate* (Mex), *jubo* (Ant), *macaurel* (Col, Ven), *majá* (Ant), *mapaná* (Col), *mazacuate* (Mex, CA) 'boa,' *mica* and *micoate* (Mex), etc. Among Spanish appellations are euphemistic *boba* (Col) for *boa; cuatronarices* (Ven), because of the shape of the mouth, and others.

On hearing the word *culebra,* some Spaniards immediately respond with ¡*lagarto!* 'lizard' to counteract or forestall the evil effect. Spanish-American writers often resort to this typically Andalusian superstition to characterize or ridicule the Spaniard. In Quintana's *Mal agüero* (Guat) we read (p. 130): "—Sí patrón, pero es la verdá: onque son animales rispetan. Lo mismo son las *culebras.* —¡*Lagarto!* —¿También los lagartos, don Manuel? —No, yo digo así para cortar el mal agüero de la palabra *culebra.* —Ah, vaya." In Clemente Palma's *Crónicas* (Peru) is an interview with the Spanish bullfighter Belmonte (p. 154): "—El presidente ... es más mañoso que una *culebra.* —¡*Lagarto!* ¡*Lagarto!* —exclamó Belmonte despavorido, y no le pude sacar una palabra más."

Bullfighters, like all groups whose success in life depends on a multitude of unforeseeable causes and who therefore may feel themselves at the mercy of some mysterious power, are especially prone to all types of superstitious beliefs and practices. It is related that in a certain Madrid café where bullfighters were wont to forgather, the café owner, during a period of depression when the habitués were unable to settle their accounts, had the cups and glasses grotesquely adorned with painted serpents. This fearsome sight caused the superstitious bullfighters to scurry away without more ado. Shouting "¡Lagarto! ¡Largarto!" they never returned.

This superstition is the basis of the punning in the following passage from *Martín Fierro* (I, vv. 859–864): "Cuanto me vido acercar: / '¿*Quén vivore?*' [= ¿Quién vive?] preguntó; / '*Qué vívoras,*' [= *víboras* 'vipers, vixens'], dije yo; /'¡*Ha garto!*' [= ¡Haga alto! 'halt,' but recalling *lagarto*] me pegó el grito, / Y yo dije despacito ['in a low voice']: / '*Más lagarto serás vos*' [*lagarto* means also 'thief']."

The counteracting words *lagarto* and *contra* are used on other occasions when evil must be forestalled. It is often accompanied with this manual gesture: while the middle and ring fingers of the left hand are turned against the palm and held down with the thumb, the index and little finger are extended to represent horns (see fig. 1). This is called *hacer* (*la señal de*) *los cuernos,* occasionally *hacer la contraguiña* (Ven, Col), from French *guigne* 'bad luck.' The extended fingers thus represent the horseshoe, often accepted as an emblem of good luck, and possibly a wishbone. Many silver or coral amulets represent a hand in this position. The gesture is sometimes made openly, and sometimes surreptitiously with the hand kept in the pocket. Since the natural purpose of the horn is to form a resistant or protective surface or even a tool or weapon, it becomes symbolical of resistance to or protection against evil influences. With the hand so shaped one touches an iron or other metallic object, such as a watch chain, a coin, a button; and to bring good luck one may touch wood. Some persons carry a piece of wood on a metal chain so that they can touch either metal (to ward off evil) or wood (to bring good luck) according to the exigencies of the moment. The Argentinian novelist Manuel Gálvez writes in *La maestra normal* (I, 1, 21): "[El señor Galiani] ... llevaba ... en un bolsillo alto del chaleco, un enorme cronómetro de oro cuya cadena ... concluía en un surtido de medallas y de amuletos contra la *jettatura*." In Spain a superstitious person on meeting three priests together or on passing a one-eyed person will touch wood with the extended fingers as described above. In many regions the superstitious consider it bad luck to meet a priest in a public place, and they immediately touch iron. It is related that one day a priest on a Buenos Aires streetcar, overhearing a boy muttering about his ill luck, pulled out a pistol and said to him: "Che, tocá fierro." In Venezuela it is considered bad luck to meet a one-eyed person, to keep a monkey in the house, to look at a tiger's skin, or to meet a funeral procession (Rosenblat, p. 137), but the evil may be forestalled with the counteracting gesture.

The gesture has been observed on the following occasions. In Barranquilla (Colombia) a young man on hearing his companion tell a falsehood, extended his index and little finger against a flat surface and said "me aislo"; on hearing the untruth repeated he held his nose and ducked his head, saying, "Yo me hundo para que pase." In Lima (Peru) one speaker remarked "Ahí viene un pesado," made the gesture, and added "¡contra!" so that the approaching bore would turn and go in another direction. A young lady, reluctant to dance with a young man she noticed at a distance, made the gesture surreptitiously and added, "Lagarto, que no venga él."

In Mexico when an actor pronounced the word *verdugo* 'hangman,' his interlocutor made the gesture and touched wood. In an Argentinian film one of the characters makes the gesture and extends his hand toward the ragamuffins stoning his coach.

In many instances of this sort the speakers, particularly women, would cross themselves (*santiguarse*) to ward off evil or to protect themselves against it.

The classic example of taboo animal names is that of the swift and ferocious weasel. Because of this animal's bloodthirsty habit of destroying poultry, many superstitions grew up around it. In the Middle Ages it was thought that the weasel conceived through the ear and gave birth through the mouth, as is attested in the Spanish saying "La comadreja pare por la boca y empréñase por la oreja," which in a figurative sense may mean that things come to us through the ear and are bruited abroad through the mouth. Latin *mustela* 'weasel' and its derivatives were frequently replaced by terms designed to flatter and pacify the animal, if it had to be mentioned at all: French *belette* (dim. of *bel* 'beautiful'), Italian *donnola* (dim. of *donna* 'lady'), Portuguese *doninha* (dim. of *dona*), Spanish *comadreja* (dim. of *comadre*) and many others: *paniquesa* (Aragón), from *pan* and *queso,* alluding to the weasel's whitish-yellow breast and its brownish-red back, *papalba* (central Asturias) 'white breast,' *donicella* (Asturias), *bonuca, monuca, villería* (Santander), and dozens of other forms (Menéndez Pidal, *Orígenes del español,* pp. 417–424). In Santander some believe the beast can be exorcized by addressing it thus: *"Villería* [= *comadreja*], Dios te bendiga de noche y día" (Pereda, *La puchera*). In Spanish America the common *comadreja* is often called *onza, oncita, collareja,* and *huroncito;* other varieties often have names of Indian origin, such as Quechua *chucuri* (Col, Ec), Quechua *unchuchuco* (Peru), Aztec *cuzatli* (S Mex), Mapuche (?) *llaca* (Chile) (see Santamaría, III, 524; Malaret, *BICC*).

The fox, Old Spanish *gulpeja* (Lat. *vulpes, vulpecula*), was also feared by peasants as ill-omened because of its predatory incursions in poultry yards. Its name was early euphemized with *raposa* (appearing in Juan Ruiz alongside archaic *gulpeja*) apparently from *rabo* 'tail' and meaning the 'bushy-tailed one.' By the Golden Age, *raposa* in turn was losing ground to its new substitute, *zorra.*

Another fear-inspiring animal was the mouse. It may be questioned, however, whether fear of it led to the adoption in Chile and Argentina of the Mapuche word *laucha* (dim. *lauchita*). Perhaps speakers tried to avoid the vagueness of standard *ratón,* since the normally augmentative suffix *-ón* seldom serves as a diminutive (*rata* 'rat'—*ratón* 'mouse'); in fact, *rata* in Chile often means 'mouse' and *ratón* may mean 'rat.' In other regions of America the difficulty is remedied by using *ratoncito* or *ratoncillo,* since the *-cito* and *-cillo* suffixes are unmistakably diminutive. Other words are *mineros* or *mineritos* (Arg: *BAAL,* X), *desmeño* (Mex), *pericote* (Chile, Arg, Ec, Peru) 'rat,' from *Pero,* old form of *Pedro* with diminutive *-ico* and augmentative and deprecatory *-ote*. Sometimes local Indian tongues provide a substitute, and there are varieties of rats and mice: *ucush* (interior of Ancash, Peru: *BAAL,* X, 203) 'common mouse,' *huarén* or *guarén* or *guareno* (Chile) 'water rat,' *cururo* (Chile) 'black field rat,' *chululo* (Chile), rare *degu* (Chile), *guachero* (Ven) 'black rat,' *guayabito* (Ant) 'common mouse,' *quimichín* (Mex) 'common mouse.'

The ubiquitous American carrion-eating 'turkey buzzard,' differing from the European *buitre* 'vulture,' has a host of local appellations, most of them of Indian origin: *caracara, carranco,* or *carrancho* (RP, Bol, Peru), *cute* and *tincute* (CA), *chícora* (Col), *chombo* (Campeche, Mex), *chulo* (RP, Bol, Peru, Col, Ven), *chupillote* (New Mex, cf. *zopilote,* with associative interference of *chupar*), *galembo* (Col, Ven), *guala* or *guale* (Col), *güisco* (Ec), *huarahuau* (Trujillo, Peru), *jote* (Arg, Chile, Peru), *noneco* (Pan, CR), *nopo* (Veracruz, Tabasco), *oripopo* (Mex), *queluy* (Chile, from Mapuche, but *jote* is more general), *shingo* (Ancash, Peru), *suyunto* (Peru), *urubú, iribú,* or *(iribú) acabiray* 'sheared head' (RP, from Guaraní), *zamuro* (Col, Ven), *zonchiche* 'redheaded' (CA, from Aztec) or *zoncho* (CR), *zopilote* and *zope* (Mex, CA, from Aztec); others are mostly Spanish, some of them of euphemistic tinge, as the more general *ciudadano* 'citizen,' *cuervo* 'crow,' *viuda* 'widow,' *gallinazo* 'big hen,' *gallote* 'big rooster,' *aura* (from the Latin *cathartes aura*), but the form *aura tiñosa* (Cuba) 'scabby' is certainly not euphemistic. Euphemistic *gualgura* is the name given in parts of Ecuador and Colombia (where *guala* is a kind of 'turkey buzzard') to a phantom chick (some think it is a hen) that utters hair-raising noises during its nocturnal wanderings and flights, playing havoc in poultry yards with its peeps and its blighting breath (see Cornejo). Among other euphemistic words denoting various birds of prey are *aurora* (Guat) 'dawn'; *bailarín* (Chile, Peru) 'dancer'; *batista* (Cuba); *bebe-humo* (Col) 'smoke drinker,' because this bird flies very low over recently burned fields in search of serpents and small mammals.

Spanish-American *chancho* 'pig' has a curious history. From time immemorial the use of pig flesh was prohibited to the Jews as unclean, and the prohibition was adopted in the Mohammedan law. Spanish *puerco* (Lat. *porcus*) and its congeners *cochino* and *marrano* fell into early disrepute. In the older language no one mentioned the unclean *puerco* without immediately adding a propitiatory "(hablando) con perdón" or "con acatamiento" or "con reverencia" or something similar. Cervantes ridiculed this custom when he wrote "un porquero ... andaba recogiendo una manada de puercos (que, *sin perdón,* así se llaman)" (*Don Quijote,* I, 2). Sometimes the word *puerco* was replaced by a metaphoric euphemism like "el de la vista baja." By the end of the sixteenth century the proper name *Sancho* (< Lat. *sanctius*) had come into use as a nickname for the lowly animal, and the conquistadores brought the term to America. Then while another euphemism, *cerdo* (from *cerda* 'shag, bunch of bristles'), was cropping up in Spain, *sancho* developed into *chancho* in most of America (see Corominas). The change of *s-* to *ch-*, consonantal dilation, is found in many endearing nicknames: *Chofi* for *Sofía, Chepa* for *Josefa, Chus* for *Jesús, Chano* for *Feliciano* (pronounced with *seseo*), etc. In some rural regions the mention of *chancho* is, in polite speech, still followed by a propitiatory phrase, as "está el chico gordo como un *chancho, dispensando la palabra*" (Peru: Benvenutto, p. 80).

The diminutive *cochino* (originally 'suckling pig') derives from the interjection *coch(e)* or *cuch(e)* used in calling pigs, an onomatopoetic imitation of a grunt, probably an early euphemism. Spanish variant *cuchi* was adopted in many regions of America as a substitute for *puerco*. Later when *cuchi* was lost in Castilian, missionaries began to register it erroneously as of Indian origin. It in turn seems to have fallen into disrepute among careful speakers. Possibly its avoidance in polite discourse accounts for the dislike among Mexicans of the onomatopoetic verb *cuchichear* 'to whisper.' Frenk (p. 142) reports: "Cuando dos personas *cuchichean* entre sí se dice que *se aconsejan.*" However, this may also be a euphemistic attempt to avoid Mexican *chiche,* itself originally a euphemistic Indian borrowing to soften Spanish *teta* or *pezón* 'teat' or 'nipple.' In Piura (Peru) vague *ave* 'bird' euphemizes *cerdo* or *puerco,* as in "Entraron *las aves* y pisotearon todo el sombrío" (Hildebrandt, p. 262). In parts of Colombia *runcho* 'a kind of opossum' is used as a euphemism for *cerdo.*

In some regions, general *pajarito* 'little bird' may indicate any bug or insect (PR), particularly a flying insect (Piura, Peru). In Peru, in rustic speech the words *piajeno* or *especie* may be used euphemistically in place of *asno* or *burro,* as in "Venía de mi chacra, en mi *piajeno,* perdonándome la palabra" and "en su *especie* iba montado, con perdón sea dicho"

(Benvenutto, p. 80). The propitiatory phrase is common in rustic speech, as in "los ladrones ... se nos llevan lo que pueden: el güey, la vaca o el *burrito, perdonando sus mercedes*" (Mex: Ángulo, p. 96). In parts of Colombia, the euphemistic *María casquito* is used for *burra,* and in Arequipa (Peru), the softer *mariano,* applied to persons, sometimes replaces *burro.*

In many regions the *lechuza* 'owl' is considered a bird of ill omen. The Spanish word is often replaced by words of Indian origin, some of them representing different local modes, others perhaps for euphemistic considerations. Among the terms registered are *alilicuco* (RP), *borococo* (Ven), *coa* (Chile), *cocorote* (Ven), *cuscungo* (Col, Ec), *chucho* or *chuncho* (Chile), *estiquirín* (Hond), *estucurú* (CR), *guacaba* (Ven), *morrocó* and *múcaro* (Ec), *ñacurutú* (RP), *ñacurubú* (Bol), *pava, pavita, mabita* (Ven), and others. Although many of them are postulated as deriving from Indian languages, a large proportion of them are probably onomatopoetic formations from the cry of the owl, particularly *chucho,* or *chuncho, cocorote, guacaba,* and the like. That the owl purportedly presages misfortune and death is attested by the sayings: "*Cocorote* canta, indio muere; no lo creo, pero sucede" (Ven: Santamaría); "Si la *pavita* canta, alguien se muere. Esto no es cierto, pero sucede" (Ven: Rosenblat, p. 131); "El *chuncho* canta, el indio muere; no será cierto, pero sucede" (Chile: Malaret). By extension, *chuncho* is applied in Chile to a person who brings bad luck by predicting misfortune and disaster. One frequently hears "no sea *chuncho*" (Plath, p. 11). Derivatives are *achoncharse* 'convertirse en brujo o serlo para hacer daño a la jente' (Lenz), *achunchar* 'frustrar a uno en sus proyectos o pretensiones, dejándolo un tanto corrido y avergonzado ...' (Román), as in "Cosa que todo el mundo sabe es que hay jugadores que, cuando están de mala suerte, creen a pie juntillas que hay algo que les está *achunchando*" (Hübner, ap. Medina). Derivatives of Venezuelan *pava* and *mabita* are *pavoso* ("Ese hombre es *pavoso*"), *pava ciriaca* ("Ese pobre hombre tiene una *pava ciriaca*"), *mabitoso, enmabitar* ("Lo *enmabitaron*," Rosenblat, p. 131). Because of its resemblance to a bird of prey, a black butterfly is considered in Venezuela to be of ill omen. Thus one may hear: "Fulano de tal es mi *mariposa negra;* me cayó la *bicha negra;* me persigue la *tara* (= mariposa) *negra*" (Rosenblat, p. 135).

DISEASES

Mention of certain diseases (the plague, leprosy, tuberculosis, epilepsy, etc.) has often been avoided by some persons who feel that such phenomena are unnatural and are caused by evil spirits. The evil spirit is irritated when the name of the disease is mentioned; if it is referred to at all it must be in vague or flattering terms lest the spirit take offense. Civilization has rejected most such beliefs but cannot eradicate completely a certain mysterious fear that still lingers. It is related that during an epidemic among the Spanish army in the African campaign of 1859, soldiers dared not mention the name of the disease for fear of irritating the evil being that was responsible for the scourge. In speaking of a stricken comrade, they would say simply "Tiene eso que corre" (Núñez de Arce, *Miscelánea,* Barcelona, 1886, p. 155).

A malign erysipelas that caused great ravage between the tenth and sixteenth centuries, particularly among wounded soldiers, was called *fuego sacro* or *sagrado,* and also *fuego de San Antón* 'Saint Anthony's fire,' *mal de San Antón* and *fuego de San Marcial,* as a sort of invocation to these saints.

Other Spanish euphemisms for dread diseases are *mal de San Lázaro* for *elefancía* 'elephantiasis' and *lepra* 'leprosy'; *mal de la rosa* for *pelagra; morbo regio* 'royal disease' for *ictericia* 'jaundice,' cf. *buenamoza* (Col); *morbo* (or *mal*) *francés* or *gálico* (whence the proper name Galindo as a euphemism) for *sífilis.* The last-mentioned disease is sometimes referred to by vague *mal de los cristianos* (cf. English 'social disease'), *enfermedad secreta* or simply *enfermedad, avería* 'damage' and *avariosis,* strange *gato* (Ven) 'cat' and vulgar *chinche* 'bedbug' (Arg, where the word may mean also 'gonorrhea'). The sufferer is *enfermo,* vulgar *meado de la araña* (Guat: Sandoval: cf. pop. peninsular *picado de la tarántula*), *quemado* (Arequipa, Peru), *echado en banda* (SD: Patín), *averiado,* etc., and is familiarly referred to in phrases like "le dieron una cogida" (Cuba: Rodríguez).

In ancient times, epilepsy was attributed to the influence of the gods or of evil spirits, and by the Romans it was called *morbus sacer* 'sacred disease.' In Spanish it is known as *morbo comicial* (Lat. *morbus comitialis*) and by another euphemism: *mal de corazón.* In many Spanish-American countries the euphemism has been shortened to *el mal,* as in "Fulano tiene *el mal"* and "En cada efecto de luna ['lunar phase'] le da *el mal* a la hija de la cocinera" (Sandoval). In Chile, *el baile de San Vito* 'Saint Vitus dance' is known as *el baile* or *el mal del zambito* 'of the little mulatto,' a case of popular etymology, *San Vito,* in rapid speech, being pronounced as *sambito.*

For tuberculosis and its sufferers we find the following euphemisms: *afectado del pecho* or simply *afectado,* as in "murió *afectado"* (Mex: León, II, 14); *calenturiento* 'feverish' and *tener calentura* 'to have a fever' may mean 'to have tuberculosis' (Chile); *dañado* 'damaged' (Col, CA; cf. *dañado* 'leper,' Canary Islands), as in "Leoncio está *dañado* por lo que pronto se va a morir" (Guat: Sandoval); *delgadito* 'very thin' (Mex); general *enfermo del pecho; heticarse* (from *hético* 'consumptive') 'to contract tuberculosis' (Ant), as in "su hermana *se heticó* a los veinte años" (SD: Patín); *maleficio* 'witchcraft, spell' (rural Col); *malograrse* 'to have an untimely end' (*ibid.*)*; picado del pecho* (Ant) or simply *picado,* deriv. *picarse* (*del pecho*), as in "la pobre joven *se picó* a causa del excesivo trabajo" (SD: Patín), and in familiar speech also "le ha *picado* el tigre" or "se halla en el 111," the symbolic number for tuberculosis being 111: "comienza *con uno,* sigue *con uno* y termina *con uno"* (*ibid.*)*; tener paletero* or *paletera* and *gusanos paleteros* 'T.B. germs' (Ec: Cornejo), from *paleta* (indicating the shape of the bacilli), as in "De improviso se incorporó para toser. Una bocanada de sangre encharcó el piso ... —Está jodido, compá— exclamó el cholo —Ésa es la *paletera"* (A. Ortiz, p. 104); *tener susto* 'to have a scare' (Jauja, Peru); *tener T.B.C.* (in doctors' parlance), as in "después se supo que su enfermedad era una *T.B.C.* en estado avanzado" (Chile: Castro, p. 299); *tisis* in *estar tisis* (similarly, *estar sífilis, estar parálisis*) for *estar tísico* in Santo Domingo, where sufferers camouflage their illness by claiming to be *enfermos del corazón* 'heart patients' (Jiménez, p. 125); *yerba* 'herb, poison administered in food' (rural Col), as in "Aquí no hay nadie tuberculoso. Todo es maleficio y *yerba"* (ap. Flórez, *Habla,* p. 203). Furthermore, one may avoid verbal reference by merely tapping one's chest or shoulder, or by touching the back of one's interlocutor.

In some parts of Peru, *paludismo* 'malaria' is sometimes called *chucho* (an onomatopoetic Quechua formation denoting the shivering caused by the sensation of cold); in Colombia it is sometimes called *fríos* or *fiebres* or *fríos y fiebres.* In Mexico, *cocoliscle* or *cocoliste* (Aztec *cocolizcli*) is occasionally used for any epidemic disease, and especially for typhus, which has practically disappeared today in the capital. To replace Spanish *alhorre,* Mexicans often employ Aztec *chincual* in referring to this itching skin eruption common in infants, especially in the posterior muscles. Figuratively, *chincual* is used to denote a love of hilarity, as in "Parece que no le curaron el *chincual"* (Santamaría) said of frivolous persons inordinately fond of revelry and merrymaking (cf. our 'to have ants in one's pants'). Derivatives are the adjectives *chincualero* and *chincualudo,* the noun *chincualeo,* and the verb *chincualear.* Standard *ictericia* 'jaundice' is euphemized by *buenamoza* (Col: Uribe), *panadizo* 'felon' by *doncella* (Col, Ven, Andalusia), and *úlcera* 'ulcer' by *lora* (Ec, Col, Ven, PR) and *lorenza* (Ven).

In some regions even the apparently innocuous *enfermo* 'sick' (but cf. *enfermo* as a euphemism for *vicioso* 'depraved' and for *sifilítico*) is avoided by using: *estar atrasado* 'to be retarded' (RP), *imposible* (Cauca Valley, Col), *inferior* and rustic *injerior* (Boyaca and Cundinamarca, Col), as in "amanecí *injerior"* (Tobón), *estar muy mucho* 'to be deathly ill' (*ibid.*), *estar uno de gravedad* 'to be critically ill', and *tener demoras* (CR) 'to be ill, weak' (lit. 'retarded, delayed'). To euphemize the noun *operación* 'operation' the expression *intervención quirúrgica* 'surgical intervention' is current everywhere; 'to commit a mental patient' is no longer *encerrar al loco* but *internar al demente,* perhaps through the French.

Of a person depressed physically or morally it is sometimes said in Mexico: "él está *achahuistlado"* or "le cayó el *chahuistle* (or *chagüiscle*)," from Aztec *chiahuiztle* 'humor' and 'plant disease' (perhaps caused by excessive humidity) and *chiahuitl* 'plant louse (of corn).'

THE EVIL EYE

In many countries the superstitious still believe that certain individuals possess an evil eye and can inflict injury, in some magical way, merely with a glance (std. *mal de ojo, aojo,* or *aojamiento;* pop. *ojeo* for *aojo,* and *ojear* for *aojar*). To refer to this *maleficio* 'witchcraft,' superstitious persons in America frequently use the more general and euphemistic noun *daño* 'harm,' as in "a este muchacho le echaron *daño,"* and the verb *dañar,* as in "¡te digo que (ella) lo tiene *dañao!"* (Azuela, *Mala Yerba,* p. 125). Also current are *guiña* (Col, Ven) from French *guigne,* as in "la *guiña* cayó sobre la familia" (Rosenblat, p. 134); Venezuelan *mayén,* as in "Le echaron *mayén* a la casa para que se fuera la gente lo más pronto" (*ibid.,* p. 135); *fucú* (Ven, Col, SD), as in "Fulano tiene mucho *fucú*" (*ibid.,* p. 136). Of African origin are Cuban *ñeque* ("Pedro no tiene amigos porque está acreditado de *ñeque,*" C. Suárez) and *bilongo* ("No comas esa fruta, que tiene *bilongo,*" *ibid.*), deriv. *bilonguero, bilongazo,* and rare *bilonguear* ("lo *bilonguearon,*" Ortiz).

The destructive influence of the evil eye is especially feared when beautiful creatures are potential victims of insidious envy masked as friendship and benevolence. Thus, when a child is praised, the speaker may add "Dios lo guarde" or "Dios lo conserve" in order to counteract the possible evil results of flattery. Elsewhere, as in rural Ecuador (see Cornejo, p. 224), the pernicious effects may be counteracted by spitting at or beating the child in response to a request by the parents. Not only children but also animals and plants may be victims of the evil eye, and magic formulae, drugs, and manipulations of a *curandero* 'quack'—euphemized to *curioso* (Peru, Col, Ven, Ant)—are used to protect them from it. A person otherwise bewitched is there euphemistically called *ligado* 'tied' or *cogido* 'caught,' as in "Mercedes tiene *ligado* (or *cogido*) al marido" (Cornejo, p. 175).

In the River Plate region, particularly, one hears *yeta,* a short form of *yetatura* (from Italian *iettatura*). The word is also spelled with *j* ("¡La pucha, qué *jetta* tengo! Cada quince días caigo," A. Mendoza, p. 9, and "La *jetta* fué que llegó la Laura," *ibid.,* p. 58), or with *g,* as ¡*Gettatore!,* the title of a hilarious comedy by the Argentinian playwright Gregorio de Laferrère, first performed in 1904 (ed. *La Escena,* III, No. 123, Buenos Aires, 1920), and later adapted to the screen. Derivative noun *yetatore* or *gettatore* means an ill-omened person ('hoodoo, jinx') who can transmit a blighting effect on those who look at him, listen to him, touch him, or get into a public conveyance with him. In standard speech one might say "él tiene mala sombra." In the popular comedy ¡*Gettatore!* don Lucas aspires to the hand of a much younger girl, who in turn is in love with a young man of her age. The younger suitor contrives to convince the girl, her parents, and other relatives that don Lucas is a *gettatore,* that his hand burns the hands he touches, and that his presence and glances may bring misfortune and even death. To counteract this baleful influence, the other characters, in his presence or on hearing his name mentioned, hastily make the appropriate *señal de los cuernos:* vigorously extending index and little fingers forward and downward several times, often surreptitiously behind their backs or under the table; the girl wears a ring made of a horseshoe nail; the maid has a horseshoe dangling from her belt; and finally, when all are convinced of don Lucas' evil power, they march solemnly through the house burning incense and making *cuerno* gestures to exorcize the harmful spirits (see fig. 1).

In some rural regions, as in the province of San Luis, Argentina (*BDH,* VII, 212) the belief exists that diseases, wounds, or pains will appear in the exact spot of the body which a speaker, in his effort to be graphic, may indicate on mentioning the circumstance. If the speaker cannot avoid touching his body, he will each time add counteracting phrases like "Dios me guarde," "Dios me libre," "Dios me ampare."

In some Romance areas, squint eyes were originally thought to have a pernicious effect. Partly perhaps from that subconscious feeling, partly for humorous effect (by way of reaction), the word *bizco* 'cross-eyed' is often distorted into facetious *bizcocho, vizconde* (as in Spain), *vizconde de Mirachueco* (fictitious proper name from mirar 'to look' and *chueco* 'twisted, crooked, awry'), *bizcochito* (Col), *bizcorneado* (SD), *bizcornete* (as in Spain), *bizcorneto* (Col, Ven, Mex), *bizcoreto* (Hond); *bizcórneo* (Ant), *bizcorneta* (Cuervo, § 672), *birolo* (Col). In Guatemala, *choco* in addition to 'minus a member' may mean 'one-eyed' or 'cross-eyed,' as in "El *choco* Hernández fué un jugador famoso" and "tengo un caballo *choco* y una gallina *choca*" (Sandoval). For Mexico are reported the metaphorical expressions *hacer chiras* (in marble playing, *chiras* means hitting several marbles at once) and *no tiene problema para ver un partido de tenis.* The proper name Casimiro is jocosely used to indicate *bizco,* or even *tuerto* 'one-eyed' and *miope* 'nearsighted.'

Although the word *sal* ('salt') may mean 'grace, charm' in Spain, it has acquired the meaning of 'bad luck' in many regions of America, since, according to a superstitious belief, salt is considered an omen of bad luck. Hence, *salar* may mean 'to bring bad luck upon, bedevil' and *tener sal* or *estar salado* 'to have bad luck, be bedeviled.' Examples: "Antes se oía decir que se *salaban* los que se cogían las lismosnas de los santos" (Guat: Sandoval), "Eso era que me habían *salao* ... Me *saló* la ñata bandida" (Ec: José Antonio Campos, *La escoba de la bruja,* ap. Cornejo), "el vulgo cree que el que le pega a un sacerdote o a sus padres se *sala*" (CR: Gagini), "El dinero que dejan de pagar no se les *sala"* (Mex: Inclán, I, 85), "Estoy con toda la *sal"* (Arequipa, Peru: Ugarte), "Estoy *salado,* nunca me saco un premio en la lotería" (Mex: Santamaría), "Fulano está *salado* en su empresa" (Cuba: C. Suárez).

PHYSICAL DEFECTS

Physical defects in general play an important part in the superstitious beliefs of the Indian. This partly accounts for the endless list of American-Spanish terms denoting types and varieties of such defects. It cannot be determined here to what extent this multiplicity of usage was originally motivated by superstition, and to what extent superstition may still cling to words taught from the beginning to Creole children by their Indian nurses. However, the superstitious element in physical defects is attested in early Indian archaeology. Afflictions were apparently imposed by the gods with magic intent. Yet the uncharitable and derisive nature of numerous present-day locutions referring to such defects, and to death itself, is attributable, according to Alatorre (No. 3, p. 12), to a typically Spanish attitude toward them. He calls this inconsiderate feeling (incomprehensible to many Europeans and North Americans) a case of *mestizaje psicológico.* But how much of this indifference is due to stoicism, likewise typically Spanish, is yet to be established. (The words and phrases discussed in the following paragraphs might conceivably be treated elsewhere under another classification, but since, at least originally, they involved superstition, they can be conveniently mentioned here.)

Almost general in popular American Spanish is the replacement of cultured (and std. peninsular) *jorobado* 'hunchback' with *curcuncho* or its variants *corconcho, corcuncho, corcucho, curcuncha,* or its shorter forms *curco, cullco* (Ec: Toscano, p. 225), *cucho, curca,* and the humorous variant *joronche* (Mex). Some have thought the word derives from Quechua *curcu* 'tree trunk' and derivative verb in *-ncha* 'to transform into a trunk' (Lenz). Others derive it from Quechua *quirquincho* or *quirquicho,* a kind of 'armadillo' (Lafone). But it may well be a mere deformation of Spanish *corcova* 'hump' or *corcovado* 'humpbacked' (see Corominas). Possibly all these influences have brought something to bear on its varying forms as used in different regions.

To avoid ill-omened *jorobado,* many other local terms have been pressed into service, among them: *accidentado* 'uneven' in *el accidentado* (for *el jorobado*) *de Nuestra Señora de París* (Miragaya, p. 22); *totuma* or *tutuma* 'calabash' and 'vessel' made of the dry shell (elsewhere humorously supplanting *cabeza* 'head'), as in "Como dicen que es buena suerte, le toqué la *tutuma*" (Chile: Rabanales, p. 172); *maleta* 'suitcase' (Col, Ant) and *petaca* 'valise' (CA), which may be compared to the use in the older language of *alforja* 'saddlebag' and *baúl* 'trunk' (see Corominas); *ñesgado* and *ñasgado* (in certain regions of Mex), probably from the older language; Mayan *p'us* (Yuc: Suárez, p. 87), etc.

Many words refer to the maiming of persons or animals. Standard *mocho* 'maimed, cut off, defective' is frequently employed, as in *mocho de un pie* for standard *cojo; mocho de una mano* for standard *manco* 'one-handed'; *mocho de un brazo* 'one-armed,' etc. When a finger, hand, or arm is missing, standard *trunco* or *truncado* 'maimed' may be replaced by *tuco* (Bol, Ec, PR, Ven), *tunco* (CA, Mex), *tungo* or *tongo* (Col), *cuto* (Guat, Salv), *coto* (Nic: "Si me dices que me vas a pegar, recuerda que yo no soy *coto*," Valle, p. 315), *sunco* or *zunco* (Chile: "—Vos dirís que soy *zunco*. Pulséame los lagartos," Del Campo, p. 65), *choco* (CA, Mex, Chile) or *soco* (Chile, PR), *sucho* (NW Arg), *chonco* or *chunco* (Bol, Col, CA). In Chile one euphemistically indicates paralysis of an arm or leg by the use of the verb *quedarse* alone; that is, instead of mentioning the disturbing word *paralizado* one may say *"se le quedó un brazo"* (Román). To be sure, *quedar* in this construction may be an extension of such general meanings of *quedar* as 'to stop, cease, remain in one state.' Referring more particularly to fingers or hands are *collota* (Arequipa, Peru), *tonino* (Mex) 'fingerless'; *maneto* and *maneco* (Col, CA, PR) 'with deformed hands'; *ñoco* (Col, Ant, Ven), as in "tengo un dedo *ñoco* de resultas de un panadizo" (ap. Malaret, *Vocabulario*); *suco* (Col), as in "Como el pobre Juan quedó *suco* de la izquierda, sólo trabaja con la derecha" (Acuña); *broco* (PR). Persons with an extra finger or toe may be called *marinamo* (Chile), *sosta* (Salta, Arg) or *socta* (Arequipa, Peru) from Quechua *sokta* 'six.'

To indicate a deformity of legs or feet, standard Spanish has *cojo* 'lame,' *renco* 'lame, hipshot,' *patizambo* 'knock-kneed,' *patituerto* 'crooked-legged, clubfooted,' *estevado* (from *esteva* 'curved plough handle') 'bowlegged,' *patojo* 'having imperfect legs, waddling like a duck (*pato*),' *zopo* 'lame, crippled,' *escaro* 'crooked-footed,' *esparrancado* 'wide-legged,' etc. In addition to these, many others are current in American Spanish. Thus, *chueco* 'crooked' is generally equivalent to *patituerto* or *cojo,* but its meaning varies slightly according to region: 'clumsy gait' (Ec), 'pigeon-toed' (Peru). In the interior of Argentina *tinco* and *tincudo* (from *tincar* 'to knock,' Quechua *tincay*) mean 'knock-kneed.' The Chilean term *guallipén* may indicate bowlegs or other deformity of legs or feet. In Araucanian mythology *huaillepeñ* was the name of an aquatic beast of ill omen, physically deformed, with a calf's head, a sheep's body, and motionless hind legs, who by frightening a pregnant woman might cause her to bring forth a child with deformed legs. A Chilean familiar nickname to indicate a bow-legged person is *patas de sauce* 'willow legs,' as in "¡Tiene que andar molehtando no má, el *pat' e sauce"* (Rabanales, p. 172). In Guatemala, *cucleto* means 'renco, de pies torcidos,' as in "Los hombres *cucletos* están exceptuados del servicio militar" (Sandoval); this form, as well as Costa Rican *clucas* 'knock-kneed,' possibly derives from Spanish *cuclillas* 'asquat' (cf. *ñangado* [Cuba] 'crooked-legged' and *ñangotarse* 'to squat'). Other terms for *patizambo* 'knock-kneed' are *maneto* and *maneco* (Col, Guat, Ven) and *corneto* (CA). Standard *pateta* 'person with deformed legs or feet' has innumerable variants in Spanish America: general *patuleco* (with the somewhat deprecatory *-eco* suffix, Hispanized form of Aztec *-écatl,* expressing a national or tribal name), *patueco* (CA), *patuecas* (CR) and *patangas, patuco* (Hond), *patulenco* (Guat), *patuleque* (Cuba), *patulejo* (Chile), etc. In Mexico one may hear (Frenk, p. 139) jocose *pata chueca, pata chula* (cf. *chulenco* in sense of *patojo*), *pata fría, pata de ala, pata de ángel,* and the nickname *El inmortal,* because "no puede estirar la pata," involving the pun on *estirar la pata* 'to stretch one's leg' and 'to die'; and also *trae ponchada una llanta* 'he has a punctured tire.'

For animals with physical defects there is a multitude of special appellations. An animal lacking a horn or having a broken or defective one (std. *mogón*) may be *broco* or *ñoco* (PR), *mogo* (Pan), *muco* (CA), *nuco* or *ñuco* (Hond), *moco* (Peru) for hornless sheep, *cuatezón* (Mex) with derivative verb *cuatezonar* 'to cut off the horns,' *corneto* (Mex, Ven) 'with a misshapen horn,' *cuto* (Guat), *mutro* (Chile) 'animal whose horns have not grown out.'

For animals, and often for persons, who lack an ear or have a lop ear, we find *mambí* (Arg; from Guaraní); *pilón* (Chile; from Mapuche); *gocho, tunco* (Col); *huanco* (Arequipa, Peru; from Quechua); *corneto, ñoclo, paco, tucungo* (Ven); *zonto* (CA), with derivative verb *zontear* 'to crop the ears'; *churuco* (Hond); *gacho* (PR, SD), which is standard for 'lop-eared'; *muengo* (Cuba, PR), etc. In Colombia, *gocho* applies not only to animate beings but also to things that normally have *orejas* 'ears,' that is, 'handles' (std. *asas*), as in "Camarera, llévese este pocillo *gocho* ['cup with a broken handle'] y tráigame uno bueno" (Acuña).

Often replacing standard *rabón* 'bobtailed or tailless animal' are *bolo* (Col, Ant), *chupino* (Arg), *choco* (Chile), *chuto* (Bol, Ven), *chucuto* (Ven), *cutucho* (Ec), *zuco* (Col), *chingo* (CA, Pan), *tunco* (Guat). In various parts of Ecuador (Cornejo), and possibly elsewhere, a tailless hen is known as *culincha, colincha, culinga,* and *culimba,* words probably based on standard *colín,* diminutive of *cola* 'tail.'

Among the words replacing standard *desnarigado, chato* and *romo* 'muti-lated or flat-nosed' are *choroco* and *chingo* in Venezuela, where *chingo* serves as a nickname, as in *"el chingo* Olivo," *"el chingo* Machado" (Alva-rado).

Replacing standard *labihendido* or (*labio*) *leporino* 'harelipped,' the following words are popular: *cucho* (Mex), *guaco* or *huaco* (Arg, Bol, Ec; from Quechua, meaning 'eyetooth'), *cheuto* (Chile, from Mapuche), *bichín* and *janiche* (CA), *chintano* (Nic), *janane* (Guat), *janano* (Guat, Salv), *jane* (Hond), *tencua* and *tencuache* (Mex, from Aztec), *xet* and *sheto* (Yucatan, Tabasco, from Maya). In some countries are heard derivatives of Andalusian *boquino,* such as *boquinete* (Col, Tab), *boquineto* (Col, Ven), *boquinche,* and *boqueta* (Col). Indicating 'blobber-lipped'—that is, having thick and protruding lips (std. *bezudo, jetón,* or *jetudo*)—are *bembo, bembón, bembudo* (Ec, Peru, Ant), and general *trompudo* from *trompa* 'snout.'

DEATH

The mystery of death has everywhere given rise to superstitious customs, including taboos of certain words and phrases. Many primitive races believe that death (like disease) is always the act of some god or personage chiefly malevolent and is often brought on by an offense against taboo or in re-sponse to offerings made by an enemy of the victim. Mention of the name of the dead was thought to provoke the ghost into wreaking vengeance upon the taboo breaker, who by speaking the name had shown that his grief was insufficiently deep and genuine. If it was necessary to mention the name, that could be done in a whisper.

Although civilized peoples have not retained such customs, most of them instinctively replace words relating to death with some euphemistic term or periphrase to soften harsh reality. The taboo acts differently according to the speaker's social plane, the place, and the occasion. The prudish carefully eschew what might in the slightest offend propriety and decorum even though they do not accept the fears of popular superstition.

Latin *mors* 'death' was superseded by *migratio, fatum, suprema necessitas,* and others. The Romans used to say *vixit* 'he has lived' meaning 'he has ceased to live' (Montaigne, *Essais,* I, 19). The horror of death was hidden under the vagueness of *decedere, obire, occumbere, recedere, requiescere, spirare, transpassare,* and the like. Spanish *difunto* 'dead' stems from a Latin euphemism: *defunctus,* past participle of *defungi* 'to acquit oneself of, perform, finish,' then *vitā defungi* 'to die.'

In addition to standard Spanish *muerto, finado, fallecido,* one often finds in America the euphemism *extinto,* as in "El cortejo fúnebre fué de la casa del *extinto* a la iglesia de San Francisco" (Ec: Cornejo), "el *extinto* profesor de Salamanca" (Arg: Herrero Mayor, *Lengua,* p. 39), and "las virtudes del *extinto*" (Peru: Ugarte). In addition to standard *morir, finar, fallecer,* and *pasar a mejor vida* we frequently find (especially in RP) *desaparecer* 'to disappear' and noun *desaparición,* as in "el décimo aniversario de la *desaparición* del compositor" (*La Prensa,* Buenos Aires, June 20, 1946); and use of the expressions *ha desaparecido* and *dejó de existir* is widespread. In Chile, "se me quedó el enfermo" means "se murió el enfermo": *se me quedó* may be elliptical for "se me quedó muerto" or an extension of the general meaning of *quedarse* 'cesar, detenerse.'

Death is one of those emotionally strong concepts that attract endlessly to themselves new expressions to renew the feeling content gradually weakened by frequent repetition of the same word. To relieve tension, the reaction to death and sorrow often assumes a facetious or derisive bent (a typically Spanish trait), as in the popular expressions *estirar la(s) pata(s)* 'to stretch one's leg(s),' *hincar el pico* 'drive in one's beak,' *liárselas* 'to tie up one's belongings (and depart),' *liquidar* 'to settle one's account,' slang *diñarla, palmar, epichar, despichar,* and others.

Among the popular American-Spanish expressions for *morir* are extensions of terms denoting hasty departure or sudden flight, as in the familiar *largarse* (Chile), *arrancarse* (Ec, Mex, Cuba), *doblar la esquina* (Chile), *aventarse* (SD, as in "en poco tiempo *se aventaron* como veinte personas," Patín), *espantar la mula* (Cuba: Rodríguez, p. 426), *rasgarse* 'tear away'

(Col: Tobón), *jarearse* (Mex) 'to run away' and 'to starve to death,' *raspar* (Ven, where *raspar* means also 'to go away,' as in "Fulano *raspó* para Caracas"), *planear* (Nic, where *planeárselas* means 'huir, escapar'), *pelarse* 'escaparse' (Col, Ven, Mex), *chiflárselas* and *piteárselas* (CA, where this verb means also 'huir'), *pelarla* (Ec), *pelar el ajo* (Nic), *pelar rata* (CA), *pelar gallo* (Mex), *pelar el castaño* (Ven), cf. *pelar el cabezal* (Andes, Ven: "Cuando llegó el médico, ya *había pelado el cabezal*," Rosenblat, p. 316), *panquearse* (Ven). This last verb *panquear* (from English 'pancake') means first 'to flap one's legs swiftly in swimming'; then, reflexively, 'to run away,' as in "cuando vieron al guardia, *se panquearon*" (Malaret); and finally, 'to die,' as in "hace dos años que se *panqueó* su abuela" (*ibid.*). The idea of departure is expressed also in the phrases *irse al otro potrero* 'to go to the other pasture' (fam. std. *irse al otro barrio*) and *irse al país de los calvos* 'to go to the land of the bald' (Guat: *Mosaico*); *irse al otro toldo* 'to go to the other hut' (Col), as in "Don Melcíades hace un año que se *fué pa'l otro toldo* y su mujer no tardará en seguirlo" (Acuña); *irse al patio de los callados* 'to go to the yard of the silent' (Chile).

As extensions of the idea of lying down, or falling down, sleeping, or stretching out, the meaning of death is euphemized by *petatear(se)* (CA, Mex) 'to lie down on the *petate* or sleeping mat'; *restirarse* and *atirantarse* (Mex) 'to stretch out'; *estirarse* (Col) 'to stretch out,' as in general *estirar la pata* 'to stretch one's leg'; *estirar los hules* (Salv) or *las de hule* (Guat); vulgar *estirar la jeta* 'mug' (Chile); *doblar los codos* 'to fold the elbows' (Nic); *parar los tarros* (= *piernas*) 'to fall' (Col: Tobón); *parar las patas* or *las trancas* (= *piernas*) or *la cola* or *el rabo* (CA, Ant), as in "A las cinco horas *paró las patas* el enfermo" (Guat: Sandoval); *quedar uno tieso* (Chile) 'to remain stiff'; *templarse* (Ec) meaning 'tenderse en el suelo'; *quedarse* (see above), and likewise vulgar *quedar con la guata* ('belly') *al sol* (Chile: Medina); rustic *clavar la guampa* (RP), in which *guampa* means 'horn,' as in "Vendré a ser dueño de una mujercita joven y linda hasta el día mesmo en que me toque *clavar la guampa*" (Lynch, p. 230); general *clavar* (or *doblar*) *el pico* (cf. pop. std. *hincar el pico*) 'to fall asleep,' then 'to die,' as in "Tan enfermo está el viejo ... que cualquier día de éstos *clava el pico*" (Acuña) and "A lo mejor ése *clava el pico*" (Ec: Gil Gilbert, p. 227).

The idea of 'packing one's belongings, cashing in' is extended in popular variants of general *entregarla* 'to give it [life?] up, hand it over' such as *entregar los aniseros* 'strength, energy' (Col); *entregar los corotos* (= *las cosas*) or *los papeles* (Ven), as in "¡Qué vida! ¡El día menos pensado uno *entrega los corotos!*" (Rosenblat, p. 155); *entregar* (or *devolver*) *el casco* 'bottle,' *el envase* 'cask' or *el equipo* 'equipment' (Mex: inf. from A. Alatorre); *entregar los costales* 'bags' (Col); general *entregar la(s) herramienta(s)* 'tool(s)'; *entregar el rosquete* (std. *rodete* 'head pad for carrying burdens'), as in "Yo en cualquier día *entrego el rosquete* y quiero dejar asegurado tu porvenir" (RP: Florencio Sánchez, *M'hijo el dotor,* II, 6), deriv. *rosquear* (Salta, Arg); *entregar la valija* (Nic). Other favorite verbs are *colgar* 'to hang up,' *dejar* 'to leave (behind),' *doblar* 'to fold up,' *largar* 'to throw away,' and *liar* 'to tie up,' as in *colgar los tenis* 'tennis shoes' (CA, Mex); *dejar el cacaste* (CA, Mex), from Aztec *cacaxtle* 'portable latticed cupboard' carried on the back for transporting merchandise and produce; *doblar el caite* 'sandal' (CA), *el maguey* (Ven), *la maleta* 'suitcase,' *el petate* 'sleeping mat' (Mex); *largar* (or *soltar*) *la chancleta* 'slipper' or *el zapato* 'shoe' or *la tira* 'rags' (Cuba), *el rosquete* (Arg); *liar el petate* (Mex; cf. fam. std. *liárselas, liar los bártulos* 'to go away').

Among other popular and slang metaphorical expressions are *cantar pa el carnero* (rustic, Arg, where *carnero* means 'charnel house'); *cuetearse* (Col), from *cohete* 'skyrocket' (cf. fam. std. *reventar* 'to burst, blow up' > 'to die'); *dar uno un susto* 'to frighten, shock' (SD), as in "el viejo está que en cualquier día de éstos *da un susto*" (Patín); *estar en pico de zamuro* 'to be in a buzzard's beak,' that is, in danger of death; *helársele a uno el sebo* (Arg); *llegarle la china a uno* (Ant), referring to the game 'handy-dandy,' wherein one child guesses in which hand the pebble (*la china*) is concealed; *pasar el alambrado* 'to cross the wire fence,' used in the sheep-raising sections of southern Chile (Plath, p. 4); *patear el balde* (CR, Hond) or *la cubeta* (Guat) 'to kick the bucket'; *ponerle a uno la cacona* (SD, where *cacona* means 'a child's best outfit'); *quedarse en actitud de firme(s) para toda la eternidad* (Mex); *retorcer la cola* (Tex) 'to twist one's tail'; *sonar* (*como harpa vieja*) (Arg); *totearse* (Col), from *tote* 'firecracker' (Cuervo, § 976); *tronar* 'to thunder' and 'to shoot to death,' as in "Jaime *tronó* hoy a las 20 horas" (Guat: Sandoval).

Euphemistic terms for the act of dying are *la desaparición* 'disappearance' or *la repentina despedida* 'sudden leave taking,' *la desgracia* 'misfortune,' *la última* (Chile), facetious *la petateada* (Mex) from *petatearse* (see above), and so forth.

Familiar and usually jocose euphemisms for *la muerte* 'death' are *la calaca* (Mex); *la carcancha* (Peru) 'the skeleton' as a symbol of death (Corrales, p. 268); *la cierta* 'the certain one'; *la china Hilaria* (Mex), a triple euphemization veiling vulgar *chingada* (but preserving its assonance: *i - á - a*), and replacing the previously current *pelada; la dientuda* (std. *dentuda*) 'the large-toothed one' (Mex); *la flaca* 'the skinny one'; *la huesuda* 'the bony one'; *la ñata* 'the flat-nosed one' (*la chata,* Andalusia); *la Pascuala* (CA), a double euphemization veiling *pelada* (preserving its initial *-p* and its assonance: *á - a*); *patas de alambre* 'wire legs' (Mex); *la pelada* and *la pelona* 'the bald one'; *la tilica* 'the skinny one' (Mex); *la triste* 'the sad one'; *la vieja* 'the old one' (CR), etc.

The lugubriousness of *entierro* 'burial' is sometimes softened, especially in newspaper reporting, by *inhumación* (verb *inhumar*) or *sepelio* (old verb *sepelir*) for Catholic burials; and *sepultación* (Chile) replaces standard *sepultura* (verb *sepultar*). The word *cementerio* 'cemetery,' itself originally a Greek euphemism meaning 'place of sleep or repose,' is further mitigated by use of *panteón* 'pantheon, temple dedicated to all the gods,' current in Andalusia and in many regions of Spanish America (Peru, Ec, Mex, and elsewhere), as in "el hilo de muertos hacia el *panteón* no se corta ni de día ni de noche" (Mex: Anda, p. 16), deriv. *panteonero* (Ec) for *sepulturero* 'gravedigger.' In Argentina one hears *chacarita* 'small farm' for *cementerio*. Perhaps we may assume both a phonetic and a semasiological connection between *sementera* 'sown land' (one of the meanings of *chacra*) and *cementerio*. Although the general cemetery in Buenos Aires is called *Chacarita,* the more aristocratic burial ground is euphemistically termed *la Recoleta,* convent or house of Franciscan friars of the Strict Observance who 'collect themselves' for religious contemplation.

KILLING

Closely related to the preceding are the many euphemistic expressions for standard *matar* 'to kill' and *asesinar* 'to murder.' The Hispanic race holds courage and temerity in great esteem, and it is natural that the ideas of dying and killing should attract to themselves a vast profusion of terms in order to maintain the emotional content at a high level. Among verbs heard in cultured speech are *liquidar, suprimir, ultimar,* and *victimar* (Chile, Ec). In some regions (especially Arg, Chile) *desgraciarse* or *tener una desgracia* may mean 'to kill someone' or 'to commit suicide' (lit. 'to bring misfortune upon oneself'). Analogous to *desgraciar* is *infelizar* 'to kill,' as in "—¡Santo Dios de los Cielos! ¡Ya me *infelizaron!*" (Mex: Anda, p. 143). Among others are *perjudicar* 'to hurt, injure' and *ningunear* (Tex) 'to annihilate' (from *ninguno* 'no one').

Rather general in America is *beneficiar* meaning 'to slaughter cattle and prepare the meat for public sale' as in "Había olido la sangre de una res que *fué beneficiada* allí en la mañana" (Gallegos, p. 336). Such usage is an extension of standard *beneficiar un terreno* 'to cultivate a plot of ground' and *beneficiar una mina* 'to work a mine for profit or benefit.' In some regions, as in Guatemala, *beneficiar* is applied to persons in the sense of *fusilar* 'to execute by shooting' and of *matar* or *asesinar,* as in "La escolta *se benefició* al reo mediante la aplicación de la ley fuga" (Sandoval). Similarly, *carnear* (RP, Chile) means both 'to slaughter animals' and 'to kill persons,' as in "Al *carnear* la cabra vieja, vendió carne de cabrito" and "Al que es confiado y no se precave, lo *carnean*" (ap. Malaret, *Bol. fil.*)

A number of colloquial expressions for *matar* represent some action of felling, lowering, unhorsing, and the like; for example, slang *acurrucar* (Nic) 'to squat,' as in "entre gente maleante *acurrucar* a una persona es darle muerte" (Valle); *achicar* (Col) 'to make small, reduce' referring to the contraction or shrinking of a body suddenly struck down; *apear* or rustic *apiar* (Col) 'to unhorse,' as in *"apié* dos pájaros di'un solo tiro" (Acuña); *bajar* (Col) 'to lower,' as in "el reo confesó *haber bajado* a cuatro y herido a dos" (Acuña); *descocotar* (SD), as in *"descocotó* a varios amigos" (Patín); *doblar* (Mex) 'to fold'; *echarse a uno* (Mex), as in *"se lo echó"; estirar* (Arg, Chile, Bol, Peru) 'to stretch out'; *quebrarse* (or *quemarse) a alguien* (Mex); *sembrar* (Piura, Peru: Hildebrandt) 'to sow'; *tirarse* (or *echarse* or *mandarse) al plato a alguien* (CA, Mex); *tronar* (Mex, CA) 'to thunder, strike down with thunder,' as in "El gobierno *truena* a los reos militares" (Santamaría); *tumbar* (Mex) 'to fell'; *volcar* 'to overthrow.'

Miscellaneous popular metaphors are likewise graphically expressive of killing. In addition to peninsular *despachar* 'to dispatch,' *despabilar* 'to snuff a candle' ("me lo *despabilaron* de un trabucazo," Pardo Bazán, *La Madre Naturaleza,* chap. x), *enviar al otro barrio* 'to send to the other quarter,' *desempadronar* 'to remove from the roll,' *apiolar* 'to tie beasts by the legs,' etc., we find in America:

achurar (rustic) 'to eviscerate' (Arg), as in "¡Pucha! ... si no traigo bolas / Me *achura* el indio ese día" (*Martín Fierro,* I, v. 600), cf. *sacar las tripas* or *entretelas; aflijir* (Mex) 'to afflict, grieve' for 'to fire from a trench upon an attacking group'; *almorzarse a uno* (Guat) 'to eat someone up'; general *apagarle a uno la luz* (*la vela*) 'to put out someone's light (candle)'; *apagar el mecho* (Col), as in "le *apagó el mecho* a la vuelta del camino" (Restrepo); *atajarle a uno el resuello* (Arg: *BAAL,* XVII, 234) 'to cut off someone's respiration'; *aventar* (SD) 'to attack,' as in "lo *aventaron* anoche" (Mal).

bailarse a uno (Mex) 'to make someone dance'; *brincarse a alguien* (Col: Tobón) 'to jump on someone.'

comerse 'to eat up,' as in "él era el hombre que *se había comido* a Cocambo y al alemán" (Ec: A. Ortiz, p. 223) and "—¿Regresó el moreno de anoche? —¡Qué va! *Se lo comieron"* (*ibid.,* p. 256); *comerse una corvina* (coastal Ec) 'to eat a bluefish,' deriv. *corvinero* 'assassin' as in "Y su bien ganada fama de *corvinero* se extendía en muchas leguas a la redonda, y jamás abandonó su revólver" (A. Ortiz, p. 55).

dar agua, used by Mexican soldiers during the revolution (Santamaría), as in "¿A poco no sabes lo que es *darles su agüita?* ¡Su medicina, hombre, pero para que se petateen luego y no sufran!" (Magdaleno, p. 255); *dar en la chapa al alma* (Mex) 'to hit the lock of the soul'; *desmondongar* 'to eviscerate' (Peru); *despalillar* (PR) 'to strip tobacco'; general *difuntear* and rustic *dijuntiar* from *difunto.*

embarrilar (Cuba) 'to barrel' (cf. peninsular slang *escabechar* 'to pickle'); *embodegarse* 'to store in a cellar' (Col: *BICC,* I, 354); *enfriar a uno* (SD) 'to chill, make cold,' as in "si me das un palo, *te enfrío"* (Patín).

hacerle a alguien chocolatito (Mex) 'to poison someone' (lit. 'to make chocolate for him'); *limpiar* (RP) 'to clean.'

medir el aceite (Cauca, Col: Tobón) 'to measure the oil'; *morir de fiebre plomática* (Ven) 'to be killed with a bullet' (lit. 'to die of lead fever').

pasar al palo (Col) 'to tie to the stake for slaughter,' as in "a fulano lo *pasaron al palo"* (Sánchez Arévalo); *pelar* 'to skin' (SD), as in "una

noche lo *pelaron* entre dos enemigos" (Patín); *petaquiar* (Col) 'to dis-
courage, debilitate,' as in "se lo *petaquiaron* en las fiestas" (Tobón); *poner
a uno un zamuro de prendedor* (Ven: Calcaño) 'to pin a buzzard on someone.'

    quebrar (Mex) 'to crush, split'; *quemar* (Mex) 'to burn (with lead).'

    sonar or *sonajear* (CA, Mex); *soplar* (Guat), as in "la policía se lo
sopló" (Sandoval).

    tocarle a uno el violín or *violón* (Arg, during Rosas' regime) 'to kill by
cutting the throat with a notched dagger,' analogous to drawing a violin bow
across the strings, as in "*¡Tóquenle el violín* a esos perros unitarios!" (ap.
Carriegos, p. 103).

    vaciarle a uno los aniseros (Col), *anís* meaning here 'strength, energy.'

Possibly some of the following popular expressions owe a modicum of
their metaphorical meaning *matar* to phonetic association of their first
sound or sounds *m(a)*: *mamarse* (Col, Pan), as in "*se lo mamó* de un tiro"
(Tobón); *mandar* or *hacer el mandado* (Col), as in "le *hicieron* bien *el
mandado*" (Tobón); *merendarse* (Col), as in "se lo *merendaron*" (Tobón);
madrugar (Mex), lit 'to rise early, attack first'; *dar mate* or *matarile* (Mex).

A verb formed by adding to the name of an animal the suffix *-ear* may
mean 'to hunt' or 'to kill' that animal: *caimanear* 'to hunt or kill alligators
[*caimanes*]'; *pavear* (Col) and *venadear* (Guat) may mean also to slay a
person in some uninhabited place usually through a paid assassin who lies
in wait for the victim as though he were a turkey (*pavo*) or a deer
(*venado*). Formations which include names of birds are common: *buitrear*
from *buitre* 'vulture'; *palomear* from *paloma* 'dove'; *pajarear* from *pájaro*
'bird'; *pichonear* from *pichón* 'pigeon'; *tortolear* from *tórtola* 'turtledove';
zopilotear (Mex, CA) from *zopilote* 'turkey buzzard,' and others.

Often the disturbing word is avoided by the use of an appropriate gesture: that of drawing the index finger (or index and middle fingers), representing a knife, quickly across the throat; for example, "—Si miente ...
—*y se pasó el dedo índice por el cuello*" (Urug: Reyles, p. 75) and "—La
cosa es que ... y el boticario, haciendo un chasquido con la lengua, *se pasó
el índice por la garganta*" (Ven: J. R. Pocaterra, *Vidas oscuras*, p. 35).
(See fig. 2.)

Another gesture represents a blow with a *machete* 'cane knife': "—Por eso creo que la justicia debe hacerse silenciosamente, sin hacer mucha bulla y personalmente—y al decir esto, hizo un gesto como *el que le da machete a un pescuezo"* (Cuba: C. Enríquez, *Tilín García,* p. 75).

The gesture of snuffing a candle ('despabilar') is widespread, as in "—¿Usted me entiende? que fué Barbacana quien ... (ademán muy expresivo de *despabilar una luz con los dedos).* —¿Dice usted que mataron a ese hombre?" (Pardo Bazán, *La Madre Naturaleza,* chap. v).

II DELICACY

Euphemisms of delicacy or politeness are more recent than those of superstition and are far more numerous today. Their number constantly increases. Speakers incessantly resort to new turns of speech to avoid uncouth, impolite, or indelicate expressions that might offend or disturb the listener. When, with repeated use, a euphemism ceases to be felt as a circumlocution and becomes directly synonymous with its bald referent and contaminated by it, it can no longer serve its original purpose and must in turn be replaced by a new expression which will again adequately veil the exposed taboo. A distinction is generally made between euphemisms that thus constantly lose their force and others that seem to retain it. If the word is employed in careful expression of a rather high style, it will be more likely to retain its euphemistic quality. If, however, it becomes current in a less careful or lower style of speech, it will soon lose its palliating force.

FAMILY RELATIONSHIPS

Standard *mi mujer* 'my wife' has fallen into disfavor in most of America, where one hears the more ceremonious *mi esposa* 'my spouse' (*esposo* for *marido* 'husband') as well as the farfetched *mi señora* 'my lady' which formerly was, and still is, courteously applied to ladies other than the speaker's wife. Good peninsular *mi mujer* has acquired unfavorable connotations in the New World; and *su mujer* 'your wife' is practically unthinkable (one must say "¿Cómo está *su señora* or *su esposa?*" see Sologuren, p. 241). Somewhat comparable is the use of *mia moglie* 'my wife' but *la sua signora* 'your wife' in Italy, and *meine Frau* 'my wife' but *Ihre Frau Gemahlin* 'your wife' in Germany.

Purists have objected to the use of *señora* in place of *mujer,* but in vain. The Colombian lexicographer Revollo remonstrates: "En Colombia antiguamente los casados decían *mi mujer, o* cuando más en ciertas ocasiones *mi esposa;* mas hoy el más pedestre, el último pichonzuelo de marido no dice sino *mi señora.* ¡Oh, si eso les da importancia!" Furthermore, one hears in not a few areas the strained, and to many ludicrous, combination *mi señora esposa.*

Since there is a natural disinclination among some newlyweds to say *mi mujer* or *mi marido,* they often resort to *ella* 'she' or *él* 'he' (see *AmSS,* p. 96). The untutored and rustics in Yucatán avoid *mi mujer* by substituting *la familia* or *mi familia.* Thus, "vine con *la familia*" may mean 'I came with my wife' (Suárez, p. 66). Some persons use the affectionately humorous *mi media naranja* 'my half orange,' *mi costilla* 'my rib,' *mi cara mitad* 'my dear half' (cf. 'my better half'), *mi peor es nada,* or *mi patrona* 'my boss,' all of which are colloquial standard Spanish. Some use, as a term of endearment, *mi vieja* 'my old lady'; but this expression is ambiguous since it may also mean 'mother' or 'mother-in-law' or 'grandmother.' Others occasionally say jocosely *mi conjunta* (Peru: Corrales, pp. 88, 122); *mi García Moreno* (Ec), the name of a former president known for his severity (Toscano, p. 213); *mi demasiado cara* ('expensive') *mitad, mi cincuenta por ciento,* and *mi medio limón* to a husband (Chile; Rabanales, "Recursos," p. 289).

One notes in America, as well as in Spain, a euphemistic tendency to avoid *suegra* 'mother-in-law' and *suegro* 'father-in-law' by substituting *madre política* and *padre político,* respectively. This is extended to such forms as *hija política* for *nuera* 'daughter-in-law' and *hijo político* for *yerno* 'son-in-law.'

FORMS OF ADDRESS

Popular euphemistic forms for *señor* 'sir,' used by a speaker to ingratiate himself with a superior or to propitiate a stranger, are such terms as *patrón, jefe, joven,* and *doctor.* Sometimes these words are used ironically or jocosely, as, for example (to a wood peddler), "—¿A cómo la leña, patrón?" (Chile: Román); (to a policeman) "—¿Cómo se llama este jirón ('long street'), *jefe?"* (Peru: Sologuren, p. 255); *el joven fulano* may be equivalent to *el sujeto ese* (*ibid.*). In many regions *joven* is used especially by taxi drivers and bus conductors, to avoid the feeling of servility implied in *señor,* as in "—No hay asientos, *joven."* The more academic *doctor,* often applied to anyone of intellectual appearance, is occasionally pronounced *dóctor,* and *profesor* is pronounced *profésor* in an attempt to recall the classical gravity of such titles (*ibid.*). The forms *taita, tata, taitito, tatay* (with Quechua suffix -*y* 'my'), and *taitacha* (with Quechua diminutive -*cha*) are employed especially by Indians, with almost filial affection, in addressing superiors (*taita Pancho, taita amo,* or merely *taita*), priests (*taita* or *tata cura*), and saints and their images.

A well-to-do white child is generally called *niño; muchacho* (or *chico*) is usually reserved for the less privileged classes, for servants, Indians, and Negroes. *Muchacho* may imply a certain authority the speaker arrogates to himself because of higher social or economic position (which also accounts for his frequent use of *tú*), as in "—A ver, *muchacho,* lústrame los zapatos" or "—*Muchacho,* dame La Prensa" (Sologuren, p. 255). The stigma of *muchacho* may be resented also by the less fortunate classes of society: "—No es *muchacho,* que es *niño*—hemos oído protestar a una mujer del pueblo en Méjico porque se le decía a su hijo en la calle: 'quítate, *muchacho'* " (*BDH,* IV, 192, n. 8). However, diminutive *muchachito* or *mi muchachito* may express deep affection, such is the euphemistic force of the suffix -*ito.*

In many regions euphemism demands that in place of *negro* 'Negro' the gentler *trigueño* or *moreno* 'brunet' be used (as even in the classical period: "ella y un hombre *moreno," Lazarillo,* I; "Enseño a tañer a algunos *morenos," Cervantes, El celoso extremeño*). Often the speaker prefers to euphemize the word by using only a gesture, usually that of moving the extended right index finger once or twice across the back of the left hand, a motion that indicates 'color of skin, Negro' (see fig. 3), or that of touching the head with the curled index finger to indicate 'kinky hair.' The word *mulato* is occasionally replaced by *pardo* 'brown, dusky.' The harshness of *indio* may be softened by substituting *indígena* or *natural* 'native.'

Polite *doña,* feminine of *don,* originally reserved for royalty and the nobility, is in America often applied euphemistically to a charwoman, a storekeeper's wife, or to others of similar social status who have attained a certain age. In Ecuador, *doña* is often equivalent to 'a married Indian woman.' In the middle and upper classes in general *don* or *doña* with the given name has yielded in Spanish America to *señor* or *señora* with the family name. However, *señorito* 'master,' respectful in Spain, is far from flattering when applied to the average Spanish-American boy, for whom it carries overtones of 'dudish, pampered.' (For these and other forms of address, see *AmSS,* pp. 423–432.)

With certain words in direct address, respectability can often be restored in polite speech by prefixing *señor* 'sir,' as in *señor guardia civil, señor chófer, señor portero,* etc. A mere diminutive ending denoting endearment can convert an unsavory word into an acceptable form of familiar address. Thus, slang *chapa* for *policía,* is in Ecuador practically an insult, deriving from a Quechua word meaning 'to spy,' but it is not disagreeable when spoken in the form of *chapita* (Toscano, p. 424). A market woman will address her customer not with the usual *casera* (std. *parroquiana*) but with the affectionate euphemism *caserita,* and in Quito with *ama mía shunguita* (the last word being Quechua for *corazoncito*) 'my dear heart' (Toscano, p. 218, n. 1).

OCCUPATIONS

Names of certain occupations easily fall to low estate. The dignity of an occupation thus affected may be raised by a carefully selected euphemism. Thus, English *mortician* has replaced *undertaker,* and *animal inspector* euphemizes *dogcatcher.* In standard Spanish *trabajador* 'laborer' has been raised to *artesano,* and the artisan in turn has been ennobled to *artista;* a present-day *farmacéutico* 'pharmacist' would no longer relish being called *boticario* 'apothecary, druggist'; the lowly *sacamuelas* 'tooth puller,' improving his technique, became *dentista* and today appears on office signs as *odontólogo,* from the Greek; *zapateros* 'shoemakers, cobblers,' *carpinteros,* and other craftsmen are addressed as *maestros* and, along with the *maestros* 'schoolmasters,' they in turn have euphemistically become *profesores.*

The same tendency is immediately apparent in every region of America. For Puerto Rico, Tomás Navarro (p. 202) lists *timonero de arado* 'helmsman of the plough' for *labrador* 'tiller'; *halador de azada* 'hauler of the spade' for *cavador* 'digger'; *mudador de ganado* 'mover of cattle' for *pastor* 'shepherd.' In Cuba, *encomendero* indicates the person who purveys meat to a town; in Peru, the same word raises the dignity of 'grocery-storekeeper.' In Venezuela and Colombia, standard *carnicero* 'butcher' becomes *pesador* 'weigher,' *pesar* (as in the older language) means 'to sell meat,' and *pesa* means *carnicería* 'butcher shop.' In Panama, *salariante* 'salaried person' may replace *jornalero* 'day laborer.' In Chile, standard *plomero* or *fontanero* 'plumber' is ennobled by the English borrowing 'gas fitter,' which the cultured pronounce *gásfiter,* as in "En la techumbre los *gásfiters* se mojaban destapando los cañones obstruídos" (Castro, p. 388; also pp. 281, 316), cf. *gasfitero* (Peru, Ec); the semicultured pronounce it *gasfíter,* and the totally untutored say *gafite* (Román). In the same country a newspaper vendor, besides being called *diariero* and *diarero* (in much of Spanish America *diario* is preferred to *periódico*), is euphemistically dubbed *suplementero,* which supposedly dates from the war between Peru and Bolivia (1879) when newspapers, normally delivered to subscribers' homes, issued for the first time extra sheets or *suplementos* sold on the streets. Furthermore, there exist in Chile the *Escuela de Suplementeros,* the *Asilo de Suplementeros,* and a Chilean novel by José Luis Fermandoiz called *El Suplementero* (Román). In some areas (RP, Peru) a common word for 'newsboy' has, since the turn of the century, been *canillita* (std. *canilla* means 'long bone, shank'), reportedly deriving from the name of the newsboy protagonist in Florencio Sánchez' play *Canillita,* as in "El *canillita* ... es un ruidoso pregonero de las noticias y titulares de los diarios" (ap. Malaret, *Bol. fil.*). In addition to *periodiquero* and *papelero,* one hears in Mexico and elsewhere (Col: Ec, particularly in the highlands) the euphemistic *voceador* (from *vocear* 'to call out, announce'), as in "Los diarios ... se encargaron de correrlo, y había que oír a los *voceadores* ... que se desgañitaban recitando a voz en cuello las veracísimas sumillas" (ap. Cornejo).

Instead of standard *limpiabotas* 'bootblack,' softer words are now used: *aseador de calzado* (Mex); *betunero* (Ec, Mex) from *betún,* the name of a former type of 'polish,' as in "El Gremio de *Betuneros* celebró ayer una importante sesión" (Ec: Cornejo); *bolero* or *boleador* (Mex) from *bola* 'ball,' as a former type of polish was called because of its shape, with derivatives *boleado* or *boleada* 'a shine' (as in "¡Una *boleada,* jefe!"), *bolería* 'shoeshine stand,' and *bolear* 'to shine'; *embolador* (Col), with derivative *embolar; lustrabotines* (Arg); *lustrador* (Peru, Ec); *salonero* (Arg: Miragaya) from *salón* 'parlor' (cf. *salón de lustrar, clínica de zapatos,* etc.).

In many regions, as in Colombia, *la maestra de escuela* 'the school-teacher' is dignified with simple *la señorita.* In rural Chile, standard *buhonero* 'peddler, hawker' is referred to as *falte,* of dubious origin, though Román suggests it may derive from the hawker's often repeated "¡Agujas, alfileres, peinetas, jabón y todo lo demás que *falte!*" Elsewhere *buhonero* becomes *achín, achimero,* or *achinero* (Guat), from *achime* 'hawker's box (of goods)'; *anchetero* (Salv, Mex) from *ancheta* 'hawker's box'; *barillero* or *varillero* (Mex) from *barilla* 'hawker's box' (see Anda, p. 16); *chuchero* (Col: "Esta navaja se la compré a un *chuchero,*" Acuña) from *chucho* 'hawker's box'; *sencillero* (Peru, Ec: Toscano, p. 390); *tilichero* (CA) from *tiliche* 'knickknack'; *truchero* (CR) from *trucha* 'hawker's box.' In Chile, *palo blanco* (std. *testaferro*) is applied to the person associated with a *buhonero* or *charlatán,* whose pretended interest in the wares attracts customers, or to the person who connives with a *martillero* 'auction dealer' by raising the bids, as in "ya están los *palos blancos* telegrafiando a los martilleros" (Rabanales, p. 193). In Mexico, *memorialista* 'public letter writer,' dating from colonial times, has become *evangelista.* In Chile, *niños* 'boys' is applied to prisoners, soldiers, or laborers, also to bandits or assassins (cf. *nene* in ironical peninsular usage). In Argentinian cant, *cambrón,* having euphemized *barredor municipal* 'municipal street cleaner' till the beginning of the century, has yielded to *musolino,* the name of a famous Sicilian bandit, Argentine street cleaners being mostly Italian (Gobello, p. 79). In Chile the garbage man is a *municipal.*

Now-distasteful *criado,-a* 'servant' was once a euphemism meaning originally 'pupil' and 'vassal brought up in the household of his master.' Just as English 'servant' has to a large extent yielded to 'domestic' or 'help,' so Spanish *criado,-a* has been euphemized. Besides standard *empleado,-a, doméstico,-a, fámulo,-a,* and *valet,* we find *concertado,-a* (CR), rare *camarista* (Mex), and *cuartelero* (Peru, Ec) 'hotel valet'; popular *chopa* (SD), *gato,-a* (Mex); vulgar *jarro* (SD), as in "A este viejo verde le gustan los *jarros*" (Patín); *mayordomo,-a* (Peru). Standard *camarera* (*doncella*) 'maid' has become *recamarera* (Mex), from *recámara* (std. *alcoba* 'bedchamber'); in Colombia *dentrodera* or *dentrera* (Antioquia, Caldas), and *criada de adentro* (CA; Bogotá: see Cuervo, § 869); in Guatemala it is *la de adentro,* as in "Se pagan ... de 12 a 15 [pesos] a la camarera, o como diríamos en Guatemala a *la de adentro*" (José Milla,

Un viaje al otro mundo, 3d ed., I, 150); in the same country, *hija de casa* is applied to a young girl taken into a household as a servant or apprentice receiving no salary beyond clothing, food, and instruction. In Mexico, and occasionally elsewhere, *mesero,-a* (from *mesa* 'table') has practically ousted *camarero,-a* and especially *mozo,-a* 'waiter, waitress.' In newspaper "want ad" columns *cocinera* 'cook' may be found ennobled to *empleada para la cocina,* and *mozo* to *niño para los mandados, joven para el aseo,* and the like (Chile: Rabanales, "Recursos," p. 280). Standard *mozo de cordel* or *de cuerda* 'porter' has been replaced by *cargador* in most of America; *altozanero* (Bogotá; Cuervo, § 869), so called because porters usually took their stand on the *altozano* 'atrium' of the cathedral; *caleta* (Col, Ven) or *caletero* (Ven; from *cala* 'hold of a ship') 'porter, carrier, longshoreman,' as in "El que nació pa *caleta,* del cielo le bajan los bultos"; *canchero* (Chile); *fletero* (Peru, Ec, Guat), from *flete* 'freight'; *changador* (RP, Bol), of disputed and complicated origin (see Corominas); *mecapalero* (CA, Mex), from *mecapal* 'rope attached to a leather forehead band,' as in "Un *mecapalero* que viene a llevar un cofre" (Salv: T. P. Mechín, *Candidato,* San Salvador, 1931, III, 6).

Among foreign borrowings now used for 'servant' (originally, for the most part, as euphemisms) are *chichigua* (CA, Mex) 'wet nurse,' from Aztec; rather general *china,* from Quechua; *garzón* (RP, Chile) 'waiter,' from French *garçon* (std. *mozo, camarero*), cf. *adición* (std. *cuenta*), from French *addition; huasicama* (Ec), from Quechua, as in "la Chasca ... hacía cerca del amo ejercicio de *huasicama"* (Cuadra, p. 141); *imilla* (Bol), from Quechua *imilla* 'girl,' as in "¿Le has dicho a la *imilla* que les dé a los conejitos?" (Díaz Villamil, *La Rosita,* Act I, sc. 7); *mucamo,-a* (RP; *mucama,* Chile), of disputed origin; *mitani* (Bol), as in "no vas a su casa a ... servir de *mitani"* (Alcides Arguedas, *Raza de bronce,* La Paz, 1919, p. 10); *ñapanga* (Col), from Quechua *llapanga* 'barefoot'; *pichín* (Peru) 'clerk in a modest *pulpería'* extended to mean any 'employee,' from Italian *piccino* 'child'; *pilmama* (Mex) 'nursemaid,' from Aztec, as in "todo el día estaba apoltronada, teniendo a la niña en brazos, y Lupe sirviéndole de *pilmama"* (Inclán, II, 121); *pongo,-a* (Bol, Peru, Ec), from Aymara *puncai* 'guardian'; *suche* (Chile) 'clerk, errand boy,' from Quechua *suchi,* as in "Manuelito era *suche* de una casa mayorista" (Carlos Acuña, *Huellas de un hombre que pasa,* Santiago, 1940, p. 63).

AGE

Mention of age and the aging seems to have been unpleasant from time immemorial and, under certain conditions, has required euphemization. The process often results in pointing up incongruous and humorous aspects. Thus, in Andalusia, *niño,-a* 'child' is applied to a person, usually unmarried, of any age whatsoever. This usage has survived in much of Spanish America, where *niña* is even extended at times to a married woman or widow, and almost anyone may be referred to euphemistically as *niño.* Similarly, *joven* 'young man (or woman)' is commonly applied to persons of middle age. Conversely, *mediano* 'medium, moderate' is a Chilean euphemism for *pequeño* 'small' referring to a young growing person and often to the youngest child in a family, as in "Me enseñó a trabajar desde *medianito*" (ap. Medina).

Standard *quedarse soltera* 'to remain a spinster' (cf. also fam. std. *quedar para vestir imágenes* or *santos,* semasiologically related to *spinster* 'a woman who spins') has in some regions been shortened to *quedarse.* Thus "las Ramírez *se quedaron* todas" (Col: Montoya) 'the Ramírez girls were all unmarried'; "haré todo lo posible para no *quedarme*" (SD: Patín). The past participle *quedada* is equivalent to *soltera* 'single' or *solterona* 'old maid,' as in "tiene tres hermanas—*quedada* la mayor, casada la segunda, y comprometida la tercera" (Col: Acuña). Elsewhere, as in Andalusia, *solterona* may become *muchacha.* One frequently hears the circumlocution *la dejó el tren* 'she missed the train.' In some regions (Arg, Chile) *cebollón,-a* 'large onion' means *solterón,-a,* perhaps derived from older standard *cebolludo,-a,* which the Academy dictionary registers as "ant. Decíase de la persona tosca y basta, o gruesa y abultada"; that is, like the head of an onion "porque tal es la forma que con los años toman muchas veces los *solterones*" (Román). In Esmeraldas, Ecuador, a *solterona* may be jocosely referred to as *almanaque,* perhaps because an almanac, after the year has elapsed, "ya es cosa inútil que nadie apetece" (Cornejo). In Guatemala the expression *estar en el décimo no codiciar* (referring to the tenth commandment) is applied to a woman who has lost her youthful charms, as in "Bernarda fué reina de belleza, pero ahora ya *está en el décimo no codiciar*" (Sandoval). In Costa Rica one hears "quedarse para servir de tapicería" based on standard "quedarse para vestir santos." In Argentina, *domar el chivato* 'to tame the he-goat' means 'to remain a spinster.'

Euphemistic *avanzado* 'advanced' often replaces *viejo* 'old man,' as in "Don Juan ya está bastante *avanzado* y, sin embargo, piensa casarse muy pronto con una mujer joven" (Guat: Sandoval). In Mexico, Central America, and elsewhere, an older person (std. *una persona mayor*) is kindly referred to as *grande* (*es* or *está grande*), as in "El Don Tranquilino es seis u ocho años más *grande*" (Mex: Inclán, I, 264) and "La suegra es una señora ya *grande,* como algunos dicen a los viejos" (Guat: Salomé Gil, *Cuadros de costumbres,* 4th ed., p. 172), perhaps by analogy with general *chico* 'small, young.' Furthermore, *abuela* 'grandmother' may be *mamá grande* and *abuelo* 'grandfather' may be *papá grande*. Sometimes *viejo* is affectionately replaced by *ruco, ruquito, rucano, rucanito, rocano* (Salv) 'old, useless.' Harsh *viejo* may be made more palatable by a phonetic distortion into *viernes,* with the retention of the first syllable, as *estar viernes* for *estar viejo;* or by *vejanco* (Santamaría), *vejarano,* and in some places by *vetarro* (cf. *veterano*), as in "Ya ña Juana está muy *vetarra*" and "Usted es un *vetarro*" (Duarte). Although *vieja* is generally deprecatory for *mujer,* younger men in Mexico, for instance, refer to all women, including girls, as *viejas,* cf. "¡La niña está retesuave ['desirable'] ... qué suertecita te cargas con las *viejas*" (Ángulo, p. 91) and "tiene una *vieja* deliciosa" (*ibid.,* p. 205); and among the lower classes ¡qué vieja! may mean *¡qué guapa!* 'how pretty' (Frenk). In Mexico the familiar *es de tiempos de don Porfirio* (president of the Republic 1877–1880 and 1884–1911, dates which mark its modern period of prosperity) refers to antiquated things in general, equivalent to standard *en tiempos del rey que rabió* or *de María Castaña* or *de cuando amarraban los perros con longaniza.*

In Mexico many other humorous metaphors abound in popular speech or slang (Frenk): *ya está anterior, ya está macicito* (from *macizo* 'solid, massive'), *ya no se cuece* (or *coce*) *de un* (or *al primer*) *hervor* 'he can't be cooked (soft) in one boiling,' cf. *ponerse maceta* (RP, Bol) 'to grow old' (*maceta* 'club, block of hard wood'). Elsewhere we find *tiene media rueda* 'to be over fifty,' literally 'to have half a wheel' (Cuba); *dobla el paquete* 'he is over fifty,' literally 'he folds the package' (PR). In northern Chile, *viejo* may be replaced by *poico,* a word of Mapuche origin which now means 'an older person' from its original application (*poicado*) to beans and other leguminous plants gone to seed. Elsewhere we find *quedarse uno para semilla* 'to go to seed.' In Chile one hears the phrase *vivir los años del tabaco* 'to live a long time,' as does the tobacco plant: "—¡Éjese [= déjese] de esas cosas, iñor! ¡Si usté va a *vivir los años del tabaco!*" (ap. Rabanales). The phrase *pedir papa* means 'to be old, grow childish,' as in "Ya Juan está *pidiendo papa*" (Román), since very old people may become like children who ask for *papa* 'pap, porridge.' In Santo Domingo, *mojar los papeles* and *ir para las mayas* ('daisies') are heard, as in "ya tu abuelo *mojó los papeles*" and "tú y yo *vamos* ya *para las mayas*" (Patín).

PHYSICAL APPEARANCE

Physical unattractiveness gives rise to many euphemisms for harsh words like *feo* 'ugly.' In some areas (Chile, Ec) *muy feo* is replaced by *desengañado* 'disillusioned.' Elsewhere, *feo* is jocosely expanded (cf. peninsular *camafeo,* ap. Wagner, p. 16) to *federal* or *federico* (Cuba, Tex), as in "es una mujer muy *federica,*" and to *feróstico* (general). For the word *bagre* (a kind of 'catfish' found in American rivers), often applied to an ugly woman, the euphemistic *la señorita de Bagrini* may be substituted.

In Chile, the Mapuche borrowing *chuchi,* applied originally to badly formed or partly shriveled fruit (*melones chuchis, duraznos chuchis*), is euphemistically extended not only to misshapen objects but also to the human face (particularly of old women)—to a person with one eye smaller than the other, or a squint-eyed person, and the like (Lenz). Quechua borrowings *güisto* and *güingo* (Ec) 'twisted,' referring to a person with a crooked or twisted mouth or face, are current also in expressions like *camino güisto, línea güista* (Toscano, p. 224), as in "Su bastón es *güingo,* pero el mío es recto" (Cornejo). Aztec borrowing *tepocate* or *atepocate* 'tadpole' may be used to indicate *feo* (Frenk, p. 135), but it is applied especially to persons with large heads. Standard *cacarañado* 'pock-marked' has derivatives *cacarizo* (Mex), *cacaruso,* and *cacuso* (Col). In Mexico it is often phonetically deformed into *estar cucaracho* or *cúcara* (Frenk, p. 140) and ironically euphemized into *cutis de colegiala* 'schoolgirl complexion' along with the nickname *el Palmolive,* since Palmolive soap advertises such a complexion. In the Antilles, *cocorioco* 'ugly person' is more usually applied to women, as in "Juana es un *cocorioco*" (C. Suárez). In Venezuela (Rosenblat, *Lengua,* p. 36) an ugly woman may be said to be *como un porrazo* (or *golpe,* or *patada*) *en la espinilla, como un tropezón en noche oscura, como un dolor de estómago, como un acreedor, fea con efe mayúscula* or *fea con empeño, más fea que un tiro,* etc. In Colombia an ugly woman may be referred to as *azarosa, garabato, rejo,* etc. (Cadavid). All such facetious and apparently uncharitable locutions may be evidence of typically Spanish indifference and stoicism.

The sting of *sucio* 'dirty' and *mugriento* or *mugroso* 'filthy, greasy' is removed in euphemistically vague *estar uno imposible,* perhaps an ellipsis of *imposible de mirar* or *de sufrir; inhumano* (Chile); *percusio* (Ven), related to standard *percudido* 'tarnished, soiled'; *cochoso* (Ec, Col) from *cocho* 'pig'; *chorreado* 'stained by a dripping liquid, or having striped skin (of cattle)' applied particularly to the dirty face of a child, as in "¡Ay! qué *chorreadita* estás, chula" (Inclán, I, 433, ap. Frenk, p. 147) and "aquel soldado ... daba dinero a su escuintle *chorriado*" (Ángulo, p. 97); *charrasqueado* (Mex), supposedly 'cut, stabbed' from *charrasca* 'side arm' but more likely related to *charrascar* 'to burn, toast, brown'; Mexican *fodongo* or *fodongón,* as in "¿Ud. cree, don Pepe, que sean tan *fodongos,* que hacía quince días que no se mudaban la camisa?" (Inclán, I, 346, ap. Frenk); *manteco,-a* (Col) from *manteca* 'lard, fat, butter' may mean 'greasy and slovenly,' as in "Por Dios, Enrique, ¿cómo te atreves a salir a la calle tan *manteco?*" (Acuña); *sucedido* (Chile), the initial sounds recalling *sucio,* the expression *jugar rucio* (Chile) for *jugar sucio* contrasting with *jugar limpio.*

Sometimes a foreign borrowing functions euphemistically for *sucio: carachento* (Arg) from Quechua *caracha* 'mange, scab'; *carcoso* (Ec) and *carquiento* (Peru) from Quechua *carca* 'crust of dirt on the body'; *chamagoso* (Mex) from Aztec *chamahuac* 'fat, coarse object' applied to a person with soiled or greasy clothes (such as a butcher or cook) and related to *chamaco* 'boy,' with parallel semasiological shift in *fodongo* 'dirty' to 'fat' (Guanajuato); *chimeco* (Guerrero, Mex) 'dirty-faced'; *huishui* (Arequipa, Peru: Ugarte) from Quechua; *intutible* (Chile), occasionally pronounced *inchuchible,* from Mapuche *tutuy* (?), an interjection of disgust (see Román), as in "mi ropa está *intutible*"; *majoncho* (Peru: Vargas Ugarte); Quechua *mapa* (deriv. *mapioso*) 'dirty' (Ec) in vocatives like *mapa sin vergüenza, mapa gringo, mapa asco* (Toscano,

p. 226), as in "Quita, *mapa alabancioso,* / más limpio ('broke, penniless') que una patena; / si tienes llena la bolsa, / de viento la tendrás llena" (ap. Malaret, *Copla*); *piñén* (Chile), from Mapuche *pigen* 'crust of dirt (especially on the feet),' as in "Mira sus manos renegridas y sus pies cubiertos de *piñén*" (Hermes Nahuel, ap. Medina); *querque* (Arequipa, Peru) from Quechua meaning 'crust of dirt'; *xuco, shuco, xongo* and *shosho* from Aztec. A metaphorical euphemism based on a foreign borrowing is *parecer un pepenador* (Mex) 'to look like a ragpicker' from Aztec *pepena* 'to pick up,' cf. *parecer un caleta* (Ven) 'to look like a porter or longshoreman' > 'to be dirty, tattered.'

In some regions *calvo, pelado,* and *pelón* 'bald' are likely to be replaced, perhaps by a foreign borrowing, like modern standard *glabro* from Latin *glaber* (through French *glabre*), such as *coro* from Quechua *kora* and *cabizcala* from *cabeza* + Quechua *kala* 'nude' (Arequipa, Peru: Ugarte); *lauco* (S Chile) from *laucar* (Mapuche *laucan*) 'to remove or lose hair or wool,' deriv. nouns *lauca* and *laucadura*. Chilean nicknames for bald head are *cabeza de coronta* = 'cabeza pelada o de pelo muy corto' because of the visual resemblance to a *coronta* (Quechua) 'corn-cob'; *cabeza de (melón) tuna; cabeza de rodilla;* and *pelado prisco* (std. *melocotón abridero* 'freestone peach'), as in "¡Qué alegay [= alegas] voh, *pelao prihco,* oo!" (Rabanales, p. 166), cf. *coco pelao* and *cascoelosa* (SD: Patín).

Standard *delgado* 'slender, thin' and especially *flaco* or *flacucho* 'lean, skinny' may be euphemized by *acabado* 'finished' (Col, Mex, CA) and by *atrasado* 'retarded' (Col), with *acabarse* and *atrasarse* for standard *enflaquecerse* 'to become lean, weak, skinny'; *distraído* (Esmeraldas, Ec). Elsewhere, *flacucho* is euphemistically distorted in familiar and popular speech into *flaquindé* (SD), *flaquinsón* (Peru, Chile), *flamenco* (Hond, Mex, PR); often other suffixes are substituted for unpleasant -*ucho* or are added to it (depriving it of its stress), as *flaquenco* (CA), *flaquerón* (Urug), and general *flacuchento*. Foreign borrowings are the Quechua word *cuico* 'earthworm' (Ec: "—Mejor callá, *cuica* desgraciada," García Muñoz, p. 68; "la *cuica* Lola," *ibid.*, p. 98); *guascoso* (highland Ec) 'tall and thin person,' from Quechua *huasca* 'rope, strap, whip'; *galembo* (Ven) 'turkey buzzard' (also *chulo*). In Esmeraldas, Ecuador, we find the localism *rechifle,* as in "—Este vestido, tan angosto, bueno está para Antonio, que es un *rechifle*" (Cornejo). Among jocose Mexican expressions are

(Frenk, p. 135) *ñango, ñenga* (shortened from *cañenga; cañengo,-a,* Col, Cuba; *cañengue,* Cuba, SD); *charaludo,* from *charal,* the name of a small fish; especially for women: (*vieja*) *momia,* ubiquitous *escoba* (or *tabla*) *vestida* 'dressed broom (or plank),' and derisive *campeona de natación* 'champion swimmer,' explained as "nada por delante y nada por detrás"; *anuncio del paludismo* 'advertisement for malaria'; and *ya vuela* or *está que vuela, es un chiflido, de perfil no se ve.* In Chile one hears *palo de ajo* 'garlic stick,' as in "Y este *palo de ajo* ¿cuándo va a engordar?" (Rabanales, p. 172); *patas de caña* 'reed legs' and *patas de colihue* 'colihue legs,' from the name of a local flower (*ibid.*), cf. general *garza* 'heron' applied to a person with long, thin legs; *radiografía, alambrito.* Elsewhere one hears *intrínsico* (SD), perhaps influenced by *tísico; jalado* (SD) from *jalarse,* as in "ella *se jaló* con el disgusto" (Patín); general *un saco de huesos* 'a bag of bones'; *un violín* (Nic: Valle); *un casco* (Cuba: Rodríguez); un *bacal* or *bacalito* 'corncob' (SE Mex), from Maya.

Among the jocose appellations heard in Mexico for a 'tall and thin person' are *kilométrico, inspector de azoteas* or *de alambres* or *de postes,* and the nicknames *la Percha* 'pole,' *la Garrocha* 'pike,' and *el Kilómetro parado* 'an upright kilometer' (Frenk, p. 136). In Chile (Plath, p. 8) one hears *caballo de la bomba,* referring to the large skinny horses that formerly drew the fire carts; and among students the nickname *Alamiro,* a play on the proper name *Alamiro* phonetically associated with *álamo* 'poplar,' as in "—Saludos te mandó *Alamiro*" (Rabanales, p. 165); likewise the nickname *Pistilo* from botanic *pistilo* 'pistil' (cf. std. *paja larga, espigado,* etc.), as in "—Vihte al *Pihtilo* ayer?" (*ibid.*); *largo viaje* 'long journey.' For Colombia are recorded *una escalera de bajar cocos* (Flórez, p. 183), *larguncho* and *pábilo* (Cadavid) for 'a tall, thin woman'; in Cuba one hears *grillo.* Everywhere the gesture of raising the extended little finger as one says "Es así" suggests skinniness (see fig. 4).

Standard *bajo de estatura* 'short' (with a shade of *rechoncho* 'chubby') becomes in familiar speech *chaparro* 'evergreen oak' and *chapaneco* (CA, Mex), with variant *chaparrón* 'somewhat chubby'; *corojito* (Cuba), from *corojo* (called also *corozo*), the name of a small palm tree; *pachacho* (Chile) and *pacho* (Chile, CA), see Corominas; *patucho* (Ec), applied first to short-legged hens, then to chubby persons; *petizo* or *petiso* (RP, Chile, Peru), from the French *petit,* applied to both persons and animals, as in "El paisano ... era un viejito de barba blanca, *petizo* y charlatán"

(Arg: Güiraldes, p. 153); *pite* (Ec), from Quechua *pite* 'poco' (Toscano, p. 225) and the more usual *omoto* 'dwarf'; *chincol* (Chile), the Mapuche name of a small bird, as in "Tan pequeño era que la banda miserable le había apodado *El chincol*" (Edwards Bello, *El roto,* ap. Oroz); *poroto* (Arg, Chile) 'bean,' meaning 'physically and morally inferior,' as in "¡Qué hables tú, *poroto* ... cuando eres un *poroto!*" (Román); *quiltro* (Chile), possibly Mapuche (Lenz), meaning *gozque* 'cur,' as in "Fulano es un *quiltro* no más" (Oroz, pp. 15, 20); *turro* and *turrete* (Col: Tobón) 'stone, piece of wood or bone' used in playing *marro,* a game resembling quoits; *viruña* (Col) 'small piece, crumb'; *zapallón* (RP, Chile, Peru), from Quechua *sapallu,* a wide, round, and flat calabash. With a stronger shade of *rechoncho* are *batato* (Col); *barraca, barraquete* (SD); *buchicacho* (Col); *butuco* (CA); *catumbao* (Peru); *conguita* (SD); *guasapo* (Guat); *guatoco* (Bol); *guatón* (Chile, Peru); *matul* 'bundle,' *patato* and *torombolo* (Cuba); *olotón* (Mex) 'big ear of corn'; *petacón* (Arg, Peru); *paturranito* (SD); *poncho* (Col); *potoco* (Chile), from *poto* 'posterior'; *rungo* and *patango* (Hond); *tango, tangano,* and *tanganito* (Mex); *retacón* (RP, Peru), from standard *retaco; sapo* (Col, CA, Mex) 'toad,' as in "Mi cuñada es muy *sapa*" (Guat: Sandoval), together with its euphemistic derivatives *sapaneco, saparruco, saporreto* (Col, Ven), and *saporro* (Col, CA).

Among Mexican slang terms for 'short' (Frenk, p. 137) are *centavo* or *centavito* 'penny'; *comino* or *cominito* 'cuminseed'; less favorable *tachuela* 'tack,' *corcholata* 'cork-lined cap of a soda-water bottle,' *pulga* 'flea,' *microbio, gusano* 'worm'; mocking *reintegro,* the smallest lottery prize, the reimbursement of a ticket having as the last figure of its number the same figure as the ticket winning first prize; *inspector de sótanos* 'basement inspector'; *de los Bajos de Jalisco* (*los altos de Jalisco* is the name of the eastern section of that Mexican state). For women especially are *chaquira* or *chaquirita* 'small glass bead'; *lenteja* or *lentejita* 'small lentil'; *mentadita,* diminutive of *mentada,* ellipsis of *mentada de madre* 'mentioning a person's mother,' which in most Spanish-speaking countries is the gravest offense (see chap. vii).

For 'shabbily or slovenly dressed' (std. *mal vestido, desaseado, zarrapastroso*) one hears in Chile and Mexico the euphemism *distraído* 'absentminded.' In popular speech *distraído* may become *distráido,* and, among the Chilean untutored, *distréido,* as in "—No fuí a misa, padrecito, porque estaba muy *distréido*" (Román). Ubiquitously *distraído* may replace unsavory *desatento* 'rude, discourteous, inconsiderate.' Other substitutes for *mal vestida* heard in Mexico are *dejada* 'abandoned,' *mal fajada* 'badly girdled,' *mal cuidada* 'ill-kept, careless,' and sesquipedalian terms like *descuacharrangada* (cf. std. *escacharrada* and *descuajaringada*), *desgarran-chada* (also Hond; cf. std. *desgarrar* 'to tear, mangle, claw'), *desguangui-lada, guandajona* (for others see Frenk, p. 146); and among metaphors: *andar toda por ningún lado*. Elsewhere are current: *cacharposo,-a* (Ec) from *cacharpas* 'rubbish'; *cucarachón,-a* (Nic); *chafalote* (Pan); general *descachalandrado,-a; descacharrado,-a* (CA), as in "Siento no aceptar la invitación para ir al teatro, pero, como ves, estoy muy *descacharrado*" (Guat: Sandoval), from standard *escacharrar* 'romper un cacharro'; *desgolletado, desguañangado, desguarilado, desmanganillado, desmangu-rrillado, desmorgallado*, etc. (Ven: Rosenblat, p. 378). In Colombia may be heard *desgualetado, guasamelletas, hecho chiras, chulo*, and *oso* (Cadavid). In the River Plate region and Chile one hears constantly *guarango* for both *zarrapastroso* and *mal educado* 'ill-bred.' Apparently it is the Quechua *huarancu* 'a thorny tree with twisted and irregular branches,' but there seems to be a confusion of terms (see Corominas); in some aspects the word may be likened to *alcornoque* 'cork tree,' which has the figurative meaning of 'persona ignorante y zafia.' In Colombia the borrowing *guache*, from Quechua and Chibcha *huacha* 'orphan, poor,' is applied to a vulgar, ill-mannered person; the feminine *guaricha* (mean-ing also *prostituta* has a verbal derivative *guachificarse* 'coger modales propios de la gente baja o guache' (Tobón). In Argentina, and probably elsewhere, *andar a la pura penca* means 'andar mal vestido, harapiento, casi en cueros,' because of a certain similarity with *penca* 'pulpy leaf of certain plants.' Among the Chilean populace one may hear *andar más hiludo* ['ragged'] *que una penca,* as in "—¡Lo hubiéray vihto; andaba má hilúo qui'una penca!" (Rabanales, p. 178); and likewise *andar como perejil* ['parsley'] *sin hojas,* which is related to standard *emperejilado* or *emperifollado* 'elaborately dressed, dolled up,' as in "—¡Qué vay a ir así! ¿Qué no veíh que *anday como perejil sin hoja?,*" and also with the ellipsis of *sin hoja;* adjective *perejiliento* may mean 'ragged,' as in "—No es dable que mientras unos andan toos *perejilientos* y casposos ... otros estén poiríos [= podridos] en plata" (*ibid.*). In Esmeraldas, Ecuador, be-sides *pichangoso* 'ragged,' we find the localism *quiebra* used adjectivally in the sense of *maltrajeado* 'badly dressed' (as well as 'poor' and 'useless'), as in "—No acepto a ese pretendiente, porque es mui *quiebra* i yo merezco algo mejor" (Cornejo).

DUDE

Words denoting a person who gives undue attention to dress, is fond of showy clothes and affects ultrafashionable styles ('dude, dandy') are fairly numerous. Many of them, originally favorable in the sense of 'well-dressed,' acquire in time unfavorable connotations of excess, ostentation, and bad taste, often through use by lower social classes in referring to the more privileged. Then new euphemistic synonyms must be supplied, particularly when styles of dress change rapidly and radically. Among familiar standard terms are *currutaco* (from nickname *Curro,* for Francisco, and *retaco* 'chubby' ?, see Corominas); adjectives *emperejilado* (from *perejil* 'parsley') and *emperifollado* (from *perifollo* 'chervil'), which compare the curled, aromatic leaves of these plants (used in flavoring soups and salads) to the lacy frills and trimmings of overdressed and perfumed fashionables; *goma* 'rubber' or *gomoso* 'rubbery'; *lechuguino* 'young lettuce' (cf. *emperejilado, emperifollado); paquete* 'package,' girt and bound like a package (?); *petimetre* or *petrimetre,* from French *petit-maître; pisaverde,* from *pisar* 'to tread, step on' and *verde* 'green,' perhaps referring to the habit of walking daintily as if on tiptoe in crossing flower beds in a garden (see Corominas).

American Spanish has developed still other terms. The word *cachaco* first meant 'untidy, slovenly in dress.' When groups of liberal students in Colombia began to take an active part in political movements (about 1830), they were dubbed *cachacos* by their opponents, but the success of the movement in creating Nueva Granada raised the lowly epithet to the meaning of 'elegant young man,' subsequently equivalent to *lechuguino* and *petimetre* (Cuervo, § 879). However, while the latter two terms have since lost caste, *cachaco* has remained highly respectable in Colombia and Ecuador: 'apuesto, elegante' (Ec: Cornejo) and 'bien vestido ... de una persona honorable, caballerosa, de maneras distinguidas' (Col: Acuña) or 'hombre de buena sociedad ... garboso, elegante, afable o cortés' (Col: Tobón). It becomes derogatory only if modified—*cachaco pobre* or *cachaco de agua dulce*—and then it means 'el que quiere ostentar, sobretodo en el vestido, una riqueza que no tiene' (Tobón). Elsewhere, however, *cachaco* has remained derogatory: 'policeman, cop' (Peru), and *cursi* 'shabby-genteel' (Chile). Although still in good usage in Colombia, it has there been in part replaced, successively, by *pepito, gomoso, filipichín,* and *glaxo* (see L. García Ortiz, *Los cachacos de Bogotá,* ap. Santamaría, I, 255). In addition to present-day *glaxo m.,* and *fosfa f.,* we may now add, for Bogotá, *cocacolo* and *cocacola,* derived from the imported drink which has found great favor among teen-agers; and by a certain linguistic permutation of an article of consumption for the consumer, the word has come to designate frivolous young people, *lechuguinos,* and the like.

Among other American-Spanish terms are the following:

cacharpeado (Chile, from *cacharpas,* of Quechua origin, meaning 'trash, old clothes, etc.'), generally said of rustics and of the lower classes, as in "—¿Y pa onde vai tan bien *cacharpiao,* como e día e fiesta?" (Del Campo, p. 100) and *"se cacharpeaban* como señoritas de ciudad" (ap. Medina); *cajetilla* (RP) 'package (of tobacco, of cigarettes),' a double diminutive of *caja* 'box' (*caja > cajeta > cajetilla*), semantically analogous to *paquete* 'package' for 'dude,' but it has lost ground to less unpleasant *fifí* (*paquete atado* may in Argentina replace *cajetilla* in the sense of 'package of cigarettes'); *catrín* (CA, Mex), widespread in the nineteenth century, has fallen into disuse except as an adjective meaning 'elegant' with a shade of irony (like *cuco, curro*), as in "Hoy está usted muy *catrina"* (Guat: Sandoval), deriv. *catrinear* 'ponerse *catrina* una muchacha' (*ibid.*); *colocolo* (Chile; not to be confused with Colombian *cocacolo,* above), from Mapuche (perhaps onomatopoetic) meaning 'a fantastic monster' or 'a wild cat,' but it may be connected with *colero* 'top hat' formerly worn by dudes, or with *Colocolo,* the name of an old Araucanian chief.

chamberí (Peru), now in disuse (having yielded to *chic* and later to other words), *chamberín* (parts of Mex), with adjectives *chamberinado* (Mex; rustic *chambiriniado*), related by Corominas to a family of words discussed under *chamba* 'chance,' and *chamarilero* 'fripper' with its overtones of 'cheap and tawdry,' and to some speakers the word may recall also *chambergo,* applied to uniforms worn by the regiment *de la Chamberga,* the bodyguard formed in Madrid for Charles II during his minority (and originally referring to the military coat worn by General Schomberg and his troops who entered Catalonia from France); *chatre* (Chile, Peru, Ec), possibly from Mapuche (Lenz), used chiefly among peasants, is the opposite of *chegre* 'poorly dressed'; *chiche* (RP, Chile, Bol) 'trinket,' from

Quechua; *chulla* (Ec); *churo* (N Arg, Bol), perhaps from Quechua *churu* 'snail' (cf. *emperejilado* with its image of curves and curls) and recalling standard *chulo* meaning a person who is loud in dress (*churo* may be used in N Arg for *lindo,* as in "¿Cómo te va? —*Churo,*" ap. Solá); *chute* (slang, Chile, with phonetic associative interference of *futre*).

fifí (Mex), largely replacing *catrín, gomoso, lagartijo,* and *roto,* as in "El llamado Tito era un *fifí* almidonado y antipático" (Azuela, *Nueva burguesía,* ap. Frenk, p. 149) found also elsewhere (Guat); *fifí de barrio,* which is an impoverished type of *fifí* (*ibid.*); *fifí provinciano* is also deprecatory, as in *"fifíes provincianos,* con los cabellos embadurnados de brillantina, mostrando una colita de rata a manera de bigote ... habían llegado a la casa sin que nadie los hubiera invitado, soñando atraerse a la concurrencia femenina con sus poses de cinemático galán desnutrido" (Ángulo, p. 62); *fifiriche* (CR, Mex) and *fifirucho* (Mex) meaning a thin and weak *fifí; filipichín* and *filipo* (Col), *filistrín* (Ven); *futre* (RP, Chile, Bol, Peru, Ec), deprecatory when used by the lower classes in referring to higher classes of society, but not necessarily so when used among those of higher social status, possibly deriving from the French exclamation *¡foutre!* repeated by wealthy Chileans returning from France and then applied by the populace to users of the word (cf. Spanish exclamation *¡coño!* used in Chile to indicate a Spaniard), or from *futraque* (now in disuse) '(frock) coat,' later meaning 'an elegant young man,' and *futreque* (Chile) for *futre* may stem from French *foutriquet* derived from *foutre* (*foutriquet* > *futreque* > *futraque* under the influence of *fraque*), with favorable derivative *futrecito* and unfavorable *futrecillo,* as in "... las vecinas, atentas a las maniobras de los *futrecitos,* que, en grupos, pasaban por la calle ... diciendo galanterías o haciendo la corte a las chicas del barrio" (Bol: Arguedas, p. 82).

lagartijo (Mex) 'lizard,' less frequent than *fifí.*

mascasebo and *muñeco* (Ven).

pachuco, a distortion of *El Paso* (Texas) influenced by *Pachuca* (the name of the capital of the state of Hidalgo), which arose in the early 'thirties along the Mexican border, later reached Mexico City, where it displaced *tarzán,* and is itself now outmoded (the typical apparel of the *pachuco* consists of long, baggy coat, trousers tapering to the ankles, flamboyant necktie, wide-brimmed hat, and large coarse shoes usually white); *padrote* (Mex), generally 'pander' but also *bon vivant* of any social class and (over) carefully dressed, an impoverished person of this sort being sometimes dubbed *padrotito de banqueta* (Frenk, p. 150), *banqueta* meaning *acera* 'sidewalk'; *palé* (Peru), from French *palais* (?), as in "está bien *palé"; paquetero* (Arg); *patiquín* (Ven: Rosenblat, p. 185); *pepe* and *pepito* (Bol, Col, Ven, Pan), *pepillito* (SD); *pije* (Chile, Bol, Peru); *pinganilla* (Chile, Peru, Ec, CR, Hond) meaning an impoverished person who strives to dress fashionably, though as an adjective *pinganillo,-a* may mean 'well-dressed' (Bol, Ec; cf. *catrín* in Mex), connected with *pingo* or *pingajo* 'cheap clothes' and the standard phrase *en pinganitos* 'in a high position,' and *en pinganillas* (Col) 'on tiptoe,' reflecting the dainty gait of the dude (cf. *pisaverde* above); now rare *pitre* (Col, Ven, Ant), a contraction of *petimetre; plantarse* (Col, CA, Mex), as in "Aquel estudiante *se planta* siempre bien" (Guat: Sandoval) and *plantificarse* (CA, Mex).

roto or *rotito* (Mex), applied to a person of little means who tries to dress elegantly, used especially by the populace in reference to the middle classes, as in "Odiaba a las elegantes, a las *rotas* que visten de seda" (Ángel de Campo, *Pueblo y canto,* ap. Frenk, p. 149); *titino* and *truche* (Col).

III MENTAL AND MORAL DEFECTS

Many concepts have powerful feeling tones that constantly seek an outlet. When a much-used word has lost its force, the speaker fills the vacuum with a new form that, because of its newness, will adequately convey the tones of feeling. This is particularly true of words in need of euphemistic cloaking. Existing forms may be altered, shortened or, by way of reaction, humorously twisted. The attraction of the concept may be so great that it draws to itself material from many sides, thus engendering a wealth of synonyms. Words denoting mental deficiencies are of this nature.

STUPIDITY

Standard *tonto, bobo, memo, mentecato,* all meaning 'fool,' originally euphemisms like *imbécil* (from *imbecillis* 'weak, feeble') are often replaced by terms of vague or general import, such as *inocente, cándido, sencillo, un alma de Dios, un infeliz, un pobre hombre, un angelito, un santo,* and *un bendito.*

Among popular American euphemisms for *tonto* are:

alforjudo (Chile) 'equipped with saddlebags' (see below); *asoleado* (CA) 'sunstruck,' verb *asolearse.*

bayunco (CA), like *guanaco,* used in Guatemala to refer to all other Central Americans, and like *guanaco* means *tonto, rústico,* deriv. *bayuncada* and *bayunquear; bembo* (Mex) 'blobber-lipped'; *bolo* (PR), perhaps from its meaning of 'tailless,' as in *"los bolos* de la escuela salían del paso con algunas respuestas fáciles preparadas de antemano" (L. Sánchez Morales, ap. Malaret, *Vocabulario*); *bombo* (Cuba) 'rattled.'

cachencho (Chile); *caldo de ave* (Chile: Plath, p. 10) 'chicken broth'; *carajo, carajete,* and *carajón* (Col) 'penis,' cf. *pistola* and *verga* below; *ciguato* (Ant), *(a)ciguatado* (Mex, Ant) from *cigua* (or *cegua*) 'phantom' (Aztec *cihuatl* 'woman'), as in "te jugó la *cegua*" (Nic); *cristiano* (CA) alongside standard doublet *cretino* (< dialectal French *crétin,* French *chrétien;* in parts of Mexico *buen cristiano* may mean 'idiot').

chambeco (Chile) in the sense of 'madcap, harebrained,' as in "Al *chambeco* de mi marido se le ha ocurrido convidar acá al imbécil de Schubert" (Malbrán, p. 10); *chaveta* (PR) 'bolt, wedge' and *deschavetado* (Chile) based on standard *perder uno la chaveta; chocho* (Nic) from standard *chocho,-a* 'doting.'

dundo and *dundeco* (Col, CA) from *duendo* 'tame' and *duende* 'hobgoblin, elf, ghost,' deriv. *dundera* for *tontería* and verbs *dundear* and *dundequear,* cf. *jugado de duende* (Nic, where *jugado de cegua* is also heard) and "se te aparecieron *los duendes*" (Nic).

fallo (Chile); *gafo* 'suffering from leprosy' > 'suffering from claw hand' > 'fool' (Ven), as in "No seas *gafo,* aprovecha la oportunidad" (Rosenblat, p. 92); *golpeado* (Los Ríos, Ec; San Luis, Arg: Vidal, p. 324), as in "Zutano es mui *golpeado* para que pueda ser el autor del hecho que se le imputa" (Cornejo); *guaile* (Durango, Mex).

jetón (Chile), from *jeta* 'snout, blobber lip,' with the euphemism *Getulio,* as well as euphemistic gestures of extending the lower lip or of pulling the lower lip downward with the index finger.

lerendo (Mex), from *lerdo* 'slow, dull'; *loco de verano, loco lindo* (Arg: Speratti, p. 172).

maje (CA, Mex), one of the popular terms applied to Indians in the interior of Mexico, as in "Convengamos, pues, en que somos *majes* de remate y que de esta coyuntura se aprovechan algunos extranjeros ... para vaciar nuestros bolsillos" (Hond: L. Adams, *Pláticas de chicha y nabo*), "¡Anda, vente, vámonos con ellas, no seas *maje!*" (Mex: Ángulo, p. 34) and "¡Cómo eres *maje!*" (*ibid.,* p. 48); general (as in Spain) *maleta* 'suitcase,' a euphemism for *malo* in the sense of *torpe* 'dull, stupid'; *menso* (Mex), as in "el *menso* se dió cuenta de la alhajita que era la lagartona ésa" (Héctor Mendoza, *Las cosas simples,* 1954, p. 19) and "¿Eres tan *menso* que no te des cuenta que esto es un puro *enjuague* ['bribe']?" (Ángulo,

p. 124); *mudo* (Ec, Guat) 'dumb' as in "Hortensia, aunque muy hermosa, es muy *muda*" (Sandoval), deriv. *mudenco* (Guat, where *mudenco* may mean also *tartamudo* 'stuttering, stammering') and *mudengo* (Peru); *muspa* and *upa* (Ec: Toscano, p. 226).

nayo and *queispo* (Salv: Tovar, *BAAL*, XV, 62); *noneco* (Pan, CA) and *nonejo* (CR), deriv. *un no nos dejes* (Gagini); *norteado* (Coahuila, Mex) 'having lost one's bearings,' as in "Ya don Juanito está *norteado*" for "Ya está bobo" (Duarte).

pelotudo and *pepa* (Arequipa, Peru: Ugarte); *pistola* (Col, Ven) 'pistol,' perhaps in the sense of 'penis,' cf. *verga,* below.

salame (rustic, Arg); *sano* (Col: Sundheim); *sincero* (Piura, Peru); *suato* (Mex), explained by Santamaría as *menos despectivo que baboso; suncuán* (Hond) 'red wasp's comb.'

tilingo (RP, Peru, Mex), deriv. *tilingada, tilinguear; tilico* (Mex).

una verga or *pija* (vulg., Nic) 'penis'; *una viñuca* or *viñurca* (Nic); *virote* (Col, Ven, Mex), deriv. *virotada* for *tontería; volado* (Peru, Mex).

zambeque (Cuba), as in "José es muy *zambeque*" (C. Suárez), deriv. *zambequería.*

Standard *tarugo* 'chump, block,' like *adoquín* 'paving stone,' *zoquete* 'block,' has come to mean 'blockhead' and, with derivative *tarugada* (cf. *zoquetada*), is frequently used in America (Mex, CA), as in "Es lástima que el hijo de un hombre tan inteligente ... haya resultado un *tarugo,* casi un imbécil" (*ibid.*). Similarly, older *cipote* 'club' (still current in Extremadura and Andalusia) today means *tonto* in Colombia (Cauca) and Venezuela (cf. *mamposta,* SD: Patín).

Perhaps the most widely used synonym for *tonto* in America is popular *zonzo* or *sonso* (< Latin *insulsus* 'saltless'), which in Spain is heard to a limited extent and usually with the meaning of its doublet *soso* 'insipid.' Shifting the main stress of an unpleasant word by the addition of suffixes often removes much of the sting and therefore acts euphemistically. This occurs with *zonzo* in *zonzón* (cf. *cobardón* for *cobarde*), *zonzorrio* (Arg; cf. std. *zonzorrión*); *zonzoreco, zonzoreno,* and *zonzoriano* (CA); *zonzaina* (Guat), *zonconeto* (Hond). Derivatives are *zoncear* or *sonsear* for *tontear, zoncera* or *soncera* for *sosera* or *tontería, asonsado* or *asonsao* for *tonteado,* and others. Examples: "—Pa esconder el delito, de puro *sonso,* la enterró" (Arg: González Arrili, p. 37); "estoy de *sonceras* hasta las narices" (*Fray Mocho,* p. 186); "anda como *asonsao* de puro pensar en vos" (*ibid.,* p. 112).

Fairly widespread in American Spanish for *tonto* is *baboso,* as an extension of its standard meaning 'driveling, foolishly sentimental' (from *baba* 'saliva, drivel'; for std. *babieca* 'idiot, dunce,' see Spitzer and Gamillscheg, p. 86). However, in some regions, particularly in Central America, *baboso* is a shade more derogatory and offensive, meaning something like *canalla, desvergonzado,* and is therefore carefully avoided: "Entre las varias acepciones de la palabra *papo* no figura en el léxico la de 'tonto,' 'simple,' 'cándido,' que por acá se le da, que es precisamente *la misma de otra que se toma en carácter muy ofensivo, y que para más señas es derivada de 'babear' "* (Guat: *Mosaico,* p. 17). The author apparently feels that *baboso* is unprintable. Its derivative *babosear* there means, among other things, 'to insult,' as in "—A mí no me *babosea* nadie, ¿oyes?" (Sandoval).

Familiar standard *pendejo* 'cowardly' (lit. 'pubes hair') has in the popular speech of many regions (Col, Ven, Ec, CA, Mex, Ant) come to signify 'tonto' (deriv. *pendejada* 'tontería,' *apendejarse* 'to become a fool,' and *pendejear* 'tontear, babear,' that is, 'to act or talk foolishly'). It is particularly harsh in Mexico, where it is considered a grave insult. Like other terms in this category, it is often euphemistically referred to by its initial sound *p* or the syllable *pen,* as in the expressions "no seas majadero ['foolish'] con *p*" or "dejé de ser majadero con *p*" (Tobón); "verle a uno la *P* en la *F* (*or* la *P* en la frente)" which means 'to consider someone a fool' (Mex, Tex); "—No sea *pen* ..." (Col: Rendón, p. 68). Furthermore, the word may be deformed, contracted, or distorted sufficiently to temper its violence with a humoristic twist, as *penitente* or *pen* ... *itente; péndolo* or *pendolo* (Antioquia: Tobón); *pendango* (PR, where it means 'cobarde'); *penco* (Mex), as in "Siempre hay otros más *pencos* que nosotros los de la sierra, ¿verdad?" (Mex: Azuela, p. 193); "Sólo a un *p* ... *escuezo* como yo pudo ocurrírselo descansar por tanto tiempo dentro del monte" (Mex: Ángulo, p. 340). Elsewhere *pendejo* may have other meanings, even diametrically opposed, such as 'appropriate, suitable' (Atlantic coast, Col), 'sharp, cunning, wily' (Peru), 'very young person,' and frequently 'insignificant' as in "Ésa es una pobre *pendeja* repetisa" (San Luis, Arg: Vidal, p. 95). In Cuba *pendejera,* the name of a plant, is euphemized by the word *prendedera.*

Standard *leso* 'hurt, wounded, disturbed, confounded' is frequently heard for *tonto* in some regions (Chile, Bol, Peru), as in the Bolivian proverb "Así se engaña al *leso,* con pan y queso." Though originally a euphemism, *leso* now appears at times to be more forceful than *tonto,* to judge from the common phrase "tonto seré pero no *leso"* and the necessity of prefixing *medio* to mitigate the blow (*medio leso; medio,* or often *media, lesa,* etc.). Furthermore, *es leso* may be euphemized by the phrase *es Lesana,* Lesano being a fictitious proper name the initial sounds of which recall *leso* but are not stressed. Derivatives are *lesear* 'tontear' and nouns *lesura* or *lesera* 'tontería,' as in "¡déjese usted de *leseras!"* for standard "¡déjese usted de *tonterías!"*

The term *opa* for *tonto* or *idiota,* common in some regions (RP, Bol, Peru, Col), probably stems from Quechua *upa* 'deaf, dumb, fool,' though other sources have been postulated (see Corominas): "accesible al más *opa"* (Arg: ap. Schallman, p. 77); "¡Qué *opas* son ustedes!" (Bol: R. Leiton, *Los eternos vagabundos,* 1939, p. 108). Derivatives are *opear* meaning 'hacer *operías'* = *tonterías; opopa; oparrón* applied in Salta to a person who appears to be *opa* but is not completely so (Solá), and *opón* for a person who is less *opa* than an *oparrón.* A common practice, already discussed, is to use foreign borrowings as euphemisms (for theories about *panolí* and *gilí* 'fool' in Spain see Clavería's *Estudios sobre los gitanismos del español,* Madrid, 1951, anejo 53, *RFE,* pp. 249–253; also *NRFH,* IV, No. 1, pp. 43–49).

River Plate slang *otario,* once widely used in popular speech, has lost its force and is being replaced by *gil* and *gilito* (Herrero Mayor, *Lengua,* p. 89; Gobello, p. 32), deriv. verb *gilear* (Peru), as in "la *gileó"* 'he made a fool of her.'

Frequently *tonto* is replaced by the name of an animal usually considered stupid, such as general *burro, asno, topo* 'mole,' *atún* 'tunny fish,' *percebe* 'barnacle,' *besugo* 'sea bream,' in addition to *animal* and *bruto.* Thus, *pavo* 'turkey,' while heard in Spain (alongside *pavisoso* and *pavitonto*) in the sense of *tonto,* is particularly widespread in familiar speech in the River Plate region and Chile. Besides familiar standard *pavada* 'tontería,' we find the following typically American derivatives: *pavería,* superlative *pavísimo* for *muy pavo,* Chilean deprecatory *pavuncio* and *pavucho,* and verb *pavear* 'cometer pavadas.' That *pavo* and *sonso* are synonymous is evident from the following quotation: "—Me parece que el único *sonso* sos vos ... —¡Oh!

no seas *pavo* ... —El *pavo* ya te he dicho quien es" (Arg: González Arrili, p. 93).

The *pavo* or *pavo común* (to differentiate it from *pavo real* 'peacock'), being native to North and Central America, has a special name in each Indian language, which has been adopted by the Spanish-speaking persons in the region concerned. In many instances the new word has acquired the additional sense of *tonto*. Thus, in Mexico we find *guajolote* (from Aztec *huexolotl*), with shortened *jolote*, euphemistic augmentative *guajolotón*, and noun *guajolotada* 'tontería, pavada.' In Central America and certain areas of Mexico one hears *chumpipe,-a* or *chompipe,-a* (and shortened *chumpe,-a* or *chompe,-a*), generally considered an onomatopoetic name imitating the cries of young turkeys. Examples: "Tu criada es muy *chumpipa*, pues todavía no puede ir sola al mercado" and "Fuí muy *chumpipe* cuando pensé en casarme contigo" (Guat: Sandoval). Derivative *chumpipada* (*chompipada*) or *chumpipeada* (*chompipeada*) means 'tontería, pavada,' as in "Es necesario que amonestes a tu hijo, a fin de que no haga tantas *chumpipadas*" (*ibid.*); deriv. *chumpipear* means 'andar vagando ... como un tonto,' as in "Anda al correo a dejarme la carta pero sin ir *chumpipeando*" (*ibid.*). In the Antilles, *guanajo* 'turkey' (from Taino or Carib, see Corominas) likewise means *tonto,* deriv. *guanajería* and *guanajada* 'tontería, pavada' as in "Vicente comete muchas *guanajadas* en cuanto abre la boca o se mueve" (Cuba: C. Suárez). There seems to be some associative interference with *guanaco* (Quechua *huanacu*) 'a kind of llama,' used always for *tonto* (Arg, Chile, CA, Mex), deriv. *guanacada, guanaqueada,* and *guanaquería* 'tontería' as in "A nosotros nos hacen gracia las *guanaquerías* de Eloísa" (Guat: Sandoval).

Colombian *pisco* (Quechua *piscu* 'bird') 'turkey' may mean not only *tonto* (in Santanderes) but also 'vain, presumptuous' and 'fellow, guy' as in "¿Quiénes serán esos *piscos* que están en la esquina?" (Acuña). The form *piscuancio* is a euphemism for *pisco* 'fool' (*BICC,* VI, 67).

An important element in the semantic change to *tonto* is the turkey's wattle (the wrinkled and highly colored fleshy process of the skin hanging from its throat or even its crop), which resembles a goiter, a physical deformity often associated with cretinism or idiocy. By synecdoche *güecho* or *güegüecho* (Mex, CA) may mean both 'goiter' and 'turkey,' and then *tonto,* as in "No soy tu *güegüecho*, Emeterio, para creer que te casarás conmigo" (Guat: Sandoval) and "No soy *güecho*" or "No tengo *güecho*" meaning 'you can't fool me' (CR: Gagini). Also *cotudo* (from Quechua *coto* 'goiter') 'having a goiter' may mean *tonto* (Ec), and standard *papo* 'crop, double chin' has come to mean *tonto* (CA), perhaps with some associative interference of *páparo* 'hayseed' and *paparote* 'fool,' as in "Serás muy *papo* si no reclamas en tiempo tu herencia" (Guat: Sandoval). Possibly there is an analogous connection between Guatemalan *cantimplora* 'goiter' (std. *cantimplora* 'canteen, siphon or tube container for liquids' is probably from Catalan *canta y plora* 'sings and weeps' because of the peculiar noise made by dripping liquids, see Corominas) and River Plate *cantimpla* 'persona medio boba' (Urug: Malaret) and 'persona que es callada y medio zonza' (Arg: Santamaría).

Other animals whose names are frequently substituted for *tonto* are the horse and the pig. Thus, *caballo* (RP, Peru, CA, Mex, Ant) and *yegua* 'mare' (CA, PR) may mean 'persona estúpida, brutal,' as in "no seas tan *caballo*" (Sandoval; deriv. *caballada* 'tontería') and "Usted es un *yegua;* muy *yegua*" (Malaret). In Colombia, *ranga* 'mare' (*rango* 'nag') may mean 'tonto, inhábil' (Tobón), 'torpe, incapaz' (Acuña), as in "El hijo de don Felipe le resultó una *ranga*" (*ibid.*). In the same country, *marrano* 'pig' may mean 'foolish' and 'unsuspecting,' as in "Aún no me ha sido posible encontrar *marrano* para que se asocie conmigo en el negocio de las esmeraldas" (Acuña), deriv. *marranear* 'to deceive, make a fool of' and *marranada* 'tontería,' as in "A Jacinto lo *marranearon* en el negocio" (*ibid.*), "Hombre, no sea bruto, no cometa semejante *marranada*" (Montoya, p. 574).

In the River Plate region the phrase *hacerse el chancho rengo* 'to act like a lame pig, to play dumb' is equivalent to *hacerse el otario,* as in "No te hagás el chancho rengo; vos lo sabés mejor que yo" (Reyles, p. 59). This construction, with the same meaning, is found with other animal names: *hacerse la cucha* 'cat' (Chile); *hacerse el peje* 'fish' (Mex, CA); *hacerse el sapo* 'toad' (Guat: *Mosaico,* p. 46, n. 5); *hacerse el venado* 'deer' (Guat), as in "Zacarías se hace el *venado* cuando le conviene" (Sandoval).

Still other animal names (including those of birds) indicating *tonto,* are *camanejo* 'louse' (Arequipa, Peru: Ugarte), deriv. *camanejada; cangrejo* 'crab' (coastal Ec), deriv. *cangrejada; garrapatero* 'a bird fond of ticks [*garrapatas*]'; *grulla* 'crane' (Chile: Rabanales, "Recursos," p. 280); *guabino* 'a kind of fish' (Col, Ven), cf. the expression *coger guabinas* (Cuba) 'estar idiotizado'; *guacarnaco* (Chile, Ec, Col, Cuba) from Quechua *huakar cunca* 'heron's long neck'; *macaco* 'monkey' (Col, PR); *marmota* 'woodchuck' (Col); *merlo* (Arg), from *merlo* or *mirlo* 'blackbird' possibly through the influence of Italian *merlotto* 'young blackbird' and 'fool'; *peje* 'fish' (Mex, CA); *torcazo* 'pigeon' (Col), the initial sounds of which recall those of *tonto; zorzal* 'thrush' may in Chile mean 'fool' or 'sucker' because of the ease with which the bird may be caught, as in "¡Ay, Usebio, cuando dejarís [= dejarás] de ser *zorzal!"* (Del Campo, p. 39), and *zorzalear* means *engañar* 'to deceive.' Strangely, standard *zorzal* may mean *astuto, sagaz* 'astute, cunning.'

Often the Indian name of some local fruit replaces *tonto* or *bobo* (cf. familiar std. examples such as *melón* 'melon' and *membrillo* 'quince'). Usually the fruit from which the name is borrowed is round or head-shaped with a soft center; the names of the various calabashes which, hollowed and dried and often brightly painted and polished, serve as bowls or cups are frequently used to express this idea. One such is Mexican *guaje* (Aztec *huaxin*), the generic term for various types of calabash (among them *bule, jícara,* and, especially in the Caribbean linguistic zone, *güira* and *totuma*). Examples: "Desengáñate, hermano, te han visto cara de *guaje,* te tienen por un ranchero simplón" (Inclán, I, 269); "El que desde chico es *guaje,* hasta acocote no para" meaning 'el que de niño es tonto, tonto será cuando sea viejo' (Darío Rubio, I, 183); *acocote* (Aztec *acocotli*) is the name of a narrow calabash, sometimes as much as a yard long, which, when perforated at either end, is used as a suction pipe through which the juice is drawn from the heart of the maguey plant. Derivatives are *guajear* 'hacerse uno el *guaje* ,o bobo' and *guajería* 'tontería.' Colombian *túmbilo,* another word for more general *totuma* 'calabash,' heard especially along the Magdalena River, is used in Huila and Tolima for *tonto* (Tobón). Among other cucurbitaceous fruits whose names have come to mean *tonto* are the *zapallo* (CA, Col), from Quechua *zapallu,* deriv. *zapallada* 'tontería'; the pear-shaped *chayote* (Mex, CA, Ant), from Aztec *chayutli* ("La sirvienta que tenemos ahora es muy *chayote"* Guat: Sandoval), deriv. *chayotada* 'tontería' ("Nunca pensé que pudieras hacer semejante *chayotada,"* ibid.); *maraca* (Col, Ven, PR), from Guaraní *mbaracá* 'calabash,' now usually a dry orange-sized calabash, containing some pebbles, with an inserted stick as a handle, and used as a musical instrument; *múcura* (Col), from Carib or Tamanaca, a large calabash-shaped earthen jar ("Por favor, no me hables en inglés, pues tú bien sabes que para los idiomas soy una *múcura,"* Acuña).

Sometimes names of fruit trees, as well as fruits, have the sense of *tonto* (cf. fam. std. *ciruelo* 'plum tree,' *alcornoque* 'cork oak'). Possibly referring to the wood ('blockhead') as well as to the fruit are *aguacate* (Col, CA, Mex, highland Ec), from Aztec *ahuacatl* 'avocado tree and its fruit,' with augmentative *aguacatón* and the still stronger expression *aguacate sin pepa,* that is, 'stoneless' (Ec: Cornejo); *arracacho* (Col) from the Quechua name of a plant (Flórez, *Habla,* p. 296); *coco* (PR) 'coconut tree' and 'coconut'; *guanábano* (CA, Caribbean zone), from Arawak; *guayabo* (Col: Montoya); *mamey* (coastal Ec: Toscano, p. 223) 'mamey tree and its fruit,' from Arawak; *papayo* (Ec) 'papaya tree,' from Carib or Arawak; *toronjo* (Col: Tobón) 'citron tree,' with phonetic association of *tonto.*

The word *papa* 'potato,' from Quechua *papa* (std. *patata* is a cross between *papa* and *batata* 'sweet potato'), having acquired the meaning of a 'worthless thing' ("no saber uno ni *papa,* no valer una cosa una *papa"*) has come to mean also *tonto* ("ser uno una *papa,* tener cabeza de *papa";* cf. *ñame* 'yam' and *ñame con corbata,* Cuba), deriv. *papada* (Guat) 'tontería' ("Lo que acabas de hacer es la mayor *papada* del mundo," Sandoval), perhaps by phonetic association with standard *papada* 'crop, double chin, dewlap.' Indigenous *papa* should not be confused with standard *papa,* which even in Latin referred to 'food' as well as to 'father.' Chilean *cosa papa* means 'tasty' and 'something pleasant,' probably deriving from standard *papa* 'food' in general and *papas* in the sense of *gachas* 'pap, porridge.' The Spanish conquerors and first settlers frequently referred to the new American *papa,* because of its shape, as *turma de tierra* 'testicle of the earth' (cf. French *pomme de terre* 'apple of the earth'). In the interior of Colombia *turma* is still heard for *papa* and, among peasants, *turma* and *turmón* for *tonto* (Tobón). Strangely, *turma* could have acquired its meaning of *tonto* either through its use as *papa* or through that of *testículo.* For instance, vulgar *cojón* and *huevo* (or *hueva*) in the sense of *testículo* have derivatives *cojudo* and *huevón* (rustic *güevón*), both of which are used in many regions with the meaning of *tonto* (similarly *pelota[s], pelotudo; boludo* and its euphemism *voluble,* RP, Chile; *par de trolas, troludo,* and *alforjudo,* Chile; *tablón* and *talegón,* Col, from *tablas* and *talegas* 'testicles'). Derivatives *cojudez* and *huevada* (especially in Arg, Chile) mean 'tontería,' and *ahuevarse* (Peru, Pan) 'entontecerse,' *ahuevazón* (Pan) 'embobamiento,' rustic *güeviar* (RP: "Nosotros estamos aquí, *güeviando,*" C. B. Quiroga, *4 á 2,* Buenos Aires, 1932, p. 29). A related word—*bolsa* 'bag, scrotum'—has derivatives *bolsetas* (Col), *bolsón* (Ec, Col, SD), *bolsota* (Cibao, SD) and *bolsudo* (Arg, Ven, Col) 'large-bagged,' all of which mean 'tonto' and perhaps also have phonetic association with standard *bobo* and *bolonio.*

In order to avoid uttering the word *huevón,* speakers may euphemistically resort to the gesture of lowering and raising the cupped hand as if trying the weight of an object; that is, with the sense progression of 'heavy' > 'slow' > 'stupid' (see fig. 5). Other euphemisms for *güevón* are *güen mozo, güenas peras,* and *güena persona* (Chile: Rabanales, "Recursos," p. 213).

Often a new euphemism is devised for a harsh word by merely changing its main stress. An added suffix, for instance, by shifting the stress to another syllable, seems to cleanse much of the underlying feeling. Thus, *bobo* is euphemized in *boberá* (Cuba), *boboliche* (Peru), *bobeta* (RP), *bobetas* (Col), *boborote* (Riohacha, Col); cf. standard *bobalías, bobalicón, bobatel, bobático, bobote, bolo* (PR); *pisco* is euphemized in *piscuancio* (Col); *zonzo* is euphemized in *zonzorrio, zonzoreco,* and the like.

Almost any word containing the initial sounds of the taboo term may become a euphemism, the initial sounds sufficing to suggest the meaning, like slang peninsular *primavera* for *primo* 'dupe, fool.' Thus, *tonto* is suggested in *tola, torcazo* and *toronjo* (Col), in *totoreco* (CA) and deriv. *totorecada* 'tontería'; *bobo* is suggested in *bonito* (cant, Chile), *baboso* is reflected in *barbeta* (Chile: "este *barbeta* no está acostumbrado a servir en la aristocracia," Pepe Rojas and Pepe Fernández, *La hoja de Parra,* Santiago, 1937, II), and since *barbeta* recalls also *barba* and *babera* 'bib' one may hear *jeta de babero* or *jete babero* (*con blonda*), reinforced with the gesture of the hand held below the chin, palm up, and moved outward, or something similar; *mudo* (possibly *mula*) is suggested in *mudenco* (CA), *mudengo* (Peru), *músico* (CA); *memo* is suggested in *menso* (Mex, *memo* + *manso* ?), *merejo* (Ec), *merlo* (Arg), *tetelememe* (Chile, Peru), and *tetelemeque* (Peru), though Román postulates *teta* and *mamar* for *tetelememe; mamar* 'to suckle,' with past participle *mamado* (Ant) 'fool,' is suggested in *mamposta* (SD) and *mamerto* (Ec), the latter recalling also *mamey* as used along the coast of Ecuador for *tonto; cándido* 'fool' is suggested in *candelejón* (Peru, Ec, Col) and *candungo* (Peru); *chiflado* is evident in *chiflis* (Mex: "¡Estás *chiflis,* completamente *chiflis!*" Gómez Palacio, p. 91); *zonzo* is suggested in *zoroco* and *zorocongo* (Col), *zorimbo* (Tabasco, Mex), *zorenco* (CA, perhaps also influenced by std. *zopenco* 'blockhead'). Standard *bambarria* 'fool' (from *bamba = bobo,* see Corominas) is reflected in *bamburrete* (Ven). Standard *zurumbático* 'lelo, pasmado, aturdido,' especially from the effects of alcohol, is euphemized in *zorimbo, zurumato* (Mex), *azurumbado* (CA: "los hijos del doctor González no heredaron la inteligencia del padre, pues resultaron muy *azurumbados,*" "no tomo otra copa más, porque ya estoy muy *azurumbado,*" Sandoval), *zurundango,* and *zurumbo* (Guat: "La calentura me tiene muy *zurumbo,*" *ibid.*). Cuban *sirimbo, sirimbombo,* and *zambeque* have a much vaguer association with *zurumbático* and perhaps recall more directly standard *zambomba* (a rustic musical instrument made by stretching parchment over a wide-mouthed clay or wooden jar and inserting through the parchment a stick which, when rubbed up and down with the moistened hand, produces a loud, raucous, and monotonous sound) and its figurative meaning of 'hombre tosco, grosero, y rudo de ingenio.'

Often a proper name, real or fictitious, containing sounds of the taboo word, is used in a phrase to suggest that the person discussed is *tonto* or *bobo.* This practise is common in peninsular conversational Spanish as well as in literature (see Wagner). Thus, *estar uno en Babia* (region in the mountains of León) means 'estar distraído y como ajeno a aquello de que se trata,' that is, *babieca* or *bobalicón* 'fool'; Andalusian *estar en Gilena* (name of a village) has reference to *gilí* 'fool.' Similar phrases abound in America. Thus, in Argentina, *pasar uno por Merlo* (a village near Buenos Aires; for *merlo* see above) means 'to be a fool,' and since one must pass through Merlo to reach the town of Luján (a place of pilgrimage famous for its Gothic Basilica), one may say "¿Has ido a Luján?" 'have you gone to Luján?' meaning 'you're a fool.' Other similar phrases are *ser Lesana* (Chile) for *ser leso; Lucas* (Mex) for *loco,* as in "Quesque un *lucas* le pegó un golpazo al señor general Díaz" (Magdaleno, p. 100); *Getulio* (Chile: Oroz, p. 55) for *jetón; Pacheco* (Col), particularly in the form *solemne pacheco* 'ignorante, lerdo' (Tobón), recalls standard *pachorra* 'sluggishness' and *pachón* 'phlegmatic.'

Other expressions containing proper names that have come to indicate stupidity are *Bartolo* (popular form of *Bartolomé*) meaning 'a clumsy, careless, lazy person' (cf. *bartolear* 'to be lazy,' Chile), perhaps from a

Christmas-play character (Boggs, p. 37); *berengo* (Mex), said to derive from the name of the viceroy Félix *Berenguer* de Marquina (1800–1803), as in "A cada paso eran los regaños, tratándome de sandio, *berengo*, imbécil" (Inclán, II, 120); *chevo*, short for *Eusebio* (deriv. *chevada* 'foolishness'), is sometimes heard in Guatemala, reportedly from *Eusebio* Ibarra, the name of a well-known *tonto* from the department of Quezaltenango (about 1930); *ser de Bainoa* (Cuba), the name of a Cuban village; *ser de Lagos* or *como el alcalde de Lagos* (Mex), alluding to a legendary mayor of Lagos, a town in the state of Jalisco; *ser de Marinilla* (Col), the name of a town in eastern Antioquia.

Euphemistic metaphors suggesting 'foolishness' in an ironic or humorous vein are prevalent in popular speech; for example, standard *chuparse* or *mamarse el dedo* (*no me chupo el dedo* 'I'm not a fool') and *no tener dos dedos de frente* 'not to have a forehead of two fingers' width,' often indicated by raising index and middle fingers to the forehead. Others are *echar globos* (Col; *globo* in the sense of *pompa de jabón* 'soap bubble') equivalent to standard *hacer uno calendarios* 'to be daydreaming' or 'estar en el paraíso de los bobos' (Tobón), alluding to the raptured delight observed on a child's face when blowing soap bubbles; *caído del catre* (Chile: Oroz, p. 54) 'fallen from the cot' and *caído de la hamaca* or *del zarzo* (Col: Acuña) 'fallen from the hammock' or 'from the attic,' since head blows occasioned by a fall may cause mental disorders (permutations indicating the cause for the result); *patinar el coco* or *el chicle* (Col; both *coco* and *chicle* here mean 'head'), as in "A fulanita le *patina*" or "le *patina el coco* (or *el chicle*)" (Tobón); *faltarle a uno un veinte* (or *una chaucha*) *para el peso* (Chile) 'to lack twenty cents of having a dollar,' that is, to have one's five senses incomplete, since a *veinte* or a *chaucha* is the fifth part of a peso, as in "Contimás que soy un leso / y que al leer esta calta / dirís a Eusebio le *falta* / *las cinco chauchas pal peso*" (Del Campo, p. 17); familiar standard *faltarle a uno un tornillo* 'to lack a screw' may be changed to *tener los tornillos sueltos* or *flojos* 'to have loose screws,' as in "chiflada de remate ... *Los tornillos* (llevándose cada índice a una y otra sien) más que *flojos; ya no hay tornillos*" (Mex: Quevedo y Zubieta, *La camada*, p. 181); *falla la azotea* 'the roof is failing,' as in "¡A este pobre le *falla la azotea!*" (Chile: Pepe Rojas and Pepe Fernández, *El gallo de las pasión*, Act II); *faltarle a uno un domingo* (Tex); *pasado por la cola del pavo, por agua tibia,* and *quedado en las huinchas* (Chile: Oroz, p. 54), the *huinchas* being the ribbon stretched across the race track and behind which the horses are lined before the take-off; *Fulano pasa en la luna* or *pasa pajariando* (= 'embobado, con la boca abierta'), or *se le van los pavos* (*ibid.*); *tener pantorrilla* or *tener muy gorda la pantorrilla* or *ser pantorrilludo* (Peru) 'to have fat (leg) calves' (see Arona).

In the minds of many speakers the word *rústico* has acquired aspects of *tonto*, just as *cándido* now may mean *tonto*. Thus, Colombian *ñuco* means both 'rustic' and 'fool'; so also *montuno* (Chile, Col, Ven, Pan, Ant) and *montubio* (Ec, Peru, Col). Phrases like *ser* (or *venir*) *uno de las chacras* 'to be from the farm' may mean 'to be dull-witted,' as in "Hay que *ser* muy *de las chacras* pa leer tanta lesera" (ap. Rabanales, p. 187).

INSANITY

Closely akin to *tonto* is the word *loco* 'mad, crazy, silly' with general euphemistic synonyms *chiflado, ido* 'gone,' *tocado* 'touched,' *barrenado* 'bored, drilled, screwed' = 'having a screw loose,' *incapaz* 'incapacitated,' *chalado, mochales* ('madly in love'), and the like. *Casa de alienados* replaces harsh *manicomio* 'insane asylum' or *casa de orates* (originally a euphemism, from Catalan *orat* 'madman' in turn from *aura* 'air, breeze'). For wealthier clientele such places are called *casas de salud* 'rest homes' (lit. 'health homes'). Additional popular euphemisms for *loco* in America are *jubilado* 'pensioned' (Col), deriv. *jubilarse* for *enloquecerse,* as in "De tanto trabajar y de tan poco comer el pobre de don Anselmo terminó *jubilado*" (Acuña); *desvirolado* (*ibid.*) from *desvirar* 'to unwind,' and *distraído* 'distracted' (Col: Cadavid), deriv. *distraerse* for *enloquecerse.*

Among the euphemistic phonetic distortions of *loco* are *colo* (slang, Arg), in which the syllables are reversed; *locaina* (Trujillo, Ven); the proper name *Leocadio,* pronounced and written *Locadio* or *Locario* (with the corresponding feminine forms *Locadia* and *Locaria*), often without capitalization: "Como que Anastasio está algo *Locadio*" (Guat: Sandoval), "¿Cómo está usted, *locadio?*" por decir "¿Cómo está usted, *loco?*" (Mex: Duarte), a usage common also in Chile (Román) and probably elsewhere since *locarias* is not unknown in Spain with the meaning 'loco, aturdido'; *Lucas* or *lucas* (Mex); *Locumba,* name of a city in Peru, used in the *replana peruana* 'Peruvian cant' for *loco; locatelli,* applied to every *loco* in Argentina soon after the Italian aviator Antonio Locatelli had made a significant flight in the year 1919 (Gobello, p. 79).

Often a mere gesture serves euphemistically to express the idea of *loco* (see figs. 6, 7, 8): the right index finger taps the right temple once or twice, or merely points to it, or rotates clockwise or, for more emphasis, makes a boring motion as if to penetrate the temple. The pointing or tapping seems to indicate something amiss with the brain or mentality; the rotation suggests that the brain is in a whirl; the boring motion (*barrenar* or *atornillar*) imitates a screw being replaced or tightened, since the familiar standard phrase for *loco* is *le falta un tornillo* 'he lacks a screw,' corresponding to English 'he has a screw loose.' Sometimes whistling (*chiflar = silbar*) is sufficient to indicate the noun *chiflado* 'crazy': "—Viejo ... *le silba como preguntándole si está chiflado"* (Arg: A. Discépolo, *Mateo,* Act III).

Writers, both peninsular and American, often indicate that a gesture is made, without explaining its exact nature: "—¡Ay, este señor no está bueno!" *Indicando que está tocado de la cabeza* (Vital Aza, *Chifladuras,* VI); "—Y dígame usted, ¿es cierto que mi suegra ... ?" *Indica que no está bien de la cabeza* (Vital Aza, *Con la música a otra parte,* Act I, sc. 5). However, the gesture is sometimes clearly indicated: "—Mi hermana Clarines ... *Barrenándose con un dedo la sien"* (Quinteros, *Doña Clarines, Teatro completo,* XII, 170); "*Manuela se tocó la frente con un dedo y meneó la cabeza.* —No, no me llames loco" (Pardo Bazán, *La Madre Naturaleza,* chap. xx); "está uté un poquirritiyo ... *Apoyando el dedo índice en la sien"* (Valdés, *La hermana San Sulpicio,* chap. x); "—está un poco ..." *Dando vueltas sobre la sien con uno de sus dedos* (Dicenta, *Daniel,* Act I, sc. 2); "—¡Este Palmarín siempre el mismo!—exclamó, *atornillándose la frente con un dedo"* (Gálvez, *La maestra normal,* II, 6); "—¿No sabís qu'está ... ? *e hizo como si atornillase el dedo índice en las sienes"* (Reyles, p. 113).

ANGER

Since displays of anger are normally considered undesirable, words pertaining to such manifestations are carefully selected to palliate unpleasant connotations or to mitigate them with a humorous turn of phrase or metaphor. Thus, neutral *nervioso* 'nervous' and *emocionado* 'moved' are often used in place of *enojado* 'angry' (more often in American Spanish than *enfadado*) or *enojadizo* 'petulant'; *torcido* (cf. std. *rostritorcido* and *rostrituerto*) and *enroscado* 'twisted' (Col: *enroscarse* 'enojarse') refer to the distortion of an angry person's face. Rather general *entromparse* (Ec, Col, CA, PR) 'enojarse' from *trompa* 'snout' refers to the thrust-out lips of angry persons, as in "Basilio *se entrompa* conmigo porque no le doy prestado el dinero que me pide" (Guat: Sandoval). In some regions (Peru, Col, Ven) *tibio* 'lukewarm' is a euphemism for *caliente* 'hot' in the sense of *enojado* (cf. our 'hot, burned up'), the change to *tibio* being occasioned by another standard meaning of *caliente*—'to be in heat.' Examples: "El corrector está *tibio* con tantos repasos confrontados" (Ven: Alvarado); "Si él está *tibio,* yo estoy bravo" (Ven), meaning 'tal para cual' (Malaret). Another euphemism for *caliente* 'angry' is *caribe* (SD), as in "Cuando le dieron la noticia, se puso *caribe*" (Patín). The adjective *bravo* 'angry,' as in "Juan está *bravo* conmigo" (Col: Acuña), is much commoner in America than it is in Spain. Common, too, is *ardido* (Bol, Ec, Col, CA) from *arder* 'to burn' and influenced by *ardido* 'courageous, intrepid,' as in "José me tiene muy *ardida* por haberse robado anoche a mi *hija de casa* ['a young servant who receives no wages']" (Guat: Sandoval).

Metaphorical are *arrecho* (CA) 'courageous, energetic' (Latin *erectus*), deriv. verb *arrecharse;* general *asado* 'roasted'; *empalado* (Esmeraldas, Ec), that is, as hard as a *palo* 'cudgel, wood,' with verb *empalarse* 'enojarse'; *encachimbado* (Nic) from *cachimbo* (or *cachimba*) 'tobacco pipe'; vulgar *emputado* (Salta, Arg; CA), cf. *emputecerse* (Col: Flórez, *Habla,* p. 213); vulgar and rustic *encojonado* (*ibid.*), as in "Julián está *encojonado* por la mala broma que le hicieron" (Cornejo), with corresponding verb *encojonarse* (formed from the original expression *meterse en cojones*); rustic *enculado* (San Luis, Arg: Vidal, p. 328); *enchichado* (Ec, Col, CA), from *chicha* 'an alcoholic drink generally made of corn,' so that the verb *enchicharse* means 'to be in a state of ferment,' as in "Amalia *se enchicha* fácilmente por lo que no conviene bromear con ella" (Sandoval) and "Si *te enchichas,* ¡te embotello!" said to a person who has lost his composure and is becoming irritated (Cornejo); likewise, the short form *chicho* (Col), as in "se puso *chicho*" and "no se ponga *chicho*" (Tobón); *estar en el arbolito* (Col); *estar de un huevo, estar de punta, estar con los pelos de punta, estar que rasca* (Nic); *estar hecho un ají, un pepián* 'highly peppered dish' (Peru), *una barba de agua, un brazo de mar* (Ec); *subir y bajar* (SD), as in "Cuando él me decía tales cosas, yo *subía y bajaba*" (Patín); *subírsele el indio a uno* (CR), because Indians are reputedly violent and irascible; *enfullinarse* (Chile, Mex) 'to be covered with soot' (modern *hollín*), semantically related to standard *subírsele a uno el humo por las narices* and *estar echando humo; sacarle a uno los choros* ['clams'] *del canasto* heard in fishing areas of southern Chile (Plath, p. 4); *ser uno* (or *volverse*) *un Zañartu* has been said to refer to a hard and stubborn magistrate named Zañartu who while constructing a bridge in Santiago, Chile, gave the working prisoners more floggings than pay (Román).

Sometimes new popular terms for *enojado* and *enojarse* are formed from the names of animals that generally exhibit irritability (like fam. std. *amoscarse* from *mosca* 'fly'). Among them are *ser avispado* (Guat) from *avispa* 'wasp' (cf. 'mad as a hornet'); *ser una chichicúa* (Guat), the name of a venomous serpent, as in "Benito es una *chichicúa*" (Sandoval); *encabronarse* (Col, Nic, Mex, Cuba) from *cabro* for standard *cabrón* 'billy goat' (cf. general *cabrearse*); *encachorrarse* (Col) from *cachorro* 'pup, cub,' as in "Tan mal genio tiene ese muchacho, que cuando ve que le van a corregir comienza a *encachorrarse*" (Acuña); *enchivarse* (Ec, Col) and *chivarse* (Ant) from *chivo* 'goat,' as in "Mi mujer *se chiva* por un quítame allá esas pajas" (Cuba: C. Suárez); *enverriondarse* (Col) 'to be ruttish,' from *verraco* 'male swine'; *empavarse* (Ec) from *pavo* 'turkey'; *ser un querrequerre* (Ven: Rosenblat, p. 41), the onomatopoetic name of a bird (*Cyanocora incas*) that reportedly dies of violent anger when confined in a cage; *montar mula* (Guat), *cabrito* (Mex), *el picazo* (RP, Bol); *tener malos totolates* (CR; *totolates* 'chicken lice'), equivalent to standard *tener malas pulgas; enchincharse* (Guat) from *chinche* 'bedbug,' as in "*Me enchincho* cada vez que por una leve causa, o por gusto, el jefe de la oficina me ragaña delante de los compañeros" (Sandoval); *estar hecho un camarón* 'shrimp' (Ec), *una coya* 'poisonous spider' (Col), *un chilincoco* 'poisonous insect' (Hond), *un chinchintor* 'poisonous snake' (Hond), *un chivo* 'goat' (general), *una tatacoa* 'a kind of serpent' (Col), *un quique* 'weasel,' and *un quirquincho* 'armadillo' (Chile); *estar hecho una bejuca* 'poisonous snake' (Col), deriv. *embejucarse,* as in "No *se embejuque* por tan poca cosa" (Acuña); *estar hecho una taya* 'poisonous snake' (Col).

To indicate states of anger one may have recourse to euphemistic movements or gestures, such as biting one's lips (to check the flow of words), beating the thighs with the fists, tapping the floor with the foot, and the like. When two persons are angry with each other, one may say "están de punta" (fam. std.; cf. *contrapuntiados,* Col), as in "Siempre *están de punta* estos gringos y gallegos" (Arg: Lynch, p. 453). As one says "están de punta" or "están así" one may strike together the points of the two index fingers (see fig. 9). Examples: "Mire usted—*chocando los dedos índices—está así* con tía Guadalupe" (Quinteros, *El centenario,* Act I); *"Juntando los índices por las puntas.* Y como el Galápago *está así* con don Calixto ..." (Quinteros, *Los galeotes,* Act III). Variations of the gesture are the following: the nails and knuckles of the two thumbs may be beaten together; the index fingers may be reinforced with the extended small fingers; the knuckles of both hands may be struck or rubbed together (see fig. 10); the right fist may be rubbed on the extended left palm (see fig. 11); the right palm may be rubbed across the left palm (see fig. 12); the chin or an imaginary beard may be seized and pulled downward (Arg: see fig. 13) in order to make someone angry, that is 'to get his goat.'

SCOLDING

The verbs *reñir, regañar,* and *reprender* 'to scold, reproach' are frequently euphemized by use of *hablar* 'to speak,' as in "me *habló* porque llegué tarde" and "no hagas eso porque te han de *hablar";* "Juan *acabó de hablar* a Pedro" means (in highland Ecuador) 'Juan insultó o reprendió fuertemente a Pedro,' apparently based on Quechuan usage in which *acabar* is a mere intensifier of the verb that follows it (Toscano, p. 278).

Other popular euphemisms for *reñir* or *reprender* (including shades of *insultar*) are *apear* (CR) 'to unhorse, take down,' as in "Mi padre me *apeó"* (Salesiano); *articular* (Chile, Col) 'to articulate'; *bochar* (Ven, Mex) 'to strike a bowl,' from *bocha* 'bowl'; *empajar* (Col) 'to cover with straw'; *glosar* (Col) 'to gloss, comment on,' deriv. *glosa* 'reprimand'; *hartar* 'to surfeit' may mean 'to insult' (Ven) and 'to slander' (Guat), as in "Anacleto no puede hablar de ti sin *hartarte"* (Sandoval); *palabrear* (Chile) 'to chatter' and euphemistically 'to insult'; *raspar, raspear* 'to scrape, scratch'; *requintar* (Peru, Ec) may mean 'to insult,' deriv. noun *requintada; repelar* (Col, Mex) 'to crop, pull out the hair'; *retar* (RP, Chile, Bol) 'to challenge,' an archaism kept alive in America, as in "Un padre *reta a su hijo porque va al teatro por motivos que no pueden aprobarse*" (R. Morales, *El buen decir,* Santiago, Chile, 1925, I, 11); *rezondrar* (Peru), as in "lo *rezondré* bien," from *rezongar* 'to grumble, scold' or a metathesis of *deshonrar; trancar* (Col), from *tranca* 'cudgel,' as in "A los obreros perezosos, se les debe *trancar*" (Acuña), deriv. adjective *trancón* 'severe,' as in "El nuevo rector del colegio es muy *trancón*" (*ibid.*)*; tuquear* (Esmeraldas, Ec), from noun *tuca.*

Many popular locutions with this meaning consist of verb *dar* or *echar* (or *pegar*) with the following nouns: *un aguacero* or *un aguaje* (Ec, CA) 'a shower,' as in "El patrón por nada y nada le *echa un aguaje* a uno" and "El coronel les *echó un aguacero* a todos los oficiales que están subordinados a él" (Guat: Sandoval); *un boche* (Ven, PR, SD), for *bochazo* 'a strike with a bowl [*bocha*],' as in "pero en cuantito lo vea le *jecharé un boche*" (PR: Meléndez Muñoz, *Yuyo,* ap. Malaret, *Vocabulario*); *los caballos* (SD); *un caballazo* (Chile, Peru) 'a horse's trampling (on something)'; (*dar*) *café* (Arg); *una calda* (CR) 'a warming,' an extension of familiar standard *dar calda* 'to stimulate'; *un chaparrón* (PR, as in Andalusia) 'shower'; *una hablada* (general); *una jartada, juagada* (Col: Tobón); ironic *echar una loa* (CA) 'praise'; *una mascada* (CA) 'chewing, mumbling, slander,' as in "Supe que anoche me *dió* usted una buena *mascada,* cuando hablaba con varias personas amigas en el café" (Guat: Sandoval); (*echar*) *la mula* (Mex); *una pachotada* (CR), metathesis of standard *patochada* 'nonsense' (see Corominas), or more likely related to apachar 'to flatten' and *pacho* 'pudgy'; *una pasada* (CA, Cuba); (*echar*) *un pavo* (PR); *un rajatablas* (Col, Ven); rather general *una raspa* or *raspada* 'a scraping'; *un rezongo* (CA) from standard *rezongo* 'grumbling'; *un respis* (CR), from standard *réspice* 'reprimand'; *una sacada a misa* (CR); *una trancada* (Col); *una trapeada,* from general *trapear* 'to mop up'; *una tuca* (Esmeraldas, Ec), as in "Por necia, recibiste ayer una buena *tuca*" (Cornejo); *una vela* (Mex); *un viaje* (CA) 'a trip' and here 'a blow'; *un zape* (Peru, Ec).

Among more elaborate vulgar metaphors expressing the idea of *reprender* are the following, current in Chile (ap. Rabanales, p. 217): *meterle a uno una luma* (*luma* is a tall and hard variety of myrtle), as in "Prepárate, que te va a *meter una tremenda luma*" (cf. *meter un palo,* Arg, PR); *meterle a uno la penca* (= *pene*)*; ponerle a uno las peras* *a cuatro; refregarle a uno el ají* 'to rub a person's nose in red pepper,' as in *"Le refregué bien el ají,* pa que no sea, no má." Elsewhere are heard *echárselo a uno* (SD), as in "Ayer *te lo echó* el jefe" (Patín); *encenderle la loma a uno* and *jartar la perra* (Col).

LYING

Although the verb *mentir,* the noun *mentira,* and the adjective *mentiroso* are not nearly so harsh as corresponding English *to lie, lie,* and *liar* (which may reflect varying moral attitudes), they have many euphemistic sub-stitutes, as similar words do in other languages. Latin *mentiri* (or *mentire*) itself may be an early euphemism, deriving as it does from *mens* 'mind' with the sense of 'to imagine, invent.' By a slight extension of its standard meaning, *hablador* 'talkative, gossiper' comes to denote *mentiroso.* This is a kind of permutation, expressing an act through the means of that act. Similar developments we find in extensions of standard *lenguaraz* or *lenguaz* 'talkative, garrulous' to 'gossiper, slanderer, talebearer,' as in the follow-ing American derivatives *lengón* (Mex) and *lenguón* (Ec, Col, CA, Mex), *lengüín* (Cuba), *lengüino* (SD), *lengüetero* (Ant), *lenguarico* (Mex); *bocón* 'big-mouthed' (Tex); *picón* 'big-beaked' (Col), *picoreto* (Ven, CA, PR). The word *mentira* is often replaced by *embuste* 'hoax, fraud' as in Peurto Rico (*Navarro,* p. 202 n.), or by plural *albures* for *mentiras* or *infundios* 'fibs, lies, humbug' (PR; std. *albur* means the first draw at a card game called *monte,* and figuratively 'risk, venture, hazard'). In Azuay, Ecuador, *cernir* 'to sift' may replace *mentir,* and *cernidor* euphe-mizes *mentiroso.*

Just as names of plants or fruits are often used to euphemize *tonto,* so sim-ilar names are substituted for *mentira,* sometimes those of fruits of soft or hollow center that suggest the unsubstantial quality of falsehoods, or fruits of pleasant or innocuous taste that are 'easy to swallow.' Thus *papa* often replaces *mentira* and is now registered in the Academy dictionary as syn-onymous with *paparrucha* in the sense of 'hoax, fake, fraud.' Example: "¡Güena la vieja pa echar *papas* más regrandes! Estuve tentao de icirle si acaso vendía la cosecha del año pasao" (Chile: Del Campo, p. 5). Since *papa* recalls *camote* 'sweet potato,' the latter has also come to mean *mentira,* particularly in Chile, where because of the vegetable's greater size it may mean *mentira exagerada,* as in "¡Chita el *camote* grande que m'estay (me estáis) contando!" (Rabanales, p. 219). Since *chaucha* (from Quechua or Mapuche) may mean 'potato' (of a certain early type, or a small potato used for seed), it also occasionally euphemizes *mentira,* especially in the River Plate area. Arawak *yuca,* the word for another root similar to the *camote,* may mean *embuste* or *mentira* (Bol, CA), as in "Esta *yuca* no entra en el costal" = 'esta bola (o mentira) no pasa' (Bayo, p. 269).

Use of the word *guayaba* (cf. *guama,* Col, Ven) 'guava,' the name of a pear-shaped and many-seeded tropical fruit, in place of *mentira,* is almost ubiquitous, especially in the phrase *echar* (or *soltar*) *guayabas* (with occasional deriv. *guayabear* 'mentir'), as in "Egberto *echa guayabas* sin tino, aun en presencia de personas formales y honorables" (Guat: Sandoval). Even in Argentina (though *bolazos* is heard more frequently there), we find it in such passages as "¡Bien haiga gaucho embustero! / ¿Sabe que no me esperaba / que *soltase una guayaba* / de ese tamaño, aparcero?" (Estanislao del Campo, *Fausto,* v. 93). In Guatemala the large, tasty *guayaba perulera,* supposedly introduced from Peru, means figuratively 'mentira gorda e ingeniosa' (Sandoval). Another fruit name similarly used in Chile is *zapallo,* as in "¡Güeno el *zapallo* grande!" (Rabanales, p. 220).

Any object with a hollow center is likely to serve as a substitute for *mentira.* Thus standard *bola* 'sphere, globe, ball' (though more akin to 'hoax' or 'canard,' an extravagant or absurd report) is synonymous with standard *pajarota, pajarotada,* and similar words. Mexican and Caribbean *bolada* (occasionally *bomba*) and River Plate *bolazo* (deriv. *bolacear*) function as (secondary) euphemisms, transferring the stress from the first syllable of *bola* to the added suffix. *Caña* 'cane, reed' (Ec, Col, Ven) means 'noticia falsa, ficción, engañifa' (Malaret); 'mentira, especie, bola, exageración' (Tobón); 'noticia falsa, fanfarronada' (Acuña), as in "Por favor, dime la verdad y déjate de *cañas,"* deriv. *cañar* 'mentir,' and *cañero* 'mentiroso, charlatán' (Tobón), 'embustero, fanfarrón' (Acuña), as in "¡Cómo te has vuelto de *cañero!"* (*ibid.*). *Paja* 'straw' may mean 'mentira, despropósito, jactancia' (Col), as in "Yo creo que de todas las maravillas que Jiménez cuenta sobre su viaje a Cartagena, la mitad es pura *paja,"* deriv. *pajudo* 'mentiroso, embustero, exagerado,' as in "A ese pisco ['fellow'] no se le puede creer ni el credo, porque es sumamente *pajudo"* (Acuña), and *pajudiar* = *echar paja* (Tobón). *Chile* 'red pepper' is common in Central America, usually in the plural, for *mentira* or *bola,* as in "Lo que me estás diciendo son *chiles* de tu invención" (Guat: Sandoval).

Other nouns meaning *mentira* are *guáchara* (Ant), which in Costa Rica is the name of an indigenous musical instrument made of cane and containing seeds or pebbles; *bunga* (Cuba), a musical instrument like the *botijuela* (lit. 'earthen pitcher'); *cují* (Pan), the name of a native plant, meaning both 'mentira' and 'estafa,' as in "Eso que me dices es *cují*" and "Haciendo *cují* gano mucha plata" (Aguilera), deriv. *cujicero* 'mentiroso, estafador'; *flota* (Ven, Col: also *flote*), meaning both 'mentira' and 'fanfarronada,' as in "Deje de echar *flotas*" (Tobón) and "Y el que le oiga las *flotas* pensará que es gente" (Rendón, p. 132), deriv. *flotear* and, occasionally, *flotante* 'fanfarrón, mentiroso'; *guillo* (Cuba), as in "Te descubrí un *guillo*" (C. Suárez), deriv. *guillar* 'mentir'; *leva* (Antioquia and Caldas, Col) 'engaño, treta, mentira,' deriv. *levoso* 'mentiroso.' Frequent in Chile is *copucha* or *cupucha,* by metathesis under influence of Spanish *capucho,* from Mapuche (or Quechua ?) *pucuchu* 'inflated animal bladder.' Now it may mean 'swimming bladder' (*nadaderas*), 'clyster' (*lavativa*), 'container for lard,' 'purse,' and, finally, 'windbag,' deriv. *copuchar* 'mentir' and *copuchento* 'mentiroso,' as in "No seas *copuchento*" = 'no seas exagerador de noticias' (Plath).

Names of animals and particularly names of birds sometimes replace *mentira* (cf. fam. std. *pajarota* or *pajarotada* from *pájaro* 'bird,' and *grilla* 'cricket'). In Chile the little *tenca* sings throughout the year, varying its song with a great diversity of tones apparently imitating the song of other birds. It is therefore called *pájaro pantomimo,* and its name has come to mean *mentira.* The same linguistic fate has overtaken *diuca,* the name of a small bird that sings early in the morning (the phrase *al primer diucazo* now means 'at break of day'). Likewise, Chilean *loica,* the name of a kind of starling whose sweet song is supposed by the Indians to presage the death or illness of some relative, as well as other misfortunes, has had the same fate as *tenca* and *diuca,* perhaps because the bird's predictions too often fail to prove true. However, *loica* may by apheresis come from *pilloica* 'mentira' (deriv. *pilloiquero* 'mentiroso, embustero,' see Román). Chilean *pocha,* a popular name for small but big-bellied fresh-water fish, often means 'mentira grande' because of the common quality of inflation or bloatedness. The Chilean phrase *echar pollitas* (lit. 'chicks') for *echar mentiras* is considered by Román a possible (secondary) euphemism for *echar pochitas* (dim. of *pochas*), or even for *pilloicas*. In some regions (especially PR) standard *gazapo* 'young rabbit' has come to mean 'fraud, deceit' (cf. French *lapin*), perhaps as an extension of one of its standard meanings 'mistake in writing or speaking, slip of the pen or of the tongue' (cf. also *dar gato por liebre* 'to deceive'). Elsewhere are heard *borrego* 'lamb' (Mex), *mula* (Arg), *meter mula* 'to deceive,' *vaca* 'cow' (Antioquia, Col: Tobón).

Other euphemistic borrowings are *macana* (RP principally), probably of Arawak origin (Friederici), 'large wooden club' with the meaning changed to '(anything) very large' > 'tall story' > 'nonsense, absurdity, artful lie' as in "déjese de *macanas*," deriv. *macanear* 'decir o hacer macanas,' *macaneador,* and *macaneo; coila,* from Mapuche *coylla* 'mentira' (S Chile), deriv. *coilero* 'mentiroso,' having phonetic and semantic association with *caula* (Chile, CA) 'deception, intrigue, lie' (stemming from std. *cábala* 'cabala'), as in "Eso que dices son puras *caulas* tuyas" (Guat: Sandoval) and "Antonio cogió las *cabullas* (or *cábulas*)" meaning *descubrió las trampas* (CR: Salesiano); Mexican *nagual* 'mentira' from *Aztec nahualli* 'witch' or person who could supposedly change his appearance by magic, deriv. *nagualear* 'contar mentiras'; *cuta* (Guat), generally in the plural, perhaps from *cuto* 'truncated, lacking a limb' and here 'short (of the truth)' as in "Lo que me cuentas son puras *cutas* tuyas," deriv. *cutero* 'mentiroso' as in "Pedro es muy *cutero*" (Sandoval); *guaragua* (Hond); in regions where English has made inroads on Spanish *blof* 'bluff' and deriv. *blofear, blofeador, blofista,* and *blofero* are current.

Among other local terms for *mentira* are *bachos* (Peru) 'embustes, cuentos, invenciones, bolas' (like fam. std. *bernardina*), now fallen into desuetude (Arona); *carraca* (Col) 'jawbone' (std. meaning 'rattle'), in the phrase *echar carraca* 'hablar mucho, sin descanso' (Tobón) and 'mentir' (Malaret); *chocheras* (Nic); *grupo* and *grullo* (Arg), deriv. *grupear* (Garzón); *iris* (Yucatán) 'rainbow,' perhaps because of the rainbow's constantly changing hues, as in "Es puro *iris* lo que te contó" (Suárez, p. 139); *jáquima* (CR) 'halter' in the sense of *estafa* 'swindle,' as in "le pegaron una *jáquima*" (Salesiano); *viruta* (CR) 'wood shavings,' as in "Qué *virutas* mete Luis" (Salesiano).

Occasionally in popular and colloquial speech the word *mentira* may be avoided by use of a gesture. Thus, when the speaker wishes to indicate that what is being said is a prevarication he may wink (this is done in all parts of the world), or pull an imaginary beard (Arg), or put his hat on askew (Ven), or hold his nose with index and thumb and duck his head, as if to say "me hundo para que pase" (Barranquilla, Col), or he may brush his fingers outward from the mouth, meaning "de dientes para afuera" or "de labios afuera," that is, what has been said is 'idle talk.'

AVARICE

Standard *avaro, tacaño, cicatero,* colloquial *agarrado* (also *mezquino, miserable, apretado, roñoso, cutre, verrugo, atacado,* vulgar *estíptico* or *estreñido,* etc.) 'avaricious,' 'stingy,' 'close-fisted,' or 'tight' have many additional synonyms in American Spanish, most of them euphemisms. Widespread are *agalludo* (Ec, Col, Ven, SD) from *agallas* 'gills of a fish,' a sign of avid devouring; *amarrado* (occasionally in Spain) 'tied up, moored' ("¿Por qué siendo don Pepe tan rico será tan *amarrado?"* Col: Tobón), and *amarrete* (especially in RP); *angurriento* (also *angurrioso,* Col), from *angurria* 'great hunger, vehement and continuous desire to eat.' Rather general is *codo* 'elbow,' *ser del codo, duro del codo, codo duro,* an extension of peninsular *darle a uno en el codo* (Andalusia) 'to strike someone's elbow' so that he will open his hand, hence 'miserly,' as in "Juan, o Juana, es muy *codo"* (Malaret). Often this expression is accompanied with a gesture, or the gesture alone may suffice to indicate miserliness (see fig. 14). In many regions the left forearm is held up with fist clenched, then the right palm strikes the left elbow (or the left elbow may strike any surface), whereafter the clenched fist opens (cf. "no suelta dinero aunque le den en el codo con un martillo"). Elsewhere, one merely touches a table with the elbow and says "es codo" or "suda antes por el codo que gastar un peso," or merely holds up the clenched fist and says "Es así." The closed fist (*puño*) has from time immemorial been a symbol of miserliness (*ser como un puño*), whence the popular peninsular euphemisms *devoto a la virgen del puño, ser como Don Alejandro Empuño, Don Juan Puño,* etc. (Wagner, p. 11).

Sometimes the synonym is the name of an animal that manifests characteristics of avarice, as familiar standard *cochino* or *puerco* 'pig.' Because of the oyster's tightly closed shell, *ostra* is used in Chile, where sea food abounds, to mean an avaricious person, as in "Él es una *ostra,* no

pienses que pueda darte algo" (Oroz, p. 19), cf. *juey* (PR) 'crab' >
'miser.' In Chile, *chincolito* (a small sparrow-like bird whose song is a
single invariable phrase which sounds like "¿Has visto a mi tío, tío Austín
[= Agustín]?") has come to indicate a person who gives very meager
tips in hotels, beach resorts, and the like (Román). In the same country,
"¡padrino *cacho!*" is what street urchins call the godfather who at a baptism
throws few coins to them; does this term derive from *cacho* 'dog,' or is
it from *cacho* ('horn') 'an unsaleable article' having as little value as a
horn? Example: "Al salir de liglesia taba la tupición de chiquillos ...
—¡Viva el pairino! *¡Pairino cacho* orejas de macho! ... Me metí la mano
al golsillo y saqué un puñao e tapas e cerveza y se las tiré" (Del Campo,
p. 107). In Guatemala one hears *chucho* 'dog' for 'miserly' (as well as
for 'gluttonous') or 'usurious' as in "El banquero Villegas es muy *chucho,*"
deriv. *chuchada* as in "Cobrar el tres por ciento de interés mensual es
una *chuchada"* (Sandoval); *lagarto* (also CR and elsewhere) 'alligator'
because of that animal's voraciousness, usually applied to a usurer, as in
"El usurero José Pinzón es un *lagarto* que da prestado dinero ... al módico
interés del 10 por ciento mensual" (Sandoval), cf. *caimán* (Col) 'alligator' > 'miser'; *mica* 'monkey' (std. *mona*) may mean 'stingy,' as in "El
mica de don Ginés oprime tanto la moneda o el billete que agarra, que
hace cagar al quetzal del escudo" (*ibid.*). Central American *piche,* the
name of a web-footed bird that habitually stands on one leg, may mean
'avaro,' as in "Don Antonio fué siempre *piche,* hasta con sus hijos" (Guat:
Sandoval). However, *piche* may well be a shortened form of ubiquitous
pichicato (see below). In Colombia and Panama, *runcho* 'a kind of
opossum' (also 'pig,' Col) means 'stingy, tight' because if threatened with
danger this animal curls up and shrinks.

Many euphemisms are borrowings from other languages. Thus, rather
general *pichicato* (Ec, Col, CA, Mex, Cuba) is apparently from Italian
pizzicato. This word and its variants *pichicate* (Mex), *pichicote* (Bol),
and *pechicato* (Cuba, Hond) contain the first syllable *pi* or *pe* associated
with smallness (*piccino, pequeño, petit*) and hence with miserliness, as
do also *pichirre* (Ven), *pinche* (Nic), *pisirico* (Salv), *pijotero* (general),
deriv. *pijotear, pichicatear, pichicatería,* and others. Chilean *pichiñique,*
related to *pichicato,* also reflects Mapuche *pichi* 'little, a small thing or
amount' (cf. *pichiruche* 'an insignificant, useless or dull person'), as in
futre pichiñique 'stingy dude,' a favorite insult applied by coachmen and

drivers to persons giving small tips. In Ecuador, *micha* (also *michoso, mitza, mitzoso*) is 'miser,' probably from Quechua *micha* meaning *verruga* 'wart,' since, according to popular belief, warts are peculiar to misers (Toscano, p. 226); cf. *misho* (NW Arg: Lizondo Borda) and *misquiriche* (Arequipa, Peru: Ugarte). In Ecuador one hears likewise *chulquero* from *chulco* 'usury,' as in "este tipo es un *chulquero* que roba a los pobres cobrando el interés del veinte por ciento mensual" (García Muñoz, p. 108). In northwest Argentina one finds *ocotudo* 'stingy' from *ocote* (Quechua *okoti*) 'anus' (Vidal, p. 316).

Other local words for 'stingy' are:

atracado (Chile, Guat; std. *atacado*).

colmillón (CR) 'eye-toothed,' that is, 'voracious'; *coñudo* and *coñón* (Ec), *coñete* (Chile, Peru), from *coño,* a nickname applied to a Spaniard because of his frequent use of this word as a vulgar interjection; *cuentachiles* (Mex); *culimiche* (Mex); *cuña* (Hond) 'wedge.'

garrotero (Chile, Cuba), from *garrote* 'club,' as in "un comerciante muy *garrotero*" (Suárez), recalling standard *agarrado; gurrugús* (CR), related to *angurriento* (?);

hambriento (Col, Ant) 'hungry,' cf. *muertodiambre* (rustic, Col); *jajá* (SD).

lanza (CR) 'lance, pike'; *lechero* (Ven, Col, Mex) and also *leche* (Col), as in "El viejo Melquisedec es muy *leche*" (Acuña).

maceta (PR); *machucho* (Col); *milañero* (SD) from *milaña* 'bit'; *muela* (Hond) 'molar,' cf. *colmillón* above and verb *muelear* (Guat) 'to eat.'

perecido (Antioquia, Col); *pesetero* (Cuba) from *peseta* '20-cent coin'; *piedra azul* (Chile), alluding to the hardness of blue stones (?), as in "Y no saben lo agarrado que es Pedro ... Es *piedra azul*" (Durand, p. 239) and "... tienen plata ahorrada, ¿no ve que son *piedra azul*? ¡más cicateros que Judas!" (Castro, p. 166); *pilinque* (Pan) from Aztec *pilihui* 'to wilt, wrinkle (of fruits)'; *pirata* (Nic); *poquitero* (Mex) and *poquito* (Ec: Toscano, p. 192).

tapado (Col) 'covered' with money; *tominero* (Mex); in Mexico one may hear "éste es de Monterrey" (perhaps accompanied by the gesture of tapping the table with the elbow), since inhabitants of that commercial city have been traditionally considered avaricious; *tragón* (Col: Montoya) 'voracious'; *truñoño* (Col), *tuñuño* (Pan); *vigilia* (Col).

DRUNKENNESS

Perhaps in no other domain of euphemism is there such a plethora of synonyms as in that pertaining to drunkenness. A man who has imbibed excessively, especially a person of some social standing, is not *ebrio* or *embriagado* or crudely *borracho* but rather is referred to indulgently as *alegre* 'gay,' *contento* 'happy,' *templado* 'tempered,' *descompuesto* 'out of order, indisposed' (Chile, Peru, CA, PR), *divertido* 'amusing,' *ido* 'gone,' *cargado* 'loaded,' *mareado* 'seasick, dizzy,' *hecho* 'done' (Arg), etc.

More direct terms are *tomado* and *tomador* (std. *bebido* and *bebedor*), since American Spanish usually substitutes *tomar* 'to take' for *beber* 'to drink,' except in reference to animals; from *mamar—mamado* (Arg, Peru, Ec), *mamerto* and *mamertín* (RP), *mamífero* (Arg, Mex); from *chupar —chupado, chupador, chupista* (RP, Ec), *chupaco, chupandín,* and *chupitegui* (Arg), *chupingo* (Chile); from *copa* and *copear—copeado, copetón* (Col), *copetinero* and *copista* (Arg), *copólogo* (Chile, Mex); *curado* (RP, Chile, Peru) 'cured, salted' (cf. fam. std. *ahumado* 'smoked' and Eng. 'pickled, stewed'), as in "divisé a un *curado* ... andaba dos pasos y retrocedía uno" (Chile: Castro, p. 418), "On Honorio *se curó* hasta las repatas y tuvimos que acostalo" (Chile: Romanángel, p. 22), cf. humorous *cureque* (Chile); *chumado, chumeado, chumo, achumado* (from Quechua *chumo*); *caneco* (Bol, Ven) from standard *caneca* 'cylindrical glazed earthen bottle,' also 'basket, usually of straw, with lateral handles, used for gathering grapes' in Mendoza and San Juan (Arg); *pipo* (Mex), *pipón* (Arg), *(estar hecho) una pipa* (Chile, Arg, Peru, PR) 'cask,' or *camisa de mimbre* (Chile), referring to the 'wicker covering' of demijohns containing wine, as in "¡Ya 'stá curao otra ve el *Camis' e Mimbre!"* (Rabanales, p. 189), both *pipa* and *camisa de mimbre* recalling familiar standard *estar hecho un cesto* ('a basket') or *una cuba* 'a wine cask,' *un cuero* or *una bota* 'a wine skin,' *una uva* 'a grape'; *grifo* (Mex) 'faucet,' though this word more generally indicates a person intoxicated with marijuana, cocaine, or morphine; *guarapeado* (Peru), from *guarapo* 'cane juice'; *guareado* (CA) from *guaro* 'cane brandy'; *tarro* (CR) 'earthen vessel for liquids'; *tragueado* (Ec, Col, Ven, CA) from *traguearse* 'to get drunk,' frequentative for standard *tragar* 'to swallow'; *traguiteado* (Guat, SD) from *traguitearse; trinco* (PR) from *trincar* 'to drink liquor.'

Some terms, like familiar standard *alumbrado, achispado,* and *encandilado,* have as points of comparison light, heat, fire, spark, and the like: *acocuyado* (Bol), from Arawak *cocuyo* 'glowworm'; *bomba* (see below); *caliente* (Arg, SD) 'hot'; *cuete* (Mex), from *cohete* 'skyrocket' > 'revolver,' as in "¡A este maje le voy a poner *cuete* en menos que canta un gallo, y entonces ... !" (Ángulo, p. 347); *chamuscado* (Arg) 'scorched, seared'; *chispo* (CA, Mex) from *chispa* 'spark'; *eléctrico* (Guat); *farolazo* (CA), from *faro* 'lighthouse, lantern,' as in "meterse un *farolazo*" 'to get drunk'; *estar en fuego* (Pan) 'to be on fire'; *prendido* (CA, Ant) 'on fire'; *quemado* (Ven, SD) 'burned'; *rubio* (Bol) 'red, blond,' cf. *estar en blonda* (Ec); *tiznado* (CA) 'sooty,' as in "Don Salustiano andaba algo *tiznado* por la calle" (Guat: Sandoval).

Among other terms meaning 'drunk' is *bolo* (CA, Tabasco) 'ninepin,' probably from the ease with which it falls; it is used in such sentences as "Estaba tan *bolo* Serapio, que no podía pararse [= ponerse de pie]" (Sandoval) and "quien nació para triste, ni *bolo* será alegre." Gagini relates that when a Salvadoran was asked in Madrid what the president of his country was like he answered, "Es peche, cuto y *bolo*," but no one understood what he meant until the interpreter explained, "Es canijo, manco y ebrio." The word *bolo* is often euphemized by the words *boliviano, boleco,* and *volatín,* in which the first three sounds recall *bolo,* but stress and spelling have changed, as in "Doña Justa ya está algo *volatina*" (Sandoval).

Still other, more or less local, words for 'drunk' or 'tipsy' are:

azurumbado (Guat), familiar standard *azumbrado,* from *azumbre* 'a liquid measure.'

briago (Mex) from *embriago* (cf. Speratti, p. 155); *bimbo* (Mex); *bufa* (Mex, Cuba); *bufandilla* (Cuba); *bútago* (Mex), from older *buétago* 'lung.'

corrido (Mex), as in "estar más *corrido* que escaso" (Malaret); *cospeado* (CR), recalling *copeado,* from *cospearse,* deriving from Aztec *cozpol* or *cuzpul* 'highly colored' ? (Gagini) or to be connected with *cuspe* (from Quechua *cushpi* 'spinning top') as used in Colombia and Chile (cf. *trompo* 'top' and *trompeta* 'drunkenness'); *cucarro* (Chile) 'faulty spinning top'; *cufifo* (Chile); *curcucho* (Guat).

chebo (Guat), as in "Marcela es buena cocinera, pero es muy *cheba*" (Sandoval); *chicoteado* (SD) from *chicotear* 'to whip'; *chimpím* (Ec, where it means also *aguardiente* 'brandy' and is therefore a permutation of the cause for the result); *chungo* (Ven).

droguista (Arg: Madueño) from *drogui* or *droga* 'drunkenness'; *duro* (RP, Bol, Mex), as in "Fulano andaba bien *duro*" (Malaret).

emparrandado (general) from *emparrandarse* (fam. std. *parrandear* 'to carouse'); *estar en pedo* (RP, Chile) from verb *peer* 'to break wind,' because of the odor of an intoxicated person (cf. *peo* in parts of Spain: Alcalá Venceslada, Iribarren; *pea:* Cuervo, § 793), as in "¿Cómo ... has encontrao cómo emborracharte? —Si no *estoy en pedo,* señor, sino medio templadito" (Ascasubi, *Aniceto el Gallo,* ap. Tiscornia, I, 57) and "El otro día debía *estar en pedo*" (Güiraldes, p. 174), cf. *empédocles* (Arg: Madueño), a facetious euphemism for *borracho,* from the name of the Greek philosopher.

fondeado (Guat) from *fondear* 'to anchor' and phonetic association with *fonda* 'inn.'

giro (Guat), as in "Mi sirvienta vino del paseo ... bastante *gira*" (Sandoval); *gis* (Mex, where *gis* 'chalk' may mean 'pulque' or any other white or colorless alcoholic drink); *gris* (Guanajuato, Mex) in *andar gris* (cf. French *se griser*).

inalámbrico (Guat), that is, 'incommunicado,' as in "Don Ignacio se mantiene *inalámbrico*" (Sandoval); *infróndigo* (Ec).

jalado (general) 'pulled, dragged' (cf. std. "beber de un *tirón*") often euphemized in Mexico by the place name *Jalisco; jumado, jumo* (general); *jumatán* (Cuba), *jumedo* (Peru); *jumético* (Ec), as in "Lástima que se ha de hacer *jumético*" (Gil Gilbert, p. 14); *jupiado* (CA) and *jupipe* (CR).

machado (Arg, Bol, Ec), also *machador, machalón,* and *macharín* from Quechua *macha* 'drunkenness'; *maiceado* (CA); *ñuto* (Arequipa, Peru) from Quechua *ñuttu* 'broken.'

pando (Mex); *peao* (Col: Tobón) and *pegado* 'stuck, plastered' (Guanacaste, CR), whence "estar más *pegado* que una estampilla" (Gagini); *pelao* (Ven: Rosenblat, p. 320) from *pelarse; perico* (Col, Ec) 'parakeet,' probably because of the bird's garrulity; general *picado* from *picarse* 'to sour (of wine),' 'to begin to rot (of fruit),' 'to get irritated, to itch, tingle,' deriv. *picón* and *picucho* 'tipsy'; *pisco* (Ven); *piscólogo* (Peru) from *pisco* 'brandy.'

rascado (general), from the feeling of roughness or dryness in the throat (?), as in "—¡Basta, basta; que se pare ese hombre si no es que está *rascao!*" (ap. Alvarado), deriv. *rascoso* (Ven) and *rascucho* (Chile) 'slightly tipsy.'

soco or *socado* (CA), as in "Don Ruperto siempre está o anda muy *socado*" (Guat: Sandoval); *suruco* (PR) 'tipsy'; *taranto* (Ven) from *taranta* 'fit of madness' and *atarantado* 'bitten by a tarantula.'

teco and *tecolote* 'owl' (CA), as in "Don Pancracio siempre anda *teco* por la calle" and "Doña Engracia comienza a ponerse algo *tecolota,* pues ya está muy platicadora" (Guat: Sandoval); *tranquilino* and *tranquilo* (Mex), euphemisms based on *tranca* 'drunkenness'; *trompeto* (Mex), from *trompeta* 'drunkenness,' suggesting *trompo* 'spinning top' and a comparison between blowing a bugle and drinking from a bottle; *turiego* (Ven), *tuturuto* (Ven, CA, Mex), perhaps a euphemistic distortion of *turulato* 'stupefied, speechless.'

vacilador and *vacilón* (Mex, Guat, PR) meaning *medio ebrio* or *calamocano* 'tipsy,' from *vacilar* 'to carouse' and 'get drunk'; *vejigo* (Mex).

zarazo or *sarazo* (Col, Ven, CA, Mex) and *zarazón* 'almost ripe' (applied to fruit), meaning 'tipsy' (Guat), as in "Don Jaime está muy decidor, señal de que ya está algo *zarazón*" (Sandoval); *zopilote* (CR) 'turkey buzzard,' as in "está *zopilote*" 'he is tipsy'; *zumbo* (Mex, parts of Spain).

Nouns denoting *borrachera* 'drunkenness' are legion, and nearly all of them are feminine. Among familiar standard terms are *cogorza* (possibly Latin *confortium* from *confortiarse* 'to comfort, console' > 'to hold a funeral feast,' see Corominas), *casco* 'helmet,' *curda, chispa* 'spark,' *filoxera* 'phylloxera,' an insect that attacks grapevine leaves and roots, *juma* and *jumera* for *huma* and *humera, lobo* 'wolf,' *melopea* 'melopoeia' or 'the art of forming melody,' *merluza* 'hake,' *mona* 'monkey,' *mordaga, mosca* (Andalusia) 'fly,' *papalina* 'cap or bonnet,' *pea* (< *pega* ? as in *pegarse una mona,* see Cuervo, § 793), *toquilla* 'hood,' *tajada* 'slice,' *turca* (originally an adjective, like *curda,* modifying *borrachera*), and *zorra* 'fox.'

Among American-Spanish words for *borrachera* are:

bebecina, bebeta, and *bebezón* (Col), *bebendurria* (Peru); *bimba* (Mex); *bolencia* (Guat), from *bolo,* as in "El indio Lucas tenía una *bolencia* tan grande, que no podía tenerse en pie" (Sandoval); *bomba* (Arg, Chile, Peru, CA, Andalusia), as in "Pedro y Juan estaban en *bomba* anoche" (Chile: Yrarrázaval, p. 121) and "Anoche se cargaba usted una *bomba* número uno" (Guat: Sandoval); *briaga* (Mex), cf. *briago; bufa* (Mex, Cuba).

candado (Mex); *cospe* (CR); *cruda* (CA, Mex), meaning also 'hang-over'; *cuesca* (Col).

chiva (Hond); *chonguenga* (Hond); *chuma* (Andean zone); general *chupa,* from *chupar* (std. 'to suck, sip, soak up'), meaning commonly in America 'to drink [*beber*]' and 'to smoke [*fumar*]'; *chupeta* (Chile), as in "A Pedro le gusta mucho la *chupeta*" (Román).

fa (Azuay, Ec), as in "¡No puede más, tiene una *fa!*" (Malaret).

gaita (Peru) 'bagpipe,' as in "zampéme *gaita* de órdago" (Corrales, p. 94); *guarapeta* (Mex, Ant) from *guarapo,* as in "se tomó las otras noches una *guarapeta* fenomenal y escandalosa" (PR: ap. Malaret, *Bol. fil.*); *guayo* (Cuba, PR) 'grater.'

huaripampeada (Huánuco, Peru).

jala (Col), from general *jalarse,* as in "Se metió una *jala* espantosa" (Tobón); *jalera* (Cuba); *jáquima* (CA) 'halter,' as in "Don Isidoro se puso una buena *jáquima* en el baile de anoche" (Guat: Sandoval); *jindama* (Cuba); *juma, jumera* (Ant), as in "¡Vaya una *juma* la de Ramón!" (Cuba: C. Suárez); *jumo* (SD), as in "se dió un *jumo* de tres pisos" (Patín).

macaca (Chile) 'monkey,' as in "agarrar o pegarse una *macaca*" (Lenz, p. 880); *macha* (Arg, Bol, Ec), from Quechua and Aymara; *machasca* (Peru); *maguey* (Mex) 'century plant,' a permutation of instrument for product; *mamona* (Ec), perhaps a cross between *mamar* and *mona; mamúa* (RP), as in "un cajetilla al cual la *mamúa* le da por llorar" (ap. Malaret, *Bol. fil.*); rare *mamada,* as in a "Carculen cómo sería / La *mamada* que agarré, / Que sin más me afiguré / Que yo era el mesmo Gobierno" (Estanislao del Campo, *Gobierno gaucho,* v. 7); *marimonda* (Col, Ven) from the indigenous name of a small monkey; *mejenga* (CR), probably related to *menjurje* 'concoction'; *mica* (CA) 'monkey,' as in "Prisciliano lucía ayer pol la calle una *mica* de padre y señor mío" (Guat: Sandoval); *metido* (SD) from *meter* 'to put in,' and *medio metido* 'tipsy,' as in "llegó *medio metido* al baile" (Patín); *montera* (Hond) 'cap,' since a heavy head feels as if it were covered with a cap (cf. std. *papalina* 'cap with flaps,' 'drunkenness,' and also *casco* 'helmet' and *toquilla* 'hood'); *mula* (CR; Tabasco, Mex; elsewhere in Mexico *mula* may mean 'bottle of liquor').

peo (Cuba), *pedo* (RP), as in "Y aquel beber tan prolijo / Que en el rico es alegría / Y en el pobre es *pedo* fijo" (Hidalgo, *Cielito,* ap. Tiscornia, I, 455); *pela* (Ven), as in "se pegó una *pela"* (Rosenblat, p. 320); *pelado* (Chile), perhaps a confusion of familiar standard *desollar la zorra* 'to sleep off a drunkenness,' *desollar* 'to skin' being equivalent to *pelar* 'to peel' (Román); *peludo* (RP, Bol) 'a kind of armadillo' but possibly a euphemistic distortion of vulgar *pedo,* or from *pelo,* a reference to accompanying dull paints at the hair roots ? (see Kröll, V, 33, who lists Portuguese *cabeleira, peleira,* and *peruca* 'drunkenness'), "Tomé en casa el otro día / Tan soberano *peludo* / Que hasta hoy, caballeros, dudo / Si ando mamao todavía" (Estanislao del Campo, *op. cit.,* v. 2); *penca* (RP) 'leaf' of a certain cactus (prepared in several ways as a remedy for a number of ailments) and also meaning *tuna* 'fruit of the cactus,' see below; *perica* (Ec, Pan, Col) 'parakeet'; *perra* (Col and Spain) 'she-dog'; *perrusquía* (Tex); *petera* (Cuba) 'fit of temper'; *pichinga* (Guat) 'small clay water jug,' as in "Juan se puso en al baile una espesa *pichinga"* (Sandoval); *pintonera* (Ven) from *pintonear* 'to begin to ripen (of fruit)'; *pisca* (Ven) from *pisco* 'brandy.'

quema (SD) 'fire,' as in "anoche tenías tamaña *quema"* (Patín).

rasca (general) from *rascar* 'to scratch, strum (a guitar),' perhaps from the resemblance of the movement of the hand in strumming a guitar to the gesture meaning 'to drink' (see below), as in "¡Qué *rasca* tienes, chico!" (Ven: Gallegos, p. 140).

sirindanga and *siringa* (Hond), for *jeringa* 'syringe, clyster'; *soca* or *zoca* (CA) from *socar* (std. *azocar*) 'to tighten,' deriv. *socarse* 'to get drunk'; *suruca* (PR).

tagarnia (Col) and *tagarnina* (CA, Mex), verb *tagarniar* (Col) 'divertirse causando bullicio, discusiones y hasta pendencias,' as in *"Tagarniaron* toda la noche y no dejaron dormir"* (Tobón); *taranta* (Mex); *tecolote* and shortened *teco* (Mex, CA) 'owl'; *tiempla* (Col) from *templarse; tomatera* and *tomadura* (Chile) from *tomar* 'to drink'; general *tranca* 'club,' perhaps the idea of something that cannot move freely or lacks equilibrium, as in "Ayer lucía usted una buena *tranca,* cuando salió de la cantina" (Guat: Sandoval) and *"—Tranca* tenés, si ya no sabés quién soy" (Arg: Lynch, *Palo verde,* ap. *AmSS,* p. 66); *trinca* (PR); *trompeta* (Mex); *trúa* (Arg, Bol), as in "estar en *trúa"* (Malaret); *trusca* (Arequipa, Peru); *tuesta* (PR, SD) 'tanning, toasting,' as in "se dió una *tuesta"; tuna* (Ven, Guat) 'vagrancy,' as in "Ya Justo está en *tuna* desde la semana pasada" (Sandoval).

vacilada (Mex) from *vacilar* 'to carouse, get drunk'; *verraquera* (Cuba), little used, from *verraco* 'male swine'; *zumba* (Mex) 'flogging, beating.'

It is worth noting that a number of nouns for *borrachera* are names of animals whose peculiarities, instincts, antics, or lumbering gait are readily associated with states of drunkenness (such as fam. std. *mona* 'monkey,' *lobo* 'wolf,' *perra* 'she-dog,' *zorra* 'she-fox,' *filoxera* 'phylloxera,' *merluza* 'hake'): *chiva* 'goat,' *macaca* 'monkey,' *marimonda* 'small monkey,' *mica* 'monkey' (similarly, German *Affe*, Italian *monna, bertuccia,* see Riegler, p. 8), *mula* 'mule,' *peludo* 'armadillo,' *perica* 'parakeet,' *pisco* 'turkey,' *tecolote* 'owl,' and others.

A number of words are euphemistic phonetic distortions of terms denoting drunkenness that have fallen into disrepute. Thus, *bebecina, bebezón,* and *bebendurria* are derivatives of *beber,* but shifting the stress from the root to a somewhat unusual suffix also shifts the attention from the unpleasant connotations and thus acts euphemistically; *borracho* may be reflected in *bolo* and *bomba,* as *bolo* is in *boliviano* and *volatín; copaiba* in Lima veils *copa de aguardiente* and *doctor Copaiba* means *pisco* 'brandy' (Tovar); *jalado* is veiled in *jalisco,* from the proper name *Jalisco; mamerto* and *mamífero* recall *mamado; peludo, pelado* and facetious *empédocles* recall vulgar *pedo; perica, perra, petera* and others euphemize colloquial standard *pea; piscólogo,* deformation of *psicólogo,* recalls *pisco* which may be *pisco* 'turkey' or *pisco* 'grape brandy' from the town Pisco, in Peru, where the brandy was originally made (noun *piscología* means 'afición al consumo de pisco'); *tranquilino* and *tranquilo* are euphemistic transformations based on *tranca; travieso* and *trabanino* (Guat) for *trago,* as in "Tomemos el último *trabanino* y te vas" (Sandoval).

Harsh *emborracharse* 'to get drunk' may be euphemized by almost any of the nouns mentioned above and a verb like *coger, ponerse, amarrarse,* or *pillarse* (cf. fam. std. *coger una mona*), as *amarrarse una perra* (Col); *ponerse* or *amarrarse una bomba, una jáquima, una mica, una juma* (Guat), general *coger una tranca, coger un guayo* (Cuba, PR). Since most of such nouns are feminine, the object pronoun *la* is often found in verbal expressions meaning *emborracharse* (like fam. std. *cogerla*), such as *ama-*

rrársela 'to tie it on' (Col, Pan, CA); *clavársela* 'to nail it on' (CA), as in "En verdad te digo que yo *me la clavo* fácilmente en una fiesta" (Guat: Sandoval); *ponérsela* 'to put it on' like an article of clothing; *no apeársela* 'not to take it off' (Nic: Valle) means 'estar siempre borracho.'

Other verbs are *bombear* (SD), as in "estuviste *bombeando* con ellos" (Patín); *cospearse* (CR); *curarse* (RP, Chile, Peru); *chicotearse* (SD) from *chicote* 'whip'; general *chumarse, chuparse; guarearse* (CA); *guayarse* (PR) from *guayo; huaripampearse* (Huánuco, Peru); general *jalarse, jumarse; jupiarse* (CA); *mamarse; macharse* (Arg, Bol, Ec); *machascarse* (Peru); *picarse; pelarse* (Ven); *quemarse* (SD), as in "cuando *te quemas,* nadie puede aguantarte" (Patín); general *rascarse,* as in "cuando yo— estando *rascao*—voy andando y de pronto me paro, me da después mucho trabajo volver a arrancar" (Col: Arango, p. 165); *rajarse* (PR); *socarse* (CA), as in "El sirviente *se socó* anoche" (Guat: Sandoval); *tarrearse* (CR); general *templarse; tiznarse* (CA) 'to smirch oneself'; *traguearse* (Ven, Ec, Col, CA) and *traguetearse* (SD), as in "él *se traguetea* con frecuencia" (Patín), and *traguitearse* (Guat); *trancarse* (Ven, Ant); *vacilar* (Mex); *vocalizar* (SD), associated with *boca,* as in "acostumbramos *vocalizar* los sábados" (Patín).

Some verbs have a prosthetic *a-: abombarse* (*bomba*), *apedarse* (*pedo*), *acocuyarse* (*cocuyo*), *achicharse* (*chicha*), *achumarse, alicorarse* (Col), *ajumarse* ("Tiempísimo que no ... *me ajumo* con un buen guarapo," Ec: A. Ortiz, p. 180) or *ahumarse, atarantarse* (Guat, Mex), *apalearse* (SD: from *palo* 'drink'), *atilamparse* (Trujillo, Ven), *atoyarse* (CR) 'to stuff oneself,' *azurumbarse* (Guat), etc. Most verbs, however, prefix *en* or *em* (std. *embriagarse, emborracharse*); for example: *embolarse* (CA, Mex); *enchaucharse* (Arg); *enchicharse* (CA, Mex) 'to get drunk on *chicha'; enchisparse; emparrandarse; empedarse* (RP); *empericarse* (Col, Ec) from *perico; empiparse* (Arg, Chile, Peru, Ec), cf. *apiparse; empolvarse* (Col); *encañarse* (Urug, Cuba) from *caña; encoparse* (Chile) from *copa; engrifarse* (Mex); *enguaralarse* (Col) from *guaral* 'cord, rope'; *enguapearse* (Mex) from *guapo; enguarapetarse* (PR) from *guarapo* 'cane juice'; *enjarinarse* (Riohacha, Col); *enmonarse* from *mona; enmoscarse* (Peru); *ensurucarse* (PR) from *suruca; entrompetar* (Mex) from *trompeta.*

Among the numerous nouns corresponding to standard *copa* 'drink' (from *copa* 'wineglass,' a permutation of receptacle for content) and that often indicate a 'blow' or 'shot' (fam. std. *latizago, lapo,* etc.) are:

buche (Ec, where are heard *fuerte, pepo, puro, quiño,* see Cornejo).

cachetazo 'slap' (Guat); *cachimbazo* (CA) from *cachimbo* or *cachimba* 'tobacco pipe'; *cantazo* (PR) 'lash'; *cañazo* and *cocotazo* (Cuba); *cohetito* (Mex) from *cohete; cospe* (CR), as in "echarse un *cospe*" (Gagini).

chicotazo (SD) from *chicote* 'whip'; *chinchorrazo* (Ven, SD) from *chinchorro* 'hammock.'

fajo 'blow with the sword' (Mex; std. *cintarazo;* cf. rather general *fajar* 'to beat' and cant *fajas* 'blows'), as in "Primero nos echaremos un *fajo* de tequila ... ¡Dos tequilazos, don Pedro!" (Frías, ap. Santamaría, *Dicc. de mejicanismos*).

jalón (CA, Mex) from *jalar,* usually 'drink from a bottle' ("Echa otro *jalón*"), diminutive *jaloncito* ("Dale un *jaloncito* a la botella"), agumentative *jalonazo* (Guat: Sandoval); *juanetazo* (PR, SD), as in "nos dimos varios *juanetazos* en la pulpería" (Patín).

matracazo (PR) from *matraca* 'wooden rattle,' deriv. *matraquearse; mecatazo* (CA, Mex), from *mecate* 'rope, whip'; *palo* and *palito* (Ven, Ant) 'stick,' as in "¿Otro *palito,* doctor?" (Ven: Gallegos, p. 138), deriv. *apalearse* (SD) and *palotearse* (Ven).

pedrada (SD) 'blow with a stone,' as in "en una pulpería de la esquina solíamos darnos una que otra *pedrada*" (Patín); *petacazo* (SD); *piedra* (Cuba).

tanganazo (Col, Ven, PR), from *tangana* 'oar'; *toma* (SD), as in "una *toma* cuesta cinco centavos" (Patín); general *trago* 'swallow, swig' and its euphemisms *travieso, trabanino,* etc. (Guat); *trancazo* (Ec, Ven, Ant); *tarrayazo* (Ven: see Rosenblat, p. 328, for many others; also Madueño).

Familiar standard metaphors for 'to drink' (*empinar* or *alzar el codo, estar entre dos luces, estar a media vela,* etc.) have many congeners in America: *alzarse la bata* (Col); *andar a toda llave* 'completely drunk' and *a media llave* 'half drunk' (Ec); *andar entre San Juan y Mendoza* 'to be tipsy' (these are the important wine-making regions in Argentina), as in "En la puerta de mi casa / tengo una piedra rocosa; / en ella tropiezo si ando / *entre San Juan y Mendoza* (Malaret, *Copla;* cf. fam. std. *estar entre Pinto y Valdemoro); cortar la mañana* or *cortar el frío* or *cortar la tarde,* and simply *dar* (or *echar*) *un corte* (Peru); *chupar el rabo a la jutía* [= 'local rodent'] (Chile); *echarle copal al santo* (Pan, where *copal* is 'resin' used for incense); *escurrir los vidrios* (Col) 'to drain the

bottles'; *estar a media bolina* or *a medios chiles* (Mex), as in "El Juez
... no había perdonado una sola copa y ... ya *estaba a medios chiles*" (Ángulo, p. 189); *estar a media caña* (Ec); *estar a media ceba* (CR); *estar a
media máquina* (Ven; for others see Rosenblat, p. 322); *estar entre pichita
y pichón* (Cuba); *estar entre Gualeguay y Gualeguaichu* (Arg); *estar
meado* (or *picado*) *de araña* (Guat); *estar picado de culebra* (Oajaca,
Mex); *ganar altura* (Mex) 'to be high' and *agarrar vapor* (Mex); *hacer la
mañana* or *la tarde* (Arg, Chile, Mex); *irse para Tomé* (Chile), a place
name recalling *tomar* 'to drink'; *meterse en caña* (Cuba); *meterse en la
botella* (Ven), *en el saco* (Cuba); *no ver sol* (Ven); *pegar un beso al jarro*
(Arg) 'to kiss the jug'; *pisar la comida* (Ant) 'to take a drink after a meal';
remojar el gaznate (Col) 'to moisten the throat'; *trabajar uno el vidrio*
(Tex) 'to drink beer'; *trabajar en el levante* (Chile); *tener media navaja
adentro* (Mex), as in "Aquél ya lleva *media navaja adentro*" (Velasco);
ser manyacaña (Arg) 'to be a cane-juice consumer.'

   Often the words *beber* and *borracho* are avoided with a significative
gesture (see figs. 15 and 16): with right thumb and small finger extended,
other fingers folded inward on the palm, the hand is moved several times
with a wrist motion toward the mouth. The hand thus represents roughly,
or seems to be holding, a wine bag or bottle, the extended thumb being the
spout or bottle neck. In local variations, sometimes only the thumb is
extended and all the other fingers are held against the palm (Col, Cuba,
etc.); sometimes thumb and index fingers are extended, the remaining
fingers held against the palm (Peru, Ec, etc.), sometimes thumb and index
finger form a circle and the other fingers are curved as if holding a glass
(Col). These gestures represent the act of drinking, but, by a permutation
of cause for effect, they may also indicate a person who is inebriated. In
Guatemala, for instance, one may indicate that a habitual drinker is at it
again by saying "está en el oficio" and accompanying these words with the
appropriate gesture. One may say merely "Está ..." or "está algo ..." and
make the gesture. Furthermore, the extended thumb (other fingers
clenched) directed toward a glass or cup may mean 'to pour,' a gesture
seen in coffeehouses when someone wishes the waiter to pour him a cup of
coffee.

   Among local terms for 'hangover' are:

   cruda and *crudez* (CA, Mex), as in "—Ya ve usted lo mal que amanece
uno al día siguiente de una borrachera ... le dije: —Anda y acuéstate, mu-

jer, para que te pase *la cruda"* (Mex: Federico Gamboa, *Santa,* 1938, p. 144).

chaqui (Bol) as in "tengo *chaqui"* (Brown, p. 86); *chuchaque* or *chuchaqui* (Ec), as in "—Y despertarse así, con *un chuchaque* monstruoso, los labios secos ... es algo que no deseamos a nuestro peor enemigo" (García Muñoz, p. 21) and "abrazaba a mi mujer y le ofrecía la cafiaspirina para que al otro día no amaneciera *chuchaque,* porque eso es lo que sucede: toma el marido, y la mujer es la que siente *el chuchaque"* (*ibid.,* p. 41).

goma (CA, Mex), as in "Tengo la boca reseca, necesito un trago para quitarme *la goma"* (Hond: Arturo Mejía Nieto, *El solterón,* p. 122) and "Me estoy muriendo del *gomón* que tengo" (Guat: Sandoval), deriv. *gomarabia, engomarse* and *engomado; guayabo* (Col), the name of a tropical fruit tree, as in "el maestro se encontraba aquel día bajo el flagelo implacable de *un guayabo* mortal" (Arango, p. 165), "¡Ah, *el guayabo!* Aquel terrible despertar del lunes" (*ibid.,* p. 159), deriv. *enguayabarse, enguayabado,* and *desenguayabar,* as in "Hay quien afirma que para *desenguayabar* lo mejor es un trago doble de aguardiente" (Acuña).

pelado (Chile), perhaps connected with familiar standard *dormir* or *desollar la zorra* since *desollar* 'to skin' is related to *pelar* 'to peel, skin' (Román), as in "—Si cuando agarra una tuna ('borrachera') está con *el pelao* ocho días" (Barros Grez, I, 2); *perseguidora* (Peru) 'the persecutor,' as in "como ayer fué su santo, debe estar con *la perseguidora"* (Corrales, p. 14).

ratón 'mouse' or *rata* 'rat' (Ven), as in the expressions *sacarse el ratón* or *matar la rata* which mean 'tomar un trago de aguardiente al día siguiente de una borrachera' (Alvarado; cf. fam. std. *matar el gusanillo* 'to have a morning drink of brandy on an empty stomach,' *matar el bicho* 'to drink an alcoholic beverage,' and French *tuer le ver*), deriv. *enratonarse* 'tener ratón'; *resaca* (SD, Urug) 'surf,' as in "Pero la tranca durmiendo y *la resaca* llorando" (Urug: ap. Madueño).

tornajuma (SD), from *juma* 'borrachera' and *tornar* 'to return'; (*estar de*) *zisca* (Guat: Madueño).

This is perhaps an appropriate place to touch on euphemisms referring to marijuana (*marihuana, mariguana*) and the intoxication caused by it. The terms mentioned below belong mostly to Mexican cant (see Rod, Chabat) and are in a state of constant flux. An initial sound or two suffice to recall the referent: *mari, mariposa, mastuerzo, moravia* (*moravio* 'addict'), *morisqueta* (*morisqueto* 'addict'), *mota, motivosa, motocicleta* (*motorista* 'addict'), *motivosa, motor* (*de chorro*). Others are *clorofila* 'chlorophyl,' *cola de borrego* (*de lion, de zorra*), *coliflor tostada, chipiturca, de la buena, doña diabla, doña Juanita, doradilla, grifa* (*grifo* 'addict'), *grilla* (*grillo* 'addict'), *hojas de alpiste japonés, Jerez seco, Juanita Salazar Viniegra, orégano, sahumerio, suprema verde de mejorana* (*de clorofila*), *tostada* (*tostado* 'addict'), *trueno verde, viniegra, yerba, yesca* (*yesco* 'addict'), *zacate inglés* (*zacatero* 'addict'). A cigarette is *chicharra* ('butt'), *chicharrón* ('lighted cigarette'), *mariposa, tecolote* ('butt'). The leaves necessary to make a certain number of cigarettes or a package containing that number is as follows: for one = *canilla,* for three = *carrujo* or *chanchomón,* for ten = *cartucho, cartón.* Verbs meaning 'to smoke' marijuana are *acelerar*(*se*), *atizar*(*se*), *dárselas, darse las de trueno verde, darse las tres* = *dar las tres chupadas, darse las tres de reglamento, darse un toque* (*de atención, de mota*), *dorár*(*selas*), *enamoriscar*(*se*), *enyerbar*(*se*), *grifear, motorizar*(*se*), *quemarse, tostárse*(*las*), and *tronárse*(*las*).

IV FINANCIAL STATUS

Since poverty (*pobreza, inopia*) is often considered humiliating, harsh reference to it must be constantly softened with euphemisms. Some of these are vaguely allusive, others purely humorous, showing a popular predilection for playful metaphor.

Standard *arrancado* 'uprooted, torn away' is in familiar speech applied to a person who, having been wealthy, is reduced to poverty. This meaning is extended in America to 'poor' in general and also to 'temporarily without funds,' like our colloquial 'broke.' In many regions derivative nouns *arranque* (Ec, Guat, Ant), *arranquera* (Col, Guat, Ant) or *ranquera* 'poverty' ("Aquí me tiene, querido amigo, en una *arranquera* espantosa," Guat: Sandoval) are further euphemized with the humorous formation *arranquitis* or *ranquitis,* as if poverty were an inflammatory disease ("Moisés padece de *arranquitis* crónica," *ibid.;* "Estar en *arranquitis,*" Peru: Ugarte). The terms may be reinforced with additions, as in "más *arrancado* que manga de chaleco" or "que una cebolla" (Santamaría); and, as a secondary euphemism, "estar como la manga de un chaleco" (Malaret), in which *arrancado* is circumspectly omitted.

It may be noted here that *mendigo* 'beggar' is in standard speech often euphemized by *pobre,* and in some regions (particularly in the Mexican zone) popular *méndigo* is offensive but standard *mendigo* is not. Standard *embromar* 'to fool, banter,' *fregar* 'to rub, scrub,' and vulgar *joder* in much of America as in parts of Spain have acquired the sense of 'to annoy, vex, harm,' physically as well as financially, so that *un embromado, un fregado,* or *un jodido* may be equivalent to both *un enfermo* and *un pobre* (RP, Chile, Col, Ant). Vulgar *jodido* is euphemized with the form *josemaría* (Ven), as in "Carlos está medio *josemaría*" (Rosenblat, p. 379).

Occasionally names of animals become synonymous with *pobre.* Thus, in Chile, *traro* (from Mapuche) 'a kind of small eagle' and *quiltro* 'cur' may both mean *pobre* (Oroz, p. 20); in Puerto Rico *estar ratón* or *ratona* means 'estar sin dinero' (cf. 'poor as a churchmouse'); in the River Plate region *pato* 'duck' may mean 'arrancado, sin dinero' as in the phrase "andar uno *pato*" (Santamaría).

Picturesque adjectives are (*estar*) *asado* or *asao* (Ven), cf. *estar frito;* (*estar*) *bruja* 'witch' (Mex, Ant), perhaps by popular etymology from English 'broke,' as in "Ven mañana que hoy *estoy bruja*" (Cuba: Rodríguez), (*ser*) *un bruja* 'to be habitually broke' (*ibid.*), deriv. *brujera* and *brujez* (Mex), *brujería* (PR); *calato* (Peru), from Quechua *kala* 'nude,' deriv. noun *calatería,* as in "Mientras más *calatería,* más batería," meaning 'mientras mayor pobreza, mayor apariencia de rumbosidad' (Arequipa, Peru: Malaret); rather general *cortado, recortado,* which perhaps refer to pockets 'cut open,' or are elliptical forms of *corto de dinero* 'short of money,' as in "A ver si me prestan unos cinco, porque yo ando muy *recortado*" (Chile: Malbrán, *Las diez de última,* p. 8), deriv. *cortadera;* (*estar*) *chonete* (CR) 'worn-out'; *desbaratado* (SD) 'ruined'; *fallenque* (Col), from *fallar* 'to fail'; *fuñido* (SD), from *fuñir* 'to bother, molest, plague,' as in "si no estuviera yo tan *fuñido* te regalaría un sombrero" (Patín); *gafo* (Guat) 'footsore, foundered,' as in "No me hables de pisto ('money'), porque ahora sí que estoy *gafo*" (Sandoval); *garifo* (Peru) 'hungry,' as in "estoy *garifo*" (Ugarte); *lámparo* (Col), as in "presumía de rico y resultó ser un *lámparo* (Acuña); *lépero* (Ec); *limpio* 'clean,' extended euphemistically to (*estar*) *en la limpia concepción* (Guat: Sandoval); *llucho* (Ec), as in "soy *llucho,* soy limpio, pero tengo honor" (García Muñoz, p. 275); *pasacantando* (SD); widespread *pelado* (from *pelar* 'to shear, fleece'), as in "A nadie le gusta casarse con una *pelada* o con mujer *pelada*" (Chile: Román), "tooh han sío *pelaoh* como la palma de la mano" (Cuba: Ciro Espinosa, p. 157), and *estar más pelado que un calvo* (Sandoval), cf. std. *pelón, pelete; planchado* (Chile, Peru, Cuba) 'ironed' flat, as in "andaban más *planchaos* que camisa e jutre en un día e fiesta" (Del Campo, p. 31) 'they were more smoothly ironed than a dude's shirt on a holiday'; *con los bolsillos planchados* or *pelados* or *limpios* or *puros* (Chile); (*ser*) *poblete* or (*estar*) *chupe* or *puro* (Chile); *seco, reseco* (Arg) 'dry'; *tener cero pesos* (Mex).

More elaborate metaphors also evince a preponderance of popular influence (cf. fam. std. *andar uno con una mano atrás y otra delante, no tener ni donde caerse muerto, no tener más que el cielo y la tierra, no tener más que el día y la noche,* etc.): *andar en la real quema* (CR); *estar en la lata* or *las latas* (Col, CA), in which *lata* is an extension of its meaning of *molestia* 'annoyance'; *estar en la* (*quinta*) *chilla* (Mex), in which *chilla* is an extension of its Mexican meaning 'piso alto de los teatros'; *quedar uno en muletas* (SD) 'on crutches,' as in "Después de la última guerra los pueblos beligerantes *quedaron en muletas"* (Patín); *comerse las uñas* (Nic: Valle) 'to eat one's nails'; *estar en la lona* (Ven), like a threadbare tire, and *estar en la carraplana,* from *carramplán < caplán* 'devil' (?) (Ven: Rosenblat, p. 382); *estar más limpio que* (or *estar como*): *talón de lavandera* (or *de angelito* or *de angelito serenao*), *una pepa de guama* (a native fruit), *pata de perro de agua, un resbaladero, cueva de loro sin pichones, un purgao, bolsillo de estudiante, sobaco de rana, espalda de frasco, hueso de sabana, la consciencia de Cristo, la mano de un santo,* etc. (Ven: Rosenblat, p. 376); *estar limpio de a huevo* or *de a locha* (Ven, where *huevo* and *locha* are names of copper coins; see *AmSS,* p. 278); *estar en la lupia* (Col), in which *lupia* means 'small change'; *no tener chapa* (Chile), the former name of a copper coin; *no tener ni para la amanezca* (Mex); *estar vaciado, estar en las delgaditas* (Col: Acuña); *estar en la raja* (Col: Tobón); *estar de* or *en ráfaga* (Ec, Peru) 'gust of wind'; *estar sin un maíz que asar* (Col, Ven, SD), since in areas where corn is of great importance, possession or lack of it may denote wealth or poverty; *estar en soletas* or *dejar a uno en soletas* (Ec), an extension of *soleta* 'patched sole of a stocking'; *estar en harinas* (Col: Tobón); *estar a tres dobles* ['knells'] *y un repique* ['chime'] (Arg, Chile, Peru); *estar a tiro de* ['a punto de'] *robar gallinas* (Col: Acuña); *estar en la prángana* (Mex, Ant) or *fuácata* (Ant) or *fuacatina* (Cuba, where interjection ¡*fuácata!* denotes a violent fall); *estar uno colgado* or *colgao* (Chile) 'to be hanging; to be disappointed,' which may mean both 'ignorant of something' (fam. std. *quedar en ayunas*) and 'impecunious,' with occasional variants, as in "Tú no sabes lo que es *andar a las cuelgas* y mirar como los otros andan ricos, y encontrarse que el bolsillo está sin chico, más pelao ['shorn' of money as well as of hair] que un conscripto militar" (Malbrán, p. 10), "amanecimos más *colgaos que una ampolleta"* (Romanángel, p. 22), "estoy *más colgao que un péndulo"* (*ibid.,* p. 127), "estoy *más colgado que un columpio"* (Malbrán, *Las diez de última,* p. 16).

In Guatemala alone are heard the following (Sandoval):

estar en la real quema, estar la patria en peligro ("No puedo hacer gastos ... porque* ahora sí *está la patria en peligro"), estar uno al corte, estar uno tronado* or *atrancado* or *atrasado* ("No he podido pagarte el pisto que me diste, porque estoy muy *atrasado,* pero el sábado cancelaré mi cuenta") or *bien raspado* or *bien rompido* (cf. 'broke'), *estar uno desnudo y sin defensa como la mayor parte de los animales* (from Miguel de Zamacois, ap. Sandoval), *estar uno en el petate,* or *en la cama* or *en la lipidia* or *en la loma del grito* or *en las cuatro esquinas* or *escuchando donde guisan* (that is, 'esperando comer en casa ajena') or *escuchando donde tortean* (= *hacer tortillas*) or *gimiendo y llorando como la Salve* or *haciendo versos, estar uno quemado* or *sin cuaco* or *sin cuas* (*cuis* in Salv) or *sin meco* (= *medio*) or *sin pisto, estar uno velando* (where *velar* 'to keep vigil' means *pegotear* 'to sponge') or *velando donde tortean.*

Elsewhere one hears: *tomar la jaba* (Cuba) 'to be reduced to begging,' *jaba* (of Carib origin) meaning a kind of basket or bag carried by beggars to hold the alms given them; *estar uno matando tigres a sombrerazos* (SD); *estar uno pasando el Niágara en un palo de fósforo* (SD); *no verle la cara a Bolívar* (Ven), referring to the coin so called.

Some metaphors contain the names of plants: *acabársele a uno el tabaco* (Arg, Chile) 'to run out of tobacco'; *estar uno más limpio* or *más pelado que una pepa de guaba* (Ec) 'to be cleaner than a guava seed', as in "Si han venido *más pelados que una pepa de guaba"* (A. Ortiz, p. 24); *ser palo delgado* (Chile: Rabanales, p. 193), by contrast with *palo grueso* 'wealthy' and *peral cargado* 'loaded pear tree'; *guayar yuca* 'to grate yuca' or *pasar yuca* (Ant), in which the *yuca,* a starchy root and basic food of peasants, symbolizes poverty.

Sometimes a gesture may be a euphemism for *pobre* or *pobreza:* that of counting money (see figs. 18, 19, 20) if accompanied with a negative sign (shaking the head, or moving the extended index finger of the up-held right forearm from side to side); tapping one's empty pockets or turning one's pockets inside out; drawing the index finger across the throat and snapping the relaxed index and middle fingers (Ven); particularly in Spain, placing right index and middle fingers on either side of one's nose and (this is optional) drawing the fingers downward (see fig. 17) —women sometimes turn the palm outward in making this gesture, "por coquetería" it is said. This last gesture corresponds to the standard expression *estar a dos velas* 'to be with two candles,' explained by Sbarbi (*Diccionario de refranes*) as follows: after church services all lights are extinguished except two candles which are left burning before the sanctuary, and since these shed but little light they may be compared to the spirit of an impecunious individual. Yet *estoy a dos velas* may mean 'I have two sails' set for opposite directions, hence the ship cannot move.

Among other gestures euphemistically indicating impecuniosity are the following: placing the slightly curved index finger on the nose (Guat); closing both eyes and holding them closed while saying *estoy así* or *ando ciego* or *estoy seco* or *ando pato* (Arg); the open hand, palm down, strikes sideways against the belt or waist (Arg, where the same gesture means 'food, eating').

WEALTH

Acquiring wealth, especially if it is done suddenly, is likewise an indelicate matter, and euphemistic expressions must be found to veil harsh words like *enriquecerse* 'to get rich.' Popular euphemisms are *aplatarse* (Cuba) from *plata* 'money'; *armarse* (CA, Mex); *chapearse* (Chile) 'to cover oneself with *chapas*' = 'metal (gold?) sheets' or from *chapa,* an old coin, as in "Fulano va a *chapearse* con el negocio del arroz; X está ahora bien *chapeado* y anda buscando auto" (Yrarrázaval, p. 157); *echar guata* (Chile) 'to get fat'; *estar de a bojote* (SD); *forrarse* (Peru, Mex, Ant), 'to line oneself, to cover oneself' (cf. fam. std. *tener uno bien cubierto el riñón* and English 'to feather one's nest'); *organizarse* (Ven) 'to get organized'; *pararse,* in many regions, an extension of its American meaning of 'to stand up, get on one's feet,' as in "Fulano *se paró* con el alza del azúcar" (Cuba: C. Suárez), "Ya *se paró* Abel con las ganancias que obtiene en cada negocio que hace" (Guat: Sandoval), "Miguel estaba en quiebra, pero recientemente hizo un buen negocio y logró *pararse*" (Col: Acuña); *pasar uno la barca* (SD); *ponerse uno pupón* (Arg), from *pupo* 'navel'; *rayarse* (Col); *taparse* (Col) 'to cover oneself (with money),' deriv. *tapado* equivalent to *rico* or *platudo; taquiarse* (*ibid.*), from *taquiar* 'to fill, stuff, wad (a gun),' in turn from *taco* 'plug, stopper, wad' (deriv. *taquiado* 'rico'), as in "El doctor López está *taquiado* de plata" (Acuña).

Among other popular adjectives and nouns are *cacaúdo* (El Cibao, SD: *BDH*, V, 192) from *cacao; chaludo* (RP, Bol) from *chala* 'corn husk,' as in "Ando *chaludo*, me pagaron las vacas que vendí" (Vidal, p. 312); *gente atesorada* (CR); *gente de bolengo* (CR), from *abolengo* 'lineage'; *estar uno de matar* and *estar uno gordo* (SD), as in "él está *gordo* y puede servirte" (Patín); *maizudo* (Guat), from *maíz* 'corn,' as in "La viuda de Taboada quedó bastante *maizuda*" (Sandoval); the proper name *Riquelme* is sometimes heard as a euphemism for bald *rico*.

MONEY

From time immemorial the representative Spaniard has been reputed to be indifferent to matters of lucre and disinclined to mention money or even to use the words *pagar, vender,* and the like, especially in polite conversation. Everywhere one hears the standard euphemisms *liquidar* and *abonar* for *pagar* 'to pay, settle an account,' and phrases like *¿Cuáles son las condiciones?* meaning 'what salary is paid?'

In the Antilles *bajar* 'to lower, come down' is slang for *pagar,* as in "Me debía cinco pesos y ayer *bajó*"; "Cada uno, para el baile, tiene que dar dos pesos, y si mañana no *bajan,* se pospondrá" (Patín). Colombian peasants often use *nombrar* for *ofrecer,* as in "Su mercesito ('your grace') me había *nombrado* unos centavitos" (Tobón). In Peru and Puerto Rico *cotizar* 'to quote prices' sometimes replaces *vender,* as in "En este sitio no se *cotiza* mucho" (Malaret). In Ecuador, Peru, and probably elsewhere, *cambiar* 'to change, exchange' may euphemistically replace *vender* when reference is made to religious items, as in "Cintas benditas *se cambian* ('*se venden*') a dos reales" (Malaret). In Mexico, *rayar* means 'to pay a man his wages' and 'to receive wages,' as in "los trabajadores fueron *rayados*" and "¿cuánto *rayas* esta semana?" (deriv. *raya* 'pay' and *rayador* 'payer'). This meaning derives from *rayar* 'to strike out' referring to the list of workers' names which are crossed off as the workers are paid.

Sometimes any noun beginning with *pa* recalls *pagar* in a more pleasant way: *pagano* 'heathen, pagan,' general (as in Spain) for *el que paga,* as in "Iremos al baño ya que tú eres el *pagano*" (Mex: Ángulo, p. 61);

paciente (Guat), as in "Jugamos cuatro tandas de tragos y yo resulté ser el *paciente*" (Sandoval); in most of America, *paganini,* from the name of the famous Italian violinist, and in Mexico the name *Pablo* may mean the person who 'foots the bill.' The word *cuenta* 'bill' itself is often avoided: in Argentinian and Chilean restaurants and coffeehouses, a diner asks for his *adición* (from French *addition* 'bill'). Examples: "Después el director pidió las *adiciones,* cada uno pagó su parte" (Eduardo Mallea, *La ciudad junto al río inmóvil,* Buenos Aires, 1938, p. 67); "después de abonar cada cual su respectiva *adición,* los circunstantes se dispersaron" (*Antología de cuentistas ríoplatenses,* 1939, p. 302).

Perhaps the word most often substituted for *dinero* 'money' in Spanish America is *plata* 'silver,' which, though also standard in Spain, is not nearly so widespread there, derivative *platudo* being equivalent to standard *adinerado* 'rich, wealthy.' In Central America, particularly in Guatemala and Honduras, one hears *pisto,* as in "A ti te gusta mucho tener *pisto*" (Sandoval). The word has many derivatives: diminutive *pistillo,* as in "Ya tengo algún *pistillo,* ganado últimamente en mis negocios" (*ibid.*) and "le presto un *pistillo* de mis ahorritos" (Torres Arjona, p. 13); *pistero* 'fond of money' and 'financial' ("cuestión *pistera*"); *pistudo = platudo;* nouns *pistal* and *pistarrajal* for *dineral* 'a lot of money,' as in "Adalberto no venderá nunca su finca, porque pide por ella un *pistarrajal*" (Sandoval). Standard *pisto* 'expressed fowl juice' derives from *pistar* 'to crush, pestle'; the meaning 'money' shows associative interference with popular *machacante* 'coin, dollar' from *machacar* 'to pound, crush.'

Popular speech abounds with ironic euphemisms for *dinero,* usually words denoting things of little or no value:

agua, agüita, agüilla 'water' (Peru, Ec), as in "mi jefe llamaba *agua* al dinero; seguramente por la facilidad con que se lo gastaba" (Ec: J. de la Cuadra, *Guásinton,* 1938, p. 30) and "(telegram) Si continúa así cortaremos (el) *agua* (a) Rosaura" (Peru: Corrales, p. 72); *alpiste* 'canary seed' (Pan; cf. 'chicken feed'); *barro* 'mud' and *bicoca* 'trifle' (Tex).

cacao 'cocoa bean' (Peru, Ant), originally used as a coin (cf. *tener un palito de cacao* 'to have available money,' Nic); *carbón* 'charcoal' (SD); *cascajo* 'gravel' (Ant); *clavos* 'nails' (Tex); *concha* 'shell' (Ven), as in "tiene sus *conchas*" (Rosenblat, p. 89).

chala (from Quechua) 'corn husk' (RP, Bol); *chauchas* (from Quechua) 'small early potatoes' (Chile, Bol, Peru), and *chaucha* is also applied to a 20-centavo coin; *chilpes* (from Quechua) 'dry corn husks' (Arequipa, Peru); *chipes,* from *chipe* 'imaginary coin of little value' (Chile), from English *chips,* especially in card playing, as in "Abro con dos *chipes,* dijo uno ... Hasta peso" (Orrega, ap. Medina); *ficha* 'chip' (Tex).

fierros (pl. of *fierro* 'iron') 'centavo coin' (Mex) and *ferros* (slang, Arg).

gasolina (cant, Peru); *guano* 'cotton-like matter' derived from the berry of the *guano,* a kind of palm tree (Ant).

harina 'flour' (Ant), as in "no se puede vivir sin *harina"* (SD: Patín), "Fulano es hombre de *harina"* (Cuba: C. Suárez), *harina bruta* (Cuba) 'hard cash' as in "Pago con *harina bruta,* y no con giros" (*ibid.*).

lana 'wool' (Mex), deriv. *lanudo* 'wealthy'; *luz* 'light' (cant, Peru).

manganá (from Guaraní) 'bee' (RP); *manguá* (Cuba); *maní* 'peanuts' (Ant); *murmunta* (Arequipa, Peru) 'raisin-like fruit of a water plant'; *música* (cant, Peru).

pasta asciutta, Italian for 'dry paste': spaghetti, etc. (Arg); *pucha* (from Quechua *puchu* 'left over') 'a small amount' and 'cigarette butt' (Col), deriv. *puchado* for *adinerado* or *platudo* 'wealthy.'

sebo (cant, Mex) 'tallow, fat' (cf. fam. std. *untar la mano* 'to grease the palm, bribe' and *unto de Méjico* or *de rana* 'money' in reference to bribing—English 'oil of palms').

tecolines, from Nahuatl *tecolli* 'charcoal' (Mex), as in "Fulano tiene hartos *tecolines"* (Velasco); *viruta* 'wood shavings' (Cuba).

Other local words for *dinero* are of various origins: *burata* (Ven); *bollos* (Nic, where *bollo* is popular for *centavo*) as in "el rico tiene *bollos* y puede gastar muchos *bollos"* (Valle); *colque* or *colquis* (Arequipa, Peru); *chavos* (PR, from *ochavo* ('eighth'), the name of an old Spanish coin; *cheles* (PR, SD), probably from *chelín* 'shilling' and also an old half-cent coin (PR), as in "Fulano es hombre de *cheles"* (Malaret, 2d ed.); *chiripío* (Hond); *chiva* 'goat' (Ven, Tex); *física* (Ec); *guitarra* (cant, Arg), from popular peninsular *guita* 'string' and 'money'; *gurbia* (CR), from *gubia* 'a kind of chisel' (?); *gurda* (Bol; cant, Arg: Gobello, p. 102) from French *gourde* (as is *gordo,* the name of a coin, SD); *jando* (Tex); *jola* (parts of Mex) and *joles* (CA); *mejengue* (PR, SD); *mene-*

guina (cant, Arg); *mergo, mergolla,* and *mergollina* (Pan), possibly connected with *mercar* 'to buy' (Aguilera); *moni* (Arg, Col, CA, Ant) from English *money,* also *monis* (cf. fam. std. *monís* and *monises); níqueles* (pl. of *níquel*) from English *nickel,* as in "Don Juan tiene sus *níqueles"* (Mex: Santamaría); *pipiolas* (CR), influenced by Old Spanish *pipión* or *pepión,* a coin of small value (?) and by Aztec *pipiolín* 'wild black bee' (?); *realero* (Ven) 'money, wealth,' from *real,* a coin equal to 12½ *centavos; sangre* 'blood' and Italian *vento* 'wind' (Arg: "Tiene *vento* en el banco y, ¡no juega ni un peso!" Mendoza, p. 24), which are comparable to continental slang *sangre, resuello,* etc. (R. Salillas, *El delincuente español,* p. 183); *tlacos* (Mex), from Aztec *tlaco* 'copper coin' (formerly), cf. *estar sin (un) tlaco* 'to be broke.'

To indicate 'small money' or 'change,' standard (*dinero*) *suelto* 'loose change,' *calderilla* 'coppers,' and *menudo* or *sencillo* 'small change' are supplemented in America with others, such as popular *feria* (Mex), deriv. *feriar* 'to make small change' as in *"Fériame* este tostón en centavos" and *"feriar* un peso en tostones" (Santamaría); *morralla* (Mex), as in "Desanuda la faja y saca billetes, pesos, *morralla"* (Anda, p. 129); *lupia* (Col) 'a small amount of money,' as in "Felizmente ya no le debo al sastre sino una *lupia"* (Acuña); *sueltos* (Ec: Toscano, p. 189). In Peru, *sencillero* may mean "el que saca la *sencilla"* (std. *sacar la sisa*) 'the one who filches,' so that *sencillero* is here equivalent to *sisador* (*BAAL,* X, 189).

To indicate 'change'—that is, the balance returned when payment is made with a coin or note exceeding the sum due—in most of Spanish America *vuelto* (*vueltas,* Col; popular *feria,* Mex) is used rather than standard *vuelta;* hence standard "Quédese usted con *la vuelta"* 'keep the change' is rendered "Quédese con *el vuelto."*

Among the many words, mostly euphemisms, applying to an additional bit of merchandise (sometimes referring to money) given gratis to a customer, or 'thrown in for good measure' by a vendor or dealer, peninsular terms are *adehala, alboroque* 'top or treat after a bargain,' *botijuela* 'small earthen jar,' *chorrada* 'jet added to the measure of liquids,' *de oque* or *de momio* 'gratis, free,' *de propina* 'as a tip,' *guantes* 'gloves, glove money, extra pay, fee, tip,' *momio* 'lean, meagre' and 'extra allowance,' colloquial *pal* (= *para el*) *gato* 'for the cat,' *pasera* (Córdoba, Spain), *refacción,* etc.

Some of the American-Spanish words are *ajuste* (Salv) 'adjustment, bargain'; *alipego* (CR), probably from Aztec *piguis* or *pihuiz* 'increase' and verb *pihuilia,* with phonetic interference of *pegar* 'to stick, adhere'; *contra* (Salv, Cuba), as in "—¿De qué quiere usted la *contra?* —De agujas" (C. Suárez); *chascada* (Hond); *feria* (CA), as in *"una feria* de higado, mondongo, caramelos," etc. (see *AmSS,* p. 305); *ipegüe* (CA), from Aztec *piguis* or *pihuiz* (as in "¿Qué vas a dar de *ipegüe?"*), variants *ipégüel* or *ipéhuel, hipégüel* or *hipéhuel, hipéhuil* (Salv), *lipegüe* (Hond, Nic) with the definite article prefixed; *llapa* or *yapa* (RP, Chile, Bol, Peru, Ec, CA) and *ñapa* (Col, Ven, CA, Veracruz, E Cuba), from Quechua *yapa,* as in "los niños ... piden al hombre *yapa* de caramelos" (for other examples see *AmSS,* p. 305); *pezuña* (Ec, Pan) 'hoof,' perhaps because butchers were wont to 'throw in' that part of the animal; *pilón* (Mex) 'counterpoise of a spring balance' used in weighing merchandise; *sope* (Chihuahua, Mex: Duarte); *vendaje* (Bol, Peru, Ec, Col, Ven, CR), an extension of the standard meaning 'commission,' as in "Usted ignora el *vendaje,* la ñapa, o el colmo de este desastre" (ap. Alvarado) in a figurative sense.

Often the word *dinero* (or *plata*) is euphemistically replaced by some gesture. Standard and general is that of rubbing the ball of the thumb against the ball of the index finger, as if feeling a texture or testing the quality of powder (see fig. 18). Often the words *de acá* accompany the gesture. In fact, the phrase *de acá* sometimes serves to indicate the money gesture, as in "ando dende tiempo bastante apurao en 'esto' ¿me compriende? —y le hizo *de acá* con los dedos" (Arg: Lynch, p. 281). This gesture probably represents the act of counting money. Examples: "—¿Y de acá? ... *Haciendo resbalar el pulgar sobre el índice"* (E. Zamacois, *Nochebuena,* Act II); "—¿Hay palomar?— preguntó Pardo. —No, señor ... *El criado estregó el pulgar contra el índice,* como indicando que no sobraba dinero para meterse en aventuras" (Pardo Bazán, *La Madre Naturaleza,* chap. xxxii); "—¿Y cómo andará la Cira de ... acá? *En señal de dinero.* —La chica creo que gana bastante" (Benavente, *Pepa Doncel,* Act I, sc. v); "—¡Pues, cualquiera le aguanta, si no suelta de aquí. *Haciendo ademán de contar dinero"* (Martínez Sierra, *Madame Pepita,* Act I).

In Spanish America this money gesture has several variants. Counting money, particularly bills, may be indicated thus: the extended finger tips of the right hand (sometimes only of the index) brush up into the open left palm (see fig. 19). This gesture was made by a Peruvian as he said, "la gente poderosa viene a la playa." It may mean *pagar* 'to pay' and may indicate people who can pay. It may mean also *págame* 'pay me.' The same meanings are to be attached to another variant made with one hand only: the fist is closed very loosely and the four finger tips then brush the palm inward several times. In the Mexican zone, particularly, and because of the abundance of silver pesos, the following gesture indicates *dinero:* the forearm is extended, palm of hand up, thumb and index form almost a complete circle, the remaining three fingers clenched upon the palm—the circle formed with thumb and index finger probably representing a peso coin, or possibly a roll of bills (see fig. 20). Example: "está para regresar de París, con su título de médico ... la fama que le han dado ... y sobre todo con esto ... Y diciendo así *figuraba con los dedos un circulito tamaño una moneda de oro"* (Nic: P. J. Chamorro, *Entre dos filos,* 1927, p. 56).

Spanish-American coins have a large variety of names. Often a coin is named from the image engraved on it. The monetary unit of Venezuela, for instance, the *bolívar,* was named after Simón Bolívar "the Liberator," born in Caracas in 1783; it is popularly known also as *simón, bolo,* and *bolante* (Grases, p. 113). In Bolivia it is the *boliviano,* as in "un *boliviano* mensual costaba la suscripción" (ap. Malaret, *Bol. fil.*). The monetary unit of Ecuador is the *sucre* ("Otra vez había reunido trescientos *sucres* de multas," ap. Malaret, *Bol. fil.*), named after one of Bolívar's officers, Antonio José de Sucre who, Venezuelan by birth, defeated the Spaniards at Pichincha, Ecuador, in 1822 and at Ayacucho, Peru, in 1824. The sucres coined during the presidency of Ayora are referred to as *ayoras* ("No te olvidaras de los tres *ayoras,"* Cuadra, p. 145), and coins of fifty centavos of the same period were called *lauras* or *lauritas,* after Ayora's wife. When sucres, no longer of silver, were introduced by a later president, Federico Páez, they were colloquially dubbed *federicos* or *fedes* (Toscano, p. 189). A sucre is often referred to as *patacón,* as in "Por imprudente, tuve que desembolsar ochenta *patacones"* (Cornejo). The monetary unit of El Salvador and Costa Rica is the *colón,* named after Cristóbal Colón (the coin is sometimes referred to as *patacón*); that of Honduras is the *lempira,* the name of an Indian chieftain who fought valiantly against the Spanish conquerors; that of Panama is the *balboa,* named after Vasco Núñez de Balboa, the Spanish conquistador who in

1513 crossed the Isthmus of Panama and discovered the Pacific Ocean; that of Nicaragua is the *córdoba,* after Francisco Fernández de Córdoba, the Spanish conquistador who took possession of Nicaragua in 1524. In Guatemala the monetary unit is the *quetzal* (pop. *queque*), the name of the brilliantly colored and long-tailed bird which has been adopted as the national symbol of Guatemala, the Indians having regarded it with veneration, reserving its feathers for native tribal chiefs. The monetary unit is popularly known as *chema* from *Chema* Orellana, the nickname of former President José María Orellana, whose bust was engraved on the bank notes issued by the Central Bank founded by him in 1924. The monetary unit of Peru is called *sol* because the Incans were sun worshipers.

Among the small coins, the one-centavo pieces are called *chico* and *cobre* (Peru); *rufo* (Cuba) but more generally *quilo* or *kilo; quilo* or *quicho* (Mex); *bollo* (Nic); *cobre, charo, chipe, chiva, churupo, chuso, níquel, nica, puya* (Ven: Grases, p. 113); *chivo* (Col); *chimbo* (Col) is a centavo coin ("Hoy amanecí sin un *chimbo* en el bolsillo," Acuña) and also a 'worn-out' or 'counterfeit' coin (Col, Ven), as in "me metieron una peseta *chimba,"* and *cheque chimbo* 'rubber check.'

Coins of 5 centavos, besides general *un cinco,* may be called *cincón* (Salv), *grillo* (Ec), *chirolita* (Arg, Bol), *ficha* (Arg, CR), *medio* (*real*) (Ec, Peru), *vellón* (Pan, PR), etc. Coins of 10 centavos, besides general *un diez,* may be called *real* (Peru); *real, ruso,* and *ruperto* (Cuba); *cucaracha* (Ec); *diezón* (Salv) and *diego* (Mex), distortions of *diez,* as in "Pero si quiere usted, compraré una caja. —¡Vaya si quiero! ¡A ver, afloje un *diego!"* (Ángulo, p. 19).

In Venezuela, a coin of 12½ centimos is the *locha* (*la ochava* > *lochava* > *locha* > *la locha*), as in "le encendí una vela de a *locha"* (Gallegos, p. 82); rarely *chola* by metathesis; and *viuda* 'widow,' that is, 'incomplete, alone,' since the coin is inconvenient to use alone and is generally used with another to complete 25 centimos (Grases, p. 112, n. 2).

Coins of 20 centavos, besides general *peseta* and (*un*) *veinte,* may be called *chaucha* (Chile, Bol) from Quechua 'small early potato' (deriv. *chauchera* 'coin purse' and *chaucheo* 'unimportant business'), as in "—Tome una *chaucha* pa la *góndola* ['bus']" (Chile: Pepe Rojas, *El gallo de la pasión,* p. 14); *chirola* (Arg, Bol); besides standard *peseta* and *beata,* Cuban terms are *perjura* 'perjurer, false,' *guaña, tapa, chapa, caña, bomba,* etc. (C. Suárez) and *cáscara* (Rodríguez); *tomín* (Bol, Col).

A coin of 50 centavos is the *tostón,* especially in Mexico. A former Peruvian 4-real coin was called *cuatro corbatones* from the image of Bolívar wearing a large *corbata* 'cravat.' A 50 centimo coin in Venezuela is a *clavo.*

Coins of one peso (former and present) are:

arzobispo 'archbishop,' *cachete* and *cachetón* 'plump-cheeked' (Ven: Grases, p. 114, n. 6), perhaps referring to engravings on the coin (peso = 5 bolivares).

bamba (Ven, CA), as in *"entierros* ['buried treasures'] de sólo *bambas";* *bolo* (Mex, Ant), perhaps from *bolo* 'tailless,' slipping away easily; jocose *bululú,* pl. *bululuses* (SD).

canalete 'small paddle' and *clavo* 'nail' (N Col), as in "cuesta tres *canaletes,"* "tal cosa vale cinco *clavos"* (Revollo); *coco* 'coconut' (Ant).

chicharrón (Cuba) 'cracknel.'

disco (Ant) 'disk'; *durazno* (Ven, as in Andalusia) 'peach,' based on *duro* 'dollar'; *estrella* (Ant) 'star.'

fuerte (Col, Ven), from *peso fuerte,* as in "tengo unos cuatro *fuertes* entre estos centavos" (Gallegos, p. 81).

grullo (Arg, Ven, Mex, Ant) 'gray horse'; *guayo* 'musical instrument' and *guayacán* 'local tree' (Ant).

loco (Mex); *loco* (Chile), the local name of a mollusk about the size of a *peso,* as in "dan más de cincuenta *locos* en cualquier parte" (Del Campo, p. 53).

machacante (Ant, as in Spain), from *machacar* 'to pound,' probably because of its weight, and *matacán* (SD), as in "gasté veinte *matacanes"* (Patín); *machete* (SD), as in "mi sombrero me costó *machete* y medio" (Patín); *mango* (Arg, Chile); *maraca* (Cuba) 'musical instrument'; *ojo de buey* (Cuba).

peluco (cant, Mex; *micho peluco* 'half a peso'), leaning on Spanish cant *peluca* 'peseta' (older Spanish *pelucona* 'large wig' = 'gold doubloon,' because of the image of a wigged king); *pesar* (N Col) 'sorrow,' based on *peso; rueda* (Ant) 'wheel.'

tabla (N Col), perhaps from its older meaning 'tablet of chocolate'; *tolete* (Ant) 'club'; *tote* (Col), as in "me dió cinco *totes"* (Tobón);

tranca (PR, SD) 'club,' as in "este sombrero me costó *tranca* y media" (Patín); *trompudo* (parts of Mex) 'blobber-lipped,' from some engraving on the coin (?), as in "Estos *trompudos* me vienen al pelo para pagar el parto de mi vieja" (Ángulo, p. 126); *tulipán* (Ant) 'tulip.'

Peruvian coins of one sol are often referred to as *barra* or *barreta* (since 'bars' of silver used to serve as money), *capulí, chórchola, mamacona, morlaco, ojo de buey, pepa, rúcano, solete, solifacio, tronco,* etc. Examples: "Cada cuchi, del peso medio de cincuenta kilos, nos servía para la confección de otros tantos de chicharrón, que vendidos al precio de dos *barras* el kilo, daba un total de cien *pepas.* El cuchi lo comprábamos de veinte a treinta *solifacios;* ganancia líquida, deducidos los gastos de elaboración como sesenta y más *soletes*" (Corrales, p. 238); "por menos de cien *capulís* no remachaba compromiso ... —Cien *mamaconas* es mucho cacao, hermano" (*ibid.,* p. 108); "pagando no cheques circulares sino *chórcholas* oro" (*ibid.,* p. 76); "iban a costar la mar de *rúcanos* al país" (*ibid.,* p. 110).

Formerly a 20-peso Mexican gold coin was known as *águila* 'eagle,' the 10-peso coin being a *media águila* 'half an eagle.'

A bank note is often referred to with a word designating or recalling its particular color. Such names may be considered permutations deriving from a concomitant circumstance, or from a quality applied to the object possessing it. Thus, *lechuga* 'lettuce' frequently denotes a green bank note, like the 20-bolivar bill in Venezuela, called also *lechugón* and *verdín;* the 50-bolivar note is *mandarina* 'tangerine' because of its orange color; the 100-bolivar note is *marrón* 'chestnut' or *chocolate,* as in "Le presté ('I borrowed') un *marrón* a Fulano, ¡y me lo dió!" (Rosenblat, p. 338); the 500-bolivar note is *azulejo* 'tile' because of its bluish tint (Grases, p. 114, n. 6). A green one-quetzal note (Guat) is a *perico* 'parrot'; a purple 100-peso note in Bolivia is a *billete morado.*

In Peru the 10-sol (= one libra) note is called *pálida* 'pale' ("ha visto en el pavimento una *pálida* desgaritada del bolsillo de su dueño," Corrales, p. 46), and also *camarón* 'shrimp' (*camarón* was formerly current in Guatemala for the 100-peso note); the bluish curlicued 50-sol (= 5 libras) note is a *pavo real* 'peacock,' as in "¿de dónde me vienen los *pavos reales,* si no estudio?"; the 100-sol (= 10 libras) note is a *colorada* 'red.'

In Colombia the peso note may be a *mango,* the name of a tropical fruit of reddish-yellowish hue; a yellow-and-black bank note circulating at the end of the nineteenth century was called the *toche* (Acuña), from the name of a yellow-breasted and black-winged songbird.

In Argentina, *canario* 'canary' is often applied to the yellow 100-peso note; *durazno* 'peach' to the peso note, phonetically associated with *duro* (= peso).

The older Chilean 5-peso note was a *congrio* 'sea eel' having a red-spotted abdomen, or *congrio colorado* ("estiró cuatro *congrios coloraos* diacinco," Del Campo, p. 30), often shortened to *colorado* ("le habís limpiao *los coloraos*," *ibid.*, p. 31); it was also called *gringo* because its reddish hue recalled that of the blond and rubicund *gringo* 'Englishman,' (and by extension 'any foreigner').

Other names for the peso bank notes are *machacante* (Col; elsewhere, as in Spain, this word is applied to the coin), as in "Necesito que alguien me preste siquiera cinco *machacantes*" (Acuña); *rúcano* (Peru, Col), as in "Cien *rúcanos* pagué por este sofá" (Acuña); *clavo* (Atlantic coast, Col) 'nail,' and *clavao* (SD). In Argentine cant *cocinero* means a 5-peso note: *cinco* 'five' by *vesrre* (= *revés*) 'in reverse' gives *cocin,* and suffix *-ero* renders the term familiar by the process of popular etymology (Gobello, p. 84); *fragata* means a 1,000-peso note, so called from the image of a 'frigate' engraved upon it (*ibid.,* p. 82).

DEBTS

The word *deuda* 'debt' is one of the harsh terms within the money complex. In some regions (Chile, Peru, Mex) *droga* 'drug,' as an extension of the figurative standard meanings 'embuste, trampa' and 'cosa que desagrada o molesta,' has been particularized to mean *deuda.* Among its derivatives are *endrogarse* 'to get into debt,' *endrogado* 'in debt,' and *droguero* 'fond of contracting debts,' with additional expressions like *hacer droga* and *echarse uno drogas* 'to get into debt.' Examples: "—Lo que podemos hacer por usted es tomarle los bienes por *la droga*" (Mex: Azuela, *Los caciques,* III, 3); "tener más *drogas* que un dueño de droguería"; "En el pueblo toda la gente se quedó *endrogándose*" (Mex: J. T. Núñez Guzmán, *Infancia campesina,* Mexico, 1937, p. 22); "los dos expendios liquidaban con pérdida y estaban *endrogados*" (Mex: Useta, *Cuentos mexicanos,* ap.

Malaret, *Copla*); "Se encontraron en quiebra y *endrogados* en dos mil duretes" (Peru: Ricardo Palma, *Tradiciones peruanas,* VII serie, *De menos hizo Dios a Cañete,* ap. Román).

Elsewhere, *endeudado* '(to be) in debt' may be *encalillado* (Chile) in which *calilla* (std. 'suppository' > in America 'bore, nuisance') has in Chile acquired the meaning of standard *calvario* in its figurative sense of 'score of indebtedness' represented by lines, bars, and crosses used in jotting down amounts of indebtedness and reminiscent of the crucifixion of Christ on Calvary showing three crosses. Examples: "Pagué las *calillas* que tenía" (Castro, p. 400), "—*Te* volvís a *encalillar* hasta este otro mes" (*ibid.*). In Panama and Colombia, *engrillarse* may euphemize *endeudarse* or *adeudarse* through its standard meaning 'to fetter' and its meaning *embaucar* (Col, PR) 'to deceive, trick, victimize' (cf. *droga* 'drug' > 'deceit, trick' > 'debt'); that is, *engrillar* may be derived from *grillos* 'fetters' and *grilla* 'female cricket' > (familar) 'fake, humbug' (perhaps because the female cricket does not chirp) > 'nuisance, trouble' (Ec, Peru, Col). The original meaning of Latin *grillus* was 'cricket,' from which was developed the meaning 'chains, fetters,' the metallic sound of the fetters being compared to that of the chirping of crickets (produced by rubbing a filelike ridge of one wing over a scraping surface of the other). Example: "Pidiendo prestado más de lo que podía pagar *se engrilló*" (Pan: Aguilera, p. 283).

In some regions (Col, Ec, Peru) a popular word for *deuda* is *culebra* 'snake,' deriv. *enculebrarse* (= *endeudarse*) 'to get into debt,' *enculebrado* (= *endeudado*), and *desenculebrarse* (= *salir de deudas*) 'to get out of debt.' Examples: "Una *culebra* aquí, una *culebra* allá: malos días te esperan" (Ec: Cornejo); "Estoy muy *enculebrado*" (Col: Tobón).

Other local formations are *encangrenarse* for *gangrenarse* 'to gangrene' (Valle del Cauca, Col); *engolillarse* (Cuba) from *golilla* 'collar' > '(gambling) debt'; *enquimbarse* (Col), from *quimba* 'sandal' > 'debt'; *jaranear* (CA) from familiar standard *jarana* and *arana* 'trick, fraud' (cf. fam. std. *trampa* 'trick' > 'debt'), and noun *jarana,* as in "Isidro está lleno de *jaranas*" (Guat: Sandoval; for doubtful origin of *harana* or *arana,* see Corominas), deriv. *jaranero* and *jaranerazo* ("No hay que dar dinero prestado a Benito, porque es *jaranerazo,*" Guat: Sandoval); *cacalota* (Hond); *cuca* (Guat), from *cucaracha* (?); *chillo* (Salv); *chorritos* (SD), as in "recibí diez pesos, pagué varios *chorritos* y me sobraron noventa centavos" (Patín); *arruga* 'wrinkle' > 'trick, fraud' > 'debt' (Peru: Benvenutto, p. 73); *matadura* 'sore' > 'debt' (Ec, PR).

Standard *quebrar* 'to become bankrupt' is euphemized as *irse uno para Quebradillas* (PR), the place name suggesting the word to be avoided; *estar en falencia* (Arg, Chile, Peru, Hond), from *fallar* 'to fail' (std. *falencia* 'misstatement, mistake'), as in "Ese comerciante *está en falencia*" (Peru: Ugarte). 'To borrow money' (fam. std. *dar un sablazo* 'to deal a sabre stroke,' that is 'to strike for a loan') may be *hacer un pechazo* 'push' (Arg), *hacer un pique* 'poke, prod' (Ec), *tirar un carro* (Ven), etc.

Pawning (std. *empeñar*) one's valuables is a delicate matter. Consequently, standard *casa de empeños* or *de préstamos* (std. euphemisms are *montepío* and *monte de piedad,* like French *mont de pitié*) is euphemized by *empeño* and *empeñito* (Mex: Speratti, p. 163), *empeñero* 'pawnbroker'; *peña* (Col, SD) 'rock'; vague *agencia* 'agency' or *casa de agencia* (Chile), as in "me debe unos veinte riales que lempresté (— le presté) una tarde, pa que sacara un par de pantalones que tenía empeñaos en la *ajencia* del Loro" (Del Campo, p. 95), deriv. *agenciero* 'pawnbroker' (std. *prestamista*), but the more cultured say *casa de prendas* (*prenda* 'pledge, pawn'); *agencia de negocios* and popular *contaduría* (Ec), *contador* 'pawnbroker.'

Standard *empeñar* finds palliatives in *meter una cosa bajo la peña* (SD), as in *"metí* mi reloj *bajo la peña"* (Patín); *llevar una cosa a estudiar* or *a estudiar* (or *aprender*) *inglés,* whence *está aprendiendo inglés* 'it is pawned' (Chile, Peru, Ec), as in "Yo no sé lo que vamos a hacer, pues hasta los anillos *están aprendiendo inglés"* (Chile: Edwards Bello, *El roto,* 1932, p. 95), "eché mano al bolsillo de atrás para sacar el revuélcate ('revolver'), sin acordarme de que este utensilio doméstico *estaba aprendiendo inglés"* (Peru: Corrales, p. 46); *está sudando* 'is perspiring,' as in "Tengo mi abrigo *sudando"* (Mex: Velasco), "Mi reloj *está sudando* desde hace varios meses" (Guat: Sandoval); *llevar una cosa a beber agua* (PR); *tener algo a la sombra* (N Chile). Peninsular Spanish is likewise rich in such expressions: "(mi abrigo) *está en casa de tío,"* in which *tío* means 'pawnbroker' (Beinhauer, p. 222 n.); *está en Peñaranda,* the name of a place in the province of Salamanca, recalling *empeñar; está en Peñíscola,* the name of a place in the province of Castellón de la Plana (see Wagner, p. 5).

V OFFENSES AND CONSEQUENCES

STEALING

Harsh *robar* (or *hurtar*) 'to steal' is usually avoided. Among popular peninsular euphemisms are *coger* 'to take,' *pillar* 'to seize, snatch,' *limpiar* 'to clean,' *apañar* 'to grasp,' *aliviar* 'to lighten,' *afanar* 'to toil, hustle,' *cachear* 'to search a person for hidden weapons,' *trabajar* 'to work,' *raspar* 'to scrape, scratch,' not to mention scores of terms common in thieves' slang to designate different methods of stealing (see J. Hidalgo, L. Besses, P. Serrano García), and nouns like literary *cleptómano* 'kleptomaniac' and colloquial *amigo de lo ageno*. General, too, are such elegant euphemisms for *robo* 'theft' as *irregularidad* 'irregularity' or *distracción* 'distraction,' especially if the victim is the government, a bank, a club, or some other public institution, which recalls the Guatemalan expression *estar asegurado contra incendio* 'to be insured against fire' referring to a person enriched by theft from the government, as in "Muchas personas *están aseguradas contra encendio,* porque han metido la mano hasta el codo" (Sandoval).

American-Spanish euphemisms meaning *robar* are legion. The verb *avanzarse* (Mex, CA) 'to advance' originated in the revolutionary practice of seizing and pilfering by soldiers while they 'advanced,' and has become synonymous with *robar* since the Mexican revolution of 1913 (Santamaría); *avanzador* 'thief,' *avance* 'theft' are derived from it. This is a permutation: the naming of an act to designate a concomitant circumstance. Examples: "Ese muchacho *se avanzó* cinco pesos de mi cartera" (Suárez, p. 137);

"Nuestras tropas *avanzaron* al enemigo toda su artillería" (Sandoval); "hacer un *avance* = realizar un robo" (Valle).

Other verbs are:

aguatusar (CR), from *aguatuso,* a game in which one boy, while another is off his guard, slaps him on the wrist and snatches something from his hands, saying "¡aguatuso!" (Gagini).

bolsear (CA, Mex) 'to pick pockets' from *bolsa* 'purse, pocket,' deriv. *bolseo* 'act of picking pockets'; *bolsiquear* (Chile) 'to search a person's pockets' > 'to pick it.'

cachar (RP, CA), from std. *cachear* 'to search a person for hidden weapons' (cf. 'to frisk' > 'to rob'); *clavar* (Mex) 'to dive (into someone's pocket)'; *completarse* (Hond) 'to steal what is lacking in order to cover expenses.'

chorrear (RP, Col) 'to spout, drip' and *chorear* (Col) may mean 'to steal, appropriate,' deriv. *chorro* (RP) and *choro* (RP, Peru, Col, Andalusia), as in "Según parece, Juan se quiere *chorrear* el libro que le presté" (Col: Acuña), "Es *chorro,* pero también trabaja" (Arg: Mendoza, p. 60), possibly because *chorrera* 'mark along a candle where wax has run off' or 'candle snuff' is standardly called *ladrón* because it 'steals' the wax (ap. Tobón).

ganar 'to earn, win' (cant, Mex: Chabat); *gavillar* (Col, SD) 'to rob, hold up (in a gang),' as in "aquellos forajidos *gavillaban* a los viajeros" (SD: Patín).

ñanfliarse (jocose, SD), as in "el empleado se *ñanflió* unos cuartos" (Patín); *ñauñar* (Arequipa, Peru), from Quechua, as in *"Se ha ñauñado* mi cuaderno" (Ugarte); *ñapear* (Riohacha, Col; Tabasco, Mex), from Quechua *yapa* 'extra gift with a purchase,' hence 'something gratis' (see *AmSS,* p. 304).

patraquear (Chile) 'to rob, swindle,' thought by Lenz to derive from Mapuche, but perhaps associated with *atracar* 'to attack, hold up,' as in "entre *patraquiar* al prójimo y no *patraquiar,* lo mejor es desvalijarlo, polque así andará más liviano" (Del Campo, p. 19), deriv. *patraquero* 'pickpocket, swindler,' cf. variant (by metathesis) *patriacar,* as in "los otros le *patriacaron* los bolsillos" (Castro, p. 418).

rupar (cant, Mex), *rupante* 'thief,' *rupa* 'pickpocket' (a cross between *robar* and *rufo* 'thief' ? See Wagner, "Mex. Rot.") and the euphemism *Ruperto* for *rupa* and *rupante.*

The phrase *echarse una cosa a la izquierda* (Chile) 'to throw a thing to the left' means 'to steal it.' From time immemorial the left hand has been associated with theft, for it was usually held out of sight inside the gown or cloak: "devoted to rest, yet being at liberty and ready to handle . . . this purloining hand thinks itselfe the proprietary of another's goods . . . To put forth the left hand as it were by stealth, is their significant endeavour who have an intent unseene to purloine and convey away something" (J. Bulwer, *Chirologia,* London, 1644, p. 133).

Other euphemistic metaphors for *robar* are *enredarse en algo* (Col: Tobón) 'to get entangled in something'; *ensuciarse en* or *con alguna cosa* (*ibid.*) 'to besmirch oneself in or with something'; *dejar a uno para el baño* (cant, Mex) 'to leave one ready for the bath,' that is, 'stripped'; *guachapear* (Chile) 'to paddle, splatter in water' may mean 'to steal smaller articles, sometimes in fun,' as in "En el teatro me *guachapearon* las llaves" (Yrarrázaval, p. 187); *soltar* or *echar el gato a retozar* (Mex, CA, Col) 'to let the cat out to frolic' is surely connected with std. *ratear* 'to filch,' *ratero* 'pickpocket' and *ratón* 'mouse' or *rata* 'rat'; *tirar al indio* (Chile) 'to fire at the Indian,' possibly from the early custom of shooting at the Indians to kill them or to frighten them away in order to purloin their property (Román), this being a permutation expressing the action for its result; *tocar lo ajeno* (Col: Tobón) 'to touch other people's property'; *volantinear* (Peru) from *volantín* 'somersault,' as in "le *volantineó* un sol" (Corrales, p. 274); *volarse* 'to snitch' (Mex), as in "¿Quién *se voló* mi lápiz?" (Velasco).

Many expressions are picturesquely based on the motions of the hand and fingers in seizing a thing, like general *raspar* 'to scrape, scratch.' Among these are *uñar* (Ec, Chile, probably *uñear* originally), from *uña* '(finger) nail,' *uñatear* (Arg, Bol), *uñetear* (Chile), deriv. *uñalarga* (Peru; cf. fam. std. *largo de uñas*), *uñetas* (Col, CA), *uñilargo* or *uñón* (Peru) 'long-nailed'; *cazuñar* (CA), from *cazar* 'to hunt' and *uña; garrear* (Arg), from *garra* 'claw'; *manotear* (Arg, Ven), from *mano* 'hand'; *mangonear* (RP, Peru, Mex, PR); *mañanear* and *maromear* (Tex) 'to dance on the rope,' this group being phonetically associated with *mano* 'hand'; *poner la máquina* (Col: Cadavid); *recortar* (Chile) 'to cut away' as with scissors, in the sense of std. *sisar* 'to filch,' as in "nunca sentí ganas de *recortar*" (Malbrán, p. 10); *tirar* or *tirar los dedos* (Chile: Vicuña) 'to draw or pull the fingers,' with noun *tiro* for *robo; tocar (el) piano* (Arg, Peru) or *tocar* (*el*) *piano al revés* (Arg, Ven, Ant) 'to play the piano in reverse' and general *tocar el arpa* (as in Spain) or *arpar* (deriv. *arpista*), and *arpiñar* (Ec) 'to play the harp,' or *tocar do re mi fa sol* (*Filología*, III, 76), often accompanied with a gesture of the hand as if playing on harp strings.

Sometimes the noun *ladrón* 'thief' is euphemized by using the name of some animal particularly thought of as engaging in thievery. Such is standard *rata* 'rat' in *ratear* 'to filch' and *ratero* 'pickpocket'; *garduña* 'marten' becomes *garduño* 'petty thief.' Others, often associated with thieves' slang, are *águila* 'eagle,' *avispón* 'hornet,' *comadreja* 'weasel,' *lagarto* 'lizard,' *lechuza* 'owl,' *lobo* 'wolf' (see Juan Hidalgo). In Spanish America we find *avispa* 'wasp' (Mex); *cafuche* (Col: Acuña) 'a kind of wild boar' > 'smuggler'; *coyote* (Mex), deriv. *coyotear; huiña* or *huina* (Chile) 'marten' (cf. *garduña*), as in "Este niño es una *huina"* (Román); *ch'uy* (Yucatán) 'a bird of prey,' from Maya (Suárez, p. 84); *gato barcino* (SD) 'white-and-brown cat'; *gavillero* (Ec, Col, Ven, SD) 'highway robber,' perhaps from *gavilán* 'sparrow hawk'; *loro* 'parrot' > 'thief acting as lookout' (Chile); *mangangá* (from Guaraní) 'bee' > 'thief' (Arg, Bol); *peuco* or *peuca* (Chile) 'hawk,' from Mapuche, meaning especially a 'chicken thief' since the *peuco* hunts birds and even doves and chickens (*peuco* is also the name of a game similar to 'hen and chickens' in which one child, the *peuco,* engages in a struggle with the hen trying to protect her brood); *zopilote* (Mex) 'buzzard,' deriv. *zopilotear,* sometimes used for *robar,* as in "en vano buscó el puñal que llevaba en la bolsa ... ya se lo habían *zopiloteado* sin sentirlo" (Inclán, I, 273).

The noun *ladrón* has euphemisms in words of identical initial sounds: *ladrillo* (Juan Hidalgo) and *lagarto,* as in "Y yo dije despacito ['in a low voice']—¡Más *lagarto* serás vos!" (Arg: *Martín Fierro,* I, v. 864). Such phonetic interference we find also in "¿*ladrónde* [for *adónde*] te compraste ese traje?" (Mex: Frenk, p. 148), when the speaker wishes to imply that the article was not honestly acquired, being beyond the economic possibilities of the wearer. With the euphemism *limpiar* ('to clean') in mind for 'robar,' the word *ladrón* may be euphemized with *tintorero* (Arg) 'dry cleaner.' The euphemism *dañino* (N Arg) 'harmful' is sometimes heard, and the standard proverb "Piensa el *ladrón* que todos son de su condición" may become "Piensa el *dañino* que todos son de su camino" (Santamaría), deriv. *dañinear* 'to steal.' The euphemism *travieso* (Piura, Peru) 'mischievous, playful' is used of a person who is a proven thief, as in "Fulano es *travieso*" (Hildebrandt, p. 266), and for the same region are recorded *hombre de caminos* for *salteador* 'highwayman' (*ibid.,* p. 264) and *manudo* 'bighanded' for *ladrón*. Others are *vago* (Col) 'vagrant' for *ladrón; niño* (cant, Chile) 'boy' for *ladrón,* as in *niño de caballería* 'a country thief' and *niño de infantería* 'a city thief'; *raspa* (general).

Often a gesture obviates the necessity of speech. Sometimes it accompanies the word. The spoken word may even have a diametrically opposed meaning or none at all. Meaning then depends solely on the gesture, which usually indicates some motion of the hand or fingers as employed in filching or in picking a pocket.

The classical *tomador del dos* 'pickpocket' ("que mete dos y saca cinco" 'who puts in two and takes out five,' R. Salillas, *El delincuente español,* pp. 139, 473) may be indicated graphically by extending thumb and index, or index and middle finger, toward a vest pocket or an inner coat pocket, closing the fingers and withdrawing them (see fig. 21). Since the fingers move in the manner of scissors they are often referred to in cant as *tijera(s),* sometimes as *el dos de bastos* 'the deuce of clubs.' Standard *sisar* 'to filch' may become *chauchar* (Ec) from *chaucha* '20-centavo coin,' as in "con esta carestía ya no podimos *chauchar* los dos riales diarios a los patrones" (García Muñoz, p. 67); *recortar* (Chile) 'to cut away,' deriv. *recorte* (std. *sisa*). *Ratero, caco* or *carterista* 'pickpocket' may become *punguista* (Arg, Ec), *punga* (Chile) or *punguero* (Ec) 'puncturer, borer' as in "Se le acercaron los *pungas*" (Castro, p. 418).

Since in some regions of Mexico *clavarse el dinero* means 'robar el dinero' according to a local meaning of *clavarse*—'to dive' (cf. American-English slang *diver* 'pickpocket'), the corresponding gesture is that used for 'diving': the right wrist strikes the open left palm, representing a diving board, then the right hand is raised over and swings downward like a person diving (see fig. 22).

Perhaps the best-known gesture for stealing is that of extending the open hand, palm down, then gradually folding the fingers, one after another, to the right, downward and inward upon the palm, beginning with the little finger, all with a fanlike motion, imitating the seizure of some object and holding it tight in the fist (see fig. 23). This gesture may accompany unfinished sentences in which the offending word is euphemistically omitted, as in "despidieron a la criada por ..." (+ gesture), "lo cogieron ..." (+ gesture), "¿te has dedicado a esto ... ?" (+ gesture), and "el libro ha desaparecido" (+ gesture). Sometimes an author describes the gesture as an aid to the reader: "—Ahora resulta que el santo presbítero se resolvió. ... Y diciendo esto *vuelve los dedos de la mano derecha en escala picaresca hacia fuera"* (Ven: Briceño, *Balumba,* 1943, p. 156); "Cada vez que lo conducían preso, los muchachos le gritaban: —Zarapico, ¿por qué te llevan? —Por nada, sino por esto. Respondía ... haciendo al mismo tiempo *un movimiento con la mano derecha, abriendo los dedos y cerrándolos luego en abanico, empezando del meñique al pulgar.* Con lo que indicaba que lo llevaban por ratero" (Ec: Alfredo Pareja Diez-Canseco, *Baldomera,* Santiago, Chile, 1938, p. 81). Sometimes the gesture contradicts the accompanying words, which are euphemistically ironical, as in "el dinero que me gané ..." (+ gesture); and the popular dialogue: "—¿Por qué te llevan? —Por nada (+ gesture for stealing). —¿Cuándo te sueltan? —Mañana (+ gesture for 'no,' that is, moving index held upright back and forth). —¿Corres peligro? —Ninguno (| gesture for hanging: moving the index across the throat)."

Although the gesture for stealing just described is common, others are substituted, perhaps because of a possible confusion with the gesture expressing doubt: moving the open extended hand, palm out, back and forth several times and with a wrist movement describing a semicircle. Another common gesture for stealing (especially in Mex, Col, Ven) is that of extending the fingers like claws and then bending the first and second joints inward as if scratching something; or the hand thus formed may be drawn down the cheek as if scratching it (Col) (see fig. 24).

Curiously, a number of verbs meaning 'to run away' may also connote theft, because of similar connotations of speed and disappearance (cf. Russian *svistnut* 'to whistle,' which may mean 'to disappear' and 'to steal' as *karandash svistnul* 'the pencil disappeared' and *kto svistnul karandash?* 'who stole the pencil?'), and vice versa (std. *robarse* in the older language meant also *huirse, escaparse;* cf. English 'to steal away'). Thus, *alzar* 'to raise' used reflexively may mean 'to rebel, to run away' as well as 'to steal' (Arg, especially among Gauchos; CA, as sometimes in the std. language): —"Y al irse *se alzó* unas guascas" (*Martín Fierro,* II, v. 2203), deriv. *alzo* 'theft,' as in "Los cacos le hicieron un buen *alzo* a don Juan" (Guat: Sandoval). Among other verbs are: *arrear* 'to drive horses, cattle,' then 'to walk fast' or 'hasten,' and finally 'to steal' particularly cattle (RP, CA, Mex), deriv. *arreada* 'theft of cattle'; while *caiteárselas* (Guat), from *caite* 'sandal,' means 'to run away,' both *cutarrear* (from *cutarras* or *cutaras* 'sandals') and *macacinear* (from *macacinas* 'sandals, moccasins') mean 'to steal,' deriv. *macacino,-a* 'thief,' as in "Salomón es aficionado a *cutarrear*" and "A Domingo le ha gustado siempre *macacinear*" (Sandoval); *espiantar* and *piantar* (cant, Arg), from Italian *spiantare,* mean both 'to run away' and 'to steal,' deriv. *espiante* 'flight' and 'theft'; *gabanear* (Tabasco, Mex) from *gabán* 'overcoat' may mean 'to run away' (by a permutation of action for means of action, or beginning of action for result) as well as 'to steal' (CA); *refalar* (= *resbalar*) 'to slip, slide' may (when used reflexively) mean 'to steal away' as well as 'to steal' (Arg, Bol): "El puñal de la cintura / Me lo habían *refalao*" (Estanislao del Campo, *Fausto,* II, v. 26).

FLEEING

The relationship between *robar* 'to steal' and *echar a correr, huir* or *escaparse* 'to run away' leads us conveniently to the wealth of words and expressions meaning 'to run away.' Most of these are euphemistic in that they seek to veil an undesirable quality of fear or cowardice implied by the original expression. They are numerous because such a strongly felt concept engenders hosts of synonyms, inevitably renewed whenever constant use has expended their force. A humorous version of the present indicative of *irse* runs as follows: *yo me voy, tú te marchas, el se naja, nosotros nos arrancamos, vosotros os largáis, ellos toman las de Villadiego.* The number of synonyms is so great that dozens of such popular versions could be added without the repetition of a single expression (*alarse, ahuecar el ala, guillarse, guiñarse, levarse, miñarse, mudarse, pintarse, pirarse, tomar soleta, tomar el portante, tomar el tole,* etc.).

Many of these verbs contain the indefinite feminine object pronoun *las* (also *la*), the antecedent being unexpressed though perhaps occasionally understood. This we find in colloquial peninsular *afufarlas* = 'tomar las afufas' (*afufa* = *fuga*), *apeldarlas, liarlas, tomar las de Villadiego* in which *las* has been thought to mean *las calzas* 'the breeches,' or more likely *las alforjas* 'the saddlebags' since Villadiego, a town in the province of Burgos, was noted for its *alforjas* (Beinhauer, p. 267).

Thus in popular American Spanish we find:

abrírselas (Col, CA), *abrir* being used for *huir* nearly everywhere ("*se abrió* como un gamo por el pasillo," Peru: Corrales, p. 63), and *mandárselas abrir* in Costa Rica, as in *"se las mandó abrir"* for *huyó* or *echó a correr* (Gagini, who thinks *las* may refer to *las piernas* 'the legs').

cabrear(se) from *cabra* 'goat' (Col); *caiteárselas* (CA), from *caite* 'sandal,' considered by Gagini elliptical for "poner caites a las patas (= los pies)," as in "Juan es ... cobarde, y cuando ve la cosa seria, pronto *se las caitea"* (Sandoval); *campaneárselas* and *campeárselas* (Guat), as in "El capitán *se las campaneó* a las primeras bofetadas que le dió un enemigo suyo" (Sandoval) and "Ortiz hizo aquí un gran alzo [robo] de alhajas valiosísimas, con lo que *se las campeó* para El Salvador" (*ibid.*).

echarlas (Chile), as in *"se las echó* a primera hora" (Durand, p. 85); *endilgarlas* or *endilgárselas* (Chile), from *endilgar* 'to direct,' as in *"las endilgó* derechito para su casa" (Guzmán Maturana, p. 112); *emplumarlas* or *emplumárselas* (Col, Chile) from *emplumar* 'to feather, moult,' as in "Esta mañana Tito Jara *se las emplumó"* (Durand, p. 85), in which *emplumarse* may first have meant "irse como el ave que ya emplumó" (Cuervo, § 570); *empuntarlas* (Col) which Cuervo (*ibid.*) explains "alude probablemente al ganado que, haciendo punta, se escapa"; *envelarlas* or *envelárselas* (Chile), a maritime expression meaning 'alzar o levantar velas, hacerse a la vela, largar las velas,' as in "—No vaya a ser cosa que on Peiro *se las envele* pa la Rinconá" (Latorre, p. 170).

hacer las (or *lo del* or *el viaje* or *correo*) *del zopilote* (Mex) 'to act like the turkey buzzard,' meaning 'to leave with some pretext and never return' and referring to the turkey buzzard which Noah dispatched to find the carrier pigeon he had previously sent: the buzzard, engaged in consuming the carrions he found, likewise failed to return; a similar explanation is usually given of *hacer la del* (or *lo del* or *como el*) *cuervo* (Chile) 'to act like the crow.'

limpiárselas (Tab, Mex) from general *limpiar* 'to clean, steal' and a local meaning 'to beat, whip' (Mex, Pan), that is, 'to clean, purify' by whipping, cf. also *limpiarse* 'to flee,' as in "El preso *se limpió"* (Mex: Duarte).

mecateárselas (Mex), from *mecate* 'string, cord' and *mecatear* 'to beat with a *mecate'* or, in the sense of 'to tie with a *mecate,'* analogous to *liarlas,* cf. also *liar los bártulos.*

picárselas (Ec, Col), from *picar* probably with the meaning of 'to itch,' as in *se me pican los pies* 'my feet are itching (to go, to dance, etc.)'; *pisársela* (Ven), as in *se la pisó* 'he fled'; *pitárselas* and *piteárselas* (CA), from standard *pitar* and American *pitear* 'to whistle,' but it may well come from *pita* 'cord' and mean 'to tie up one's belongings' as does familiar standard *liarlas* and Mexican *mecateárselas; ponérselas* (Ec); *prenderlas* (Col), from *prender* possibly from its meaning of 'to kindle, light, catch fire.'

rasparlas (Chile, Ven) from *raspar* in the sense of 'to steal, carry off,' as in "—A tranco largo *las raspó* pa la calle" (Guzmán Maturana, p. 20).

tejérselas (Cuba) from *tejer* 'to weave' and *templárselas* (Cuba, Mex), probably from *templar* 'to trim the sails to the wind'; *tomar* (or *pelar,* Bol) *las de gaviota* (Arg); *tomar las de Villahuaico* (Ec: Toscano, p. 459).

Verbs meaning 'to run away' that have also acquired the meaning of 'to die' have been discussed (see chap. i); among them are *arrancarse, chiflárselas, doblar la esquina, jarearse, largarse, panquearse, pelar el ajo, pelar el castaño, pelar gallo, pelarla, pelar rata, pelarse, piteárselas, planear, rasgarse, raspar.*

Some expressions are formed with *alzar* 'to raise, pick up' or with *parar* in its American sense of 'to raise': *alzar el poncho* (Arg); *alzar pelo* (CR), probably from *alzarle pelo a alguno* 'to be afraid of someone' ("Fulano *le alza pelo a* zutano" = 'le tiene miedo,' Gagini), an expression taken from cockfighting, for when one of the contenders becomes frightened its head feathers stand on end, an expression related to *parar la moña* (Col); *parar el rabo* or *la cola* (CA, Mex, Ant), as "vino un agente de policía y muchos *pararon el rabo*" (SD: Patín), *parar la guajana* 'sugar-cane stalk' (PR). These expressions might be classified as permutations indicating either concomitant circumstance or naming an action for its result. In this same category could be placed *apretarse la iraca* (Col), *apretarse el gorro* (Arg, Ven), *ponerse uno las botas* or *las de hule* or *los caites* or *los de hule* or *los de suela* (CA) or merely *ponérselas* (Ec: Cornejo, p. 244); *ponerse uno las cotizas* (Ven, Col), *cotiza* being a kind of rustic sandal; *pegar los baúles* or *las petacas* (Ven); *coger brisa* (PR), a nautical expression.

Other miscellaneous metaphors for *huir* are:

alcanforarse (Col, Ven, CA), from *alcanfor* 'camphor,' alluding to its volatility; *ariscarse* (PR), from *arisco* 'shy, timid,' as in "Yo seguío *me arisqué*" (ap. Malaret, *Vocabulario*).

borrarse 'to erase oneself' (Pachuco).

dar agua a los caites (CA); *despintarse* (Col) 'to fade, wash away' (cf. colloquial Russian *smütsa* 'to wash oneself off'), as in "Quédate aquí guardando los canastos y *no te despintes"* (Acuña), cf. *hacer pinta* and *pintar el venado* (Mex) 'to play truant' and general slang *pintarse* 'to flee'; *dar cureña* or *tusa* (Cuba: C. Suárez); *despezuñarse* (Chile, Col, CA, PR) 'to get sore hoofs.'

embalar and *embriscar* (PR, SD); *empolvarse* (SD), cf. familiar standard *poner pies en polvorosa;* slang *espiantar* (Arg, Chile) from Italian *spiantare,* deriv. *espiante* 'flight,' and the phrase "tocar la polca del *espiante"* meaning 'marcharse con la música a otra parte' (Malaret).

ganarse en (Arg, Chile) or *ganar para* (Col, Ven, Guat); *grillarse* (Ant), probably from familiar standard *guillarse* 'to fly, scoot.'

hacer el corcho (Chile) 'to be a cork, play the role of a cork,' that is, to disappear quickly, like a cork snapping from a bottle, cf. *destaparse* (SD) 'to uncork oneself,' as in "cuando lo supo en la calle, *se destapó* para su casa" (Patín).

pendonearse (SD), from familiar standard *pendonear* 'to gad, wander about,' as in "algunos, viendo que arreciaba el desorden, *se pendonearon"* (Patín); *picar los cabos* (Ven); *pirarse* (Cuba, Mex), as in Spanish cant (see Wagner, "Mex. Rot."), as in *"se piró* de la cárcel" (C. Suárez); *plumearse* (SD), as in "cuando vieron la cosa fea, *se plumearon"* (Patín); *hacerse perdiz* (Arg) 'to become a partridge.'

rajarse (Arg, Ant); *ranclarse* (Ec), perhaps associated with *arrancarse; raspar la bola* (Chile), like standard *escurrir la bola; rajarse* (Cuba); *raspar la hebra* (Arg).

tocar la nina (SD), as in "a la hora del peligro algunos *tocaron la nina"* (Patín); *tocar el pito inglés* (Cuba) 'to blow the English whistle'; *tomar el polvo* (Chile); *trucarse* (SD) "cuando sonó el tiro, todos *se trucaron"* (Patín); *no ver ni el polvo* (Mex.)

Sometimes a mere gesture obviates the necessity of the spoken word. Thus, snapping the thumb against the middle or index finger, with forearm usually raised upward and outward, generally indicates 'rapidity' and by extension it means 'flight.' The standard phrases for 'to snap the fingers' are *chascar* or *chasquear los dedos* and *castañetear los dedos,* the latter from *castañuela* 'castanet,' which is from *castaña,* the word for the similarly shaped chestnut. Hence, *hacer castañetas* or *castaña(s)* may mean 'to snap one's fingers.' In American Spanish one often hears *chicotear los dedos* 'to snap one's fingers' from *chicote* 'whip' (std. *látigo*), as in "—Cuando te haga seña te vení—concluyó *chicoteando el dedo índice contra el pulgar con un movimiento rápido de la mano y el antebrazo,* signo que quería decir 'a todo meter' " (Urug: Reyles, p. 29).

Another common gesture expressing 'to run' is to extend one or both outstretched hands and move them alternately and rapidly up and down, palms facing each other, imitating the rapid motion of the feet in running. This gesture may accompany such phrases as "se marcha la gente," "agua que no has de beber, déjala correr," "me anda persiguiendo," or "la procesión va por dentro," or it often suffices without words to represent flight, through its essential indication of haste. Sometimes this gesture is preceded by a single clap of the hands. It may also accompany such neutral phrases as "voy a casa," "voy a pie," or "el camino es recto." Again, one may place the open right hand on the open, slightly curved left, palm to palm, then drawing the right forcibly backward. Sometimes a sharp whistling sound indicates rapid motion, in accordance with the expressions *pitárselas* and *piteárselas, chiflárselas,* and *tocar el pito inglés.* Example: "—¡Arre, arre, mulitas! En ocasiones agregaba *el silbido* que era como la misma orden de caminar" (Mex: Gregorio López y Fuentes, *Arrieros,* Mexico, 1937, I, 3).

PLAYING TRUANT

Playing truant from school or business may well be considered here. Numerous euphemisms palliate such acts, especially when reference is made to 'cutting classes' or 'playing hooky' (from slang 'to hook it,' meaning 'to run away').

Among familiar standard locutions are *hacer novillos* 'to play young bulls,' that is 'to act' like or 'to fight' young bulls (older *irse a novillos* referred to young men leaving their native villages to see the world and returning after a brief absence as if they had merely gone to a neighboring fair to buy bullocks), deriv. *novillero* 'truant'; related *hacer corrales,* from *corral* 'barnyard' or 'playhouse, theater'; *hacer bolas,* related to *escurrir la bola* 'to flee' or to *bolas* 'a game of bowling,' deriv. *bolero* 'truant'; *hacer* (*la*) *rabona,* from *rabón* 'docked, bobtailed (animal),' perhaps 'turning one's tail on' (cf. German *die Schule schwänzen,* from *Schwanz* 'tail,' deriv.

Schwänzer 'truant'); *hacer marro* 'to fail to keep an appointment,' from *marro* 'game resembling quoits'; *hacer mico,* from *mico* 'monkey'; *hacer el cuco,* from *cuco* 'cuckoo' or 'a sort of caterpillar' (?); *hacer tuna,* from *tuna* 'vagrancy, truancy'; *hacer zorra,* from *zorra* 'fox'; *fumarse la clase* or *la oficina,* and others.

Among Spanish-American expressions are many referring to animals (like std. *hacer novillos*) and involving the idea of running away or of playing:

hacer(se) la cimarra (Chile, parts of Arg, Peru), from *cimarrón* 'wild (animal),' formerly also 'runaway slave,' deriv. *cimarrero* 'truant' and rare *cimarrear* 'to play truant' (for disputed etymologies, see Corominas), as in "Pedro permaneció silencioso y recordó su niñez, cuando montaba a caballo y *hacía cimarra*" (Chile: Edwards Bello, *Criollos en París,* chap. xlix); *hacer(se) la cuca* (Santiago del Estero, Arg) 'to play the cuckoo.'

hacer(se) la chancha (Chile) 'to play the sow,' as in "—Si yo pudiera ir a la escuela como vo, no *haría la chancha*" (Guerrero, p. 126), probable deriv. *chacharse* (La Paz, Bol), as in "Los niños *están chachando*" (Brown, p. 85); *hacer(se) la chupina* (Arg) 'to play the tailless animal' (cf. std. *la rabona*), usually assumed to be from Quechua *chupo* 'tumor' but may also be related to Spanish *chupín,* diminutive of *chupa* 'undercoat with flaps *or* coattails.'

hacerse la pava (Ec) 'to play the turkey,' deriv. *pavista, pavero,* and *paviolo* 'truant' (Cornejo) and verb *pavearse* (Ec, Pan), as in "Mañana *me* voy a *pavear*" (Brown, p. 124); *hacerse la pelada* (Urug), from *pelado* 'a kind of hairless dog'; *hacer (la) pinta, estar de pinta, irse de pinta* or *pintar* (Mex), probably alluding to *(vaca) pinta,* where *pinta* is a shortened form of *pintado* 'mottled (usually black and white).'

hacer la erre, in which the letter *erre* (multiple *r*), being the initial sound of *rabona,* suffices to recall it; *hacerse la rata* (Arg) 'to play the rat' (*BAAL,* XVII, No. 64, p. 253).

hacer vaca or *hacerse la vaca* (Peru) 'to play the cow,' although some persons feel that *vaca* in this phrase derives from *vacar* 'to cease work temporarily' (see Arona), and Wagner (p. 20) postulates *hacer vaca* as an original locution on which standard *hacer novillos* is based as a continuation of the metaphor; *pintar un venado* or *venados* (Mex) 'to paint a deer' or 'to paint deer' may mean 'to deceive' and also 'to play hooky,' as in "un muchacho no dejará de ser muy hombre porque *pinte venado,* fume, beba una copa y robe a sus padres" (Nervo, ap. Santamaría, *Dicc. de meji-canismos*); *correr la venada* (Tex), *correr venado* (Guat).

hacer la yuta (N Arg, Bol), from Quechua *yutta* 'partridge, tailless par-tridge, any tailless bird, animal or thing,' deriv. *yutear, yutero,* and *yutería,* as in "fuí ... *yutero* destacado ... para que pudiera conocer el halago de la *yutería*" (ap. Malaret, *Bol. fil.*).

Other locutions expressing 'to play truant' are:

aventarse (*de la escuela*) (CR) 'to run away, escape (from school).'

cachar (Santanderes, Col), involving its local meaning of 'conversar y más frecuentemente conversar, los novios o personas que se quieren bien' (Tobón) or that of *jugar al cacho* 'to play dice' or general *cacho* 'horn'; *capar a* (*la*) *clase* (Col), and *capear* or *capearse* (Chile, Guat), possibly derived from one meaning of *capar,* that of 'to castrate, to cut' (cf. 'to cut class'), and syntactically influenced by *faltar a la clase* (suggested by Cuervo, § 634) or *capear* 'to fight the bull with a cloak' (thus related to *hacer novillos*), deriv. *capeón* or *capeador* 'truant' and verbal noun *capeada,* as in "Por más enfermo que me sienta, no quiero *capar* oficina" (Col: Acuña) and "Es bueno que te fijes en tus hijos, porque son muy *capeadores* y van a salir mal en sus exámenes" (Guat: Sandoval); *comer guásima* (parts of Cuba) 'a kind of tree' or *pelar guásima* (Brown, p. 98); *comer jobos* or *jobillos* (PR) 'to eat *jobos,*' tropical fruit resembling yellow plums, as in "un día tras otro se pasa *comiendo jobos*" (ap. Malaret, *Vocabulario*), deriv. *jobero* 'truant' and *jobear,* as in "era grande amigo de la mayor parte de los *joberos*" and "Cansado ya de *jobear* por la histórica Peña de la Fortaleza ..." (*ibid.*); *cortar clases* (PR) 'to cut classes,' based on the English.

darse (or *pegarse* or *ponerse*) *la leva* (Col) 'to flee,' in which *leva* may be felt as the American form of standard *levita* '(frock) coat,' as in "se puso la *leva*" 'he played hooky' or 'he stayed home from work' (Brown, p. 89), but cf. fam. std. *irse a leva y a monte* 'to run away.'

futigarse or *futivarse* (parts of Cuba: *ibid.,* p. 98).

hacer brusca (PR) 'to make kindling wood'; *hacer chuela* (Veracruz, Mex, where *chuela* means 'hoax, jest'); *hacer la chuña* or *hacer chuños al sol* (Bol), in which *chuño,* from Quechua, means 'dried or frozen potatoes' or 'potato starch,' deriv. *chuñista* 'truant'; *hacer la gacha* (Santanderes,

Col) 'to make porridge'; *hacer hoja* (Ec), in speaking of two or more pupils, from the local sense of *hoja* 'group of persons addicted to some questionable amusement or vice,' as in "ese hombre es de *la hoja"; hacer la machancha* (San Luis, Arg), from local *macharse* 'to become inebriated' and phonetic interference of *chaucha* (?), deriv. *machanchero* 'truant,' synonym of *rabonero,* as "Los van a llevar a la polecía a los *machancheros"* (Vidal, p. 266); *hacer pifia* (PR) 'to whistle'; *hacer puts'* (Yucatán, Mex), from Maya, as in "Juan *hizo* hoy *puts'* escuela" or "hoy *hice puts'* trabajo" (Suárez, p. 97); *hacer la rocha* or *rochearse* (Cochabamba, Bol), probably related to *rochela* 'spree, gang' and perhaps to *Rocha,* the name of a famous colonial counterfeiter from Potosí (cf. *moneda rochuna* 'false or badly minted coin'); *huirse de la escuela* or simply *huirse* 'to run away (from school).'

irse a la jiriola (Tex, where adjective *jiriolo* means 'self-satisfied in spite of unfavorable circumstances').

jubilarse (Ven, CA) 'to retire,' in which the idea of rest predominates.

mamarse (de) la clase or *la escuela* (Antioquia, Col), perhaps from its local meaning 'to deceive, kill,' as in "cuando yo *me mamaba de la escuela* ... me iba a la zapatería" (Arango, p. 15), cf. fam std. *fumarse la clase.*

pintar un violín or *violines* (Mex).

ranclarse (Ec) 'to run away,' deriv. *ranclón* and *rancla.*

sacar cera (Ven) 'to extract wax (from beehives)' and figuratively 'to exploit a matter,' deriv. *sacacera* 'truant,' but perhaps the expression is to be associated with older *cerero* (from *acera* 'sidewalk') 'loafer'; *salarse* or *salar la escuela* (Mex), in which *salar* seems to mean 'to get into bad luck, to dishonor,' as in "A veces invitaba a sus compañeros de colegio para *salar,* es decir, para faltar a las clases" (García Cubas, ap. Santamaría, *Dicc. de mejicanismos*).

JAIL

Euphemisms for standard *cárcel* or *calabozo* (fam. *chirona*) 'prison, jail' are numberless. Some of them imply a haven of rest, of free food and lodging: *casa de tía* 'auntie's house'; *pensión Rosales* (= *la cárcel del paseo de Rosales* in Madrid, see Beinhauer, p. 35); *quinta* 'country house,' as in "nos llevaron a *la quinta* ... ei [he] pasao veraniando en *la quinta* por la fuerza" (Chile: Del Campo, p. 60); *la casa blanca* (cant, Mex: Wagner, "Mex. Rot.") 'the white house'; *la juiciosa* (Arg) 'the judicious' (Gobello, p. 101); "lo mandaron *de vacaciones*" (Nic) 'he was sent on a vacation'; *estar uno de orden* (Guat), a euphemistic shortening of *estar preso de orden superior* (Sandoval); *veranear* (cant, Mex) 'to summer.'

In the sense of a place of safekeeping or confinement, *cárcel* in popular speech may be replaced by *alcancía* (cant, Mex) 'charity box'; *archivo* (cant, Chile, Mex) 'archive,' deriv. *archivar* 'to imprison, jail,' as in "El lunes pasao habían *archivaos* en el calabozo lo menos setenta rotos" (Del Campo, p. 23); *buchaca* (Hond), from *bolchaca* 'pocket, bag'; *bote* (Mex, CA) 'jar, jug, can,' as in "los gendarmes pretendieron llevársela al *bote* por escándalo en la vía pública" (Ángulo, p. 44), also *boticheli* (Mex: Alatorre, No. 3, p. 11); *cacharro* (CA, PR) 'earthen pot'; *canasta* 'basket' (retaining the initial syllable of *cárcel* and *calabozo*), with shortened *cana* (though *cana* is by some considered an Italianism, see Wagner, "Apuntaciones," p. 192), and deriv. *encanastar* and *encanar* (Arg, Chile, Col), as in "Pónele una vela a la virgen pa que no me *encanen* ... ¡Y mi marido, esperándome! ¡A lo mejor lo *encanaron* también!" (Arg: Mendoza, p. 9); *capacha* (RP, Chile, Bol, Ec) 'hamper,' as in "¿No tienen ustedes miedo de venir a la *capacha?*" (Ec: García Muñoz, p. 96); *cueva del rey Inca* (N Chile); *chipa* or *tipa* (Arg, Bol, Col) 'basket, bag,' from Quechua-Aymara; *guandoca* (Col: connected with *guandolo?* 'leather bag' for *chicha* 'beverage made of corn or fruits' and *guarapo* 'cane juice'), as in "No siga bebiendo, que lo meten a la *guandoca*" (Tobón); *joyolina* (Guat); *meter,* euphemistic shortening of *meter en la cárcel,* as in "Ayer *metieron* a tu amigo" (SD: Patín); *tinaja* 'large earthen jar' formerly used in referring to water-soaked underground dungeons (Mex), which were abolished after the revolution of 1910 (Velasco).

For lack of heating in the *cárcel,* it is sometimes called a *nevera* (Col, PR) 'icebox.' For its lack of cleanliness, it is called a *pocilga* (Col) 'pigsty'; *pulgosa* and *pulguero* (Peru, Ec, Col, Ven, CR) 'place abounding with fleas,' as in "Nos metió al *pulguero*" (Ec: García Muñoz, p. 95); *chinche* (Mex) 'bedbug' or *chinchero* 'place abounding with bedbugs'; *chiva* (Ven) 'goat,' as in "lo metió en la *chiva*" (Rosenblat, p. 141), rustic *chivunga* (Valle del Cauca, Col); *chichera* (CA) from *chicha; leonera* (Arg, Ec, PR) 'lion's den'; *ratonera* (Ec) 'mousetrap'; *tigrito* (Col, Ven) 'wildcat'; *bartolina* (CA, Mex, Ant; cf. Bartolo 'clumsy, lazy, careless person'), as in "una horrorosa *bartolina* que por su hediondez ... había quedado en total abandono" (Mex: Inclán, II, 219).

The word may be a borrowing: *chipa* (see above); *cafúa* (RP) from Portuguese *cafua* 'cave'; *cufa* (cant, Arg) from Genoese *cuffa* (Gobello, p. 202); jocose and now rare *terpiloya, tlalpiloya,* and *trampiloya* (in parts of Mex), from Aztec *teilpiloyan* (Robelo, Santamaría); *tambo* (NW Mex), conjectured by Santamaría to be from Quechua *tampu* 'country inn' > 'prison' (since *bote* 'jar, can' may mean 'jail' in Mexico, *tambo* has also come to mean *bote*); *tipa* (RP, Bol) 'bag, basket,' from Quechua, as *meter en tipa* = *meter en la cárcel*.

Other words heard in familiar speech and in slang are *barra* (Chile), for standard *cepo* 'stocks, pillory,' as in "Si no te asosegái te pongo en la *barra*" (Del Campo, p. 20); *cachaco* (Lima, Peru), now obsolete; *calabuitre* (Peru), based on *calabozo; cambulera* (Col); *cuchuflí* (Cuba); *chero* (Mex); *chico* (Peru); *chirola* (CA, Ant), probably from general familiar *chirona; chucho* (Chile) 'owl,' as in "ei estao en el *chucho* remuchísimas veces" (Del Campo, p. 20); *foco* (S Chile) 'focal point'; *jeruza* (CA); *tabique* (Tex) 'partition wall'; *trancar* (SD) 'to jail,' as in "A tu cuñado lo *trancaron* por propagandista" (Patín); *separo* (Mex), as in "salieron mujeres desgreñadas, conducidas luego a calabozos llamados *separos*" (Quevedo y Zubieta, *La camada,* p. 41).

For older peninsular colloquial speech and thieves' slang Juan Hidalgo lists among others: *angustia* 'anguish,' *banasto* 'basket,' *banco* 'bench,' *confusión* 'confusion, shame,' *horno* 'oven,' *temor* 'fear,' *trápala* 'confusion, noise,' *tropel* 'rush, bustle,' and *tristura* 'sadness, blues," some of which are still current.

Euphemistic gestures may suffice to indicate *cárcel,* such as extending the fingers of the right hand over the extended fingers of the left to form a kind of grating suggestive of prison bars (see fig. 25). This gesture may accompany words like the following: "¿Te acuerdas de aquel individuo calavera? Pues ahora ... (+ gesture)." In another gesture the spread fingers cover the face, as one says "¡Qué pena!" or something similar. Again, the right hand may seize the left wrist to suggest handcuffing, as one says something like "Si tú sigues en ese camino"; or the gesture may be made without words: "hice señas a mi comadre ... y arqueando las cejas y *cogiéndome con la mano derecha la muñeca izquierda,* le dí a entender que había peligro que su marido cayera preso, si no seguía mi consejo de quedarse en casa" (Nic: Calero Orozco, *Sangre santa,* 1940, p. 6). In Mexico one may cross the index and middle fingers of both hands (see fig. 26), which may also indicate a *julia* 'police wagon.'

POLICEMAN

Along with euphemisms for *cárcel* are terms for standard *policía* 'policeman,' a word that has equally unpleasant associations, particularly for malefactors. For the older language, Juan Hidalgo lists *buho* 'owl,' *fiera* 'wild beast,' *guro* from *gurapas* 'galleys,' *harpía* 'harpy,' *mastín* 'bulldog,' *papagayo* 'parrot,' *posta* 'relay,' *rayo* 'bolt,' *señal* 'signal,' *soplón* 'informer'; for modern usage Besses gives, among other words shortened *poli* and phonetically associated *polilla* 'moth.'

Similarly, because certain animals have characteristics popularly associated with the activities and attitudes of policemen, in colloquial American Spanish their names are synonymous with *policía*. Among them are *camarón* (SD) 'shrimp,' which quietly lies in wait, used for *espía* 'spy, detective,' as in "varios *camarones* visitaban el cafetín" (Patín); *conejo* (Guat) 'rabbit' with its long ears > 'secret police'; *chiva* 'goat' and *chivato* 'he goat' (cant, Mex) for *delator* 'informer'; *chota* (Mex, Cuba, Tex) 'sucking kid'; *gallo* (S Chile: Vicuña) 'cock'; *gallote* (Pan) 'buzzard'; *grulla* (Tex) 'crane' (cf. 'to crane forward' in order to see better, to spy, etc.); *güitre* (Chile) = *buitre* 'buzzard, vulture'; *mono* (N Chile) 'monkey'; *palomo* (Chile) 'pigeon,' probably because of the policeman's white (summer) uniform; *perro* (Chile) '(watch)dog.'

The following are popular euphemistic borrowings:

cana 'jail' and also 'policeman' (Arg), as in "un *cana* me agarra por alboroto" (Mendoza, p. 79); *cosaco* 'Cossack' (Arg) formerly applied to mounted police; *cuico* (Mex), derived by Robelo from Aztec *cuica* 'to sing,' a name given at first to night watchmen whose duty it was to sing out the hours of the night and the condition of the weather (std. *sereno*), as in "¡Pobre de ti si lo denuncias, o haces que vengan esos *cuicos* de la Diputación a cogerlo!" (Payno, *Fistol,* II, chap. xii), "cuando los *cuicos* me sacaban del calabozo ..." (Anda, p. 103); *cuilio* and *cuiliote* (Hond, Salv), as in "lárguese o llamo a un *cuilio*" (Hond).

chapa and *chapita* (highland Ec, and Nariño, Col), from Quechua *chapana* 'to spy,' as in "Al *chapita* le faltaban brazos para dar direcciones a los vehículos" (Ec: García Muñoz, p. 134), deriv. *chapería* 'group of policemen' and 'police barracks'; *chapol* and *chapolo* (Col), perhaps connected with *chapulín,* of Aztec origin, meaning 'grasshopper' and applied to the *policía* because of his formerly green uniform (others think it derives from *chapó,* French *chapeau,* because of the high-crowned hat once worn by Bogotá policemen; still others consider it a phonetic distortion of metathesized underworld *cia-poli* from *poli-cia,* see Tobón), as in "Si me sigue molestando, llamo a un *chapol*" (Acuña).

genízaro (Mex) 'janizary,' the three initial sounds recalling *gendarme,* as in "Este hecho atrajo a los gendarmes ... La Guanga no se amilanó con la presencia de los *genízaros*" (Ángulo, p. 44); *guairuro* or *huairuro* (Peru), from the Quechuan name of a plant and its podded seeds of brilliant red with a spot of black, used by the Indians in necklaces, for buttons, and formerly as dice.

paco (Chile, Ec, Col, Pan), possibly from Quechua, was applied originally, some believe, to a policeman because his *poncho* 'cape' was red, the color of an animal called *paco,* but *Paco,* a nickname for *Francisco* and Chilean nickname for *Pascual,* may well be a proper name in appellative use (cf. 'bobby' in England, 'Gianni' in Italy), *pascual* itself being current in Chile for 'policeman,' as in "Vamos a vel qué tengo que saber pa ser un *pascual* de pelo en pecho" (Del Campo, p. 20) and "Ligerito llegaron los *pascuales* y arriaron con toítos pal *chucho* ['jail']" (*ibid.,* p. 103); *paco* is sometimes disrespectfully modified to *paco asoleado* because the policeman stands in the sun, and to *paco porotero* because his nourishment consists mostly of *porotos* 'beans.'

teco and *tecolote* (Mex), from Aztec *tecolotl* 'owl,' applied because the policeman's nighttime vigilance suggested the nocturnal activity of the bird with the large all-seeing eyes; *tombo* (Peru, Col); *topile* or *topil* (Mex), from Aztec *topilli* 'staff of justice' and 'person who carries it'; *trintre* (Chile), from Mapuche *thinthi* 'curly' referring to chicken feathers that are sparse and seemingly grow inward, deriv. expression "feo como un pollo *trintre*" (Lenz).

Among miscellaneous popular and slang words for *policía* are:
aguadulcero (Caldas, Col) 'fond of soft drinks or sugared water'; *azulejo* (Mex, Cuba), because of the blue uniform, as also *el del azul* (PR).
bombacho (Santanderes, Col).

cachucha (Tex) 'cap'; *catarato* (Mendoza, Arg), from *catarata* 'waterfall'; *colimocho* (Chile) 'rural policeman,' from *cola* 'tail' and *mocho* 'cropped,' alluding to his short jacket or to his bobtailed horse (?) (Vicuña).

chonte (Guat), a phonetic variation of the last two syllables of *polizonte* 'policeman, cop'; *chota* (slang, Mex, Cuba), from peninsular cant *chota* 'informer.'

germán and *gervasio* (formerly, Mex), proper names in appellative use, the two initial sounds recalling *gendarme; gobierno* (PR) 'government, law.'

julia (New Mex); *jura* (Guat, Cuba, Tex).

milico (Chile), recalling *miliciano; mordelón* (Mex) 'traffic cop,' because many of them accept *mordidas* 'bribes'; *morfil* (cant, Mex), from *marfil* 'ivory,' applied because of the policeman's white trousers (?).

oreja (Guat) 'ear' and *orejón* 'big-eared' for 'secret police, spy, investigator,' as in "Tenga cuidado ... lo están vigilando muchos *orejas* conocidos" (Sandoval).

paquete (S Chile) 'elegant,' also 'policeman'; *parca* (N Chile) 'death'; *pasma* (parts of Mex, Spain), *pasmo* (PR); *pastora* (Mex), perhaps a euphemization of *pasma; perjuicio* (Chile) 'harm, nuisance,' recalling *perro* 'dog' in the sense of 'gendarme,' as in "Atención, compañeritos, / que viene allí un *perjuicio;* / conviene espirar [= huir] muy luego / y evitar un precipicio" (ap. Vicuña, p. 123); *pescado* (Peru, Ec) 'fish,' recalling *pescar* 'to catch' and a euphemistic distortion of *pesquisidor* 'secret police, detective,' similarly *peje* 'fish,' as in "a causa de haber espías austríacos creyéronme *peje*" (Peru: Corrales, p. 83); *pesquisa* (RP, Ec) 'investigation, search' for *pesquisidor,* a permutation of action for agent, as in "el ojo inquisitivo del *pesquisa*" (Arg: Mallea, ap. Schallman, 182), "Mi vecino, no cabe duda, es *pesquisa*" (Ec: García Muñoz, p. 92).

soplón (Mex) 'gendarme,' elsewhere 'secret police,' from *soplar* in the sense of 'to spy, inform,' as in "creo que el ser *soplón* no deshonra ... Soy *soplón* y soplo como un fuelle ... a todos lados" (Peru: Corrales, p. 13).

tira (Arg, Chile, Col) 'policeman, detective,' as in "Ayer los *tiras* fueron a incomodar a la pobre vieja enferma" (Arg: ap. A. Castro, p. 152); *técnico* (Mex) 'trained, uniformed policeman' as opposed to the common *tecolote, vecino* and *cuico,* as in "Favor, señor *técnico* ... Se trata de un grave delito" (Azuela, *La luciérnaga,* 1932, p. 151).

varita (Arg) 'small rod' > 'traffic cop' because of the rod he carries; *verde* (N Chile) 'green' because of the carabinero's yellowish-green uniform, as in "Brotaban *los verdes* de los matorrales como los moscones del estiércol" (ap. Rabanales, p. 193); *vecino* (Mex), as in "yo no soy *vecino;* yo soy un gendarme técnico y pa eso jui a la escuela" (C. Rojas, ap. Santamaría, *Dicc. de mejicanismos*).

yerba (Chile) 'grass,' because of the green uniform, as in "¡Lorea [= observa], parece que vienen *loh yerba!*" (*ibid.*).

Curiously many of these terms refer to the color of the uniforms worn by the various types of policemen. Such words are permutations naming an article of dress or its color for the person wearing it: *azulejo* 'blue' as a tile, *chapol* 'green' as a grasshopper, *guairuro* 'red' as a *guairuro* seed, *paco* 'reddish' as a *paco,* *morfil* 'white' ivory, *palomo* 'white' as a pigeon, *yerba* 'green' as grass, and simply *verde* 'green.'

Sometimes a gesture conveniently suffices to recall the unpleasant term. Thus, to indicate *oreja* or *orejón* a speaker may merely touch or pull his ear lobe or push it forward slightly as if eavesdropping. He may also fold a corner edge of his coat to represent an ear, as observed in Guatemala. For *soplón,* the speaker may pucker his lips and blow (since the original sense of *soplar* is 'to blow'), as observed in Guayaquil, when a hat vendor on boarding the ship and noticing a policeman stationed there to seize contraband goods, whispered "¡Cuidado! Ése ..." and puckered his lips as if in blowing. To indicate to another driver that a *mordelón* (Mex) 'traffic cop' is following, one may bite the ends of the three middle fingers.

BEATING

Many circumlocutions seem to attenuate or mollify the act of beating (std. *pegar*) in one way or another. Some of them tend to justify the attitude of the person administering the beating; others, perhaps because of a humorous slant, apparently lessen the humiliation of the one who is beaten. The long list of familiar standard expressions synonymous with *pegar* includes *apalear,* from *palo* 'club'; *aporrear,* from *porra* 'club'; *azotar,* from *azote* 'whip'; *cascar* 'to crack, break into pieces'; *dar* (less often *atizar*) *una azotaina* or *azotina, capuana, escurribanda, felpa, leña, mano, paliza, pega, pisa, soba, solfa* (or *un solfeo*), *somanta, sotana, tanda, tentadura, tocata, tollina, tunda,* (*un*) *vapuleo, zamanca, zurra, zurribanda; descalabrar* and *descrismar* 'to give a blow on the head'; *pencar,* from *penca* 'pulpy leaf of some plants' and figuratively 'cowhide for flogging culprits'; *sobar el pellejo* 'to massage someone's hide'; *tundir el paño* 'to shear someone's cloth'; *vapul*(*e*)*ar; zurrar la badana* 'to tan someone's hide,' etc., all of which mean 'to beat, drub, flog, lash, lick, thrash, whip,' etc.

In addition to the forms just mentioned, American Spanish has numerous terms and metaphors that, in the beginning at least, were euphemisms and seemed to lighten the form and the shame of castigation. Many are phrases consisting of *dar, echar, pegar, arrear, arrimar, asestar,* or a similar word, and a noun; whence *dar* and *arrimar* are sometimes used alone, the noun being euphemistically omitted, especially in addressing children (*arrimador* is *el que arrima a los chicos* 'the one who beats children,' Mex: Santamaría). Among such phrases are:

dar una bejuqueada (Peru, Ec, Guat, PR), from *bejuquear,* and *dar una bejuquiza* (Ec).

dar caballazo (Chile) 'to trample on with a horse' > 'to beat violently,' as in "me *pegó un caballazo ... miarrió* [me arreó] otro *caballazo* pior" (Del Campo, p. 28); general *dar cuero,* from *cuero* 'leather strap, whip,' and *dar una cuereada* (Col, CA, Mex) or *una cueriza,* as well as *cuerear.*

dar una chilillada (CA) from *chilillo* 'whip.'

dar fuete (Ant), from French *fouet* 'whip,' *fuete* being general for standard *látigo.*

dar garroteada (from *garrote* 'club' and *garrotear* 'to club'), *garroteadura* (Peru), *garrotera* (Col: "Si ese muchacho continúa tan travieso se va a llevar una *garrotera,*" Acuña), or *garrotiza* (Ec, Mex); *dar una golpiza* (Ec, Mex); *dar goma* (Cuba), since the club is often of *goma* 'rubber'; *dar guantes* (Chile), *guante* 'glove' being a euphemism both for *disciplina* 'whip, cat-o'-nine-tails' and for *disciplinazo* 'blow with the whip' on the hand as formerly administered in schools, as in "te doy una docena de *guantes*" (Román); *dar guasca* (Arg, Chile, Peru, Ant), from Quechua *huasca* 'rope, strap, whip,' also *guasquear; dar guiza* (CR), *güiscamo* (Hond), from the name of a tree.

dar huira (Chile), from the name of a tree, the bark of which is twisted into ropes, straps, and whips.

dar meremere (Ven) usually with *con pan caliente* added, as in "Me las he robado como aquellas otras, por las que *nos dieron meremere con pan caliente*" (Urbaneja A., *En este país,* ap. Alvarado).

dar monda (Col, Mex, Ant) or *muenda* (Col), from *mondar* (see below), as in "Si no te portas bien te voy a dar una *muenda* que no la vas a olvidar en los días de tu vida" (Acuña); *dar membrillo* (Guat), in which *membrillo* means 'a sprout of the quince tree' used for whipping culprits, as in "Al infeliz preso le dieron *membrillo* para que confesara el delito" (Sandoval).

dar palo is euphemized to *dar palomo* in Mexico (Wagner, p. 19, who mentions the peninsular euphemistic phrases *dar unto de Palermo* and *San Benito de Palermo*); *dar una pela* (Ven, Col, CA, Mex, Ant); threatening *dar a uno para su chocolate* or *para su fruta* (cf. fam. std. *dar para peras a uno*) or *para sus dulces* (Guat), ironical euphemisms, as in "Si no te sosiegas, niño, te voy a *dar para tu fruta*" (Sandoval); *dar una planiza* (Ec); *dar a uno para tabaco* (Arg).

dar reata or *rejo* (CA, Col), both words meaning 'rope, whip,' as in "Al que me siga molestando le doy *rejo*" (Col: Acuña).

dar suiza (Ec, Ven, CA, Cuba), perhaps from the rope-jumping game known as *suiza* (std. *comba*).

dar tabaco (Arg).

dar una veteada or *vetiza* (Ec), from *veta* 'strip of leather' used as a rope; *dar vergajeada* or *verguiza* (Ec) and verb *vergajear* (std. *verguear*), from *vergajo* 'bull's pizzle' used as a lash.

dar yaya (Cuba), the name of a tree the flexible wood of which is used for clubs.

Other terms are *aflijir* 'to afflict, grieve' (Mex); *bañar* (Nic) 'to bathe' and *dar una bañada; bejuquear* (Peru, Ec, Guat, PR) from *bejuco* 'a climbing plant'; *cajear* (Peru, CA); *cascundear* (CA); *cuajar* (CR); general *fajar* 'to girdle' but here in the sense of using the *faja* 'belt' as a 'whip,' as in "El maestro albañil le *fajó* diez cuerazos al chunero ['apprentice'] por respondón" (Guat: Sandoval); *festejar* (Mex), as in "mi padre hacía seña de que me *festejaran* recio" (Inclán, I, 250); general *fuetear* and *afoetear* (Peru, Col, PR), from French *fouet* 'whip'; *guaraquear* (Chile, Ec, Col), from Quechua *huaraca* 'sling,' as in "Hay que castigar al cuerpo pecaor ... ¡emprencipien a *guaraquiarse!*" (Del Campo, p. 85); *huaripampear* (Arequipa, Peru) 'to beat, overcome,' from Quechua, as in "Lo *huaripampeó*" (Ugarte); *mamonear* (SD), from *mamona* 'chuck under the chin,' as in "dos jovencitos *mamonearon* a tu hijo" (Patín); *mapolear* (Col); *meterle a uno* (SD), as in "anoche *le metieron* a tu hermano con un garrote" (Patín); *mondar* (Col, Mex, Ant, Andalusia) 'to cleanse, trim, peal,' less common than *dar una monda,* as in *"mondé* al muchacho porque me faltó al respeto" (Cuba: C. Suárez); *sonar* and *hacer sonar* (Chile, Ec, Mex), as in "Cuidado con que te *suene";* *vetear* (Ec) from *veta* 'piece of string'; *poner en juicio* 'to bring a person to his senses,' usually applied to children; *ripiar* (Ant) 'to shred,' as in "entre los dos *ripiaron* a tu compañero" (Patín); general *pelar* 'to skin' (see Rosenblat, p. 308).

More elaborate metaphors are *calentarle la cotonía* (trouser material) *a uno* (Ven: Rosenblat, p. 308); *componerle* (or *regarle* or *quebrarle*) *los tabacos a uno* (Col), literally 'to fix (or water or break) someone's tobacco leaves,' figuratively meaning 'to fell someone's horse' and consequently 'to injure, to beat him'; *darle un baile a una persona* (Arg: Saubidet, p. 29) and *hacer bailar a uno* (Arg: Lafone Quevedo) 'to make a person dance' (cf. *bailado* 'fisticuff' in Bogotá slang, and popular French *danse* 'shower of blows,' Wagner, "Apuntaciones," p. 188); *encenderle la leva a uno* (Cuba) 'to set fire to someone's coat'; *matar los piojos,* literally 'to kill lice' means 'herir en la cabeza,' as in "El más engolosinao / Se me apió con un hachazo, / Se lo quité con le brazo, / De no, *me mata los piojos"* (Arg: *Martín Fierro,* I, vv. 1597–1600); *menear a uno el guarapo* (Ven, Cuba) 'to stir someone's cane juice'; *pelar la cola* (Arg) 'to skin the tail'; *volver charqui a una persona* (Peru) 'to make jerk beef of someone,' etc.

Standard *bofetada* or *bofetón* 'slap' has many popular synonyms: *capirotazo, capón* and *coscorrón* 'fillip on the head,' *chuleta* 'chop,' *galleta* 'biscuit,' *guantada* or *guantazo* 'blow with a glove,' *hostia* 'host' (wafer), *mamporro, mojicón, morrada* 'blow on nose or mouth,' *sopapo, soplamocos* 'blow on the nose,' *torta* 'round cake,' *tortazo,* and others.

Spanish America has many more or less local congeners. Among these are Argentinian *bife* 'beefsteak,' which perhaps by phonetic association recalls *bofetada* and, like the semantically analogous *chuleta* 'chop,' compares the flat open hand to a flat piece of meat of about the same size. Examples: "Entonces Jacques ... comenzó lisa y llanamente a hacer llover sobre Corrales una granizada de trompadas, *bifes,* reveses ..." (Miguel Cané, *Juvenilia,* 1939, p. 75); "Y ahí no más me le acomodó *el bife*" (Lynch, p. 357). Other popular synonyms current in Argentina indicate some kind of food, vegetable, and the like, perhaps vaguely recalling in shape the type of blow administered (with the open hand, with closed fist, on the mouth, on the head). The idea of a slap may suggest feeding, or a color may indicate that of the resulting bruise: *bollo* 'roll'; *castaña* 'chestnut' or *castañazo* (cf. popular French *marron* 'chestnut' with the same meaning); *miqueta,* from Italian *miccheta* 'long loaf of bread'; *piña* 'pineapple.'

Among other expressions are:

bicoca (Chile, Bol) 'cap, bonnet' (from std. *bicoquete* or *bicoquín* 'cap with ear flaps') which means 'rap or fillip on the head' (fam. std. *coca* and *capirotazo*); *biaba,* from Piedmontese *biava* 'beating,' as in "Te voy a dar una *biaba* que te vas a acordar por mucho tiempo" (Forgione, p. 63), deriv. *biabar.*

cachimbazo (CA), from *cachimbo* or *cachimba* '(tobacco) pipe'; *cachucha* (Chile) 'cap' may mean both 'slap' and 'fillip,' so that both *bicoca* and *cachucha* may be considered double permutations indicating (1) receptacle for content ('cap' or 'bonnet' for 'head') and (2) name of a place for the act of striking it; *cantazo* (Col, Ant) 'blow with a strap, belt, rope,' as in "a ese muchacho le hacen falta dos o tres *cantazos*" (Patín); *catorrazo* (Mex), less frequently *cato, catorro* and original Spanish *cate* of disputed origin (see Corominas); *cocacho* 'rap on the head' may become *coscacho* (Arg, Chile, Ec, Peru), probably by analogy with its standard synonym *coscorrón,* deriv. *coscachear; combo* (Chile, Peru) 'sledge hammer' (a permutation of instrument for action), as in "cuando friega [= molesta] una suegra, ya sabes que muere a *combos*" (Malbrán, p. 11), "me escupí la mano y le enrielé un *combo* etrás e loreja" (Del Campo, p. 24), "un *combo* en la oreja" (Corrales, p. 59); *cuesco* (Col, Mex) for *coscorrón.*

chirlazo (Arg, Chile, Ec), based on standard *chirlo* 'facial gash, wound, scar') and 'blow with index and middle finger on hand or forearm,' deriv. *chirlar, chirlear; chope* (Mapuche) 'shovel' and *chopazo* (Chile).

gasnatón (Col, CA, Mex), standard *gaznatada* 'blow on the *gaznate* [neck, throat]' (cf. std. *pescozón* from *pescuezo* 'neck'), but generalized to *puñada* 'fisticuff, blow (in general),' as in "Por faltarme al respecto le tuve que dar sus *gasnatones*" (Acuña); *gualetazo* (Chile), from *aleta* 'fin'; *guamazo* 'fisticuff' (Ven, CA, Mex), as in "Los rijosos se dieron de *guamazos*" (Mex: Velasco); *guante* (Chile) 'glove' > 'cat-o'-nine-tails' > 'blow on the hand' as punishment, a permutation of instrument for action, as in "Te doy una docena de *guantes*" (Román), deriv. *guantada,* and *guantonear* (Arg: Vidal, p. 161) from *guantón* 'slap'; *güizarazo* (CR) 'fillip,' blow on the head given with the nail of the middle finger snapped from the ball of the thumb.

huaracazo (Peru), from *huaraca* 'cord.'

láminas (Chile) 'engravings, prints,' referring to the imprints left on the face by slapping (Vicuña); *lapo* (Arg, Chile, Peru, Mex) 'blow with the fist,' from standard *lapo* 'blow with a stick, cane, belt, etc.,' as in "Le di cuatro *lapos*" (Peru: Ugarte).

ñeco (Ec) 'blow with the knuckles.'

quenque (Peru), as in "largándole al suelo de un *quenque*" (Corrales, p. 60); *quiño* (Peru), as in "Lo arrojaron al suelo de un solo *quiño*" (Ugarte).

seco (RP, Chile, Peru, Mex), as in "le mandé un *seco*" (Peru: Corrales, p. 60).

tabaco (Mex, Cuba), perhaps from the color of the resulting bruise or from the shape of a tobacco leaf; *tapazo* (Peru, Ec), from *tapa* 'lid' (cf. fam. std. *tapaboca* 'slap on the mouth'), as in "A Ricardo le dieron un buen *tapazo,* por grosero" (Cornejo); *tatequieto* (Chile) = *estáte quieto* 'be still,' as in "te voy a dar un *tatequieto*"; *viaje* (SD), as in "le dió a su contrario un *viaje* en el ojo derecho" (Patín).

The gestures for beating, used either alone or accompanying some verbal expression, vary considerably. The two chief gestures, however, are (1) raising and extending the clenched fist, a gesture used in all parts of the world; (2) moving the open hand, palm up, with several lateral wrist strokes from right to left, slightly downward and inward, usually at the chin level (see fig. 27).

MISCELLANEOUS

Harsh *despedir* 'to discharge, turn away' is attenuated in *darle a uno las gracias* 'to thank someone'; *mandar cambiar* (or *mudar*) *a uno* (Chile, Ec, Peru), as in *"Mandé mudarse de aquí a mi sirviente,"* "Mi amo *mandó mudarme"* (Román); *bolear* 'to blackball' (rather general); *darle su pasaporte a uno,* as in "A la sirvienta hay que *darle su pasaporte";* slang *darle el espiante a uno* (Arg, where *espiantar* < Italian *spiantare* means colloquially 'to go away, flee,' and *espiante* means 'flight, departure'), as in "Su novia *le dió el espiante"* (Brown, p. 82), corresponding here to standard *darle calabazas* 'to jilt, give the gate to'; *darle galleta* (Col: *"Le dieron galleta* a Federico, y eso que llevaba diez años trabajando en esa oficina," Tobón), and *galletear* (RP: "A Fulano lo *galletearon,"* Garzón), from a standard maritime expression (ironical) *colgar la galleta* ('wine bottle, drinking vessel') 'to deprive a sailor of his post'; *darle ayotes a uno* (Guat) 'to jilt,' in which *ayote* is a euphemistic borrowing from Aztec meaning 'squash'; *cortarle el rabo a uno* (CR) 'to cut off someone's tail,' as in *"Me cortaron el rabo"* 'I was fired' and "Mi novia *me cortó el rabo"* 'My girl friend gave me my walking papers' (Brown, p. 91); *desgomar* (SD) 'to ungum,' as in "Ayer *desgomaron* a varios empleados" (Patín); *volar* (SD) 'to blow up, explode,' as in "Ayer *volaron* a siete empleados de instrucción pública" (Patín); *raspar* (Ven: Rosenblat, p. 69), and *cortarle el cambur,* of a public officer (*cambur* 'banana' > 'public office').

Being out of work or loafing is often *medir* (or *aplanar*) *calles* 'to measure (*or* flatten) streets,' deriv. *aplanacalles* or *aplanador de calles* 'loafer' (cf. fam. std. *azotacalles*); *andar desempedrando las calles* (Ven) 'to unpave the streets'; *andar de florcita* (RP, Chile, Bol); *estar de ñango* (Col: Tobón), in which *ñango* refers to the 'coccyx' or end of the vertebral column, 'to be sitting down'; *hacer San Lunes* means 'not to work on Mondays.'

Standard *casa de vecindad* 'tenement house,' having come into bad odor, was replaced in many regions (RP, Chile, Bol, Peru) by *conventillo* 'little monastery,' each religious occupying a cell being equated to each family supposedly occupying a room or apartment, as in "Alquiló un cuartito en un *conventillo* de la calle de Rivadavia" (Arg: ap. Malaret, *Bol. fil.*). But *conventillo,* in turn, has lost its repute, and now a new euphemism, French borrowing *cité,* currently designates a 'tenement' or 'apartment house' (Chile). A building of larger dimensions and greater elegance is termed *casa de departamentos* (Arg). The Argentinian playwright Florencio Chiarello gives to his play *Casa de departamentos* (1939) the subtitle *Conventillo de cuello duro* 'stiff-collar tenement house.' Perhaps together with *cité* came *locatario* and *locador* (from French *locataire, locateur*) for old-fashioned *inquilino* or *arrendatario;* deriv. *conventillero* means 'gossipy.' The older but now lowly *casa de huéspedes* 'boardinghouse' has yielded to standard *pensión* (from French); *casa de asistencia* or merely *asistencia* (Col, Mex), deriv. *asistente,-a* 'boardinghouse keeper' ("Doña María está ahora de *asistenta,"* Santamaría); *casa residencial* (Chile); in some areas (N Mex, Tex, Cuba, PR) *bórdin,* a shortening of 'boardinghouse,' deriv. *bordante* 'boarder' and *bordinguero,-a* 'boardinghouse keeper.'

Standard transitive *no aprobar* (*desaprobar, reprobar, suspender, dar calabazas*) 'to fail, (slang) to flunk' in an examination, always a humiliating occurrence, finds mitigation in many local terms (most of them slang), among them: *aplazar* 'to postpone,' analogous to standard *suspender* 'to suspend, postpone,' meaning 'to postpone the (re)examination to a later date'; *bochar* (Arg) 'to strike with a bowl [*bocha*]' in the game of bowling; *bolear* (Chile, Peru, Col, Ven, Pan), from *bola* 'ball,' cf. 'to blackball,' that is, 'to vote against' as by putting a black ball into the ballot box; *bombear* (Urug); *colear* (Chile) 'to fell a bull by pulling its tail'; *colgar* (Nic) 'to hang'; *corchar* (Col) 'to cork' and 'to show up someone's ignorance'; *cortar* (SD) 'to cut,' as in "lo *cortaron* en física" (Patín); *echar en banda* (SD), as in "le *echaron en banda* la botánica" (Patín); *jalar* (Peru) 'to pull, drag,' as in "Me *jalaron* en álgebra" (Ugarte); *liquidar* (general); *partir* (esp. Chile, Col) 'to split,' as in "Mira, Pedro, que si continúas tan desaplicado en tus estudios te van a *partir"* (Acuña); *pelar* (Pan) 'to skin' (*BAAL,* XX, 482); *quebrar* (Ven) 'to break'; *rajar* (esp. Chile, Col) 'to split,' as in *"Rajaron* a Enrique en aritmética" (Román), "El profesor *rajó* a diez alumnos de matemáticas y tan sólo aprobó a dos" (Acuña); *raspar* (Ven) 'to erase, scrape,' as in "lo *rasparon* en química"; *tirar* (Peru) 'to throw (away)'; *totear* (Col) 'to burst, explode,' as in "Si no dedico todo el día a preparar el examen de álgebra mañana me pueden *totear"* and "Alfonso resultó *totiado* en química" (Acuña); *tronar* (Mex) 'to thunder' and locally 'to kill, execute by shooting,' as in "A Juan lo *tronaron* en álgebra" (Suárez, p. 141). Cf. peninsular slang *catear, escabechar, cargar,* and *cepillar,* as in "Me *catearon* en álgebra."

Among other euphemisms are:

aburrición (Ec, Col, PR, SD), for standard *aburrimiento* 'annoyance, boredom' and now meaning *antipatía, odio* 'dislike, hatred,' as in "le tengo *aburrición* a esa persona" (Malaret), a kind of euphemistic litotes with possible interference of *aborrecer* 'to abhor'; *alentado* (Chile) 'encouraged,' for *audaz, fresco* 'bold, fresh,' as in "Fulano es bien *alentado,*" said of a check forger or party crasher and the like (Yrarrázaval); *apretado* (Mex) 'close, dense,' for *presumido* 'conceited, presumptuous'; *articular* (Chile) 'to articulate' may mean *disputar, altercar.*

blata (Chile), the scientific term for *cucaracha; brisa* (N Col) 'breeze,' for the 'strong north wind' that blows from December to March.

capitana (cant, Mex: Wagner, "Mex. Rot.") for *la pena capital* 'capital punishment'; *carilimpio* (Pan) 'clean-faced,' for *desvergonzado* 'shameless'; *cariñosa* (Pan) 'affectionate' replaces *sarna* or *roña* 'itch, mange'; *confite* 'round candy,' for 'bullet,' as in "[telegram] bajando cabeza no fuera caerme *confite*" (Peru: Corrales, p. 76).

chocolate (*chocolata,* Arg: Selva, *BAAL,* p. 10), for *sangre* 'blood,' as in "No me digas nada, porque puedo sacarte el *chocolate*—dice un muchacho a otro" (Ec: Cornejo), deriv. *chocolatera* (Ec) 'chocolate pot' for *nariz* 'nose,' as in "Si continúas molestándome, te rompo la *chocolatera*" (*ibid.*).

de respeto (Col) 'respectable,' for *terrible,* as in "Juan es *de respeto*" (Tobón).

edificante (Chile) 'edifying,' an ironic euphemism for *escandaloso* (*proceso edificante*), for *deshonesto* (*conducta deshonesta*); *emponchado* (RP) 'wrapped in a poncho' may mean 'astute, hypocritical'; *enterado* (Chile) 'upright, firm' may mean *orgulloso* 'proud'; *estar* or *quedar en evidencia* removes the sting from *estar* or *quedar en ridículo,* a situation Spanish-speaking people regard as humiliating; *este pues* (Ec) replaces deprecatory adjectives, as in "¡Vea que don Sofronio es bien *este pues!*" (Toscano, p. 183).

flojo (CA) 'loose, weak, lazy,' for *cobarde* 'coward.'

gamín (Col), for *golfillo* 'street urchin,' a French borrowing.

homenaje (Chile) 'homage,' for *don* 'gift,' as in "Me hizo *homenaje* de un precioso libro" (Medina).

inconveniente (Col) 'inconvenience,' for *disgusto, riña* 'annoyance, fight.'

lámina (Ec, Col) 'engraving, picture,' representing an ideal, is an ironic euphemism for *bribón* 'scoundrel' (cf. std. *tipo* 'type, pattern' > 'fellow, guy').

llamarse (Mex) 'to back out, not to keep one's word' (corresponding to popular *rajarse*), deriv. *llamón* 'coward.'

maleta 'suitcase,' general for *malo* in the sense of 'dull, stupid' (as in Spain), for *despreciable* (CA), for *travieso* (PR), for *perverso* (Mex); *maleza* (Chile) 'underbrush, weeds,' for *piojos* 'lice,' for *pus* (Arg); *ma(n)ganzón* (Peru, Ec, Col, CA, Ant), for *holgazán, perezoso* 'lazy,' deriv. *magancear* and *maganzonear* (Col), from standard *mangón* and *mangonear; mandioca* (Peru), for *revólver,* as in "Se puso pálido de ira y su primer impulso fué sacar la *mandioca*" (Corrales, p. 61); *mojarra* (the name of a sea fish), for *mojado* 'wetback,' a laborer who crosses the Rio Grande and illegally enters the United States.

niño contemplado (Antioquia, Col), for *niño consentido* 'spoiled child.'

ocuparse (Col), for *murmurar* 'to gossip'; *oído* 'sense of hearing, inner ear,' for *oreja* '(outer) ear,' perhaps because of the association with the long ears of a jackass, as in "hablan y ríen con la boca llena o se rascán *los oídos* y las piernas" (Col: Rendón, p. 68), and also for *oreja* in its sense of 'handle' (Col: Tobón); *orfelinato* (Col), for *orfanato* 'orphanage.'

palabrear (Chile), for *insultar,* deriv. *palabrudo* for *malhablado* 'foul-mouthed'; *peseta* (Cuba), for *pesado* 'bore,' as in "No seas *peseta*" and "Fulano es un *peseta*" (C. Suárez); *píonono* 'Pius IX,' for *piojo* (cant, Arg); *prosa* (Chile), for *altanería* 'arrogance,' as in "Don F. se gasta una *prosa* al dirigirse a sus empleados" (Yrarrázaval).

resbaloso (Mex) 'slippery,' for *desvergonzado* 'shameless.'

simple (Col), for *soso* 'tasteless, insipid,' as in "sopa *simple*" (Obando).

tomar 'to take,' for *beber* 'to drink,' since *beber* is by many persons considered applicable only to animals.

Often real or fictitious proper names are colloquially used when one or more syllables recall the word to be avoided, sometimes merely for humorous effect. The following are among those recorded for Mexico (ap. Wagner): *venga por Acámbaro* (the name of a place in Guanajuato) for *venga por acá; Cayetano la botica* for *cállate la boca; no es para Miguelito* for *no es para mí; mi Querétaro* (capital of the state of Querétaro) for *mi querido; Tampico* (the name of a river port) for *tampoco; Zacatecas* (the name of the capital of the state of Zacatecas) for *sácate de aquí.* Elsewhere are heard *Calletano* or *Cayetano* (general) for *callado; estar en Calleuque* (the name of a town in Chile) for *estar callado* (Rabanales, "Recursos," p. 214), and *Calleuque es muy buen lugar,* which one says when one recommends discretion or silence; *Daniel* for *dado, danieles* (Ven) for *dados* 'dice'; *dar la Covadonga* (the name of a village in the province of Oviedo, Spain, where Pelayo routed the Moors in the year 718, marking the beginning of the reconquest) for standard *dar coba* 'to flatter'; *Maluenda* for *malo; Mateo* for *mate* (Arg), as in "¿Dónde estás, don *Mateo,* que no te veo?", and for 'boner, one who studies hard' (Chile) from *mate* 'head' (Rabanales, "Recursos," p. 213); *Miranda* (Chile) for *mirón* 'bystander, rubberneck'; *Nicomedes* (Salta, Arg), recalling *no comer,* meaning a person who has not eaten, as in "¿Qué te pasa? —Es que estoy *Nicomedes"* (Solá, p. 202); *Porfirio* for *porfiado* 'obstinate' (Rabanales, *ibid.*); *Poblete* for *pobre; Riquelme* for *rico,* etc.

The following metaphors have been selected at random from the group corresponding to the division containing euphemisms of delicacy or politeness, in which the speaker attempts to avoid wounding either his interlocutor's feelings or his own (intonation plays an important role in such euphemisms): *bajar la prima* 'to lower the first string (of a musical instrument)' may mean, particularly in Argentina, 'to moderate one's language' and *subir la prima* 'to raise the string' may mean 'to use harsh sarcastic words,' as in "—Mira, Natalia ... respetá a la polecía ... y no *subás la prima"* (*Fray Mocho,* ap. Garzón); *cantarle el magnificat* (popular *la magnífica*) *a uno* (Col: Restrepo) is an ironical euphemism for *decirle cuántas son cinco* 'to tell a person off,' referring to the song of thanksgiving *magnificat anima mea Dominum* 'my soul doth magnify the Lord,' ascribed to the Virgin Mary (Luke 1:46–55) and later incorporated into the service of vespers; *hacer uno la chica* (Chile), in which *chica* is an ironic euphemism for *grande,* and the omitted noun equates *acción* or *avería* 'damage, harm,' the whole expression meaning 'to cause much damage,' 'to commit a crime,' etc. (Román); general *planchar* (or *aplanchar*) *el asiento* 'to iron out the seat,' sometimes shortened to *planchar* or expanded to *hacer oficio de planchadora* (Chile), replaces standard *comer pavo* (lit. 'to eat turkey') meaning 'to be a wallflower' at a dance, etc.; *sacarse el clavo* (Arg, Col) 'to pull out the nail' may replace *vengarse* 'to take revenge, get even'; *tocar el piano* (Tex) 'to play the piano,' may, because of a similarity of appearance, replace indelicate *tomar las huellas digitales* 'to take fingerprints' (elsewhere *tocar el piano* may replace *robar*); though deceptive cognate *tráfico* 'commerce, trade' has with many speakers replaced *tránsito* in the latter's true meaning of 'the passing of vehicles and persons in a city street,' some speakers prefer standard *tránsito* partly because *tráfico* is often too closely associated with illegal trading (narcotics, white slavery, etc.).

VI DECENCY: THE BODY

Under euphemisms of decency are classified those indicating certain parts of the body and various physiological and sexual functions. Unlike some taboos (those for death, for instance, that are practically universal) the so-called taboos of decency may vary according to the culture and customs of any given linguistic community. Each period has its specific taboos, and the people of each period wonder at the freedom of speech of their predecessors. Words used freely in one period become in time so closely and immediately associated with the referent that they no longer serve as a screen through which the hearer assimilates the meaning gradually and painlessly instead of being rudely struck by it.

Words signifying certain parts of the body are in careful speech generally replaced by euphemisms. Having banned the nude, modern civilization bans also verbal expressions of it. Thus, *desnudo* 'naked, nude,' besides standard *desvestido* 'undressed,' familiar *en cueros* or *en pelota* (*piel* 'skin,' *pelar* 'to skin') 'in the skin,' may in colloquial American-Spanish become *encuerado* ("muchachos *encuerados,*" Mex, ap. Speratti, p. 164) and *empelotado* (as in Andalusia and other areas), or shorter *encuero* (or diminutive *encuerito*) and *empeloto* (Arg, Col), with corresponding verbs *encuerarse* and *empelotarse* (as in Andalusia, see Acalá Venceslada), as in "Para poderme reconocer el médico me hizo *empelotar*" (Col: Acuña), "Yo no *me empeloto* para dormir" (Cuba: C. Suárez), "*Encueraron* (*encuerar* is commoner in Cuba than *empelotar*) al niño" and "me *encuerariá* los días calurosos" (*ibid.*). Among more local expressions for *desnudo* are *a espuela limpia* (SD), as in "se bañaron *a espuela limpia;* él duerme *a espuela limpia"* (Patín); ironic *estar a rey* (rural PR), as in "No me quea una gallina. Mi marío la ja vendío toas pa jartarse de romo (= ron, aguardiente). Y los nenes ... *'stán arrei"* (Laguerre, *Solar Montoya,* ap. Álvarez Nazario, p. 119); *en almendra* (Col: Cadavid); *en bolo* or *en bola* (Col), *en bolas* (RP); *pelucho* and *pilucho* (Chile); (*andar*) *pila* (NW Arg, Bol); *rabón* (Chile).

Many of the euphemisms for *desnudo* are borrowings, which for the speaker are not surcharged with the same disagreeable associations as the corresponding term in his native tongue. Among them are *biche* or *viche* (NW Mex) from the Indian name of a leguminous plant; *cala* and deriv. *calato* (Chile, Peru, Ec) from Quechua *kala* 'nude,' deriv. *encalatarse* and *calatearse* (or *ponerse calato*) = *desnudarse, calatería = desnudez,* as in "El calor nos invita a andar *calatos"* (Peru: Corrales, p. 249), *"Me* voy a *poner calato"* (*ibid.,* p. 117), *"Nos encalatamos* y ... nos agarramos a una tanda de palos" (*ibid.,* p. 182); *chirisiqui* (highland Ec) from Quechua *chiri* 'cold' and *siqui* 'posterior' (Cornejo, p. 329); Latin *in puribus naturalibus* (often shortened to *in puribus*) and *in albis* have given rise to facetious *in Adamis* (Ec) and have influenced *in viringuis* (Cuenca, Ec: Toscano, p. 328) from *viringo* (Ec, Col) or *veringo* (Col), as in "Había visto negritos *semiviringos* como él, pero también los había visto mejor vestidos" (A. Ortiz, p. 12), deriv. *veringuearse = desnudarse, en virote; en* (or *a la*) *pampa* (Chile); *llucho* (Ec) 'naked' (also 'poor'), as in "¿Así *llucho* tuviste valor de exhibirte?" (García Muñoz, p. 47).

BODILY ODORS

Bodily odors generally find euphemistic expression in careful speech. Thus, standard *maloliente, hediondo* and *fétido* 'foul-smelling, stinking' often yield to *fuerte* 'strong.' Noun *fortaleza* 'strength' may be heard (especially Chile, Mex) for standard *mal olor, hedor, hediondez* and the like. In fact, *fortaleza,* having in turn worn off its euphemistic cushioning through constant use, has found refuge in its antiquated synonym *fortitud,* at least on one occasion, according to the story related by Román: "Como en Chile tiene *fortaleza* este significado (*hedor*), una señora muy pulcra, al hablar de los dones del Espíritu Santo, llamaba el de fortaleza, don de *fortitud,* prefiriendo así pasar por arcaísta antes que por mal educada."

Other popular euphemistic terms relating to 'bad odor' are:

abajarse (PR) 'to sink,' as in "El pescado *se abajó*" (Malaret), cf. *bajo* (SD), as in "en este sitio hay un *bajo* insoportable" (Patín); *apedrear* 'to stone' > 'to smell' (Mex), as in "A X le *apedrea* la boca" (Velasco), cf. *golpe* 'blow' > 'stench' (cant, Mex).

bufarle el cacle ('sandal') *a uno* (Mex) 'to have smelly feet.'

cantar (Cuba) 'to sing,' as in "Ese pescado *canta*" and "A fulano le *cantan* los pies" (C. Suárez); noun *catinga* (RP, Chile, Bol), from Guaraní *catingá* 'stench' applied to plants, animals, and human beings, especially Indians and Negroes, deriv. *catingoso* and *catingudo*.

chucha (Col) 'armpit sweat' from *chucha* 'foul-smelling fox' (Tascón).

dentina (Pan) 'stench' (std. *hedentina*).

estocada (Guat) 'stab, thrust,' defined as 'mal aliento de una persona, el cual se siente al hablar con ella,' as in "Celmira da unas *estocadas* tan certeras que nadie se libra de ellas" (Sandoval).

grajo (Peru, Col, Ant), similar in meaning to *catinga,* deriv. *grajiento; panteras rugientes* 'roaring panthers' > 'foul-smelling feet' (cant, Mex: Rod).

patada and *patrulla* (*ibid.*)*; patinar* (Chile) 'to skate,' having phonetic association with *pata* 'paw, foot,' has acquired the meaning 'hederle los pies a uno,' that is, 'to have foul-smelling feet'; *pesuña* or *pezuña* (Peru, Ec) 'toe, hoof' may mean 'foul-smelling and perspiring feet,' as in "Báñate y cúrate esa *pesuña* ... que te vuelve intolerable" (Cornejo), deriv. *pesuñento* or *pezuñento,* as in "¡Vete de aquí *pesuñento* ... o lávate los pies!" (*ibid.*) and "esta niña dice que le es usted antipático y *pezuñento*" (Peru: Corrales, p. 66); *pécora* and *trepadora* (synonyms of *pezuña*), but *pécora* is immediately noticeable and *trepadora* 'creeps up' gradually (Peru: Corrales, p. 272); variants *pecuaca* and *pecueca* (Col, Ven) have the same meaning as *pesuña,* deriv. *pecueco,* as in "¡Quítate de aquí, indio *pecueco!*" (Acuña); *pitarle la boca a uno* (PR), said of a person whose breath smells, from *pitar* 'to whistle, hiss.'

respetarse (jocose, SD) 'to respect oneself,' ironical, as in "esa joven *se respeta*" (Patín).

violín (Ven) euphemizes 'foul-smelling mouth,' as "fulano tiene *violín*" for "le hiede la boca" (Malaret), (cf. *cantar* above).

UNDERWEAR

Articles of clothing covering certain parts of the body are frequently euphemized in polite speech, particularly underwear. Thus, *cariocos* (Col) may replace *calzones de mujer* (Tobón) 'women's drawers'; *calcinaguas* (Col) is a combination of *calzones* and *enaguas* 'underskirt' for *pantalón de mujer; combinación* may be 'blouse and drawers' or 'blouse and underskirt' (PR) or 'shirt, drawers, and girdle' (Peru); *franela* (Col) 'flannel' or *interior* may replace *camiseta* 'undershirt'; *interior* (Col) may replace cruder *calzoncillos* 'drawers'; *pantaloncillo* (PR) for *calzoncillos* 'drawers'; *panti* (Pan), from English 'panties'; standard *sostén* 'supporter' for 'brassière' often becomes *sutién* (Arg), Hispanization of French *soutien,* and *corpiño* (Arg) 'bodice'; *tijeras* 'shears' and *tijerales* 'gable frame' may mean 'trousers' (Chilean slang), and in familiar speech *tijeral* may mean also *pierna* 'leg,' as in "cayó con los *tijerales* abiertos" (Román).

BELLY

Coming to the body itself, we find standard *vientre* or *barriga* (of the same root as *barril* 'barrel, cask') almost as unsavory as English 'belly.' Some of the substitutes stem from native Indian tongues. Undoubtedly a major factor in the adoption of words of this nature is the influence of Indian nurses who in chattering with their nurslings employed their native terms, to them infinitely more expressive. From Mapuche comes *guata* or *huata* (Arg, Chile, Bol, Peru: "tengo una cicatriz en la *guata,"* Castro, p. 281; "proceder a mi autopsia, abriéndome *la huata* de par en par," Corrales, p. 231); deriv. *guatón* 'big-bellied' (std. *barrigón, barrigudo*), *guatitas* 'tripe' (std. *mondongo, tripas, callos*) as in the Chilean street vendor's cry "¡Patitas y *guatitas!"* (or *"¡Guatitas* y patitas!*), guatero* 'vendor of *guatitas'; echar guata* means *engordar* 'to put on weight, get stout,' and figuratively 'to get rich.' From Mapuche has come also *contri* or *contre* or *conti* ('gizzard'; std. *molleja*), as in "acabo de quemarme *el contre* diuna chupá [= de una chupada] que leí [= le dí] a este mate" (Chile: Del Campo, p. 40), "Emprencipiamos una noche a acarriar baldás [= baldadas, from *balde* 'bucket') diagua, y había que verlas [las chiquillas] mojaítas hasta *el contre"* (*ibid.,* p. 56), with figurative *hasta el contri* 'to the innermost recess.' From Aztec *petlacalli* 'wicker basket' has come *petaca* 'box, trunk,' deriv. *petacón, petacudo* (Col) = *barrigón, barrigudo;* in Honduras *petaca* may mean, in slang, "el vientre de las mujeres preñadas cuando están en meses mayores" (Membreño). From Italian are (now rare) *busarda* (Arg: Genoese *buzza,* Italian *buzzo*), and *buseca* (Milanese *busecca*) 'entrails,' as in "Con tanto pimentón en la *buseca*" (Arg: Vacarezza, *El fondín de la alegría,* 1930, ap. A. Castro, p. 156).

Other popular words current for *barriga,* from various sources, are *caja del pan* (or *panadera*) 'breadbox,' as in "un cabezazo en la *caja del pan*" (Peru: Corrales, p. 59); *lipa* (Ven), as in "El que va a tener la *lipa* grande, aunque lo fajen chiquito" (Alvarado), deriv. *lipón* = *barrigón; pipa* (general) 'cask,' deriv. *pipón, pipudo; protocolo* (Nic), suggesting the referent through phonetic association: *pro-* 'before,' and perhaps *culo* 'buttocks'; general *tonel* 'barrel' and *timba* (CA, Mex, Ant), as in "era conocido con el nombre de Chico *Tonel,* debido a la enorme *timba* que tenía" (Guat: Sandoval), deriv. *timbón, timbuco,* and *timbudo* (Guat).

As substitutes for *ombligo* 'navel,' borrowings are frequent, again in large part through the influence of Indian nurses. Among them are *pupo* (N Arg, Chile, Ec, Peru) and *puputi* (Arequipa, Peru), from Quechua *pupu,* deriv. *pupulo* (Salta, Arg) 'deep-naveled person'; *maruto* (Ven); *mushush* (Salv); *mush* (Guat); jocose *mote* (Col), from Quechua *mutti* 'cooked corn,' probably because the navel looks somewhat like a boiled grain of corn, deriv. *motoso* 'large-naveled child'; *tuch* (Yucatán, Mex), from Maya, as in "no se le ha caído el *tuch* al niño" (Santamaría).

BREASTS

Original *tetas* (now restricted by some speakers to animals) 'teats' and *pechos* 'breasts' are, in standard speech, euphemistically replaced by *senos.* Noun *seno* (< Latin *sinus,* English *sinus*) means 'sinus, cavity' including the 'thoracic cavity'; plural *senos* has come to mean 'pechos' perhaps through the euphemistic influence of French *seins;* but *seno* 'space between chest and dress' may, by a permutation of proximity, have come to mean '*pecho*' (cf. English *bosom*). Because of the phonetic association with *senos,* standard *sien* 'temple,' especially in America, is euphemistically referred to as *sentido* 'sense,' as in "le pegó en el *sentido*" (Chile: Oroz, "Metáforas," p. 93), "Me duele mucho el *sentido* derecho," and "El dolor de los *sentidos* se cura con aspirina" (Gaut: Sandoval). In America a

widespread euphemism for *pecho* is *chiche* or *chichi* (variant *chicha,* CA),
perhaps an apocopation of Aztec *chichihualli* 'pecho, teta' (Robelo) or
from verb *chichi* 'to suck,' deriv. *chichigua* 'nurse,' cf. euphemistic distortions *chichornias* and *chimeneas* (cant, Mex: Rod, p. 135); elsewhere perhaps from Quechua *chucho* 'nipple,' though similar forms in parts of Spain
may show that all are onomatopoetic. Example: "Las *chichiguas* ... dando
la *chiche* a los niños" (Guat: *Mosaico,* p. 341). On the coast of Colombia
niple (< English 'nipple') designates a small tube resembling a *pezón*
'nipple' (Revollo). In Jalisco (Mex) *petacas* (< Aztec *petlacalli* 'wicker
basket') may mean *pechos.*

Names of certain fruits, because of a similarity of shape, are often used
facetiously, particularly among men, as euphemisms for *pechos.* Among
them are *chirimoyas* and *guanábanas,* tropical fruits; *limones* 'lemons';
membrillos 'quinces'; *manzanas* 'apples,' familiarly among women, as in
"¡No se te vayan a caer *lah manzana!*—le dice una mujer a otra, cuando
va corriendo o está saltando" (Chile: Rabanales, p. 160); general *naranjas*
(*chinas,* Cuba, PR) and *peras; tecomates* (Guat) 'cone-shaped calabash
bottles,' with phonetic association of *tetas* (Sandoval, II, 238).

Among other popular designations are *agarraderas* (Guat) 'handles; influence'; *alforjas* (Nic) 'saddlebags'; *educación* (cant, Mex), as in "esa
chamaca tiene buena *educación"; frente* (PR) 'front,' as in "ella tiene buen
frente"; ovillos de hilo (Peru) 'balls of yarn,' especially in referring to young
girls, as in "Ya están con los *ovillos de hilo"; maceteros* 'flower-pot
stands,' *pirámides, porongos* 'milk cans,' and *repisa* 'shelf' (cant, Peru:
Bonilla Amado); *parachoques* (Peru) '(automobile) bumpers,' as also in
Portuguese, see Kröll, "Termes," p. 28 (cf. 'headlights'); *teteras* (Bol,
Peru) 'teapots,' *tetuanes* and *totorretas* (cant, Peru), euphemistic in that
some of the sounds recall the referent but with shifted stress.

POSTERIOR

We find a legion of euphemisms for familiar standard *nalgas* 'backside,
buttocks' and vulgar *culo* 'anus' (std. *ano* extended to mean also 'nalgas,'
neither of these, however, being quite so shunned as the English equivalent 'arse.' Among general synonyms are *asentaderas,* from *asentar* 'to seat,
sit down' and suffix *-dero,-a* expressing fitness to perform the action of the
verb; *caderas* 'hips'; *mapamundi* 'map of the world'; *nalgatorio,* deriv. of

nalga, acting euphemistically because of the removal of the original stress; *pompi; popa* 'poop, stern'; *posaderas,* from *posar* 'to sit down, repose'; *posteridad* 'posterity'; *rabel,* the name of a round musical instrument phonetically recalling *rabo* 'tail'; *rulé,* a Gipsy word; *salvohonor,* cf. such phrases as "en salva sea la parte," "la parte donde la espalda pierde su honesto nombre" (Beinhauer, p. 100); *compredón* among Oriental Hebrews, a corruption of *con perdón,* added whenever the original word was mentioned, English "pardon the expression"; *silla* 'seat'; *tabalario,* from *tabal* 'drum'; *tafanario* and *antifonario* 'antiphonal, anthem book'; *tras* and *trasero* 'hind(er)'; *trascorral* 'back courtyard,' *traspontín, trastorno.*

American Spanish offers an equally impressive list, which includes:

abeja (E Col: Tobón), deriv. *abejorriar = tocar las piernas a otra persona; albóndigas* (Nic) 'meat balls'; *aquello* (PR) 'that thing.'

balde (Nic) 'bucket'; *banco* (Nic) 'bench,' a permutation of container for content; *bombito* 'drum' and *pandero* 'tambourine' (Arg: *Filología,* III, 55); *botamais* (Nic: Valle) 'anus,' from *botar* 'to throw away' and *maíz* 'corn.'

cachetes 'fat cheeks' and *cojines* 'cushions' (Chile: Oroz, "Metáforas," p. 98); *cola* 'tail'; *común* (Mex), antiquated; *culantro* (Mex), retaining the initial sounds of *culo* and shifting the stress; *chiquito* (CA, Mex, Ant) 'anus.'

desafío (SD) 'challenge'; *el de atrás* (PR).

fondongo and *fondoque* (Cuba), from *fondo* 'bottom'; general *fundamento, fondillos* 'seat of trousers,' *fundillo; fuste* 'saddletree' (Ven, Pan, CA); *fundango, funfún* (Pan); *fuí* (jocose, SD) 'anus,' cf. "hubo una madre que llegó a prohibir a sus hijas que usaran en la conversación el pasado perfecto del verbo *ir*" (Lockward, p. 33).

hopo, with aspirated *h* and hence often spelled *jopo* 'bushy tail' (from Old French *hope,* mod. *houppe*), a permutation of proximity (Atlantic coast, Col: Revollo), perhaps an older peninsular usage.

joyete (PR), diminutive of *hoyo* 'hole'; *juanetes* 'hips' (Hond), from standard *juanete* 'bunion, prominent cheekbone.'

melón 'melon,' because of similarity of shape, as in "estoy de barriga en el horno con el *melón* afuera" (Peru: Corrales, p. 55); *nalgamentorio* (Col).

ojo 'eye' (std. *ojete* 'eyelet' may mean 'anus') as euphemistically used in compound *lameojos* or *lambeojos* (Ant) for vulgar *lameculos* 'flatterer, fawner, bootlicker,' and occasionally in *lambiocho* in which *ocho* phonetically recalls *ojo* with perhaps a still further facetious play on *siete, ocho,* etc.; *oribamba* (Cuba: Rodríguez, p. 436).

popó (Chile), euphemism among children for *poto* (see below), cf. German *Popo*.

siete (general), a euphemistic modification of standard *sieso* 'anus' (Latin *sessus* 'seat'), as in low 'hijo de la gran *siete*' (*siete* 'seven' means also 'rip' or 'tear,' because of its similar shape); *sisiflís* (Hond) and *sisirisco* (Mex), distortions of *sieso,* as in "en cuanto pasaba cercas de un nopal, se le fruncía el *cicirisco;* ansina a mí, en cuanto oyía hablar de guerra" (Anda, p. 47).

taburete (Nic) 'stool,' a permutation of container for content; *totó* (some parts of Chile and Peru), cf. *popó; trasandino* (Ec) 'transandean' phonetically recalls *trasero; traste* (Chile), as in the sayings "Para eso es el *traste,* para que se gaste" referring to a person who sits on the floor or who remains seated anywhere for a long time (Román).

Many of the Spanish-American euphemisms are borrowings (cf. English use of French *derrière*), mostly native Indian words originally introduced by Indian nurses. Among them are *callana* (Chile, Bol) 'a wide, earthen bowl,' from Quechua (Oroz, "Metáforas," p. 98); *canco* (Chile) from Mapuche *canco* 'water jug, flowerpot' and *canque* 'posterior,' as in "ella tiene un enorme *canco*" (Lenz), deriv. *cancona* and *cancu(d)a* 'large-hipped woman'; *cinco* (Mex) from Aztec *tzintli* 'posterior, anus,' as in "Si no me das la lección te doy doce azotes en el *cinco*" attributed to former schoolmasters (Robelo); *mataco* (Peru), presumably from some African tongue (Malaret); *ocote* or *ocoti* (NW Arg, Peru) 'anus,' from Quechua; *petacas* (Mex) from Aztec *petlacalli* 'wicker basket' (in turn from *petla* 'mat' and *calli* 'house'), deriv. *petacona* 'large-hipped woman' of whom one may say "para *petacas* las mías" (Frenk, p. 137) which is also the slogan of a luggage shop in Mexico city (playing on the double meaning of *petaca* 'suitcase, trunk' and 'posterior'); *upite* (Arg), from Quechua (?); *poto* and *potito* (Arg, Chile, Bol, Peru) from Mapuche *poto* 'anus' and by extension 'buttocks,' as in the proverb "el mal del tordo ('thrush'), las piernas flacas y el *poto* gordo," in which local *poto* has replaced *culo* of the original standard version, and standard "sana, sana, *culito* de rana, si no sanas hoy, sanarás mañana" (said to a child who has bumped himself and as one rubs the sore spot) becomes in Chile "sana, sana, *potito* de rana, si no sanas hoy, sanarás mañana" (Román). Furthermore, a certain sea anemone is called in Chile *poto de mar* because when irritated a central orifice emits a substance muddling the water, and then puckers up until the danger has disappeared. The place names *Potosí* and *Potojunco* (Peru) are double euphemisms for *nalgas:* the stress is removed from its original syllable, and the place name retards the process of identifying the referent. Because of similarity of shape *zapallo* (Chile), from Quechua *sapallu* '(a kind of) pumpkin,' may mean 'posterior,' deriv. *zapallón* and *zapallito,* as in *"¡zapallito* que te gahtay [= gastas]!" (Rabanales, p. 164).

Among humorous metaphors we cull *sentido común* 'common sense' (with phonetic interference of *sentar* 'to sit, seat') for *posterior,* as in "Y m'encajó tan tremenda patá en el *sentío común,* que casi me quebró la cola" (Chile: ap. Oroz, "Metáforas," p. 98).

SEX AND SEX ORGANS

In mentioning the sex of a person, many speakers avoid *hembra* 'female' because it refers also to animals, like *macho* 'male,' and they substitute *mujer* 'woman' or *varona* (from *varón* 'male') even for newborn babes, as in "Éstos eran dos muchachitos, *mujer y varón* ['girl and boy'] que no tenían mamá" (CR: María de Noguera, *Cuentos viejos,* 1938, p. 137), "En tantos años de casados tuvieron mucha familia, pero siempre *mujeres,* nunca un hombrecito" (Chile: A. Jarmillo, *La buenamoza y el toro,* 1951, p. 61), "Dos hijos, un varón y una *mujercita"* (Peru: Benvenutto, p. 81).

For the word *virgen* 'virgin' may be substituted the euphemistic phrase *como Dios manda* (Guat) 'as is fitting' (lit. 'as God commands'), as in "esa chica está *como Dios manda";* the word *niña* (SD: *BDH,* p. 220); the word *señorita* 'young lady,' as in "Fulana está *señorita"* (Col). (For Boyacá, Colombia, Tobón registers *señorita* as used by peasants in referring affectionately to the Holy Virgin.) Elsewhere, the word is popularly euphemized by *coco* (Ec: Cornejo) 'hymen' and by extension 'virgin,' as in "—¡Y es *coco,* jefe! ¡Virgen doncella!" (Cuadra, p. 174); *mate* (Chile) because of the opening in this small calabash used for drinking tea, as in "Ella le dijo que estaba *mate* y el tonto se la tragó [= creyó]" and maliciously referred to in the proverb "Mientras uno calienta el agua, el otro se toma *el mate*" (Rabanales, p. 178), further euphemized by the proper name *Matilde;* vulgar *cartucho,-a* (Chile, Peru), referring to either sex (as "¿Creíh qu'ese cabro [= joven] ehtá *cartucho?*," *ibid.*), said first of a male child because of the similarity of his foreskin to the flower of a plant called *cartucho* (*antirrhinum majus*)—from *cartucho* 'paper cornet' or 'cornucopia' (std. *cucurucho*)—and later applied analogically to females. Verb *desvirgar* 'to deflower' may be *arruinar* (general) 'to ruin'; *descartuchar* (Chile); *descorchar* 'to uncork' (Col: Cadavid); *hacer el mandado* (Col), which also means 'to steal' (Acuña); *pasar por las armas* (Guat) 'to execute by shooting' with the association of marginal meanings (*pasar* 'to pierce, penetrate,' *arma* 'weapon'), as in "esa *patojita* [= muchachita] ... ya *está* (o ya *fué*) *pasada por las armas*" (Sandoval); *romper el pomo* (cant, Peru: Bonilla Amado).

Words indicating genital organs are usually banned from polite speech, except in scientific language. When mention of them is necessary, recourse is had to such vague terms as *naturaleza* 'nature,' *partes* 'parts,' *pobreza* 'poverty,' *desnudez* 'nudity,' *sexo* 'sex,' *cosita* 'little thing' and the like. Popular speech, on the other hand, has a great number of metaphoric euphemisms (now mostly vulgar) usually based on some exaggerated resemblance of form.

Among colloquial peninsular substitutes for standard *pene, miembro viril,* and *verga* are *aparato* 'apparatus,' *badajo* 'bell clapper'; *berenjena,* the name of a cylindrical type of eggplant; *bolo* 'ninepin'; *caña* (*de pesca*) '(fishing) rod'; *cipote* 'club' (Besses, Corominas); *chorizo, longaniza,* and *morcilla,* names of sausages (hence, in some areas, for *chorizos* 'sausages' the euphemistic phrase *unos tras otros* is substituted, see Toro y Gisbert, p. 112, and Barreto, II, 20); *chorra; chuzo* 'pike'; *flauta* 'flute'; *hermano pequeño* 'little brother' (Besses); *nabo* 'turnip'; *palo* and *porra* 'club'; *pepino* 'cucumber'; *pera* 'pear'; *pijo, pija, picha, pichina,* from older onomatopoetic *pixa,* whence older *pinjante* 'pendant' is euphemistically replaced by French *pandantif; pilila; pito* 'whistle, fife tube'; *plátano* 'banana'; *polla* 'pullet, young hen' (see Beinhauer, p. 99).

Indecent but known in every Spanish-speaking country is *carajo,* of disputed origin (see Corominas), although its sexual meaning is less apparent in America. As an interjection, this offensive word has given rise to an interminable list of harmless euphemisms, phonetically deformed but retaining a sufficient number of the original sounds to make identification unmistakable. Among these are *canarios, canastos, cará* (SD), *caracoles, carachas, caraches, caracho, caraj, caramba, caray, cáspita, carifo, carijo* (rustic, Cuba: *"¡Carija!* y qué mala debe sel la muerte,"* Espinosa, p. 475), *barajo, barájoles, baramba(s)*, and *pispajo;* elliptical *ajo,* as *echar ajos* ("echaba chispas por los ojos y unos *ajotes* por la boca que retumbaban," Corrales, p. 63), or *echar ajos y cebollas* (play on *ajo* 'garlic') or *echar una ristra de ajos* ('string of garlic'), or simply *ajear* (Peru). One finds such vague allusions as "¡ni qué *carga de leña!";* *canijos* (lit. 'weak, infirm'), as in "Si no me equivoco, estos *ca ... nijos* son de los de nosotros" (Mex: Ángulo, p. 101); *capones,* as in "¡Adelante, *ca ... pones,* echen bala!" (*ibid.,* p. 35); sometimes written as *c ...* , as in "¿Vas a venir o no vas a venir? *¡C ... !"* (Arg: Lynch, p. 226); *carbón,* as in "Cual más, cual menos ... todo mundo un *car ... bón!"* (Mex: Anda, 77); *cáscara de ajo,* as in "¿Qué *cáscara de ajo* me importa?" (Cuba: ap. Rodríguez, p. 414).

Among additional substitutes found in popular American Spanish for *pene* are:

bicho or *bicha* (Ant; *bicha* for *culebra*), whence *bicho* in its standard meaning ('insect, animal') is avoided in favor of *insecto* or *animal; burundanga* (parts of Mex), cf. older *borondanga* and *morondanga* 'insignificant thing, hodgepodge' and *cosita.*

cabezón (PR) and *cabezona* (Nic) 'big-headed'; *camarón* (Veracruz, Mex) 'shrimp'; *cicuta* (Guat) 'hemlock'; *collofe* (Chile) from Mapuche *collofi* 'edible seaweed,' as in "¿No queríh ehte *collofe,* mejor? —le suele decir un muchacho a otro, cuando éste le pide alguna cosa" (Rabanales p. 161); *corneta* (Mex) 'horn, mushroom'; *la cosa* or *el chunche* or *el virote* (Nic) 'thing, trash, utensil, tool,' etc.; *cuca* (CA) '(a kind of) caterpillar.'

chaira (Yucatán) 'cylindrical steel for sharpening knives'; *chile* (Mex) 'red pepper,' whence *enchilada* 'coition'; *chilillo* (Nic) 'rope, whip'; *chimbo* (Col) from *chimbo* 'piece of meat' (?); *chincol* and *chincolito* (Chile), a kind of small bird (Lenz); *chivo* (cant, Mex) 'he-goat'; *choclo* (Chile) 'ear of corn,' as in "¿Cómo te veríay [= verías] con ehte *choclito?"* and "ir a pelar *choclos"* 'to go to husk corn' meaning 'to go to a brothel' (Rabanales, p. 216); *choto* or *chota* (Arg) 'sucking kid'; *chuto* (Arg, Bol) 'short tail.'

daga (PR) 'dagger'; *dedo sin uña* (Nic) 'nailless finger'; *diuca* (Chile), the name of a small bird.

fierro 'iron tool' (Mex); *fifiriche* (Guat).

guama (Col), the name of a fruit; general *gusano* 'worm'; *huevo* (Ven). *lulo* (Chile) 'cylindrical object.'

macana (RP) 'club'; *machete* (RP, Ven) 'cutlass'; *masacoate* or *mazacuate* (Mex), a kind of 'boa,' and by extension anything long and thick; *mondá* (N Col); *morongo* (CA) 'thick blood sausage'; *morsolote* (Mex).

pájaro (general) 'bird' (cf. French *oiseau* and Italian *uccellino,* Riegler, p. 101); *paloma, palomita* 'dove'; *penca* (Chile), pulpy 'thistle leaf' and 'cowhide whip' often ending in a knob, whence the punning in the following passage concerning religious flagellation: "... entraron toítos a la capilla ... unos con rebenques ... otros con *pencas* con plomo en la caeza [= cabeza], quiabía que verla cuando 'staba tiesa" (Del Campo, p. 85); *pepe* (Cuba); *picaporte* (Guat) 'latch bolt,' a euphemistic distortion of *pico* (*pene*), especially in the phrase "Ya no se le paraguay el *picaporte*" (Sandoval), in which *paraguay* euphemizes *parársele* 'to have an erection'; *pelao* (PR); *pichi, pichilo* (Bol); *picho, pichón* (general) 'pigeon,' or from *picha* ? (see Corominas), *pincho* (Peru) 'goad, prod'; *pichula* (Chile, Peru), from general *picha* or Mapuche *pichol* (?) 'a needle used for sewing up bags'; general *pico,* whence Chileans avoid its homonym *pico* 'a bit' in phrases like "las dos y *pico*" 'a little after two,' in which they substitute *tanto* or *pucho* (from Quechua *puchu* 'left over'), as "treinta pesos y *pucho*" (Román); general *pingo, pinga* (from older *pingar* 'to hang'); *piocha* (Mex) 'pick(axe),' as in "El médico te ve los dientes, te examina los pulmones, te pela *la piocha* para ver si no estás enfermo de allí" (Ángulo, p. 22), here with punning overtones of *pelar la piocha* 'to cut the beard'; *pipe* (Guat); *piola* (Arg) 'cord, rope,' erroneously conjectured by Lenz of Mapuche origin (see Corominas, *Indianoromanica,* p. 61); *pipiriche* (Guat); *pisco* 'bird,' from Quechua; *pistola* (Arg) 'pistol'; *popa* (PR) 'stern'; *pirinola* (CA, Mex) for *perinola* 'spinning top.'

rábano (Chile) 'radish'; *reata* (Mex) 'whip.'

sable 'sabre' (Peru, Ec), whence *limpiar* ('to clean') and *afilar* ('to sharpen') *el sable* may mean 'to copulate.'

tiliche (Guat) 'thing, trifle'; *toche* (Santanderes, Col), a kind of bird; *tomín* (Col); *tordo,* a kind of small black bird, and *tortolito* 'small dove,' both in reference to children (Chile); rustic *tripa* (Arg: Tiscornia, II, 91; Peru) 'tripe'; *tronco* (Chile) 'tree trunk'; *turca* (Nic).

virtud (Cuba) 'virtue'; *yuca* 'manioc root.'

For Mexican cant alone we find registered the following fifteen terms (Rod, p. 119): *bastardo, basto(n), cabeza de gato, chambarete, chucumite, fierro, masteo, mastiachi, monda, mosquete, pescuezo, retazo macizo, riata, rienda, sancho.* For Peruvian cant (*replana*) the following have been listed (Bonilla Amado): *cabra, calero, callampa, comba, chopi, huaraca, huasamandrapa, huasamayeta, pata, tolete, trola, verdura,* etc.

A remarkably large number of words begin with *pi* or simply *p,* to suggest the referent *pene* or *picha.* Many of the terms, originally euphemisms, are now more vulgar than the word they have supplanted.

Sometimes a word of the foregoing type may be phonetically distorted for satirical or merely humorous reasons, as in "con el cargo y comisión / de Pleno—*sipotenciario* (association with *cipote* 'pene') / a la ciudá de London" (Arg: Ascasubi, *Trovos de Paulino Lucero,* ap. Tiscornia, II, 89); *Vergacruz* for *Veracruz* (*ibid.,* p. 90); *tripagofría,* rustic and malicious for *tipografía,* with play on *tripa* 'pene' (*ibid.,* p. 91). Standard *hacer un pito catalán* 'to make a Catalan fife,' that is, 'to thumb one's nose,' a derisive gesture (the "Shanghai gesture"), the extended and waving fingers resembling those of a fife player (see fig. 28) may have been euphemized to *hacer un grito catalán* (especially Arg), although the meaning of *apito* (*de pastor*) has in some areas (Salamanca, Spain, see Corominas) developed into the meaning of *grito* (*de pastor*) by simple transfer.

Because of a resemblance of form, a common euphemism for *testículos* 'testes' (vulgar *cojones*) is *huevos* (*huevas* in Chile, Col, and elsewhere) 'eggs.' In speaking of animals, *criadillas* 'lamb fries' was also a euphemism, deriving from *criadas de tierra* 'truffles' (lit. 'the earth-created'), but now the term may need further euphemization as in Lima, where *criadillas* are sometimes called (allegedly by nuns) *adefesios* (lit. 'nonsense, ridiculousness,' from *ad Ephesios*) *del carnero* (Benvenutto, p. 80). In many regions *tener huevos* is a vulgar expression for *tener valor, fuerza, energía,* as in "tengo más *huevos* que tú" which a Mexican market woman said to her male companion, meaning 'I am more courageous than you'; "Asustados con los relatos truculentos de la anciana, exclamaban los mozos: ¡Carajo! ¡tenían güevos! —Ese era el tributo que rendía la gente nueva a los abuelos tallados en madera de roble y de encina" (Hond: Carías Reyes, *La heredad,* 1931, p. 36). However, adjective *huevón* may mean 'stupid' (Chile) or 'lazy' and 'slow' (Mex, CA). Use of the feminine form *huevona* attests the loss of its primitive meaning. The vulgar phrase *tener huevos* may be euphemized by *ser bragado* 'to be breeched' (also fam. std.): "Las hembras compiten con los machos, y a veces son más *bragadas* que el negro más valentón" (Col: Carrasquilla, I, 61); "Era mujer muy *bragada* y montaba a caballo mejor que cualquier dragón" (Mex: Ángulo, p. 43).

Because of the now ill-sounding *huevos* (or *huevas*), the word is in some regions avoided by careful or fastidious speakers even in its standard sense of 'eggs.' Among its euphemistic substitutes are *blanquillos* (Mex, CA), as in "Decile a la cocinera que entibie [*entibiar* 'to soft boil'] un par de *blanquillos*" (Guat: Sandoval), "Matilde quiebra un *blanquillo* al borde de una cacerola humeante" (Azuela, *Las moscas,* 1931, p. 29); *cascarones* (Peru, especially by women in Ferreñafe and Piura, see Benvenutto, p. 80) 'shells,' a permutation expressing a part for the whole (synecdoche), or receptacle for content; *huvos* (*ibid.*), a slight phonetic distortion sufficing to ennoble the word; *lisuras de gallina* (*ibid.*), *lisura* meaning 'maliciousness, obscenity,' perhaps influenced by standard *posturas de gallina* (from *poner* 'to lay'); *yema* or *ñema* (Ven, Mex) 'yolk,' by synecdoche, and even preceded by 'con perdón de la palabra' (Piura, Peru: Hildebrandt, p. 263).

Children are sometimes reprimanded for using *huevo* in its standard sense of 'egg': "¿Y quién fué Colón? —¿El del *huevo,* papá? pregunta Marlene. —No seas mal educada, Marlene. ¡Qué son esas palabras!—le reprende su madre, al tiempo que le clava una mirada inquisidora" (Ec: García Muñoz, p. 226). A certain so called 'historical' tale begins as follows:

> Un día Doña Bruna, no se sabe por qué rara casualidad, mentó la palabra *huevo,* en lugar de *postura de gallina* o de *óvalo blanco, hijo de la esposa del gallo,* como ella los llamaba. Dió muestras de grande arrepentimiento, se lavó la boca, se la persignó; pero todo esto fué poco para tan grave falta, y resolvió irse a confesar, como en efecto lo hizo, etc. (Nic: Barreto, II, 112).

Among other euphemisms, most of them now vulgar, for *testículos* are:
aguacates, from Aztec *ahuacatl* 'testículo,' euphemized by some speakers to *frutas de San Jerónimo* (Nic: Barreto, II, 20); *ayotes* (Mex) from Aztec *ayotl* 'gourd.'
berocos or *verocos* (Cuba); *bilunchas* (Chile: Medina), especially those of a ram; *bolas* (general).

caimas (Col), fruit of the *caimo* tree; *candongas* (Ec, Col), of disputed origin (see Corominas) but equivalent to *pendientes* 'earrings' or anything hanging (Col, Ec), whence its present euphemistic use; *cocos* (Chile, Ec: Cornejo) 'coconuts,' as in "Jugando a la pelota, le pegaron una pata(da) en *loh coco*" (Chile: Rabanales, p. 162); *compañeros* (Esmeraldas, Ec; Pacific coast, Col) 'companions'; *coyoles* (Guat) from Aztec *coyolli* (lit. 'bell') 'palm-tree fruit' that hangs in large clusters, as in "A Juan le dieron un balazo en los *coyoles*" (Sandoval); general *chuspa* 'bag, scrotum,' from Quechua.

fruta (Chile), that is, resembling fruit hanging from trees, hence the representative gesture of the cupped hand moving upward and downward.

gandumbas (Ven); *granos* (SD); *guayabas* (*ibid.*), the name of a pear-shaped fruit; *gumarros* (cant, Mex) from cant *gumarra* 'hen.'

huanquis (*ibid.*), the name of a local plant with small edible bulbs.

matate (Guat) from Aztec *matatl* 'hanging nest, bag'; *mochilas* or *muchilas* (Col) 'saddlebags (made of rope)'; *obstáculos* (cant, Mex).

papas (Chile) 'potatoes,' but only in the expression alluding to a stout woman: "es mucha carne pa *doh papas*" (Rabanales, p. 163; cf. "es mucho jamón para dos *huevos*," Mex: Frenk, p. 137); *peras* (Chile) 'pears,' as in "¡Oye, no se te vayan a caer *lah peras!*—le dice uno a otro, cuando va corriendo" and "¡Buenas *peras!*, con que se zahiere la torpeza de una persona" (Rabanales, p. 163); *riñones* (cant, Mex) 'kidneys.'

tablas (Col); *talegas* (Santa Cruz, Bol) 'bags'; *tanates* or *tenates* (Mex) 'leather bags,' from Aztec *tanatli; timbales* (SD) 'kettledrums,' used also for 'bravery, courage'; *trolas* (Chile, Peru) 'hanging things'; *tunas* (N Arg, Chile) 'prickly pears,' as in the expression *gustarle a uno las tunas* 'to be effeminate': "—Entonces al Flaco le gustan *las tunas,* resumió alguien" (Lautaro Yankas, *Rotos,* ap. Rabanales, p. 163), and in San Luis, Argentina, *tuna* is avoided in favor of *penca* (lit. 'leaf').

Standard *castrar* or *capar* 'to castrate' is euphemized by the vague *arreglar* (general), cf. 'to alter'; *aviar* (as in Andalusia) 'to repair, fix up'; rustic *beneficiar* 'to benefit, improve' (Santamaría); *componer* (RP, Chile, Mex) 'to repair, fix up,' especially of cats (but also of other animals), as in "Que venga el aguador a *componer* este gato; el otro está ya *compuesto*" (Mex: Icazbalceta); *hacer la operación,* as in "si se pone pesao, le *hago la operación*" (Mex: Anda, p. 104); *quebrar* (parts of

Mexico), 'to crush, break.' In peninsular *llevar a Capadocia* (ap. Wagner, p. 5), the place name euphemistically veils *capar*.

Likewise *vulva* (vulgar *coño*) has a variety of substitutes and metaphoric euphemisms, most of which are also based on some resemblance of form. Many of these are names of plants or animals (cf. Italian *monna* 'monkey,' French *chat* 'cat,' German *Maus* 'mouse,' *Schnecke* 'snail,' etc., Riegler, p. 235). Among popular peninsular words are *almeja* 'clam'; *conejo* 'rabbit,' probably a phonetic distortion of vulgar *coño* used much less in America than in Spain, where it is a common vulgar exclamation, with euphemistic *concho* and *córcholis; crica; chocho* 'lupine' ? (confused derivation, see Corominas); *higo* 'fig'; *papo* 'double chin, maw, gizzard,' which, because of its association with *vulva,* has in its original sense been replaced by *buche* in some regions, as in Chile (Lenz, II, 562), and it is phonetically distorted for satirical reasons in "Era un gringo tan bozal, / Que nada se le entendía / ... lo único que decía / Es que era *pa po-litano* [= napolitano]" (*Martín Fierro,* I, v. 852).

In addition to many of the foregoing peninsular terms, American Spanish possesses an interminable list of synonyms. The following have been registered in various parts of Mexico (Duarte, Santamaría): *biscocho* 'sweet roll'; *camote* 'sweet potato'; *chango* 'monkey,' as in "las Santas de Durango esconden las patas y enseñan el *chango"* (Ángulo, p. 35); *chayote* (Oaxaca), a kind of 'calabash' shaped like a prickly pear, wherefore some speakers in referring to the plant euphemize its name into *espinoso* 'thorny'; general *empanada* 'meat turnover'; *gusano* (Zacualtipán) 'worm'; *jetas* (Orizaba, Cuernavaca) 'blobber lips, snout'; *mamey* and *papaya,* names of tropical fruits; *mojina* (Tabasco), a kind of 'turtle'; *mono* 'monkey'; *ñame* (Tobasco) 'yam'; *pájara* (PR), *pájaro* (Veracruz) 'bird'; general *panocha* 'cone of brown sugar' and *paparrucha,* probably a derivative of *papo; pepa* 'large seed'; *perdigón* 'young partridge'; *pinche* (Guadalajara), whence standard *pinchar* 'to prick' is replaced (in some regions *pinchar* means *copular*) by *ponchar* ("la llanta se *ponchó,"* from English *puncture*) and by *picar; pochitoque* (Tabasco), a kind of 'turtle'; *raja* 'crack'; *rul* and *rulacho,* cf. popular peninsular *rulé* 'posterior'; *sancha* 'lamb'; *sapo* 'toad'; *saraguato,* a kind of 'monkey'; *sartén* 'frying pan'; *tamal* (Tabasco, Zitácuaro) 'tamale'; *tamarindo* 'tamarind'; *tocino* (Yucatán) 'bacon'; *tortuga* (Tabasco) 'turtle'; *tuche* (Tabasco), from Maya *tuch* 'navel.'

From other countries we glean:

arepa (Col) 'round corn-pancake'; *argolla* (RP) 'ring.'

bollo (Ant) 'roll, penny loaf,' whence it is avoided in this sense; *burro* and *asno* (Piura, Peru: Hildebrandt, p. 263) 'donkey, ass,' whence these words are replaced in their original meaning with the euphemism *piajeno* (*pie ajeno*).

caimito (Cuba), an orange-shaped mucilaginous fruit; *cajeta* (Arg) 'box,' hence this word in its original sense and diminutive *cajetilla* (*de fósforos, de cigarrillos*) are avoided (*cajetilla de cigarrillos* may be called there *paquete atado*); *cachimba* (CA) '(tobacco) pipe' and 'fired car-tridge'; general *concha* 'shell,' cf. peninsular *almeja* 'clam' (in antiquity a type of clam, symbol for the vulva, was used as an amulet; even today it is worn round the neck, in some regions, to ward off the evil eye, see Wagner, p. 22), whence mention of the *Río de las Conchas* in Argentinian classrooms arouses the pupils' risibilities (A. Castro, p. 126); *congola* (Col, Ec) 'pipe' (cf. *cachimba*), of African origin (?); general *la cosita* or *la cosa* 'the thing,' also *cosiaca* (Arg: Vidal, p. 338); *cotorra* (RP) 'parrot'; *cresta* (Chile, Peru) 'cockscomb,' with vulgar ¡*por la (re)cresta!* euphemized by ¡*por la recoleta* (or *reverenda*)!; *cuca* (Peru, Ven) 'a round cookie'; *cueva de los leones* (cant, Peru); vulgar *culo* in many regions, a permutation due to proximity (replacing also *nalgas*); *cuchara* (Ven, CA) 'spoon,' as in the play on words in the phrase overheard at a picnic "tanta *cuchara* y estamos comiendo con la mano."

chaca (Chile), a kind of mollusk, from Mapuche; *chimba* and *chocha* (Col); *chochada* and *el chunche* (Nic) 'indefinite thing' like *la cosa; choro* (Chile) 'clam,' from Quechua, deriv. *chorear* 'to cohabit'; *chucha* (RP, Chile, Bol, Peru), probably related to peninsular *chocho* and native *chucha* 'a kind of clam,' whence the vulgar Chilean interjection and oath ¡*por la chucha!* (and the grave insult ¡*vete a la chucha de tu madre!*, cf. "—No traten de arrancarse *ch ... de su madre* porque los baleo hasta que caigan los dos," Castro, p. 308), euphemized as ¡*por la chita!* or ¡*por la chupalla!* or ¡*por la (re)chuata* (or *entrechuata*)! (Rabanales, "Recursos," p. 213); *chuspa* (parts of Ec) 'bag,' from the Quechua.

erizo (Chile) 'sea urchin'; *gato negro* (Nic) 'black cat'; *guillave* (Chile), pear-shaped fruit of the *quisco,* a kind of cactus.

maco (Cuba), from the Carib, a kind of mollusk resembling a snail with an egg-shaped shell; *mico* (CA) 'monkey.'

olisque (Col), from *oliscar* 'to smell, sniff'; *oreja* (SD) 'ear.'

pan (Santa Cruz, Bol) 'bread, roll,' whence *pan* in its original sense is replaced by *hornea(d)o,* as in "Véndame *horneao(s),*" heard among all classes (a large loaf is *marraqueta*); *papa* (Peru); *papada* (Hond, Tabasco), from *papo; papaya* (Ant, CA, Mex, parts of Chile), perhaps a phonetic distortion of *papo,* whence careful speakers, especially in Cuba, substitute *fruta bomba* in referring to the fruit *papaya; pelúa* (PR) = *peluda* 'hairy'; *pepe* (Cuba), of African origin (?), meaning *concha* 'shell' (Ortiz); *pepita* (SD) 'kernel, seed,' whence speakers use *semilla* for 'seed'; *pitón* (PR) 'protuberance'; *pupusa* (CA) 'meat turnover' (cf. *empanada,* above).

shusho, from Maya *xus* 'wasp.'

taparcuá (Col); *tola* and *toto* (Peru), the name of a sea animal; *tontona* (PR); *zorra* (Chile, Bol) 'fox.'

BODILY EXCRETIONS

Everyone avoids, as far as possible, mention of natural bodily needs. When it is necessary to mention them, however, the speaker is likely to use veiled words or vague terms conveying the requisite meaning without offense to his own sensibilities or to those of his interlocutor. If the new euphemism, however, becomes current in careless speech of a lower style it will soon be immediately associated with its bald referent and contaminated by it. Then the careful speaker will seek a new term. This process accounts for long series of successive euphemisms, such as English *privy, backhouse, toilet, (water) closet, washroom, lavatory, bath, necessary, comfort station, rest room, lounge, powder room, cloakroom,* and *John and Mary.*

Among standard Spanish terms are *retrete* 'retreat, private room'; *excusado,* shortened form of older *cuarto escusado* (derived from *absconsus*) 'room hidden or separated from the others, used originally as a storeroom, but today only as *retrete,* and popularly considered elliptical for *el que es excusado* ['exempt'] *mencionar por su nombre* or connected with *excusar* 'to prevent, avoid, dispense with,' as in "entró en una callejuela para facer aquello que non podía *excusar*" (*Conde Lucanor,* No. 46) and "Si le ha venido gana de hacer lo que no *se excusa*" (*Don Quijote,* I, 48); *necesaria, privada* or *secreta,* originally adjectives agreeing with *pieza* or *habitación* 'room'; *garita* 'sentry box'; (*lugar*) *común,* as in "a un lado de la puerta del corral, con grandes letras rojas: COMUN" (Mex: Anda, p. 92); *WC* or *W.C.* (from English *water closet*) shortened and pronounced *váter,* as in "no hacer uso del *WC* en las paradas" (on trains) and "ahí quedaron tres *W.C.,* y a un lado hizo hacer un urinario de cemento" (Chile: Castro, p. 393); *inodoro* 'odorless,' a euphemism by irony; *aseo* 'cleanliness'; *baño* 'bath,' short for *cuarto de baño; servicio* or *servicios,* now (for how long?) the term most widely used in polite speech, as in "Dónde está *el servicio?"* or "Dónde están *los servicios?"; tocador de señoras* 'boudoir.'

Among additional words found in Spanish America are older *casilla* (as in Ec) 'box, hut'; *cuartico* (Antioquia, Col) 'small room'; *chicago* (Peru), a place name recalling vulgar *cagar* 'to defecate,' as in "Hemos puesto cocina económica, *chicago* moderno, y cambiado el mobiliario de la sala" (Corrales, p. 105), "estaba yo sentado sobre la tapa del *chicago"* (*ibid.,* p. 107); *descanso* (Chile) 'rest' (though *excusado* is commoner); *sanitario* (Col: Acuña); rare *ñipa* (Curicó, Chile), the name of a certain bush of strong and offensive odor (Rabanales, p. 203); and probably many others that will be replaced after a brief existence.

Vulgar *cagar* (Latin *cacare*) 'to defecate' is often euphemized by phonetic distortion, especially in vulgar peninsular oaths or exclamations containing the first person present indicative of this verb, such as *me caigo en Dios, me caigo y me levanto, me cacho en diez* (= *Dios*), *me caso con veinticinco, me caso,* innocuous *mecachis,* whose connection with the original verb is so tenuous that it may be used by anyone in familiar speech (Beinhauer, p. 51; Vidal, p. 203), and *mecachis en la mar,* in which *mar* euphemizes *madre* (*de Dios*). In the periphrase *ir a ca García* (Andalusia) *ca,* meaning 'a casa de,' suffices to recall the referent sufficiently to make the whole phrase a euphemism for the taboo verb under discussion (Wagner, p. 22).

Among other peninsular euphemisms are *desembargar(se)* (antiquated) 'to free oneself,' as in "tomó talante de *desembargar* ... entró en una callejuela para facer aquello que non podía excusar" (*Conde Lucanor,* no. 46); *hacer aguas mayores,* as in "pregunto ... si acaso ... le ha venido gana y voluntad de *hacer aguas mayores* o menores, como suele decirse" (*Don Quijote,* I, 48); *defecar* 'to purify'; *deponer* 'to depose, deposit'; *desocuparse; obrar* 'to work, operate' ("siempre que orino al ratito *obro,"* Castro, p. 355), wherefore some speakers jocosely attempt to euphemize the place name *Chicago* by saying *Chiobro; hacer sus cosas,* as in "el gato por defecto de educación en vez de irse al techo *hacía sus cosas* en el sofá" (Corrales, p. 105); *hacer lo que otro no puede hacer por uno;* general *hacer pupú* (of children), onomatopoetic; *hacer del cuerpo* or *de(l) vientre; evacuar* or *exonerar* or *mover el vientre; ensuciarse* 'to soil oneself,' designating an involuntary act, synonymous with *zurrarse* and *zurruscarse,* as in "casi *ensuciáronse* de risa" (Corrales, p. 76), "¡Ay! me voy a tener que *ensuciar* en la cama" (Castro, p. 354), "Cambiar un enfermo *sucio* era trabajo serio" (*ibid.,* p. 355); *irse al zurullo* (see Cuervo, § 672).

In addition to most of the preceding expressions, American Spanish has others more or less local and involving all manner of semasiological changes:

amarrar la perra or *el zorro* (Santanderes, Col: Tobón) 'to tie up the dog' or 'the fox,' cf. 'to see a man about a horse or a dog,' 'to see Miss Jones,' etc.; *asustarse* (Ven) 'to be frightened,' a permutation expressing an act for its result.

bostear (RP, Chile, Bol), used in speaking of animals and jocosely of human beings, from *bosta* 'dung,' as in "las vacas han *bostiau* [= bosteado] todo el camino" (Vidal, p. 153, where we learn also that in San Luis, Argentina, *bostear* is facetiously substituted for *vosear*—the use of *vos* for standard *tú*—as in "Eran tan amigos que *se bostiaban*").

calzonear (Mex), from *calzón* 'breeches,' the change being an adequation; rustic *cantar* (Mex, Col: Acuña, "Vocabulario campesino," p. 135), influenced by the first two sounds of *cagar* and leaning on *cántaro* 'jug,' since one hears also *andar a cantaritos* (Wagner, "Mex. Rot.," p. 527); *comunicarse* (Mex), euphemizing *común* (= *excusado*) and semantically related to the metaphor *poner un telegrama* (below); *corregir* (Ant, occasionally Mex) 'to correct, remove, remedy,' possibly with phonetic association of *correr* 'to run'; *cortar flores* 'to cut flowers' and *cortar tucas* 'to cut pieces (of anything)' (Nic), related to *poner un telegrama* (below); *cuitear(se)* (CA), from Aztec *cuitlatl* 'excrement' principally of birds, as in "las gallinas *cuitearon* el corredor" and "el zopilote *se cuiteó*" (Gagini).

dar del cuerpo (Col, Ven, Pen, Ant), a variation of familiar standard *hacer del cuerpo; destrancar* (Chile) 'to unbar, deobstruct' (std. *desatrancar*), said of a person who is *estíptico* or *estreñido* 'constipated.'

feriar (Mex) 'to buy, sell, trade.'

gobernar (Mex: Duarte) 'to govern, regulate'; *guanear* (Arg, Chile, Bol, Peru), from *guano* 'excrement,' said of birds and facetiously of humans, as in "en el campo la gente se va a *guaniar* a los yuyos no más" (Vidal, p. 153).

hacer un mandado (Pan) 'to do an errand' (Aguilera, p. 143).

ir al monte (rustic, Bol, Ven, PR, and elsewhere) 'to go to the woods'; *ir a la huerta* (Peru) 'to go to the orchard,' *salir al campo* or *salir a campear* (Col: Montoya, No. 88), which may be considered relational shifts (beginning of the act for the act itself).

jiñar (vulgar, Cuba), from *jiña* 'excremento.'

poner (or *pasar*) *un telegrama* 'to send a telegram' (general), leaning on standard *deponer,* and referring to dots and the varying length of lines or sounds in telegraphic codes, recalling sounds made in voiding excrement (cf. the insulting *está pasando telegrama a* ... followed by the name of an unpopular politician), consequently some speakers prefer to substitute *mensaje* 'message.'

salvar (Santiago, Arg) 'to escape from danger, overcome a difficulty.'

There are many euphemisms to indicate the taboo verb especially when the act is involuntary and precipitate ('to have a sudden call of nature'), as that of children or of patients in bed (std. *zurrarse*). Among these are *componerse* (Col) 'to adjust, restore oneself,' as in "Del susto que la dió *se compuso* en los calzones" (Acuña); *chuquearse la ropa, schuquearse* or *enschucarse uno* (Salv); *churriquearse* (Cuba); *churrusquearse* (Hond, Mex); vague *desgraciarse* (Arg, Chile) 'to get into trouble'; *embolsarse* (Col); *hacerse* (general), with ellipsis of the taboo word, as in "la niña *se hizo* en la hamaca" (Suárez, p. 139); *embarrarse* from *barro* 'mud' as in "Este niño está todo *embarrado*" (Ven: Rosenblat, p. 405; Ec: cf. Icaza, pp. 114, 115).

Other terms may denote more specifically *diarrea,* or more vulgar *cagalera* 'diarrhea.' Among standard expressions are *cámaras, cursos, desconcierto, despeño* 'flinging down a precipice,' *escurribanda, flujo de vientre, soltura* 'looseness,' and familiar *seguidillas* 'lively dance and tune' with phonetic association of *seguir* 'to follow, continue.' The sufferer is referred to as *camariento, corriente,* or *suelto* 'loose.'

Many American-Spanish synonyms are based on *curso* 'course' or *correr* 'to run.' Among them are *cursear* or rustic *cursiar* (from std. *cursos* 'diarrhea' and *cursar* 'to do anything frequently'), as in "El guagua está *curseando*" (Ec: Toscano, p. 451) and "Le dieron una purga que *cursió* todo el día" (Arg: Vidal, p. 157), with verbal noun *curseada* ("El niño se largó una *curseada* por las piernas," *ibid.,* p. 224) and general adjective *cursiento* ("Tener la muerte de la urraca, / *cursienta* y flaca," *ibid.,* p. 345); *correr el chancho* (Salta, Arg) means *estar con diarrea;* nouns *correñañito,-a* (Salta, Arg) and *correquetealcanzo* (Mex) 'run or I'll overtake you'; adjectives *correoso* (Chile) and *correlativo* (Cibao, SD).

A whole series of words is based on standard *churre* 'thick, dirty, dripping grease' or anything resembling it. Among derivatives are *churra* (PR) and *churrias* (Col, Mex), as in "El zumo de limón es el mejor remedio pa' las *churrias*" (Acuña); *churrear(se)* (Córdoba, Arg; Hond, PR), with adjectives *churriento* and *churroso; churretearse* (Arg, Bol, Ec, Peru), as in "Comió peras verdes y *churretió* todo el día" (Vidal, p. 165), deriv. *churretoso; churriquearse* (Cuba); *churrusquearse* (Hond, Mex).

Others are *currumbamba* (Pan), perhaps onomatopoetic (Aguilera); general *flojera* 'looseness,' as in "Estoy con *flojera* y no puedo salir a la calle" (Guat: Sandoval); *obradera* (Col, Pan, Guat), from *obrar* 'to defecate,' as in "Tengo mucha *obradera*" (Sanchez Arévalo), and euphemism *operación* (Col) for *defecación* (Tobón); *quechera* (Peru), from Quechua *kechay* of same meaning.

Among the metaphors are *estar a tres tusas* (Ven); *estar con asientos* (Guat), since *asiento* means 'chair, stool,' as in "El niño *está con asientos* desde que le comenzaron a salir los dientes" (Sandoval); *estar con la vara de alcalde* (Nic: Valle) 'to have the mayor's rod of authority,' that is, 'something light or easy,' and *esto no es vara de alcalde* means there 'this is a burdensome and difficult task'; *aflojársele a uno el tornillo* (Mex) 'to have one's screw come loose,' as in "¿—Qué tiene el enfermo?" —"Que *se le aflojó el tornillo*" (Duarte); *perder las llaves* (CR) 'to lose one's keys' or *estar con las llaves perdidas* (Guat); *estar uno del pin al pon* (SD: Patín).

Vulgar *mierda* (*caca* and emphemistic *caquita* in speaking of infants) for standard *excremento* is in most situations avoided by careful speakers. The first sound *m* (pronounced *eme*) suffices to convey the meaning as in "vaya usted a la *m* (or written as pronounced: *eme*)" equivalent to 'go to h——,' sometimes reinforced with "vaya usted a la *m grande*" (Beinhauer, p. 152). Examples: "—Andá, andá, indio de *m*..." (Bol: Céspedes, p. 165); "—Todavía me discute esta *m*... Y con la derecha le lanzó una bofetada" (Chile: Castro, p. 389). The word is often replaced by a euphemism the initial sounds of which suggest the referent, such as *miércoles* ('Wednesday'): "Si tuviera un espejo ... Pero ... ¡qué va a tener uno en esta desolación de *miércoles!*" (Arg: Lynch, *De los campos porteños,* 3d ed., p. 14), and as an interjection of anger or pain: "—¡Nadie le pega a Picón, *miércoles!*" (Chile: D'Halmar, *La Lucero,* in *Obras,* I, 145); in the exclamation "¡Viva Chile, *mi hermosa* patria!" the syllables *mi* (*h*)*er* veil the word under discussion; Chilean exclamation *¡miéchica!* is a fusion of the offensive word with *meca* (from Mapuche, of similar meaning), as in "*¡Miéchica,* que me quemé los dedos!" (Román). Vulgar *come m* ... 'gullible person, dupe' is in Cuba euphemized by *come bolas* (general *tragabolas), come contra, come cantúa* (confection of yams, coconut and sugar), *come catibia* (confection of yams and sugar), *come jana* (Rodríguez, p. 416).

Frequently, borrowings of the same meaning serve as euphemisms: *aca* (Salta, Arg), from Quechua with a possible phonetic leaning on general *caca; catinga* (RP) 'human excrement sticking to underclothes' (Garzón), from Guaraní *catingá* 'strong, disagreeable odor'; *cuita* (Mex, CA), as well as *cuital, cuitla,* and *titilcuite* (Salv), from Aztec *cuitlatl,* originally of birds, but extended also to human beings; *chicuca* and *chilila* (of birds) (Trujillo, Ven); *chichina* (Hond), from Aztec *chichinoa* (?) 'to burn, scorch'; *guano,* from Quechua, originally of birds, but extended also to other animals and occasionally to human beings, as in "¡Y pensar que ... una bala perdida le pueda perforar los intestinos y derramarle el *guano!*" (Col: Arango, p. 30); *huacacara* 'cow dung' (Arequipa, Peru), from Quechua; *hucha* (*ibid.*) '(llama, sheep, rabbit, rat) dung,' from Quechua; *meca* (Chile) from Mapuche, wherefore euphemistic *¡vete a la Meca!* and *echar a uno a la Meca,* playing upon the proper name *Meca* 'Mecca' for vulgar *¡vete a la m...!;* many terms beginning with *ñ,* some of them of Indian origin, others perhaps coined: *ñaña* (CA), *ñeñe* (Hond, Nic), *ñinga* (Pan, Cuba, Ec: "—¿Qué me ves tanto? ¿Tengo *ñinga* en la cara?" A. Ortiz, p. 29), *ñisca* (Col, CA: *ñisco,* Peru: "tenía olor a *ñisco* en todo el cuerpo," Corrales, p. 130), *ñola* (Col), *ñoña* (Chile, Ec, Andalusia), *ñusca* (Col, Guat); *ta'* (Yucatán), from Maya (Suárez, p. 86); *tusi* (Arequipa, Peru), from Aymara.

Terms of general import or that have some vague resemblance to the referent in color, shape, or consistency (like std. *mojón* 'heap, landmark') are *barro* 'mud' (Ec, Ven), whence *barro* in its original sense is euphemistically replaced by *pantano* 'swamp, marsh' (Ven), as in "Ese carro me salpicó de *pantano*" (Rosenblat, p. 405); *bollo* (Chile, Col) 'small loaf, roll,' usually when the referent is hard or cylindrical; *brea* (Mex) 'pitch, tar'; *cacana* (Arequipa, Peru), from *caca; cerote* (CA), augmentative of *cera* 'wax'; *cerullo* (CR), apparently a fusion of *cera* and *zurullo; galleta* (Col: Tobón) 'biscuit'; vulgar *jiña* (Cuba); *plasta* (Chile, CA, Mex) 'anything soft and flat,' referring to round and flat excrement, *plastada* (Col: Revollo); general *porquería* 'filth'; *tigre* (Arg, prison jargon) 'tiger,' because of color, and prisoners who cleaned the toilets were called *tigreros* (Gobello, p. 9); general *torta* 'round cake'; *tusa* (Nic) 'piece of anything'; *vidrio inglés* (Ant) 'English glass'; *zoquete* (Arg) 'chunk, block' (Santamaría).

Some of the foregoing terms applied originally to dung but have been extended to human excrement. Other words refer generally to animals: *beneficio* (Chile) 'enrichment (of soil)' for std. *estiércol; chirria* (Chile) phonetic distortion of standard *sirria* (*sirle*) 'sheep dung, goat dung,' frequent in the exclamation *¡por la chirria!* (Román); general *guano* 'sea birds' dung'; *muñiga* (Peru, Col, Pan, CA), from std. *boñiga* 'cow dung'; *leña de vaca* (*de oveja*) 'cow (sheep) firewood' and *carbón de pingo* (Arg) 'horse charcoal,' that is, 'dry dung used for fuel,' like standard *burrajo* 'dry stable dung,' from *burro; pajoso* or (by metathesis) *pasojo* or more usually *pasojos* (N Mex, in the interior) 'horse manure,' perhaps from *paja* because of its straw color.

Various euphemisms express the act of stepping on excrement (*pisar un excremento*): *cortarse* (Col, Ant, parts of Spain), 'to get cut,' as in "cuidado si *te cortas* con ese vidrio inglés" (SD: Patín), "*se cortó* con vidrio inglés" (Cuba: Rodríguez, p. 437); "*¡cuidado te muerde la culebra!*" (coastal Ec: Cornejo) 'careful or a snake will bite you'; *quemarse* (Peru, Col) 'to get burned,' etc. *Papel higiénico* 'toilet paper' is sometimes euphemized by *papel indispensable* or *papel toilette* (Col).

Popular and vulgar *mear* 'to urinate' has standard euphemisms in *orinar* and *hacer aguas* or *hacer aguas menores,* further euphemized by shortening to *hacer,* as in "—Ya *hice,* mamá ... —¡Otra vez, anda!" (Quevedo y Zubieta, p. 16) and "—*¡Hiciste!* ... como chiquita de un año. Tienes doce bien cumplidos" (*ibid.,* p. 31); general *hacer pipí* (said of children), onomatopoetic. Among American-Spanish euphemisms are *bix* (Guat), especially of children, probably onomatopoetic from Maya ("El nene quiere

hacer *bix,"* Sandoval), spelled also *uix* and *wix* (Yucatán: Suárez, p. 86),
deriv. *uixar; cambiarle el agua al canario* (Ven) 'to change the canary's
water' (cf. humorous peninsular *mudarle el caldo a las aceitunas* 'to change
the pickled-olive brine' (Beinhauer, *Umgangssprache,* p. 121, n. 40); general *cortar* (or *coger*) *una flor* 'to pick a flower'; *pasa el río* (Chile), said
of a child, means *se orina en la cama* (Yrarrázaval, p. 358); such a child
is called *guacapa* (Esmeraldas, Ec: Cornejo), from the name of a fish that
exhales a similar odor. Vulgar *meadero* '(public) urinal' has been euphemized with cultured *urinario* and *mingitorio;* in limited areas (Chile:
Román) *vespasiana,* from the French *vespasienne,* a public urinal in the
shape of a column with cubicles, derived from the name of the Roman
Emperor Vespasian (A.D. 9–79) who reportedly established public urinals
in Rome.

Standard *bacín, bacinilla,* or *tiesto* 'chamber pot' euphemized by *vaso de
noche, bañado,* or *servicio* has still other synonyms in American Spanish.
Among these are *canco* (Chile) 'earthen water jug,' from Mapuche; *cantora* (Chile, Peru) 'singer,' probably because of the peculiar sounds made
when in use (whence *cantora,* according to some speakers, is avoided in its
sense of 'singer' in favor of *cantante); comadre* (CR) 'aunty'; *china* (Peru)
'servant'; *dichosa* (Bol) 'the happy one'; *disimulada* (Córdoba, Arg) 'the
reserved or sly one'; *escupidera* (RP, Chile, PR, Andalusia) 'cuspidor,'
whence *escupidera* in its original meaning is replaced by *salivadera* or *sali-
vera,* and verb *salivar* replaces *escupir* 'to spit' especially in signs displayed
in public places: "Prohibido *salivar,"* "Se prohibe *salivar* en el suelo";
huámpar (NW Arg) 'horn,' from Quechua; *mica* (Col), probably from
mico 'monkey,' since names of animals who prattle and chatter are frequently applied to the *bacinilla* (cf. *mono* in Andalusia: "Se veía el *mono*
debajo de la cama," Alcalá Venceslada); *necesaria* (Arg); *novia* (PR)
'sweetheart'; *porcelana* and *borcelana* (Mex) 'porcelain,' a permutation of
material for an object made of it; *solera* (Arequipa, Peru); *tibor* (Cuba)
'large, decorated earthen jar'; *tirirú* (Bol), from Guaraní, a *mate* or vessel
used by the poor as a chamber pot.

Urinals for bed patients generally have the vague form of some animal
and are frequently thus designated, as: *cotorra* (Tabasco, Mex) 'parrot';
pato (Mex, Ant) 'duck'; *cola de pato* (SD) 'duck's tail'; *pava* (Chile)
'turkey hen' (because of its shape, *pava* means 'teakettle' in Argentina),
deriv. *pavero* 'person who empties the urinals'; *loro* (Chile) 'parrot.' Stand-

ard *silleta* 'bedpan,' diminutive of *silla* 'chair, seat' becomes *chata* (Chile, as in Spain) from *vasija chata* 'a flat vessel' as in "al ratito obro, póngame la *chata*" (Castro, p. 355).

When standard *estreñir* (Latin *stringere* 'to contract, tighten') specialized its meaning in 'to bind, constipate' (*estreñido* 'constipated,' *estreñimiento* 'constipation'), its more general sense of 'to tighten, contract' was to a large extent assumed by *estrechar* (from *strictus,* past participle of *stringere*). Adjective *estíptico* (from Greek στυπτικός 'astringent,' the root being related to that of Latin *constipare* 'to press, stuff') became a medical term in standard Spanish, deriv. *estipticar* and *estipticidad.* This medical term is in most of America a euphemism for *estreñido,* deriv. *estítico* (or *estíptico*) and *estitiquez* or *estiptiquez* as in "hasta ahora no me ha sentado bien ninguno de cuantos remedios me han recetado para la *estitiquez*" (Col: Acuña). Among other popular and local terms are *atrancar* or *trancar* (NW Arg, Chile) 'to bar, obstruct' (from *tranca* 'bar'), as in "*Trancado* con piquillín (a local fruit) se murió un niñito de los Sosas" (San Luis, Arg: Vidal, p. 330), hence *destrancar* (Chile) 'to unbar' or 'evacuar el que está estíptico o padece de estreñimiento' (Román); *prendido* (Chile), deriv. *prendimiento;* Quechua borrowing *quixqui* 'a narrow, tight thing' is the root of *quisquirse* (NW Arg) 'to stuff' (deriv. *quisquido* or *quixquido*) especially when the condition is due to overeating *tunas* 'prickly pears' or cheese, and also of *aquisquinar(se)* (deriv. *aquisquinado* and *aquisquinamiento*), as in "El pobre muchacho *si aquisquinó* comiendo tunas y casi se murió" (Vidal, p. 167).

Standard *enema* or *clister* or *lavativa* (or *lavamiento*) have general euphemisms in vague *ayuda* 'help, aid' and *servicio* 'service.' In addition to these standard forms we find local euphemisms in Spanish America, such as *cayetana* (Col), probably an extension of *cayetano* used in euphemistic *quedarse cayetano* for 'quedarse callado' or 'guardar un secreto' (Sundheim, Revollo); *colirio* (Cauca, Col) 'collyrium, eyewash' which means 'enema' unless specifically indicated as for the eyes (Tascón); *cupucha* (Chile) 'animal bladder,' by metathesis from Quechua borrowing *pucuchu* (Román) or *phukuchiy* 'hacer o dejar soplar' (Lira) referring to the 'syringe'; *lava,* shortening of *lavativa* (Grases, p. 123); general *lavado,* as in "póngale pronto un *lavado* de agua tibia" (Guat: *Mosaico,* p. 296); *pera* (Chile) 'pear' applies to the syringe because of similarity of shape, and also to the enema itself, as a permutation of instrument for action, as in

"A este niño hay que ponerle otra *perita* para que le baje la fiebre" (Rabanales, p. 206); *visita* (Peru, PR) and *visitadora* (Hond, Mex, PR, SD) meaning either 'enema' or 'syringe,' as in "¿Pero no te jan puesto ninguna *visita* ni jas tamao pulgas [= purgas] ni gomitivos?" (Menéndez Muñoz, *Yuyo,* ap. Malaret, *Vocabulario*).

By the end of the sixteenth century old standard *regoldar* 'to belch' had fallen into discredit among careful speakers, who adopted the euphemism *eructar* (Latin *eructare* 'to eruct or eructate'), popularly pronounced *erutar*. Everyone will remember Don Quijote's advice concerning good conduct given to Sancho Panza:

Ten cuenta, Sancho, de no mascar a dos carrillos, ni de *erutar* delante de nadie. —Eso de *erutar* no entiendo—dijo Sancho. Y don Quijote le dijo: —*Erutar,* Sancho, quiere decir *regoldar,* y éste es uno de los más torpes vocablos que tiene la lengua castellana, aunque es muy sinificativo; y así, la gente curiosa se ha acogido al latín, y al *regoldar* dice *erutar,* y a los regüeldos, *erutaciones;* y cuando algunos no entienden estos términos, importa poco; que el uso los irá introduciendo con el tiempo, que con facilidad se entiendan; y esto es enriquecer la lengua, sobre quien tiene poder el vulgo y el uso (*Don Quijote,* Part II, chap. xliii).

The verb *eructar* has since become popular and in turn is being replaced by other expressions, such as *hacer el chancho* (Chile) 'to play the pig.' Since in popular and rustic speech *eructar* is pronounced *erutar,* and *eruptar* 'to erupt' is often pronounced *erutar* (*erucción* for *erupción*), the original semasiological similarity between these verbs has become greater and in the minds of many speakers the two verbs are one and the same.

Spanish *vomitar* (or *basquear*) 'to vomit,' because of various figurative meanings developed later, is perhaps not so offensive to the ear as English 'to vomit.' Yet euphemisms are often employed to lessen unpleasantness: *almadiarse,* from *almadía* 'raft'; *arquear* 'to arch,' perhaps because of the shape of the body, deriv. *arcada* and *arqueada; arrojar* 'to throw (away)'; *avanzar* 'to advance,' a permutation of an action for its result; *lanzar* 'to throw, launch'; *marearse* 'to be seasick, dizzy'; *nausear* 'to feel nausea'; *provocar* 'to provoke,' perhaps the shortening of a phrase like *provocar a nauseas,* or a permutation of an action for its result; *rendir* 'to give back'; *revesar* 'to reverse'; *trocar* 'to exchange'; *volver* 'to turn (inside out).'

Among Spanish-American synonyms are *almariarse* (Arg), a cross between *almadiarse* and *marearse* 'to get seasick' (see Corominas, under *mar*); rather general *ansias* (as in parts of Spain) 'anxiety' for *náuseas* or *bascas,* and *ansioso* for *nauseoso* or *nauseabundo; avanzar* (Ant) 'to advance,' as in Spain; *buitrear* (Chile, Peru), from *buitre* 'vulture,' a kind of adequation, referring to the vultures' custom of gorging themselves until half torpid and, when danger arises, disgorging what they have eaten, as they take to flight (they also disgorge the food from their crop to feed their young), deriv. *buitreada* for *vomitona* 'violent vomiting'; *brisar* (SD), from *brisa; debocar* (Bol, Peru) and *trasbocar* (Arg, Chile, Col, Yucatán), as in "Cuantito *trasbocó* el niñito, se mejoró que era una maravilla" (San Luis, Arg: Vidal, p. 144); *deponer* (CA, Mex) 'to depose,' as in "Quizá me hizo mal la comida, porque la *depuse* toda" (Guat: Sandoval); *golmar* (SD), from older standard *gormar; revulsar* (Peru: Corrales, p. 273), perhaps a cross between *revolver* and *repulsar; tener un reboso* (SD), from *rebosar* 'to overflow' as in "el borracho tuvo un *reboso*" (Patín).

Among metaphors of a facetious nature, especially those having to do with seasickness or drunkenness (pop. peninsular *cambiar la peseta*), are *aflojar* (or *soltar*) *la mascada* (Arg) 'to release one's cud'; *amarrar zope* (Guat), referring to the buzzards' habit of disgorging what they have eaten (*zope* is an abbreviation of *zopilote*)*; darle a la volteadora* (Hond: Membreño) 'to go in for acrobatics'; *echar la casa por la ventana* (Arg, Bol) 'to throw the house out of the window'; *echar la ceba* (Col: Tascón), in which *ceba* supposedly replaces standard *cebo* 'priming of guns,' cf. *estar a media ceba* (CR) 'to be half drunk'; *largar el chivo* (RP) 'to release the goat'; *largar el rollo* (RP) 'to release the scroll,' which may also refer to a speech, an allegation, etc.; *largar los chanchos* (Arg) 'to release the pigs.' Noun *vómito* is euphemized by *vocación* (Col), a phonetic distortion the first syllable of which suffices to recall the referent, as in "Aquella *vocación* tan juerte que no me dejaba naa en el estógamo" (Pimentel y Vargas, *Escenas de la gleba,* ap. Flórez, *BICC,* I, p. 321).

Standard *hurgarse las narices* 'to pick one's nose' is euphemized in popular peninsular *hacer albondiguillas* 'to make little meat balls,' and *sacarse los muebles* 'to remove one's furniture' (Beinhauer, p. 25). Elsewhere we find *sacarse pan* (PR) 'to take out rolls *or* bread'; *sacar* (*los*) *loros* (Chile) 'to pull out parrots,' perhaps because of the similarity of the action of catching young parrots, which must be drawn from their caves with sticks or hooks, and possibly because of a resemblance of color.

VII DECENCY: LOVE

Matters of love, perhaps more than any other, require veiled allusions, mostly euphemisms, to screen them from indiscreet ears and eyes. Among standard expressions are *enamorarse, prendarse* 'to fall in love' (fam. *amartelarse, chalarse, despepitarse, enamoriscarse, encalabrinarse, encapricharse, enloquecerse, estar loco por, enquillotrarse, quillotrarse*), *hacer el oso* ('to play the bear,' that is, to expose oneself to derision and pity by doing or saying foolish things, then 'to court, woo, flirt, keep company with'), *pelar la pava* ('to pluck the turkey,' then 'to talk by night at the window,' said of lovers; *comer* or *mascar hierro* in Andalusia), borrowings *coquetear* (from French *coqueter,* lit. 'to act like a cock among hens'), and *flirtear* (from English *flirt,* lit. 'to run about with a desire to attract notice'). Many of these expressions have in Spanish America been superseded by others, particularly in familiar speech, the standard forms being often limited to literary style.

Perhaps the most curious verbs are *afilar* (RP) and *pololear* (Chile, Bol, Peru, Ec). Standard *afilar* 'to sharpen, grind, hone (a razor), whet' came to mean 'to flatter, stimulate, incite,' then 'to stimulate with attentions, to court, woo' (RP), as in "Me gusta también el caldo / cuando la gallina es gorda / y *afilarme* la mucama / cuando la patrona es sorda" (ap. Malaret, *Copla,* p. 16). This present usage has been the subject of much discussion. Monner Sans (*Disparates usuales en la conversación diaria,* Buenos Aires, 1923) quotes Leonardo de Argensola: "Mirando Cloris una fuente clara / donde otras veces *afilar* solía / las armas desdeñosas con que hería / y en vano ahora contra mí prepara," ap. Gobello (p. 92), who in turn postulates slang *filar* with its general meaning of 'relatar una historia fingida para obtener algo de una persona, engañándola.' Verb *pololear* (Chile, Bol, Peru, Ec) derives from *pololo* (in turn from an onomatopoetic Mapuche name of an insect or fly that buzzes around flowers and lights), with an early meaning shift of 'to bother, molest insistently' (cf. fam. std. *mosconear* from *moscón* 'large fly, bumblebee'). It may apply to either sex: "Pedro *pololea* con Juana, y María *pololea* con Diego" (Román). Rarely is *pololo* 'gallant' applied to a person having illicit relations (like std. *querido, cortejo,* fam. *cachirulo*), but rustic *lacho,* of disputed origin, and its derivative verb *lachear* (older and less refined than *pololear*), as in "¿Estás *lacheando* con alguna niña?" (*ibid.*), may have this meaning.

Among other verbs substituted for *enamorarse* are:

apestillarse (PR), from *pestillo* 'boy friend,' meaning *juntarse dos novios,* as in "Y esta noche, yo lo juro, / que aunque surja una garata ['fight'] / Bajo esa luna de plata / Me *apestillo* con Arturo" (Amelia Ceide, ap. Malaret, *Vocabulario*).

cachar (Col) 'to chat, flirt' from *cacho* 'joke,' as in "Ve a Pedro *cachándote* desde el café" (Cadavid); *cantinear(se)* (CA), as in "Ese turco está *cantineándose* a la japonesita" (Guat: Guzmán Riore, p. 49); *carretear* (Ec) 'to court,' as in "Fulano anda *carreteando* desde hace días a Zutanita" (Toscano, p. 451); *cucarachear* (Cuba), cf. *mariposear; cuentear* (Antioquia, Col), as in "la *cuentié* como con fines de que nos casáramos" (Flórez, *Habla,* p. 148); *cuzquear* (Arg), from *cuzco* 'small dog.'

dar chamico (a narcotic plant) and *enchamicar,* as in "Estos dos andan *enchamicados*" (Ec: Toscano, p. 440), cf. general *enyerbar, envenenar; dragonear* (RP), from its meaning 'to boast,' as in "el botija [= muchacho] ya *dragonea*" (Herrero Mayor, *Lengua,* p. 68).

encabarse 'empezar a tener relaciones amorosas' (Col: Flórez, *Habla,* p. 145); rather general *encamotarse,* from *camote* 'sweet potato' and 'sweetheart,' as in "Y vos ... ¿tuavía *estay* [= estás] *encamotado* con la Soleá?" (Chile: Guzmán Maturana, p. 59), also *estar camote, tener camote a; encampanarse* (Col, Mex) 'to rise up' from *campana* 'bell'; *encanicarse* (Tex); *encolinarse* (Col) 'to elevate oneself,' from *colina* 'hill'; *enverracarse* (*verraco* 'male swine') and *empapayarse* (Cuba) from *papaya; empelotarse* (Mex, Cuba, Tex), as in "Moisés se *empelotó* con Juana" (C. Suárez) and "fulano anda *empelotado* por zutana" (Malaret).

fajar (Cuba), as in "Fulano le está *fajando* a Fulana."

estar gas por (Guat), as in "Mercedes ya no puede disimular que *está gas por* Alberto" (Sandoval); "José *se puso bien gas* por ella" (Quintana, p. 152).

hablar a (Mex); *hacer brujitas* (Col: Flórez, *Habla,* p. 223); *hacer el sebo a una persona* (Ven) = *enamorarla.*

jalar (CA), from *halar* 'to haul, pull,' as in "ella y yo *nos jalamos";* *pastorear* (RP).

templarse (Arg, Chile) 'to temper oneself,' as in "X está muy *templado* de la Z" (Yrarrázaval), "es más *templao* quiuna abeja" (Del Campo, p. 51), and *"se está templando"* (Garzón).

volar (Mex), as in "Pedro anda *volando* a Juana" (Malaret).

Among more elaborate metaphors are *comer jiguillo* (PR), from the Indian name of a plant, equivalent to *pelar la pava* (cf. Andalusian *comer hierro*), as in "y los mozos charlaban en el batey [= plazoleta] ... pelando la pava o *comiendo jiguillo,* como también se suele decir" (González García, *El tesoro del Ausubal,* 1913, chap. vi); *dar de alazo* 'to flirt,' as in "Fulano me *da de alazo"* (Mex: Velasco); *darle vuelta al charqui* (Chile) 'to turn the jerked beef' so it will not burn > 'to court a woman assiduously' and 'to be importunate in some request'; *derraparse* (Mex) 'to slip, slide, skid,' as in "él está que *se derrapa* por ella," often with an accompanying gesture like that which expresses anger (see fig. 12); *estar más enamorado que un cuchucho* (Ec: Cornejo), in which *cuchucho* is a local rodent; *quemársele el arroz a una* (CA, Mex) 'to have one's rice burn,' as in "A María *se le está quemando el arroz* por Luis" (Villegas, p. 28); *rascar* (std. *arrastrar*) *el ala* (Guat), as in "Dicen que usted le *rasca el ala* a la vecina de enfrente" (Sandoval).

CONCUBINE

Among standard synonyms, originally euphemisms for *concubina* 'concubine, mistress' are *amante; amasia; barragana,* deriv. *abarraganarse* 'to enter into concubinage'; *amiga* 'girl friend,' *amistad* 'concubinage'; *manceba,* deriv. *amancebarse; moza; querida* and *querindanga; quillotra;* and others.

Among American-Spanish terms we find the following words.

amachinarse (general), possibly from *Machín* 'Cupid,' but certainly with phonetic interference of *macho* 'male' and *china* 'girl, concubine, etc.' evidenced by synonym *achinarse,* as in "fulano está *amachinado* con fulana"; *amachimbrarse, amachembrarse,* and *amachambrarse* (Chile) from std. *machihembrar* (*macho* 'male,' *hembra* 'female') 'to dovetail,' meaning in carpentry 'to fit tightly a tenon or tongue (shaped like a bird's spread tail) into a mortise or socket'; *acortejarse* (PR), from *cortejo,* as in "seguíamos viviendo *acortejados"* (Malaret, *Vocabulario*); *ajuntarse* (Col) from std. *juntarse* 'to get together,' as in "¡No eran casados! ¡No estaban sino *ajuntaos,* como dicen en el Chocó!" (Arango, p. 92); *amañarse* (Col) 'to become accustomed to, adapt oneself to'; *apatronarse* (Chile, Peru) 'to get a job, a patron or protector,' said of women; *aplazarse* (Cuba, SD), from *aplazar* 'to postpone,' that is, *promesa de matrimonio aplazado* 'promise of postponed marriage'; *aqueridarse* (PR), from *querido* 'lover'; *arrejuntarse* (Mex, Tex) 'to get together' (std. *juntarse*); general *arrimarse* 'to join, come close to'; *arrincharse* (Trujillo, Ven), with noun *arrinche* 'concubine.'

comprometerse (as in Andalusia) 'to bind, pledge oneself,' deriv. *comprometido,-a* 'concubine' and *compromiso* 'concubinage' (std. *amancebamiento*); *conglomerada* (Peru), as in "de noche me disfrazo ... y me pego un brinco a Mapiri para visitar a mi *conglomerada,* porque no es bueno dejar solas a las mujeres" (Corrales, p. 55); older *conocencia* (Peru) 'girl friend,' as in "lo vi con su *conocencia"* (Sologuren, p. 244); *cristiano,-a* (Guat), as in "Ramón es el *cristiano* de Josefa" (Sandoval).

chepa (Chile), short for *Josefa; chey* (Chile), probably from Mapuche *che* 'people,' as in "Un muchacho gordo decía—Le trae dinero ... ¡Es su *chey!"* (Edwards Bello, ap. Medina); *churo,-a* (NW Arg, Bol), probably from Quechua *churi* 'male' with interference of std. *chulo.*

emplearse (rustic, SD) 'to get employment' (cf. *apatronarse,* above), as in "Ella, cuando *se empleó,* tenía quince años" (Patín); *encuerarse* (Ven) from *cuero* 'prostitute, concubine' in many regions; *endamarse* or *adamarse* (Guat), as in "Abel y Sara se *endamaron* y viven maridablemente" (Sandoval); *enmancuernarse* and *mancornearse* (cf. std. *mancornar* 'to tie together, couple'); *enmozado,-a* (Col: Acuña) from *moza* 'concubine.'

flete (Peru) 'freightage' > 'boy friend, girl friend' in a favorable sense; *forro* 'lining, cover,' *fuste* 'saddletree' (Mex).

garraleta (Mex: Duarte); *galleta* 'hardtack' > 'soldier's girl' (Mex);

guachiconga, guariconga (Col); *guajolota* (Mex) 'turkey hen'; vulgar *guaricha* (Peru, Ec) 'soldier's concubine' who sometimes follows him to the battlefield (from Quechua *huarucha* 'prostitute'), meaning elsewhere 'concubine' (Ven), 'wench' (Col, Pan), as in "Junto con las demás *guarichas,* sus mujeres seguían al batallón" (Ec: Cuadra, p. 111).

interesado,-a (Cuba); *izquierda, por* or *a la izquierda* (PR), as in "tener una mujer *por la izquierda";* *jaña* (Nic).

lacho (vulgar, Chile, Peru); *lapa* (Chile) 'limpet,' a shellfish adhering to rocks, hence a soldier's 'concubine' who like a limpet attaches herself to him and follows him everywhere.

machucada (Bol) 'soldier's concubine,' from *machucar* 'to crush, bruise'; *madama* (Guat), as in "Rosa ya es *madama* de Luis" (Sandoval); *malamistado,-a* (Chile); *marchante* (Ec: Toscano, p. 400); general *meterse con,* as in "Dicen que la Manuela ya *se metió con* Basilio" (Sandoval); *mina* (general), from Italian jargon in which *mina* means 'woman'; *mula* (interior of Peru) = *barragana de sacerdote católico* (Malaret), since, according to legend, such a concubine expiates her sin by wandering about at night in the shape of a mule.

paloma (Col) 'dove,' as in "Al Juancho se le escapó *la paloma"* (Acuña); *pécora* (Ec); slang *percanta* (Arg) 'princess,' from Italian (?); *pieza* and *piezo* (Cuba); *pichicuaraca* (Mex), as in "Fulano tiene su *pichicuaraca"* (Duarte); *pilguaneja* (Mex), from Aztec *pilhuan,* plural of *pilli* 'hijo'; *piusa* (Mex); *peoresnada* (Chile), as in "Me priduntó (preguntó) si acaso teníai [tenías] *pioresná* [*peoresnada*]."

rabona (Chile, Bol, Peru) 'soldier's concubine,' from its local meaning 'in one's shirt' or 'completely nude.'

segura servidora (Bol); *subsistir* (Peru: Benvenutto, p. 73).

vivir de asiento con (Ec, Peru) 'to settle down with,' as in "Pedro *vivía de asiento con* la negra Tomasa; ella es su *querida de asiento"* (Malaret), "habíale propuesto tenerla como *mujer de asiento"* (Ec: A. Ortiz, p. 63).

General *casarse por detrás de la iglesia* 'to be married behind the church' may become *casarse por la montaña* 'married in or by the woods' (Chile, among Araucanians); *casarse por el (cura) Palqui* (Chile), in which *palqui* is the Mapuche name of a bush (*hijo del palqui* or *palquiado* 'illegitimate child'; abusive *guacho* ['orphan'] *palquiado* is a vulgar insult applied to an illegitimate child), as in "¿Quién no sabe que esos *se casaron con el cura Palqui?"* (Rabanales, p. 211).

The gesture of bringing both index fingers together, or index and middle finger of one hand (see figs. 29 and 30) may mean 'juntarse,' thus obviating the necessity of mentioning *amancebarse* or any of its synonyms.

PROSTITUTE

Words indicating 'prostitute' (std. *meretriz, ramera, mujer alegre, buscona, mujer de placer, mujer pública, mujer de la vida,* fam. *niña, dama de buena voluntad, fulana, individua, prójima, socia, mujer de mala vida, vendedora de amor, moza de fortuna* or *del partido,* vulgar *churriana, lea, tusona, pesetera,* from *peseta* 'a 20-cent coin,' *pendona* 'a seasoned prostitute,' etc.) have followed a variety of patterns. Foreign borrowings, at least at first, do not have the undesirable associations with the referent that are awakened by the native word. Borrowings may be words of identical meaning or words of a vague or general sense, originally euphemistic metaphors themselves. Among them are:

bayusera (Cuba) 'woman who frequented a *bayú* 'red-light district' (formerly), from French *bayou.*

carrusiana (Col), from French *carrousel* 'merry-go-round'; general *cocot, cocote* or *cocota,* from French *cocotte,* an onomatopoetic formation as an infantile term for 'chicken,' and originally also a euphemism for the referent under discussion (Nyrop, p. 302); *coscolina* (Mex) 'mujer de alegre vivir pero algo recatada' (Santamaría); *coya* (Col), from Quechua *koya* 'queen, princess,' an ironical euphemism, but in some areas it means a 'worm' resembling the silkworm (Cauca: Tascón), elsewhere a venomous 'spider' (N Col: Sundheim, Revollo).

chapola (Nariño, Col), from *chapola* 'butterfly' (related to Aztec *chapulín* 'grasshopper' ?), therefore indicating flightiness, inconstancy; *chincola* (Chile), from *chincol,* a Mapuche name for a kind of 'songbird.'

gaucha (Arg: Garzón); *giranta* or *yiranta* or *yira* (RP), from Italian *girare* 'to move around, walk about' (cf. std. *buscona* 'one who roams the streets in search of clients'), as in "La audacia de que hace gala la *giranta* cuando se lanza, se respalda en el hombre, en el 'marido' ocasional" (Mendoza, p. 44), deriv. *girar,* as in "la prostituta que *gira* clandestinamente" (*ibid.,* p. 45); *guaricha* (see above); *güila* or *huila* or *güilona* (Mex, CA), from Aztec *huilana* 'andar arrastrándose' (Robelo), that is, 'dragging oneself along' because of deformed legs, as in "ya no 'stará triste su mercé, ya le jallamos una *huila* ... Chona había enrojecido de rabia al oír que la llamaban *huila"* (Ángulo, p. 346), "agentes de sanidad que andan detrás de las *güilas"* (Anda, p. 133); *güiñachishcas* (Ec) from Quechua, as in "Ese recuerdo vivo de las *güiñachishcas* que se sabían acostar con los arrieros en las cunetas" (Icaza, *Cholos,* p. 137); *güisa* or *huiza* (Tex), from Aztec *huitztli* 'thorn' *or huitzilin* 'humming-bird' (?).

mameluca (Chile) 'mameluke' (the mamelukes were originally Turkish slaves brought into Egypt and later formed the dynasty of Egyptian sultans from 1250 to 1517), in familiar standard speech 'simpleton, dolt'; *maraca* (Chile), from Guaraní *mbaracá* (?), the name of a musical instrument made with a dried calabash containing pebbles or hard seeds, and also (in Chile) a type of 'dice game' (Román).

pepereche (Salv), perhaps from Aztec *pepena* 'to pick up, gather' (cf. std. *buscona*)*; pípila* (Mex) 'turkey hen,' supposedly from Aztec *pipilpipil* 'children' and by extension meaning offspring of the turkey hen, which the Spaniards called *pípila* because it was the mother of the *pipilitos* or *pípilos* (Robelo); *pisca* (Col), from Quechua *pisco* 'bird,' later 'turkey' and 'fellow'; *piscamocha, piscapocha* (Mex), see below; *piscuaraca* (Nariño, Col), from Quechua *piscua* + *raca* 'vulva.'

pichuncha (Chile), from Aymara *phichunchaa* 'bird of ill omen,' and sometimes meaning 'concubine.'

quilombera (Arg), from native Brazilian *quilombo* 'a place or house where refugee Negroes were beaten' and now (RP, Bol, Peru) 'brothel.'

rapariga (Peru) from Portuguese *rapariga* 'girl' and, in parts of Brazil, 'concubine' and 'prostitute.'

Often euphemisms derive from names of animals that in some way suggest similar characteristics or activities, like standard *araña* 'spider' (which lies in wait for *la mosca* 'money' [lit. 'fly']), as in "Y eres *araña,* que andabas / Tras la pobre mosca mía," Quevedo, *Letrilla burlesca,* No. I), *cabra* 'goat,' *tusona* (from *tusa* 'she-dog'), *zorra* 'fox' (Riegler, p. 47, thinks this meaning of *zorra* may derive from a peculiar manner of fox hunting: a female fox is tied to a tree in the forest to entice male foxes, which are then caught in the surrounding net).

Among American-Spanish terms, in addition to those mentioned above (*cocot, coya, chapola, chincola, huiza,* etc.) are the following.

bacalao (cant, Chile) 'codfish,' referring to the dried variety and meaning 'prostituta vieja y sucia' (Vicuña); *bagre* (CR) 'catfish,' meaning also 'ugly woman.'

camaronera (Nic); *cogedora de mariposas* 'butterfly catcher' (cant, Mex: Rod); *congria* 'eel' (Mex); *cusca* or *cuzca* (Mex), a variant of *gozque* 'cur' (Corominas).

chiva 'goat' because of its lasciviousness (Ec, Ant), as in "mi padre llamaba *chivas* a esas tristes infelices que son conocidas ... por *mujeres de vida alegre*" (Ec: Cuadra, p. 76), cf. std. *cabra; chivatera* (Peru) is a 'prostituta de última clase' (Vargas Ugarte); *chucha* (Chile) from *chucho* 'dog' or from *chucha* 'vulva' (?); *chuchumeca* and shortened form *meca* (Catamarca, Arg; Chile, Peru), perhaps from standard *chuchumeco* 'contemptible little fellow,' having phonetic associative interference with *chucho* 'owl' or 'dog' and with the *chichimeca* Indians; *chusca, chusquisa* (Chile), *chuquisa* (Catamarca, Arg; Peru), of uncertain origin, perhaps related to standard *chusco* 'droll, merry, pleasant.'

gallina (Guat) 'hen' (Sandoval); *ganado* (Col) 'cattle,' and less frequently *orejinegro* 'black-eared cattle' (Tobón); *ganso* (Chile) 'gander,' meaning 'ramera disimulada, no profesional' as in "Fulano tiene su *ganso;* Esa Fulana es un *ganso*" (Oroz, p. 24); *gaviota* (Chile) 'sea gull'; *guajolota* (Mex) 'turkey hen.'

jíbara (SD), meaning *cimarrón* 'wild' or 'undomesticated.'

lagartija (Peru) 'lizard'; *leona* 'lioness' (CA, Mex); *loba* (Peru, Col) 'she-wolf,' as in "En ese barrio no habitan sino *lobas*" and "Solamente las *lobas* usan la falda de esa forma tan indecorosa" (Acuña).

oveja (Arg) 'sheep,' perhaps referring to 'lost sheep'; *polilla* (Peru) 'moth.'

sapo (Cuba) 'toad' and a kind of 'fish,' deriv. *sapear* 'ejercicio de la prostitución con reservas; no públicamente' or 'indagar o buscar mujeres que ejercen la prostitución con alguna reserva,' and *sapería* 'sitio donde abundan las mujeres que *sapean*,' as in "un barrio de mucha *sapería*" (C. Suárez).

vaca (cant, Chile) 'cow'; *torera* 'bullfighter' (cant, Mex: Rod).

Among metaphorical terms are:

alegrona (general) 'gay'; *andadora* (Mex); *arepera* (Ven) 'arepa maker or vendor,' *arepa* being a flat corn tortilla often sold in the streets; *arrastra-*

dora (Peru) 'dragger'; *aviadora* (Chile) 'aviatrix,' from *aviación* 'aventura de amores fáciles,' with the idea of flightiness.

bicicleta (Arequipa, Peru) 'bicycle,' which 'gets around'; *bondadosa* (Mex).

cachera (Guat), from *cachar* 'to obtain, solicit, steal,' as in "Se asegura que Serafina es una de las pocas *cacheras* que hay aquí" (Sandoval); *campechana* (Tex) 'frank, hearty, liberal'; *casco* (Ant) 'cask, bottle'; *catrera* (Peru), from *catre* 'bed'; *congalera* (Mex) from *congal* 'brothel'; rather general *cuero* or *cuerito* (Col, Ec, Ven, Ant, Mex), though *cuero* (Mex) may also mean 'a beautiful girl,' as in "¡Mira qué rico *cuero!*" (Malaret), "Déjala ... lo que sobra en nuestra carrera (de soldado) son los buenos *cueros*" (Ángulo, p. 49), and "acabo de conseguirme un *cuerazo* morrocotudo, una chulada de morena que ya está aburrida de su marido" (*ibid.*, p. 205), cf. *pellejo* (Ven) 'skin, hide' meaning 'ramera vulgar,' Portuguese *coira* 'concubine,' French argot *cuir* (or *peau*) *de chien* 'prostitute,' and Russian *shkura* 'skin, hide,' meaning also 'prostitute.'

chacuelera (Peru) 'small-business woman'; *changadora* (RP) from local *changador* (= std. *mozo de cordel* 'porter'), cf. Chilean *cortera* 'ramera buscona' from *cortero* 'porter,' a person who runs errands and does any small odd job called *corte,* cf. also Cuban *fletera* 'prostitute,' from *flete* 'freightage' and *fletar* 'to hire a vehicle to transport persons or cargo,' deriv. *fletear* 'to walk the streets' in search of *fletes* 'conquests'; *chilena* (Peru) 'Chilean girl' perhaps because many prostitutes at one time came to Peru from Chile.

flauta (Bol) 'flute'; *fundillo* (Mex) 'posterior'; *horizontal* (general).

loca (general) 'crazy, silly,' because of her behavior; (*de la*) *lucha* (Mex) '(of the) struggle.'

maduja, maleta, and *maraquera* (cant, Peru); *mina* (rather general), whence *ingeniero de minas* 'pander' (cant, Peru).

nochera (Col), from *noche* 'night,' because of the time of her activity.

patinadora (Chile, Peru) 'skater'; *pirata* (cant, Mex) 'pirate'; *pisadora* (CA), from *pisar* 'to cohabit'; *piscamocha* or *piscapocha* (Mex), possibly from *piscar* 'to harvest' and *pocha* (Tabasco) 'gain' or from popular Tabascan *piscapocha* (or *piscamocha*) 'money'; *pluma* (RP, Bol, Mex) 'feather,' because of her flightiness, deriv. *plumear* (Arg) as in "Esta chinita no sirve pa nada, se lo pasa *plumeriando* en el pueblo" (San Luis, Arg: Vidal, p. 165).

serrucho (Cuba) 'handsaw,' referring to certain movements; *sajuriana* (Piura, Peru, where she is also *mozamala*), a word which in Chile means a kind of dance, now fallen into desuetude, similar to the Chilean *cueca*, performed by two dancers waving handkerchiefs and beating time with their feet.

tusa (CA, Ant) 'cornhusk,' 'a thing of little value,' or std. 'dog'?

volada (Mex), *volantusa* or *volantuza* (Chile, Bol, Peru, Ec) from *volar* 'to fly' and *volante* 'unsettled.'

Often phonetic distortions of the taboo word render it acceptable in general usage. Thus, *pelandruca* and *pelambrusca* (Cuba) replace standard *pelandusca,* of uncertain origin. Euphemistic distortions of harsh and vulgar *puta* (originally a euphemism meaning 'young girl,' cf. *niña* and French *fille*) 'whore' are numerous. As an interjection, this word, used among men to express surprise, admiration, alarm, disgust, and even joy, is in careful speech veiled by *pucha(s)*, *puchita(s)*, *ta* (only the second syllable of *puta*), *cha* or *chas* (the second syllable of *pucha* and *puchas* respectively), *chitas, pita, puchas digo* (in Chile *diego* or *Diego*), *puya, pulga, punta,* and other words, which, having lost their offensiveness, are occasionally used by women, especially in rural areas, as in the Chilean folk stanza: "Así me icía mi maire, / Así me volvió a icir: / El día que yo me muera / ¡—ta! que vay a sufrir" (for more examples, see *AmSS,* p. 433).

The vulgar phrase *hijo de puta* or *hideputa* 'son of a prostitute,' no longer current in polite society as it occasionally was in Cervantes' day (*Don Quijote,* Part II, chap. xxxi) is still heard among the populace, both in censure and in praise. In Spanish America it assumes euphemistic forms varying from region to region, but all belonging to the category of *mentadas de madre.* Reduced alterations, generally rustic, with complete omission of *puta,* are *ahijuna, hijuna, jijuna, hijue* (= *hijo de*) *juna* or *junagran,* or simply *jijo.* Again, offensive *puta* may be replaced by almost any word containing one or more sounds of the original that suffice to suggest its meaning, such as *país, palabra, p'arriba, perra, pinta, pita, puerca, punta, puya, república* ("hijuna grandísima *república,*" Chile: Del Campo, p. 48), *de la familia Putiérrez* 'prostitute' (cant, Mex: Chabat), or simply *p* ("el señor *'h de la p' ";* "el tocayo Meshe no se casa ni con la *p*... de su *m*..., hom," Peru: Barrantes, p. 156; "—¡Ríndete, Nicolás! —¡Tu *p*... madre!" Mex: Ángulo, p. 144).

In the Mexican zone (including Central America) the word is replaced among the populace by *chingada,* a word that has become even more unsavory, in such phrases as *hijo* (or *jijo*) *de la chingada,* occasionally found in print, as in "¡Nos volveremos a ver, *hija de la chingada!* —¡Tú chinga a tu madre, cabrona! Así se despidieron mis hermanas" (Galeana, p. 42). It may be clipped in print, as in *"¡jijoj de un ch...!"* (Taracena, p. 128). It may be euphemistically distorted, as in "¡Ah, qué *jijo de la chicharra!"* (Gómez Palacio, p. 106), "¡Pero qué suerte *jija de la chicharrona* me he cargado hoy!" (Ángulo, p. 130), *hijo de la china Hilaria,* in the common exclamation *¡Ah, Chihuahua!* (a place name serving as the veil), and in occasional phrases like *¿Cómo está suchi?* or less evident *¿Cómo está susana?* The exclamation *¡Me lleva la ... !* may be euphemized, as in *¡Me lleva ... el tren!* (Alatorre, No. 3, p. 11), then by use of any other word having initial *tr* or *t,* often preserving the *á–a* assonance of the offending word, such as *trampa, trompada, tía de las muchachas,* and the like.

Originally a euphemism, *tiznar* 'to smirch, smudge' is now equally opprobrious in *hijo de la tiznada* (or *tostada*). In Urquizo's *Tropa vieja* (1943, p. 106), a sergeant shouts to a soldier, *"Tizna* a tu madre," and a corporal yells "¡Carbón!" ('coal,' referring euphemistically to *carajo* and to *tiznado* 'blackened'); but realizing that the soldiers no longer react to his insults, the corporal elaborates simple "tizna a tu madre" into rhetorical "Anda y retizna a tu rejijo de un tiznado madre, tal por cual."

That these insults, through frequent repetition, often lose their original sting is indicated not only by the fact that many of the soldiers laugh in the corporal's face but also by the lack of grammatical agreement among the words used. The soldier himself comments: "hasta bonito se oye la retajila [= retahila] de insolencias" (*ibid.,* p. 107). Furthermore, in some regions, notably Alvarado, the use of such abusive *mentadas* (*de madre*) may be fairly common among friends as terms of endearment; that is, they may be classified as metaphors based on similarity of emotive effect. This does not generally hold, however, of other regions.

Among euphemistic substitutions one finds *hijo de la chesna* or *cherna* = 'jewfish' (SD), *hijo de la grand madre, hijo de la guayaba, hijo de la Gran Bretaña, hijo de la que no tiene nombre, hijo de la gran siete, hijo de la esposa del gallo* (= *gallina* = *puta*), *hijo de la repintada, hijo de siete mil tostadas,* etc.

MENTAR LA MADRE

We may now consider more fully the grave insults just mentioned which are known as *mentar* (sometimes *sacar*) *la madre a uno* 'to mention someone's mother' (in which 'to mention' euphemizes 'to slander, vilify') or *echar mentadas* (*de madre*) or *echar madres*. Other expressions are *rayársela a uno* (Col, Mex); *mentar* or *arrear la grande* (Col); *sacarla al sol* (Guat); *requintar* (Peru), as in "se puso a *requintarlo* a gritos" (Corrales, p. 149), *requintada* being explained as "la incontenible tendencia a extender a los parientes del interlocutor injurias que no se merecen, puesto que no son parte de la querella. Casi siempre ... viene la agarrona a mojicones, palos y botellazos" (*ibid.,* p. 273). The scurrilous phrase is often euphemistically shortened to general ¡*su madre!* or ¡*tu madre!*; ¡*va la madre!* ¡*va la vieja!* ¡*va la grande!* as well as less offensive ¡*va la gorra!* (Col: Tobón).

The insults referred to in the following passages are of the kind just described: "De un momento al otro llegaban a las manos. A falta de insolencias suficientemente incisivas, acudían a *nombrar padres y madres* en el bordado más rico de indecencias" (Mex: Azuela, p. 70); "Un nombre de combate resuena, y estalla el conflicto en aquel sector ¡Guineo ... Guineo ladrón! ... *Las madres* sacuden el ámbito y la piedra rumba [= *zumba* 'buzzes around']" (Col: Bernardo Toro, *Minas, mulas* y *mujeres,* Medellín, 1943, p. 10).

Needless to say, these abusive words make the offended one's blood boil. This is evident from the following passages: "Uvieta llegó y llamó como antes usaban llamar las gentes cuando llegaban a una casa: —¡Ave María Purísima! Por supuesto que al oír esto, los demonios se pusieron como si *les mentaran la mama* (CR: Lyra, p. 97); (description of a prison) "El que tiene comida, porque se la llevan de su casa, la comparte con el que no la tiene, y al que no le ven cobija, *mientan la madre,* con solicitud, *para que se caliente*" (Mex: Rubén Romero, *La vida inútil de Pito Pérez,* 1938, pp. 116–117).

Just as many Andalusians shudder at the word *culebra* and counter with *lagarto* (see chap. i), so the offended person shudders—but for a different reason—at *madre* and counters with ¡*la suya!* or ¡*la tuya!* Thus: "—¡Ladrón! —¡Tu *mae* [= *madre*]! —¡*La tuya!* ... seguían insultándose, poniendo en juego ese vocabulario de rudeza canalla en donde siempre triunfa el máximo ultraje, expresado en dos palabras" (González Eiris in *Antología del cuento moderno venezolano,* 1940, II, 325–327); (in a fight between two women) "Cada una escupió en dirección segura de los pies de la otra. —¡Anda, verásle *a tu madre!* —¡Anda, verásle *a la tuya!* —Fué la declaración de guerra" (Ec: J. de la Cuadra, *Los Sangurimos,* 1934, p. 137). Occasionally a speaker, suspecting that his interlocutor may be merely thinking the insult without expressing it, will remark *"la tuya,* por si acaso" (Guat: Sandoval). In some Geography classes, mentioning the island of Sumatra is bound to elicit the retort *¡la sutra!* (Ven: Rosenblat, p. 30).

The challenge is usually met with violence, and often has a tragic ending, for example: "Añadí agravios a las respectivas *mamas;* enfurecido uno ... se me vino encima cuchillo en mano" (Peru: Corrales, p. 82). "—Le *mentó la mama* y Tomaj se le jué encima con un cuchillo hasta dejarlo moribundo" (Mex: Taracena, p. 121); "éste que contesta con una *mentada de madre* y aquél que saca la pistola y éste que le madruga" (Mex: Gómez Palacio, p. 75). The story goes that a Mexican sentinel, aware of approaching steps in the darkness, shouted "¿Quién va?" 'who goes there?'; on hearing the reply "¡Tu madre!" and mistaking the words for an insult, he raised his gun and killed his own mother.

Many cautious speakers avoid the use of hazardous *madre,* generally substituting *mamá* (rustic *mama*) or diminutive *mamita,* as in some of the preceding examples. Sometimes these words are used euphemistically, sometimes facetiously, as in: "—¡Miserables! Esas burlas vayan a hacerlas a *las mamitas* que los parió" (Peru: Corrales, p. 224); "Si algún Mañara ... le soltaba al paso un 'adiós, prenda,' con desenfado, capaz de poner a raya al más osado, respondía: *'Tu mama,'* y seguía su camino como si tal cosa" (Col: Rendón, p. 86); "Las vendedoras siguen insultándose a voz en cuello. Y en cada insulto, hacen mención de sus respectivas *mamás*" (Ec: García Muñoz, p. 69); "En algunas regiones del país no suele decirse *"¡tu madre!,"* sino *"¡tu máma!"* (SD: Jiménez, p. 138). In Ancient History classes pupils sometimes refer to "la *mamá* de Nerón" (Ven: Rosenblat, p. 29).

The euphemization of *madre* may also be effected by use of a feminine noun containing the first syllable *ma,* such as *madrina, mañana, máquina,* and even *mula,* which contains only the first sound (Rivera, p. 181). Examples: "—¿Qué le duele, tía enjurtido? —¡Tu *ma ... drina!* ... (Azuela, *Mala yerba,* p. 126); "—¡Me da la propaganda o me la llevo presa! —¡Ay, hijo de la *mañana!*—pensé—¡cómo me estás jodiendo!" (Galeana, p. 122);

"Chona, ¡jala pues con nosotros ... tendré así la ventaja de llevar conmigo una 'ametralladora!' —*¡Tú máquina,* mula desorejada! ¡Si un hombre le hubiese mencionado *a la autora de sus días,* involucrándola con el asunto de sus orejas despuntadas, muy caro la habría pagado! Pero ... él no iba a pelearse con aquella hembra guapota" (Ángulo, p. 322).

Another method of euphemizing *madre* is the use of vaguer or further removed degrees of kinship, like *abuela* 'grandmother,' *familia* (*orden familiar* for *mentada* in Mexican cant), *parientes* or *parentela* 'relatives,' *la quinta generación* (Peru) 'the fifth generation' (based on *requintar* and *requintada*), or by periphrases like *la hermana de su tía* 'your aunt's sister,' *la más vieja de tu casa* 'the oldest woman in your house,' *la progenitora inmediata* 'your immediate ancestor.' Examples: "A mí naiden me ha mentao a *mi familia*" (Azuela, p. 71); "declaro que lo insulto ... y hago arrancar el insulto ... desde *la quinta generación* inclusive" (Peru: Corrales, p. 142); "reniega hasta de *su quinta generación*" (*ibid.,* p. 158); "—¡No me diga 'sté esas cosas, porqui onde me lo repita, va 'sti a hacer que me ricuerde de *la hermana de su tía!*" (Mex: Rivas Larrauri, p. 23); "¡Esas bromas guárdatelas para la *más vieja de tu casa!*" (López y Fuentes, p. 19); "Cuando entre las injurias se saca a relucir a *la progenitora inmediata* del injuriado, se dice 'le echaron la viga de la madre' " (Rivera, p. 181).

We find euphemistic irony in *echar la loa* 'to praise' (Veracruz: Rivera, p. 181); *alabarle a uno la mamá* 'to praise someone's mother,' as in "También he oído por ahí ... que *usté le alabó la mamá* al Director" (Arg: Manuel Gálvez, *La maestra normal,* II, 2); *su muy distinguida progenitora* (Guat: Sandoval).

Occasionally a very vague reference suffices: In Veracruz it is related that during a heated football game, players insulted the spectators (with *mentadas de madre*) and were consequently jailed. Once freed, they limited themselves to the vague euphemism of *¡No se te olvide!* 'don't forget it' and the counter (instead of *¡la suya!* or *¡la tuya!*) became *¡Ni a tí tampoco!* a practice that soon became general in that locality.

Although *mentada* gestures made in lieu of uttering the insulting words have lost much of their softening effect, they are more readily accepted than the scurrilous words they suggest. A widespread gesture, though not used in all regions, is the Spanish *corte de manga* 'sleeve cut' (Italian *manichetto,* Portuguese *armas de São Francisco*). It is usually made by bending the left forearm vigorously upward, with fist clenched or middle finger extended, and thrusting the extended right hand into the inner bend of the left arm (see fig. 31) and is accompanied by an utterance like ¡*ésta!* or ¡*toma!* (¡*tomá!* in *voseo* regions) or ¡*toma por aquí!* and in Cuba with ¡*ñinga!* (Rodríguez, p. 411). In Spain one may hear ¡*Móntate y verás Madrid!* or ¡*Por aquí se va a Madrid* (or *a París*)!

In Peru and Ecuador the *corte de manga* is known as *yuca,* the name of a long thick edible root which is similar to a potato and sometimes reaches the size of the forearm. The expression *hacer un corte de manga* there becomes *echar* (*dar* or *tirar*) *una yuca.* Examples of its execution are: "Y mandones, aguántenlos ustedes, porque lo que es nosotros, ¡eéstaa! (= an emphatic ¡*ésta!*) ... y *se mide con una mano el antebrazo de la otra*" (Peru: Barrantes, p. 90). On a train from Guayaquil to Quito, two boys who were hanging on the back platform jumped off when threatened by the conductor and made the disgraceful gesture at him—that is, *le echaron una yuca.*

Other gestures of similar meaning are the ubiquitous *higa* 'fig' (see Gillet, III, 285), in which the thumb is thrust between index and middle fingers of the same hand (see fig. 32); the middle finger is extended erect as a phallic symbol, and the other fingers are bent into the palm (a sort of diminutive *corte de manga*) (see fig. 33); the so-called *pistola* 'pistol,' in which the extended right index is briskly thrust between extended or circled left thumb and index (see fig. 34): "—¡Loco está el hombre! ... Al oír esta afirmación ... hizo Felix *un semicírculo con el pulgar y el índice de la mano izquierda, manteniendo cerrados los otros tres dedos, y por ese arco invertido dejaba caer y hacía pasar rápidamente el índice de la derecha muy tieso y erguido,* en tanto que gritaba ... ¡*Tenga!* ¡*Tenga!*" (Mex: Valle-Arizpe, *El canillitas,* 1941, p. 318); jerking clenched fist downward below the waist as one says *acá* 'here'; the so-called *violín* (Mex) 'violin,' in which index and middle fingers of one hand are placed on either side of the nose and moved downward as if a bow were being drawn over violin strings (see fig. 35): "—¡Te has rozado las verijas! [to a woman soldier]. [Ella] Se vuelve bruscamente ... se la ve *ponerse índice y cordial a los lados de la nariz. Ejecuta un movimiento de arriba abajo.* Está furiosa" (López y Fuentes, p. 31). Ragamuffins are known to make four *violines* at once, with quadrupled force of the insult: the little finger is placed below the mouth, the tongue extended, ring finger placed below nose, middle finger below eye, thumb behind ear (see fig. 36). Since the phrase *hacer el violín* has fallen into disrepute, it is frequently rephrased into vague *hacer un instrumento musical con los dedos.* More delicate *mentadas* which may be made by women are these: moving the fingers between collar and neck as if brushing back hair behind the ear, with a facial expression of annoyance, or moving index and thumb back and forth on the neck (see fig. 37); the *araño* gesture (Mex), in which the open hand is extended with tips of fingers curved inward as in the act of scratching, which may be either a *mentada* or its counter (*contramentada*), and the word *araño* itself may be euphemized with some elaborate phrase like *"hará año* [= *araño*] y medio que no la veo."

Furthermore the *mentada* is often expressed with rhythmic beats, as ′◡◡′◡ (Mex) corresponding to the stresses of *chinga tu madre,* euphemized into *palmas de tango* when one claps the hands with this rhythm; or the feet may stamp out the rhythm at a bullfight or at the theater when a delay or a poor performance proves annoying. The counter or reply is this rhythm: ◡′◡◡′◡◡′◡, corresponding to *¡la tuya que esté en vinagre!,* or something similar. The dialogue of *mentada* and *contramentada* is often carried out with automobile horns when one motorist wishes to reproach another for careless or inappropriate driving. Or the rhythm ◡′◡, corresponding to *su madre* or *tu madre* or *la vieja,* may be whistled (especially CA), with its counter in the same rhythm corresponding to *la suya* or *la tuya.*

All these insulting gestures may serve also to express strong incredulity or vigorous negation and, used jocosely among intimate friends, may even be signs of endearment. Many of them are akin in feeling to the various shades of 'go to hell,' 'God damn it,' and the like, cf. "Yo cogí algunos bocablos, / como el de 'guate' por agua; / déme es 'guime'; 'jor' cabayo; / 'blac' es negro; 'jos' es casa; / un 'estope' es esperate; / un 'olraites' a la marcha; / el 'cotejel' es mistao / y el 'gordemis' es *tu mama"* (rustic, CR: Aquileo Echeverría, *Concherías,* 3d ed., p. 145).

PANDER

Standard *alcahuete* 'procurer, pander' is often euphemized, especially in cant, by words having the same initial sequence of sounds amply suggesting the offensive term. Thus, peninsular *alcarreña* ('inhabitant of Alcarria') may mean *alcahueta* (Wagner, p. 15), and *alcamonías* ('seeds for seasoning foods') may mean *alcahueterías*. Among the euphemisms heard in America are *alcachofa* (Peru) 'artichoke'; *alcalde* (rather general) 'mayor,' upon which Cornejo (Ec) comments: "A los alcaldes propiamente dichos ... no ha de saberles a caramelo esta nueva acepción de la palabra que los nombra, por mucho que estén convencidos de que algunos de ellos son alcahuetes i alcaldes en una sola pieza"; *alcalde de la ciudad de Huete* is the more common expression in Peru (ap. Cornejo), in which a fictitious place name supplies the last two syllables of *alcahuete; alcanfor* ('camphor') and *alcanforado; alcancil* (Arg) 'wild artichoke'; *alcohol, alcasétzer,* and *ahuehuete* (Mex: Alatorre, No. 3, p. 11). The feminine form *alcahueta* may be replaced by *comadre* (general), and by *abadesa* 'abbess' (which in popular speech often euphemizes *dueña de mancebía* 'brothel keeper'). Closely allied *rufián* 'pander' may be transmuted into the euphemism *rufino* and *rufo.* Other euphemisms are *cinturita* (Mex), *comefrío* (Col), *ingeniero de minas* ('prostitutes') and *violinista* (Peru).

Borrowings are numerous: *cacahuate* (Mex); *cafiche* (Chile, Peru) from Argentine slang *cafisho* (*BAAL,* VI, 137), and its still later euphemism *cafiolo* (Oroz, *El elemento afectivo,* p. 56); *caften* (RP) 'owner of a brothel' or 'white slave trafficker' (from Turkish), as in "la burguesía comete una injusticia con los *caftens"* (Mendoza, p. 45); *canaca,* from Polynesian *kanaka* 'man' > 'a native Hawaiian,' is in Chile applied to members of the yellow race, particularly Chinamen, and since these are often proprietors of restaurants, coffeehouses and brothels, *canaca* is now equivalent to 'brothel owner'; *canfi, canfinfla, canfinfle, canflinflero* (Arg); *chichigua* 'wet nurse' (Mex); general *gígolo,* from French; *guayabito* (Cuba) from *guayabo* (Arawak or Carib ?), the name of a fruit tree, or from its meaning of 'mouse' ? ; *lacho* (Chile), of disputed origin; *macró* (especially Peru) from French *maquereau* which French speakers themselves have euphemized by shortening it to *mac* and by metaphor to *dos vert* 'greenback' (in turn shortened to *dos* 'back') because the back of the *maquereau* 'mackerel' is marked with bluish-green spots (Nyrop, p. 299); *pepenche* (Mex), from Aztec *pepena* 'to pick up, select,' meaning *hombre que vive a expensas de una mujer.*

Vulgar *cabrón* 'cuckold' (lit. 'billy goat') has in many areas (RP, Chile, Peru, Col, Ven) come to mean *rufián* or *padre de mancebía;* most Spanish Americans therefore prefer the old form *cabro* for 'billy goat' rather than modern *cabrón.* Standard *padre de mancebía* 'procurer' is often *padrote*

(Mex), in the service of the *madrota* 'brothel keeper'; sometimes the softer words *papá grande* (in cant) and *padrotón* (deriv. *padrotear* and *padrotería*) are used, or the still more euphemistic *padroterapia* (Santamaría).

BROTHEL

Standard *burdel, casa de lenocinio, lupanar, mancebía, prostíbulo,* etc., meaning 'brothel,' have a variety of euphemistic appellations: *casa de camas,* 'house of beds,' *casa llana* 'plain house,' *casa pública, casa de tolerancia, casa de trato* 'house of traffic,' etc. In America still others are current: *bayú* (formerly, Cuba) 'red-light district'; *casa de cita* or *de asignación* or *de convivialidad* (Mex); *canaca* (see above) 'brothel owner' and 'brothel,' deriv. *canaquear* 'to frequent brothels'; *comedero* (Col) 'feeding trough,' but the meaning *barrio de mujeres públicas* 'red-light district' is more general; *congal* (Mex), see Speratti, p. 158; *huerto* (N Chile) 'garden,' explained as 'sitio donde *se planta* y *se siembra,* y donde hay muchas *plantas*' (Vicuña Cifuentes); *pecadero* (Chile, Peru), from *pecado* 'sin'; *picadero* (Cuba), probably from the standard meaning 'stamping ground for bucks in rutting time'; *tocinería* (Yucatán) 'bacon shop'; *tumbadero* (Cuba), from *tumbar* 'to fell.' Many of them contain animal names: *gallera* (Guat) 'breeding place for game cocks' (*gallos*)*; lagartero* (Guat), from *lagarto* 'alligator' and 'lizard'; *leonera* (Salv) 'lion's den'; *sapería* (Cuba), from *sapo* 'prostitute' (lit. 'toad'), etc. Among borrowings are *queco* and *quenco* (Salta, Arg) from Quechua *kqencu* 'cosa de muchas vueltas y escondrijos' (Solá); *quilombo* (RP, Chile, Bol, Peru), from a Brazilian Negro word; *tambo* (slang, Arg), from Quechua *tampu,* 'country inn.'

EFFEMINACY

Familar standard *marica* (< *María*), *marico* (especially Col, Ven) and *maricón* (fam. and vulgar) meaning *afeminado* 'effeminate' (often in the sense of *cobarde* 'cowardly, sissy': a mother may say to her crybaby "no seas *maricón*") have undergone phonetic deformations to produce euphemisms generally retaining the sounds *maric, mari, mar,* or *ma,* such as *mamita* (CR); *mampucho* and *mapuchín* (Col, Pan), from local *mampucho = rechoncho* 'chubby'; obsolescent *mandarina* (Antioquia, Col) 'tangerine'; *maraco* (Bol); *maricantunga* (Chile); *maricontento* (Ec: Wagner, p. 24); *maricueca* (Chile, Peru), as in "Llegó el Arica / tocando cueca / para que bailen / las *maricuecas*" (Malaret, *Copla*); *maricueco* (Pan), now shortened to *cueco; marimari* (Chile, see below); *marinero* (general) 'sailor'; *mariposón* (Peru), augmentative of *mariposa* 'butterfly'; *mariquito* (Cuba); *marisco* 'shellfish' (Ven); *ave marica* (Col), from *ave maría; marta* (cant, Mex: Rod); *mayate* (cant, Mex; see below).

There are also many euphemistic deformations of *hermofrodita* 'hermaphrodite,' from a late story in Greek mythology according to which Hermaphroditus, son of Hermes and Aphrodite, having rejected the love of Salmacis, the nymph of a fountain where he was bathing, became, at her prayer to the gods, joined in one body to her, and a being resulted half male and half female. Polysyllabic *hermafrodita* is altered by popular etymology to general *manflorita, manfrodita* (Navarra: Iribarren), *monflorita* (Murcia), *manflora* (RP, CA), *manflor* (CA, Mex), *mamplor* (Guat), *mamplora* (CA), *manflórico* (Col, Ven), *manfloro* (SD), and still further distorted in *mafrito* (E Mex), *mofrado* (Hond) and *floripondio* (Esmeraldas, Ec; Lima, Peru), the name of a flower (cf. *flora*, Andalusia). See also A. Rosenblat in *Filología* (Buenos Aires), V, 1959, pp. 38–40.

Just as *marica* and *maricón* derive from *María,* so other names or adjectives applied to the feminine sex may come to mean 'effeminate' (cf. English *Nancy, Nance;* Portuguese *aninha,* from Ana): *coyón* (Guat), from *coyo,* nickname of *Socorro* and meaning more generally 'cowardly,' as in "El general ... no fué *coyón,* sino ... desafortunado en sus acciones de armas" (Sandoval); *chabelón* (Guat) from *Chabelo = Isabel,* also in the sense of 'cowardly'; *güitalolo* (Jalisco, Mex: Duarte), from *Lola* (?); *josefino* (Col) from *Josefina* (Caution: *josefino* may be the inhabitant of any city called *San José,* as the capital of Costa Rica, for instance); *pituco* (Arg) from *Pituca,* diminutive of *Petrona; loca* (RP, Peru, and elsewhere) 'mad, silly, wild'; *mino* (Arg slang), from *mina* 'mistress,' further euphemized by *ministro,* containing the first three sounds of *mino* (Gobello, p. 79); *nagüilón* (Guat) from *enaguas* 'underskirt,' more in the sense of 'cowardly,' as in "El general ... demostró ser un gran *nagüilón* en la batalla" (Sandoval); general *niña* 'girl'; *ñato* (Pan) = *chato* 'flat-nosed' used as a term of endearment; *pollerón* (Atlantic coast, Col), from *pollera* 'skirt'; *rosita* (CR).

Among euphemistic borrowings are *acaschao* (Salta, Arg: Solá) from

Quechua; *apapayado* (Serena, Chile) from *papaya* 'vulva' (Rabanales, p. 186); *cachero* (Chile, slang), from an Aymara root meaning 'unnatural intercourse' (Vicuña); *caucho* (Ec) from Quechua *cauchu* 'rubber,' used particularly among students (Cornejo); *cundango, cundingo* (Ant) from an African word with 'bird' as one of its meanings (Ortiz); *cuilmas* (CA, Mex) and *cuilón* (Mex), from Aztec *cuiloni* 'sodomite'; *chocollo* (Arequipa, Peru), from Quechua, 'pederasto pasivo'; *chucheta* and *chuchón* (Chile), used as vulgar insults, derivatives of *chucha* 'vulva,' possibly from a native word indicating a kind of 'clam' (see Lenz); *chuchinga* (Chile, CR) meaning also 'cowardly, weak'; *freshco* (Peru) from Portuguese *fresco* 'fresh'; *guarmilla* (Ec), from Quechua *huarmi* 'woman'; *güilón* (Hond) from Aztec; *mandinga* (CR) from African *mandinga* 'devil'; *mayate* (Mex), from Aztec *mayatl* 'a beautifully colored beetle,' sometimes applied to a person who escapes with someone's money, in cant 'active pederast'; rare *pichicón* (Chile), possibly from Mapuche *pici* 'small' and augmentative *-ón,* as in *maricón* (Lenz); *marimari* (Chile), a greeting current among Chilean Indians; *puchungo* (Ven).

Some words refer to animals: *ave negra* (Caldas, Col) 'bird of ill omen'; *buey* (cant, Mex) 'ox' for 'active pederast'; *burrero* (Col) from *burro;* *caballo* (cant, Mex) 'horse' for 'passive pederast'; *cabritilla* (Peru) 'kid'; *cabro* (Chile) 'goat'; *cacorro* (Col), perhaps deriving from the onomatopoetic cockfighting phrase *pedir cacao* referring to the crow made by the cock when it flees the fight (Cuervo, 659); *cangrejo* (Mex, Ant) 'crab, lobster'; *cigarrón* (Col) 'grasshopper'; *cocheche* and *cochon* 'pig'; *congrio* 'eel' and *culebro* 'snake' (cant, Mex: Rod); *chivato* and *chivo* (cant, Peru) 'kid'; *gallo-gallina* (Mex); *gaviota* (N Col) 'sea gull'; *león* 'lion' and *leo* (*pardo*) (Mex); *mariposón* (Peru) 'big butterfly'; *mula* (cant, Mex) 'she-mule' for 'passive pederast'; *pájaro* or *pajarito* (Cuba) 'bird'; *pato* (Ven, Nic, PR) 'duck'; *pocholito* (Chile) 'chubby' from *pocha,* a fish.

Miscellaneous forms (std. *sarasa; apio, canco,* Andalusia) are:

alfarero (Veracruz, Mex) 'potter'; *argolla* (Ven) 'ring'; *aviador* (Cuba) 'aviator,' a later euphemism for *pájaro.*

bufo and *bufarrón* (Arg), *bugato* (SD), *bujarro* (Ven), from standard *bujarrón* (< Latin *bulgarus* 'Bulgarian' meaning also 'heretic' (since many of the inhabitants of Bulgaria were heretics) coming into Spanish through Catalan *bujarró,* French *bougre* and *bougeron* (see Corminas); *culero* (Salv).

cafiaspirina and *colifor* (cant, Mex); *cuarenta y uno* or *cuarentiaiuno* (Mex) 'forty-one,' reportedly referring to the number of persons, some dressed as women, arrested during a raid in Mexico City in 1901, whence "41," having become synonymous with *maricón,* is avoided in assigning numbers to any group of persons (see Boggs, p. 36).

chulo (Salv); *hueco* (Guat) 'hollow, hole' for 'passive pederast.'

dañado (Col) 'damaged, bewitched'; (*ser*) *del otro lado* (Ven) '(to be) from the other side,' or *de los otros* (Mex), cf. peninsular *de la acera de enfrente.*

fifí (general); *izquierdo* (Nic) 'left.'

joto (Mex), of uncertain origin (Aztec *xote* 'lame' is conjectured by Santamaría); *joven* (Mex); *juaniquillo* (Ven).

loca (general); *lumio, lumnio* (cant, Mex).

mostacero (Peru) 'mustard pot'; *mujerengo* (CA); *naco* (CA).

pastilla, pirujo, pújiro (cant, Mex); *patiquín* (Ven: Rosenblat, p. 187); *petitero* (Bol); *popis* (Antioquia, Col: Tobón); *puto* (Mex); *puto culero* (Nic).

rechivuelta (Nic); *redondo* (Nic) 'round'; *rosca* and *rosquete* (Peru) 'circular cake'; *rueda* 'wheel, circle' and *rueda chata* (Nic).

simbólico = *sin bolas* (Rabanales, "Recursos," p. 213); *sol y sombra* (Mex); *sonámbulo* (Mex).

tilico (SA), *tucuco* (Peru); *vegetariano* and *venenosa* (cant. Peru); *Wilfrido* (Mex).

Gestures are often euphemistically employed to indicate effeminacy, obviating the objectionable words, which must then be supplied by the reader or interlocutor, as in "el sacristán nuevo me parece un poco ... (*con fino ademán da a entender que le parece afeminado*" (Quinteros, *El amor que pasa,* Act I). Some of these gestures are quite ancient and ubiquitous; we read: "To wag the hand in a swinging gesture . . . denotes a kind of wantounesse and effeminacy . . . the gate, the turning of the eye, the finger on the head" (Bulwer, pp. 73–74) and "to scratch the head with one finger" (*ibid.,* p. 172). Among those observable in Spanish-speaking countries are the following: the left forearm rests on the supporting open palm of the right; the raised index touches the left cheek; the head is bent toward the left; the open right hand clutches the left wrist (see Flachskampf, p. 248). Variations of these are found in Spanish America: with elbows close to the body, the extended open hands are waved to and fro from the wrist, as if they were wings (observed in Barranquilla, Col); extended index touches chin and a smile on the lips (general); left wrist is seized with the right hand and is moved with a circular motion (observed in Peru); a complete circle is made with thumb and index, remaining fingers bent in on the palm (CA); but if index and thumb do not form a complete circle, the gesture indicates 'money' (see fig. 20).

Euphemisms for *marimacho* 'tomboy, mannish,' are less abundant. Many of them are formations or deformations based on *macho* 'male,' such as general *macha; machona* with augmentative and deprecatory suffix *-ona; machanga* (Cuba), with deprecatory *-anga,* also the name of a monkey; *machetona* (Guat, Mex), leaning both on *macho* and on *machete* 'cane knife'; general *maricona* and *machorra* (std. meaning is 'barren, sterile'), as in "—Pa mí no hay mujer *machorra!*" (Ec: Cuadra, p. 118); *marota* (Mex), as in "[mi hija] es media *marota,* pica de jinete y decidora" (Inclán, I, 290).

Among the many other euphemisms of the same or similar meaning are *calincha* (Arequipa, Peru), from Quechua *karincha; carishina* (highland Ec) 'mannish,' from Quechua (Toscano, p. 339); *chepe* (Mex), diminutive of *José; chirota* (CA); *chirriona* (Mex, where it means also 'coquettish'), from *chirrión* 'whip'; *chiva* (Chile, Hond) 'goat'; *gaucha* (RP) feminine of *gaucho; sargento, sargentona* (Arg: Selva, p. 189); vulgar *tortillera* ('*tortilla* maker') for standard *lesbiana* 'Lesbian' often becomes *arepera* (Col, Ven), from *arepa* 'a kind of *tortilla,*' because of the clapping of the open palms in flattening the cake (see Acuña, *Vocabulario campesino,* p. 134). Standard *tortilla* 'flat omelet' is known in parts of America as *tortilla de huevos* (Mex) or *torta de huevos* (CA) since in these regions *tortilla* means a 'flat maize pancake.' Derivative *tortear* (Guat) is equivalent to *hacer tortillas,* and, like *chapear* (lit. 'to cut the underbrush close to the ground with a *machete*'), is used in a euphemistic figurative sense, as in "Margarita dice que no le gusta dormir con Serafina, porque luego trata de *tortear*" (Sandoval) and "A Rosa le gusta *chapear* con su amiga Serafina" (*ibid.*).

COITION

Vulgar *joder* (older *hoder, foder* < Latin *futuere*) is euphemized by *cohabitar, copular, hacer coito,* and other words, and has assumed the meaning of *molestar* 'to molest, annoy' equivalent to Spanish American *fregar*. This figurative meaning predominates in the mind of most Spanish-American speakers. Past participle *jodido* may mean 'in a sorry plight, ruined, poor, sick,' and even 'sly, astute, unscrupulous,' as in "Hay que tener cuidado al negociar con los gitanos porque son muy *jodidos*" (Col: Acuña). Even in the restricted sense of *molestar* the verb is extremely vulgar and is variously euphemized: for uncouth *¡no joda!* 'don't annoy, talk nonsense, kid,' etc., the softer expression *¡no friegue con jota!* is sometimes used, in which the veiled verb is sufficiently clear through mention of its first letter (*j = jota*); the proper name *José María,* is, because of the two initial sounds *jo,* sufficient to suggest any finite form of the verb, as in "Yo no me dejo *José María* [= *joder*] de nadie" and "Ya se *José María* [= *ha jodido*] el negocito que había establecido y en el cual me iba tan bonito" (Guat: Sandoval); cf. *jolín* and *jolines* (Madrid), and Andalusian *¡Josú!* for *¡Jesús!* (Beinhauer, *Umgangssprache,* p. 73).

Standard *coger* 'to take, pluck, seize' has also the meaning of *copular,* particularly in reference to animals (like *cubrir, prender*). In parts of America this meaning has become uppermost, particularly in areas, like the River Plate region, where cattle raising has always been of paramount importance. In the River Plate zone, then, and to a lesser degree in Venezuela and Mexico (as also in parts of Spain, see Llorente Maldonado, p. 168), the verb *coger* in its meaning 'to take, pluck' has lost caste, and is by some speakers scrupulously avoided. As early as 1910, Garzón remarked in his *Diccionario argentino:* "La inmoralidad y malicia precoces de la juventud han llegado a tal extremo, que no puede uno hacer uso de este verbo tan castizo en las acepciones que le son propias, sin exponerse a provocar la risa de los que lo toman en doble sentido." For other regions we read: "En Caracas ya no se puede usar el verbo *coger*" (ap. Alvarado), though it is still common there; "en Méjico lo evitan a veces personas remilgadas, pero nunca la gente culta" (*BDH,* IV, 49, n. 1). The verb most widely substituted in such areas is *agarrar* 'to seize, clutch,' from *garra* 'claw' and therefore much more forceful than the verb it replaces. One may hear: "*agarrar* (for *coger*) frutas de los árboles; *agarrar* una violeta, un resfriado; *agarrar* para tal parte; me *agarra* (for *coge*) el sueño; *agarrar* el tranvía," etc. In Argentina the taboo reaches derivatives like *acoger* 'to welcome,' *encoger* 'to shrink,' *escoger* 'to select, choose,' *recoger* 'to gather, pick up' and even innocent bystanders like adjective *cojo* 'lame' (Corominas). From an Argentinian school publication this sentence was culled: "Los estudiantes de la facultad deben *excogitar* buenos delegados," in which *excogitar* (lit. 'excogitate, meditate') euphemizes *escoger* 'to select' (Herrero Mayor, *Lengua,* p. 38). Standard *encogerse uno de hombros* 'to shrug one's shoulders' often becomes *alzar los hombros,* like French *hausser les épaules.* Euphemy may be attained also by adding an innocent word after a slight pause, as *coger ... mariposas* 'to catch butterflies' or *coger ... ratones* 'to catch mice' (cant, Mex: Rod).

Among the general and vaguer euphemisms are *conocer* 'to become acquainted with,' *ofender* 'to offend,' *deshonrar* 'to dishonor,' *tener historias con* 'to have an affair with,' *tener que ver con* 'to have something to do with,' *tener un descuido* 'to be careless, make a slip,' *resbalarse* 'to slip' ("La muchacha *se resbaló* con el amigo"), *tener una desgracia* 'to have a misfortune,' *juntarse* 'to get together,' and, among prostitutes, *ocuparse* and *hacer un trabajito* 'to do a little job,' as in "Ahora de cuando en cuando *hago un trabajito*" (Mendoza, p. 16), "Quería que le *hiciera un trabajito*" (*ibid.,* p. 26).

Among the more or less local Spanish-American terms, of various shades of delicacy, are:

afilar (Peru, Ec; *afilar el fierro,* Mex) 'to sharpen, grind' (*fierro* and *sable* are euphemisms for *pene*), whence Cornejo (p. 6) sounds a note of warning to Argentinians who may come to visit Ecuador or Peru, since *afilar* in Argentina has for half a century or longer been current with the more innocent meaning of *pelar la pava* or *hacer el oso* 'to flirt, court, woo,' or, as Segovia explains, 'cotejar a una dama desde cierta distancia';

atropellar 'to trample on, knock down,' as in "Al encontrarse solo con Vitalia quiso *atropellarla* y ante su resistencia, la tendió de una bofetada" (H. Jaramillo, *La buenamoza y el toro,* Santiago, Chile, 1951, p. 67);

arreglarse 'to get together, come to an agreement,' as in "Parece que en la noche aquella *se arreglaron* Eulalio Villegas y la Trompitas; amanecieron muy amartelados" (Mex: Urquizo, p. 162).

brincar (general) 'to leap, jump, skip,' applied also to animals in the sense of standard *cubrir* 'to cover' (cf. English 'to leap' and 'to cover' in the same sense), as in "El potro del vecino *se brincó* mi yegua mora" (Col: Acuña).

cachar (Peru), probably as an extension of its meanings 'dar con el cacho ('horn'), robar, engañar,' or from *cacha* 'buttock, vulva,' also *cachimbear; cargar* (CA, Mex, Ant) 'to charge,' used especially in speaking of animals, as in "El toro *cargó* dos vacas mías" (Guat: Sandoval); *clavar* (Mex) 'to nail, force in'; *comerse a una* (SD) = *robarle la doncellez,* as in "a la más pequeña de las hermanas, dicen que *se la comió* un ministro" (Patín); *coyolear* (Mex) 'to gather *coyoles* (fruit of a palm tree)'; *culear* (vulgar), as in "están *culeando*" (Ec: Icaza, p. 59); *cutarrear* (Guat), perhaps from its meaning 'to steal' (cf. *hurtar* 'to steal' used in Chilean *coa* in the sense of *cohabitar con la mujer de otro*).

checar (Tex); *chichar* (PR); *chimar* (CA) 'to skin, scratch'; *chimbear* (Col), from *chimba* 'vulva'; *chinastear* (CA), from Aztec *xinachtli* 'seed,' used particularly in reference to barnyard fowls; *chingar* (Mex, PR), of complicated origin, perhaps from a Gypsy word meaning 'to fight,' then 'to molest,' mixed later with Indian derivatives, which may explain its varying meanings throughout America (see Corominas), or its original sense may have been *copular,* as in Spanish *caló* and in Mexico (cf. the Cuban variant *singar*); *chivar* (SE Mex), probably from *chivo* 'goat' because of that animal's lasciviousness; *chorear* (Chile), from *choro* ('clam') in its meaning of 'vulva'; *chuchar* (Col, CA), from *chucha* 'vulva.'

desfundar (cant, Mex); *dormirse a una mujer* (Cuba) in the sense of 'to deceive.'

echar and a noun (like general *echar el ajo, un brinco, un palo, un polvo, una pera,* etc.), as *echar cola* ('tail'), euphemized in Chile (Vicuña) as *ir a Colina; echar un dagazo* (PR), from *daga* 'dagger'; *echar un fierrazo* (Arg) 'brand stamped with a hot iron'; *echar guata* (Chile) 'belly'; *echar güevo* = *huevo* 'egg, testicle' (Col: Acuña); *echar un palo ... a la lumbre, echar un rápido, echar reata* 'whip' (Mex); *empaquetar* (Nic) 'to pack, stuff'; *empelotarse* (Mex), from its meaning of *desnudarse* 'to undress' or possibly from *pelota* 'prostitute'; *enverijarse* (Mex), from *verija* 'region of the genitals.'

gatear (Ec: Cornejo), from gato 'cat,' an extension of its general meaning 'to be involved in love adventures' and of the Mexican sense of 'to court maidservants [= *gatas*].'

hincar (Arg) 'to drive in, thrust in' (Tiscornia, II, 87) which the Gaucho had in mind when he transformed *Ingalaterra* into *Inca-la-perra:* "Hasta un inglés sangiador / Que decía en la última guerra / Que él era de *Inca-la-perra* / Y que no quería servir (*Martín Fierro,* I, v. 327); *hostigar* (Mex) 'to lash, molest.'

jalar (CA), from the nautical term *halar* 'to draw, pull,' which, in addition to other meanings (*emborracharse, largarse*), may signify *hacer el amor* 'to make love,' as in "Ella y yo *nos jalamos;* ella *está jalando* con otro" (Malaret).

machucar (Peru) 'to crush'; *mancornearse* (Mex), an extension of standard *mancornar* 'to join (of oxen)'; *mechar* (Cuba), from *mecha* 'shaft'; *machetear* (Arg), from slang *machete* 'penis'; *meter* (general); *mojar* (PR) 'to moisten.'

parchar (Mex) 'to patch'; *picholear* (Chile), *from pichula* 'penis'; *pinchar* (Bol); *pingar* (NW Arg); *pisar* 'to step on, trample on' and 'to copulate' (< *pinsare,* a variant of classical Latin *pinsere* 'to beat, pound,' cf. French *battre* 'to beat' and 'to copulate'), used particularly in referring to doves (std.), is extended to all animals and to human beings (CA, Ant), deriv. *pisuña* (by analogy with *pezuña* 'hoof'), as in "A don Eliseo le gusta mucho *la pisuña*" (Guat: Sandoval), wherefore *pisar* in its sense of 'to step on someone's foot' is avoided by use of "me *puso el pie,* me *pateó,* no me *ponga* los pies encima, cuidado que te vas a *patear* la pluma que se me cayó" (Sandoval) and "me *majó* el pie" (CR); *pepenar* (Nic), meaning *recoger* 'to pick up' and therefore a euphemism for *recoger* 'to copulate'; *pichar* (general) from *picha:* planchar (Peru) 'to iron'; *potear* from *poto* 'posterior' and by proximity 'vulva' (Chile, Bol), cf. vulgar *culo* 'anus, posterior' and 'vulva'; *punzar* (Bol) 'to prick.'

raspar (Ven); *rebanar* (Mex); *recoger* (Nic); *remangar* (Nic) 'to roll up the sleeves' and by extension 'to skin'; *rempujar* and *arrempujar* (CA, Mex) 'to push,' as in "Hombre joven aún y perverso ... era el que, al decir de los soldados, se *arrempujaba* a la generala" (Mex: Robles Castillo, *¡Ay, Jalisco, no te rajes!,* 1938, p. 42).

sapear (Cuba) from *sapo* 'vulva' and 'prostitute'; *soplar* 'to blow' (cf. *follar,* Besses), as in "Pedro se *sopló* a Juana" (Chile: Román), cf. *cepillarse a una* (Madrid), and "El coronel, mi jefe, ya se *sopló* a esa muchacha que va por la otra acera" (Guat: Sandoval), cf. the common Mexican phrase "tú ya no *soplas*" used "para zaherir a la persona ya exenta de las incitaciones de la carne" (Santamaría).

tapar and *taponear* (general) 'to cork, plug'; *templar* (Cuba); *tirar* 'to throw (down)' and 'to pull' (cf. *jalar,* above) in Spanish argot and in much of America (particularly Chile, Peru, Col, Mex, Cuba), whence in its sense of 'to throw away' it is avoided in favor of *arrojar* and *botar;*

tronar (CA) 'to thunder' and 'to kill,' as in *"tronarse* a una mujer" (Sandoval); *tumbar* (Ec) 'to throw down,' as in "El mismo día que la *tumbó* en el linde del maizal ..." (A. Ortiz, p. 30).

Some metaphorical phrases are *dar barra* or *darle dulce a la cintura* (Cuba); *afilar* (or *limpiar*) *el sable* 'to sharpen (to clean) the sword' (Peru, Ec); *formar el Ayuntamiento* (Mex), with a pun on *ayuntamiento* 'town hall' and 'copulation,' as in "¡Ya van tres veces que ella y yo formamos el *Ayuntamiento!"* (Ángulo, p. 205); *ir al maqui* (Chile), in which *maqui* is the name of a high bush, as in "¿Vamu' al maqui? es la invitación que él le hace a ella" (Rabanales, p. 213); *refundir el botón* (Nic) 'to recast the crankpin'; *subir al guayabo* (Tabasco, Mex), with a play on the two meanings of *guayabo* 'guayaba tree' and 'vulva'; *tomar mate* (Chile), with a play on the two meanings of *mate* 'tea' and 'virginity' or 'vulva,' as in "¿(V)amo a tomar *mate,* m'hijita? suele decirle un hombre a una mujer, cuando va pasando por la calle" (Rabanales, p. 123); *mandarse al plato a una mujer* (Guat).

In addition to the general gestures explained previously (the fig gesture, *pistola, corte de mango,* etc.), there are others used in many regions to indicate without words the act of coition. Among them are the following: the extended left fist is jerked downward or sideways from a loose wrist two of three times, either in the air or against a surface (see figs. 38 and 39); the open right palm is slapped down two or three times on the extended left fist held upright or in oblique position, as if pushing a cork into a bottle (this gesture sometimes means 'to silence someone' when it accompanies words like "lo callaron" or "le metieron un tapón," etc.) (see fig. 40); the extended forearms and fists are jerked backward and downward toward the body (see fig. 41), but this gesture, which has become extremely vulgar, is sometimes euphemistically abbreviated (a kind of synecdoche) to a mere shrug of the shoulders (observed particularly in Venezuela).

ONANISM

Originally a euphemism, the general vulgar term for *masturbación* is *paja* 'straw,' and *masturbarse* is expressed by *hacerse la paja,* deriv. *pajero, pajista,* and *pajearse* (CA). Commoner in Mexico is the diminutive *pajuela* (std. meaning 'sulphur match, fuse'). Some speakers, therefore, in referring to a 'straw for sipping liquids' (std. *caña* or *bombillo*), avoid the words *paja, pajita,* and *pajuela* and substitute for them borrowings such as *popote* (Mex), from Aztec *popotl* 'straw'; *calimete* (SD), from a diminutive form of *cálamo* 'reed, pen, ancient flute,' cf. *calumet* (Cuba: *Macías*) 'stem of a pipe,' French *chalumeau* 'straw,' cf. *sorbete* (Urug, PR) for 'straw.' Speakers often avoid the word *pajuela* by using a phonetic deformation like the proper name *Pascuala* (SE Mex), in which various sounds suggest the referent.

Originally meaning 'a kind of frilled cuff,' *puñeta* (from *puño* 'fist'), its derivative *puñetero* (euphemism *peinetero*) and verbal form *hacerse* (or *correrse*) *la puñeta* were formerly more current in vulgar speech than they are today. Adjective *puñetero* is used with a noun to express anger or disgust ("en esta *puñetera* vida"); the phrase *vete a hacer puñeta* or, less crudely, *vete a hacer puños* has lost its original meaning and now is equivalent to 'go to hell.'

Among other vulgar American-Spanish terms are *ahorcar el pato* (Nic) 'to hang the duck'; *canfinfia* or *canfiruleta,* as in "—¿De qué padece Fulano? —De *canfinfia*" and "N es amigo de la *canfiruleta*" (Yucatán: Duarte); *cascársela* (cant, Cuba: Rodríguez, p. 430); *hacerse la cuzca* (Arg: Garzón), in which the noun may derive from *cuzco,-a* 'lap dog,' one of a series of onomatopoetic variants (including *gozque*) containing a syllable *quis* or *cus,* used in calling or in frightening away dogs (see Corominas), or it may be related to *cusca* 'dado, entregado' (Garzón); *hacerse callos* (or *pelos*) *en la palma de la mano* (CA) 'to get a calloused palm'; *hacerse* (or *volarse*) *la chaqueta* (Salv); *hacerse la manigueta* (Nic) 'hand cart' and general *la manuela,* euphemisms in which the first three sounds suggest the referent by recalling *mano* 'hand,' as also in the euphemistic expression of similar meaning *gustarle a uno la Manuela Palma* (or merely *la Manuela*), in which the word appears as a proper name; *hacerse la pera* (Bol) 'to shape one's goatee'; general *hacérsela* 'to do it to oneself,' containing indefinite feminine *la* (most nouns thus used being feminine); *pelársela* 'to skin it'; *pescar* (Col) 'to fish' > 'to play pocket pool'; *pichulear* (Chile) from *pichula* 'penis'; *remangársela* (CA) 'to roll it up,' from *remangar* 'to roll up the sleeves' and then 'to skin.'

PREGNANCY

Standard *preñada* 'pregnant' has many euphemisms: *embarazada* (further euphemized in Mexican cant with *estar en baras,* see Wagner, "Mex. Rot.," p. 524); *encinta; estar esperando* 'to be expecting'; *estar ocupada; estar en estado interesante,* often shortened to *estar en estado,* and euphemistically altered in Venezuela (when children are present) to "estar en el estado Táchira *or* Trujillo" or any other of the Venezuelan states. Among other expressions, some of them less delicate, are *(estar) adelantada* (Col) 'advanced'; general *(estar) cargada* 'loaded, heavy,' as in "como ya están *cargadas* las vacas, producen poca [leche]" (Mex: Inclán, II, 112); *andar con bombo* (Arg: *Filología,* III, 55) 'to have a bass drum'; *coger barriga* (Col: Tobón) 'to be getting a belly'; *(estar) de encargo* (SD); *(estar) gorda* or *gruesa* '(to be) stout, fat'; *estar con* (or *tener) tamaña barriga* (or *panza)* 'to have a large belly' (Guat); *estar en alpargatas* (Col); *(estar) templada* (Col), deriv. *templar* for std. *empreñar* 'to impregnate,' as in "A la Juanita disque la *templaron* por andar sola de noche" (Acuña); *(estar) en valija* (Guat); *(estar) con el rancho ardiendo* (Col) 'to have one's shack afire,' as in "—¿Cuántos hijos tiene Juana? —Cinco ya, y *el rancho ardiendo*" (Acuña); *(estar) como el pan de la Perdomo, con la ganancia adentro* (Guat: Sandoval), referring to the custom of advertising groceries *con ganancia* 'with a bonus' of a certain percentage of the sale price: when customers requested the bonus from the bread vendor Perdomo, she would reply "mi pan lleva la ganancia adentro."

GIVING BIRTH

Standard *parir* 'to give birth to' has such euphemisms as *alumbrar, dar a luz, salir de su cuidado,* and many new substitutes current in America. The verb *parir* is often avoided even in the consecrated expressions "la madre que te *parió,*" which one may hear in an altered form as "que te echó al mundo," facetious "que te tiró de las patas," and abbreviated "que te ..." (Vidal, p. 203). The following euphemisms are permutations expressing the beginning of the birth: *acostarse* (CA) 'to go to bed,' as in "Doña Marina *se acostó* ayer tarde" (Guat: Sandoval); *coger cama* or *caer a la cama* 'to go to bed,' as in "Cuando mi mujer *cayó a la cama,* me tocó abandonar la labranza" or "Mi comadre está para *caer a la cama*" (Col:

Acuña), simply *caer* in "¡mi vieja está para *caer!*" (Mex: López y Fuentes, p. 168); general *enfermarse* 'to be taken ill'; *guardar cama* 'to stay in bed,' which Buenos Aires newspapers sometimes employ in their social columns lest they offend their readers with standard *dar a luz* (A. Castro, p. 128); *estar sufriendo,* as in "¿Cómo está la comadre? —*Está sufriendo,* le oímos responder al pícaro. Había parido la paz-puerca, y el bribonazo del indio llamaba a eso *estar sufriendo*" (ap. Barreto, II, 16). Other euphemisms are *alentarse* (Col, CA) 'to recover from illness,' as in "Anoche *se alentó* María de un par de cuaches ('twins')" (Guat: Sandoval); *componerse* (Guat) 'to be restored, recover,' as in "Mañana al hacer efecto la Luna, es seguro que *se compondrá Emilia*" (Sandoval); vulgar *desbarrigar* (Cuba), from *barriga* 'belly'; general *desembarazar,* as the counterpart of *embarazar; desocuparse* (Arg, Chile, Ven) 'to become free'; vulgar *desembuchar* (Mex) 'to disgorge,' as in "Estos cincuenta trompudos ('pesos') me vienen al pelo para pagar el parto de mi vieja que ya está por *desembuchar*" (Ángulo, p. 126); general *tener familia; tener guagua* (general in SA) 'to have a baby.' A euphemism used in several parts of Colombia for the noun *aborto* 'abortion' is *novedad* 'news, surprise' (Tobón); and in Chile a woman who gives birth prematurely is sometimes called 'mujer *chaucha*' (Lenz), from *chaucha* 'an early variety of potato.'

Standard *partera* (or *comadre*) 'midwife,' ennobled to *profesora de partos,* may be euphemized by *obstétrica* or *obstetriz* (CA); *madama* (RP, Bol), rustic; *recibidora* (Peru) 'receiver' when unlicensed; *pepenadora* (Tabasco, Mex), from Aztec *pepena* 'to pick up, gather, seize.'

CUCKOLD

Under "Euphemisms of Superstition" (chap. i) was discussed the significance of a *contra* 'counter' used to ward off evil and made by extending index and small fingers (preferably of the left hand), middle fingers bent inward on palm and thumb holding them in place. This gesture, representing *cuernos* 'horns,' is employed also to mean *cornudo* 'cuckold' (lit. 'horned person'), but in these cases the gesturing hand is usually held near or over the forehead (see fig. 42). The gesture is sometimes varied by holding both index fingers above the temples. A circular movement of the head may serve to indicate a bull, particularly when he is *manso* 'tame, meek,' a euphemism for *cornudo,* cf. *agachón* (Mex) 'with lowered head, meek' >

'cuckold.' Although, according to Bulwer (*Chirologia,* p. 183), "your broad verball jest is nothing neare so piquant as these foul habits of reproach by gesture," yet they were and are euphemistic devices.

They must not be confused with similar gestures having other meanings. For instance, when the hand is not held near the forehead the gesture may indicate (Mex) *los picudos* (lit. 'peaky, pointed, sharp') 'the sly, cunning, malicious, perverse'; when the hand is held vertically (rather than horizontally) in gesturing toward a glass it may mean facetiously 'dos dedos de vino,' etc., that is, 'two fingers of wine.'

Offending *cornudo* (fam. std. *cabrón*) and *cuerno* have from an early period been euphemized by phonetic distortions, vague references, and metaphorical paraphrases. For example: "Liévate dende, *cornejo,* non busques más contienda" (Juan Ruiz, *El libro de buen amor,* v. 980); "vuestro putativo padre, hijo de *Cornelio* Tácito, por via de hembra" (*La pícara Justina,* II, 76); "al viejo que se casa con moza, todos los miembros del cuerpo se le van consumiendo si no es *la frente, que le crece más*" (Espinel, *Marcos Obregón,* chap. v); "Echote una pulla ... que tu mujer te haga *ciervo* y te llamen todos *cuclillo*" (H. de Luna, *Diálogos,* ap. Sbarbi, *Refranero general,* I, 235); "he rehusado en mi mocedad tomar este cargo (de casarse) sobre mis hombros, ¿y la había de tomar ahora *sobre mi cabeza?*" (*ibid.*); "¡Y era público que su esposa le *coronaba!*" (Valle-Inclán, *Los cuernos de don Friolera,* in *Opera omnia,* XVII, 44); "¡Su mujer le va poniendo *hecha un bosque la cabeza!*" (Felipe Trigo, *El médico rural,* in *Obras completas,* XXII, 143).

When *cuerno* is mentioned in its original sense of 'horn' some writers and speakers soften the effect by adding a phrase like *con perdón* or its equivalent, as in "entró un ... porquero: conocíle por el—*hablando con acatamiento—cuerno* que traía en la mano; que para andar al uso, sólo erró en no traerle sobre la cabeza" (Quevedo, *El buscón,* Madrid, 1927, chap. xi).

Sometimes innocent words that vaguely recall the referent are frowned upon or are even taboo with certain speakers. The word *alcornoque* 'cork oak,' for instance, is in bad odor because of the two syllables *corno,* as in "—¿Por qué habían comprado esos albaricoques y le ofrecían uno?—¡Era para tratarle de *alcornoque!*—¡Oh, fuerza del consonante!" (Quevedo y Zubieta, p. 192). Some persons avoid the innocuous adverb *hasta* 'even' since it is homonymous with *asta* 'horn' and thus too clearly suggests *cuerno.* They are likely to replace *hasta* with *incluso* (or *inclusive*) as in "adoptaba una seriedad de palabras y una gravedad de aptitudes *incluso* excesivas" (Luis de Oteyza, *Anticípolis,* chap. xi); "y la firmeza ... dábale *incluso* elocuencia para sostenerlas (*ibid.,* chap. xix); "le importaba poco irse a vivir sola ... *Incluso* parecíale que viviría mejor" (*ibid.*); "*incluso* llegó a sonreír ... parece que *incluso* contienen la respiración" (Jardiel Poncela, *¡Espérame en Siberia!,* pp. 279, 306).

American Spanish has inherited the same tendencies. In many areas standard *cuerno* has been replaced by *cacho,* of disputed origin (but more probably from *cacho* in the sense of *cacharro* 'earthen pot' or 'piece of an earthen pot,' since horns frequently served as vessels for liquids, see Corominas), as in "le pusieron *los cachos.*" In the River Plate region, *guampa* (from Quechua ?) may be heard for *cuerno* 'horn.' Vulgar *cabrón* in America usually takes the form *cabro* or *chivo.*

Among euphemistic phonetic distortions for *cornudo* are *cornelio* (Arg: Gobello, p. 79); *cornúpedo* (Col), from standard poetic *cornúpeta* 'animal in the act of attacking with its horns,' as in "Según dicen por ahí las malas lenguas Melitón es un *cornúpedo*" (Acuña); *coronado* (RP, Peru, Ant) 'crowned.'

In Mexico, *cornudo* is euphemized by *buey* 'ox,' and *llaves* 'keys' may replace *cuernos del toro;* hence the proverb "El que nació para *buey,* de arriba le caen *las llaves*" (Rubio, I, 191). But since *buey* has become extremely offensive, the euphemism *un Piedras Negras,* from the name of a place in Coahuila where Piedras Negras bulls are raised, is used, as in "Te van a dejar tan adornado como a *un Piedras Negras.*" An analogous proverb in Argentina (Santiago) runs "El que nace pa *guampudo,* dende chiquito es *frentón,*" in which *guampudo* (RP, Bol) 'cornudo' is a derivative of *guampa* 'horn' or 'drinking vessel' made of a horn. In Argentina, too, *cuerno* is frequently replaced by *aspa* (lit. 'cross' or 'wing or sail of a windmill') probably because of phonetic interference with standard *asta* 'horn,' deriv. *aspudo.* Thus, standard *coger el toro por los cuernos* or *por las astas* may in Argentina become 'agarrar al toro por las *aspas.*'

A very vague euphemism for *cornudo* is *desgraciado* 'unfortunate, wretch,' which is current in many regions (Peru, Ec, CA, Mex). Since it has also come to mean *hijo de mujer pública,* it is one of the most offensive insults and is carefully avoided in polite speech. Among euphemistic phrases of humorous intent referring to the inconvenience of horns are *no puede ponerse sombrero* 'he can't put on a hat,' *tiene que bajarse cuando pasa por las puertas* 'he must stoop when he passes through doors,' and *se enreda en los alambres de la luz* 'he gets tangled in the electric wires' (PR).

Standard *poner cuernos a* (or *encornudar*) 'to cuckold' is euphemized by *atrasar* (Peru) 'to push back,' as in "La mujer lo está *atrasando,*" and "Su amigo lo *atrasa* con la mujer," deriv. *atrasador;* general *coronar* 'to crown'; *correrle la carne a uno* means 'quitarle la mujer' and *corrérsele la carne a uno* means 'írsele la mujer con otro' (Cuba: Rodríguez, p. 426); *hacer guaje* or *maje a* (Mex) 'to make a fool of'; *jugársela* (SD), as in "ella *se la jugó* a su primer marido" (Patín; cf. fam. std. *pegársela*); *poner las botas a* (Mex) 'to put the boots on' may refer to reciprocal cuckolding; *ponerle a uno chaparreras* ('leather overbreeches for protection against *chaparros* or rough-leaved bushes') (Mex), as in "una mujer *pone chaparreras* al marido, cuando lo engaña" (Velasco); *quemarle a uno la canilla* (Guat) or *el horno* (Hond); *tarrear* (Cuba), from *tarro* 'horn'; *poner el gorro a,* or *gorrear* (Chile) 'to put the cap on' (cf. fam. std. *llevar una gorra con mangas* 'to wear a cap with sleeves [= horns]'). The metaphor of cap or hood with pointed top recalling a horn is referred to in the following sentence: "Porque nos pusimos los impermeables con *capuchón* ['hood'] para pasear sobre la cubierta azotada por la lluvia, discurrió que *le hacíamos cuernos* con el pico del capuchón para atormentar su presente y su porvenir" (Quevedo y Zubieta, p. 191).

APPENDIXES

APPENDIX I

Many words are only locally taboo; that is, they may be taboo in one or more regions and respectable in others. Some of them, although contaminated with the offensive meaning, may have maintained their original sense sufficiently to offset destructive inroads of euphemistic substitutes. Such words may evoke either sense according to the context and level of speech. Again, a form associated with a taboo meaning can destroy all other respectable meanings it may have. The Spanish mind, with the help of a similar sound or two, makes unusually swift associations between words that may have nothing else in common or may even have diametrically opposed meanings.

Most of the terms mentioned below have been listed in other connections (see Word Index), but they can be helpfully regrouped here in alphabetical order.

The following words are often avoided in polite and prudish speech:

abeja ('bee') in Los Llanos, Colombia, where it means also *nalga* 'buttock.'

abusador ('abuser') in Santo Domingo, where it is a grave insult, just a degree below that of *¡tu madre!* (see chap. vii), whence a murderer sometimes attempts to justify his act by saying "me dijo *abusador*" 'he called me an abuser' (Jiménez, p. 138).

acabar ('to finish') in Argentina, where one of its old standard meanings (*tener orgasmo*) is threatening to oust its other senses (A. Castro, p. 127).

afilar ('to whet, sharpen') in Ecuador, where it means also *copular,* wherefore Argentinian visitors must be especially circumspect lest they use it when they mean 'to court, woo,' its sense in their own country.

alzado in the River Plate region, particularly, where it means *estar en celo* 'to be in heat'; in many other regions its central or normal meaning is 'insolent' and even 'drunk' (Col).

barro 'mud' in Venezuela, where it means 'excrement' and the euphemistic *pantano* 'swamp, marsh' replaces it, as in "Ese carro me salpicó de *pantano*" (Rosenblat, p. 405).

bicho ('insect') in Puerto Rico, where it means *pene;* in its original sense it is replaced by *insecto* or *animal.*

bollo ('roll, loaf') in Cuba, where it means 'clitoris.'

brincar ('to leap, spring') in Peru and other areas where it means *copular,* an extension of its standard application to animals.

buitrear ('to hunt vultures') in Chile and Peru, where it means also 'to vomit.'

burro and *asno* ('donkey, ass') in Piura, Peru, where they mean 'vulva' and in their original sense are replaced by *piajeno* (= *pie ajeno*), preceded in conversation by *con perdón de la palabra* (Hildebrandt, p. 260.)

cachar in Peru and elsewhere where it may mean *copular;* in some of its local peninsular meanings of 'knife handle, buttock, vulva, etc.,' it may have some connection with *cacha,* and elsewhere it is used in a variety of senses including 'to break into pieces,' 'to scoff, deceive, gore (from *cacho* 'cuerno'), steal, take, seize,' as a euphemism for *coger* in *caché el tranvía* (Arg; perhaps from Italian *cacciare* or English *catch*), of complicated and mixed etymology (see Corominas).

cachumbo ('in heat') in Spain (euphemized by *cachondo*); to Colombians it means *rizo* or *bucle de cabello* 'curl' or 'ringlet of hair.'

cajeta ('box') or *cajetilla* ('little box') in Argentina, where it may mean 'vulva' (*cajetilla* is also unpleasant in the sense of 'dude').

calentarse ('to get warm') in the River Plate region and Chile, where its standard meaning 'to be in heat' (of animals) is extended to human beings; in other regions (Ec, Peru, Col) *calentarse* may mean figuratively *enojarse, enfadarse* 'to get angry,' *calentura* 'enojo,' and *caliente* 'enojado,' as in "Tan violenta fué su *calentura* que insultó a toda la servidumbre" and "Cuando oyó el relato de lo sucedido se puso *caliente*" (Col: Acuña); in both the River Plate region and Chile *calentura* 'fever' yields to *fiebre* and *acalenturarse* 'to be feverish' to *afiebrarse.*

calzonarias ('suspenders' in central and southern Colombia, standard *tirantes*) in northern Colombia and Ecuador, where it means *calzones de mujer* 'panties.'

cantora ('singer') in Chile, Bolivia and Peru, where it means 'chamber pot,' and in its standard meaning always yields to its common variant *cantante.*

casilla ('post-office box' in RP, Chile, and Peru for std. *apartado*) in Ecuador, where it means *excusado* 'privy.'

catira ('blond') in parts of Colombia, where it means a *vivandière* (that is, a woman accompanying a regiment as a vendor of provisions and liquor to the soldiers) and is considered an insult (Montoya, no. 88).

cerote ('big zero,' augmentative of *cero* 'zero') in Central America, where it means 'excrement'; an anecdote tells of a Spanish priest who, not knowing the local meaning, said to his pupils "les voy a poner no un cero sino un *cerote.*"

cipote (meaning in most parts of Spanish America: 'child, simpleton, plump,' etc.) in northern Colombia, where it may mean *pene,* as in vulgar peninsular speech.

cocacolo ('cocacola') in Colombia, where (though generally meaning 'teenager' by a permutation of symbol for a thing symbolized) it may mean *marica* 'cowardly, effeminate.'

coger ('to catch, seize, grasp, pluck') in the River Plate region and to a lesser extent elsewhere (Peru, Ven, Mex), where one of its standard meanings ('to cover,' said of animals) has ousted all others and the word is replaced by verbs *agarrar, tomar,* etc., wherefore still greater caution must be observed by persons from countries where *cogerse* has acquired new respectable meanings like 'to get along well' and 'to get accustomed' (SD, PR), as in *"me cojo* en esta casa," *"me cojo* con Fulano," *"no nos cogemos"* (Malaret), or 'to make a mistake' or 'to commit a crime' (SD), as in *"te cogiste,"* and other meanings closely allied with standard usage (Jiménez, pp. 59–61).

colirio ('collyrium, eyewash') in the Cauca Valley, Colombia, where it may mean 'enema.'

concha ('shell, mollusk') in the River Plate region, Chile, Peru, northern Colombia, and Puerto Rico, where it may mean 'vulva.'

coño in nearly every country (where its std. meaning is 'vulva'), though to Chileans (and to some Mexicans) the word is not obscene but merely a nickname for 'Spaniard' because Spaniards use it frequently as a vulgar interjection, cf. "(el español) tenía un genio de diablo y cuando se disgustaba o sufría alguna emoción, vomitaba más *coños* que los emitidos en su país natal por cinco generaciones de sus compatriotas" (Ángulo, p. 244).

cortarse ('to cut oneself') in Puerto Rico, where it may mean 'to step on excrement.'

criadillas ('lamb fries') in Lima, Peru, by a few prudish persons who are likely to substitute *adefesios de carnero.*

cuarto in Colombia, where it may mean *alcahuete* 'procurer'; it is very offensive in Nariño.

cuchara ('spoon') in Venezuela, where it may mean 'vulva.'

cuero ('leather, leather strap') in many regions (Ec, Col, Ven, Ant, parts of Mex) where it may mean 'prostitute'; Mexicans who are inclined to use it in the sense of *mujer guapa* 'beautiful woman' find it necessary to be especially cautious.

cuita ('grief, trouble') in Mexico and Central America, where it means 'excrement' (from Aztec *cuitlatl* 'bird excrement').

culearse = *copular* nearly everywhere; Guatemalans must watch their speech since in their country the verb may mean merely 'to go back on one's word,' as in "En los tratos con Pastor hay que ser uno [sic] precavido, porque siempre anda *culeándose"* (Sandoval).

culebro,-a ('snake') in Boyacá and Cundinamarca, Colombia, where among the common people these words are considered atrocious insults, like *tayo,-a,* the name of a venomous snake (Tobón).

chayote ('pear-shaped calabash') in Oaxaca and Orizaba, Mexico, where it means 'vulva' and the euphemism (*fruto*) *espinoso* is often substituted when the original meaning is intended.

chicha in Costa Rica, where it means 'breast,' is usually avoided in the plural.

chiche ('breast') in the Mexican zone (CA, Mex); visitors from Chile, the River Plate, and Bolivia must watch their speech, for its predominating meaning in their countries is *alhaja, dije* 'jewel, trinket,' as in the intended compliment a Chilean ambassador reportedly made to a much bejeweled Central American lady: "Qué *chiches* más bonitos tiene usted, señora."

chilena ('Chilean woman') in Bolivia, where in some regions it means 'prostitute.'

chinche ('bedbug') in Argentina, where it may mean 'syphilis' or 'gonorrhea'; visitors from Antioquia, Colombia, where it may mean 'street urchin' or 'young thief' (perhaps with phonetic interference of local *chino* 'boy, urchin, rogue'), must make a special effort to avoid its use.

chingar in Mexico, where it may mean *copular;* elsewhere it has various meanings, the most widespread (RP, Chile, Peru, Col, CA) being *fracasar* 'to fail, miscarry, fall through' and *no estallar* 'to fail to explode,' as used by a Chilean lady, who in the midst of a huge throng of Independence Day celebrants in Mexico City, exclaimed in disappointment when a skyrocket failed to explode, "*¡Se chingó!*" —to the amused astonishment of the bystanders (cf. also "*Se chingó* la zorreadura" 'the fox hunt was unsuccessful,' Chile: Latorre, p. 198; "¿Aquí anduvo Satanás / Hasta oír sonar la descarga? / —Esta vez *se le chingó* / El cuete ..." Arg: Del Campo, *Fausto*, v. 1201).

chucha ('dog' and other local meanings) in the River Plate region, Chile, Bolivia, Peru, and northern Colombia, where it means 'vulva' (see Corominas for etymology of local meanings). *Chucha,* a familiar diminutive of *Jesusa* in many parts of Latin America, occurring frequently in a certain Mexican screen play, had to be changed to something else when the film was shown in Chile.

chulo in Spain and many regions of America where it means *rufián* 'pander'; visitors from Mexico and Central America must watch their speech, for in their countries the adjective *chulo,-a* means *bonito,-a* 'pretty' (as in Andalusia).

chuspa ('bag' of any kind, from Quechua), especially in Nariño, Colombia, where it means 'scrotum.'

deponer ('to depose') in Mexico and Central America, where it may mean 'to vomit' (and is a std. euphemism for *defecar*).

desgraciado ('unfortunate, wretched') in several regions (Ec, Peru, Guat, Mex) where it is a grave insult meaning 'cuckold' or 'son of a prostitute.'

desgraciarse ('to fall out with,' 'die young,' etc.) in the River Plate region and some other areas where it may mean 'to soil one's clothes with a sudden call of nature,' 'to kill someone,' 'to have an illegitimate child,' as in "el hombre *se desgració* con la mujer."

embolar in Venezuela (except in limited areas), where it means 'to entangle, mess up,' especially by speakers from Colombia, where it means 'to shine shoes,' as in "¿Le *embolo* los zapatos, señor?"

escupidera ('cuspidor') in the River Plate region and Chile, where it means *orinal* 'urinal' and in its original sense is euphemized by *salivadera* (and *escupir* by *salivar*).

flete in Cuba, where it applies to a 'streetwalker's conquest' (*fletera* 'street-walker'); visitors from Peru, where it may mean 'boy friend' or 'girl friend' with favorable connotations, should exercise caution in its use.

fotingo ('dilapidated automobile,' from *Ford* and depreciatory suffix *-ingo*) in eastern Cuba, where it means 'rectum,' perhaps with phonetic association of Catalan *fotre* and of African words of similar root and obscene meaning (Ortiz, p. 206).

fula in Puerto Rico, where it means 'bird droppings,' especially by speakers from Panama, where adjective *fulo,-a* means 'blond.'

guano ('sea birds' dung' or 'manure,' from Quechua) should be avoided in South America by persons from Cuba, where *guano* (from Carib) means a kind of 'palm tree' whose leaves are used for thatching roofs (*casa de guano*).

hincar ('to drive in, thrust in') in rural Argentina, where it may mean *copular*.

huevo ('egg') in regions where one of its general meanings (*testículo*) has overshadowed the others, and euphemisms—*blanquillo* (Mex, Cuba), *yema* or *ñema* (Mex, Ven), *cascarones* 'shells' or *lisuras de gallinas* (Peru)—have replaced it in the sense of 'egg.'

josefino (inhabitant of any town called *San José*) in Colombia, Central America, and elsewhere where it means 'effeminate.'

joto in Mexico, where it means 'effeminate'; visitors from Colombia, where it means *envoltorio* 'package, bundle,' must watch their speech.

machete ('cane knife') in Venezuela, where it may mean *pene*.

madre (especially *su madre*) 'mother' in many regions where it is a grave insult (see chap. xii) and *mamá* is used instead.

pajaro ('bird') in regions and circles where one of its acquired general meanings (*pene*) predominates; and in Cuba, where it means 'effeminate.'

pajuela (std. 'match'; 'toothpick,' Chile, Bol, Col) in Mexico, where it may mean *masturbación*.

(*echar un*) *palo* (= *copular*), by persons from the Caribbean zone (PR, SD, Ven), where it means 'to have a (strong) drink,' since such drinks hit the imbiber as if with a *palo* 'cudgel,' as in "—¡Otro *palito*, mi negro! ¡Échele!" (Ven: Díaz-Solés, ap. *AmSS*, p. 128), and a certain kind of rum from Santo Domingo is called *Palo viejo* (Jiménez, p. 149).

paloma ('dove') in regions or circles where one of its acquired meanings (*pene*) seems to predominate; a Mexican schoolmaster, desiring to entertain two Nicaraguan guests with an instrumental rendition of the well-known Mexican song *La Paloma*, said to his pupils "Tóquenles *La Paloma* a esos señores," whereupon the visitors withdrew in all haste.

pan ('bread, roll') in Santa Cruz, Bolivia, where it means 'vulva'; there all classes use the word *horneado* for 'roll' and *marraqueta* for a large loaf.

panocha ('cone of brown sugar,' Mex; 'a kind of *tamal,*' Chile, Col, CR) in parts of Mexico and especially in the Cauca Valley, Colombia, where it may mean 'vulva.'

papaya ('a tropical fruit') in the Antilles and parts of Mexico and Chile, where it may mean 'vulva,' and in Cuba, where in its original sense it is replaced by *fruta bomba.*

pato ('duck') in Venezuela, Nicaragua, and Puerto Rico, where it may mean 'effeminate,' and in many other regions (Col, Ven, Guat, Mex, Ant), where it may mean 'urinal.'

patrón ('employer') in Chile, where *apatronarse,* having come to mean 'to enter into concubinage,' has contaminated *patrón;* a Spanish preacher shocked his audience by advising poor jobless women to find a good *patrón* whom they might serve (Román).

pendejo ('fool') in Mexico and Puerto Rico, where it is a grave insult; speakers from other regions where it is far less offensive must exercise caution.

pepe in Cuba, where it may mean 'vulva' as well as *'pene'* (Ortiz); in other regions this word has a variety of meanings: *petimetre* 'dude' (Bol, Ven), *biberón* 'feeding bottle' (CA), *pedigüeño* 'persistent in asking' (Hond), *huérfano* 'orphan' (Guat), etc.

pepenado (past participle of *pepenar* 'to pick up, gather,' Col, CA, Mex) in Tabasco, Mexico, where it is an insult equivalent to *hijo de puta,* and in Nicaragua, where *pepenar* may mean *copular.*

pepita ('kernel, seed') in Santo Domingo, where it may mean 'vulva' and *semilla* replaces it in its original sense.

pera ('pear') in Bolivia, because of the expression *hacerse la pera* (= *masturbarse*), and in Chile, where *peras* may mean *testículos.*

pico ('beak, pickaxe') in Chile, where it means *pene.*

picha in Spain and other regions where it means *pene;* visitors from Chile must exercise care since in their country *picho,-a* means *perro,-a* 'dog'.

pinchar ('to prick') in Peru, where *picho* or *pincho* may mean *pene,* and *pinchar* is often euphemized with *hincar,* and in Mexico, where *pinche* (std. 'scullion') is an insult in the sense of 'low, lousy' ("un *pinche* empleo, una *pinche* fiesta, un *pinche* escuincle"); *pinchar* 'to prick' is avoided in favor of its synonym *picar* ("me *piqué*" for std. "me *pinché*") and of *ponchar* (English 'punch, puncture'), especially in referring to an automobile tire ("se *pinchó* la llanta" for std. "se *pinchó* el neumático").

pingo in Colombia, where, though it may mean 'horse' in some cities (as in RP, Bol, Chile, Peru), may elsewhere mean *pene.*

pisar ('to step on') in Cuba and Central America, where one of its standard meanings (*copular* of birds) is extended to human beings, and consequently standard *dar una pisotada* (or *un pisotón*) is also taboo; especially by persons from Venezuela, where *se la pisó* means *huyó* 'he fled.'

pisca ('harvest of corn,' Mex) in Colombia, where it may mean 'jade, prostitute.'

pringar ('to soil with grease') in Chile, where it may mean 'to transmit a contagious disease, particularly a venereal disease' (Román); in some regions (Ven, CA, SE Mex) *pringar* (*pingar* in parts of Spain) may mean *lloviznar* 'to drizzle' ("Me despido, porque ya comenzó a *pringar*" Guat: Sandoval).

provocar (= *vomitar*, shortened from *provocar a vomitar*, see Flórez, p. 233) in Ecuador, Venezuela, and Colombia, where this verb is used in the sense of *apetecer* 'to like' ("¿le *provoca* una copa de vino?").

puto in Mexico, where it means 'effeminate'; in Peru, it means 'woman chaser.'

quemarse ('to get burned') in Boyacá and Cundinamarca, Colombia, where it may mean 'to step on excrement.'

requintar in Peru, where it means 'to insult'; in Ecuador it means merely *regañar* 'to scold.'

rica ('rich') in Peru, where one of its standard meanings ('delicious, exquisite') is extended beyond standard limits to mean 'desirable' when applied to women; hence for *rica* in its sense of 'rich' *adinerada* 'wealthy' is used.

romper el cartucho in Chile, where *cartucho* may mean 'virgin'; in Ecuador it means 'tener ánimo para realizar una acción.'

sable ('sabre') in Ecuador, where it may mean *pene*.

sapo ('toad') in Bolivia, where it may mean 'vulva' and euphemistic words are substituted for it.

talegas ('sack, moneybags') in Bolivia, where it means *testículos*.

tamal in certain circles in Mexico, where it may mean 'vulva.'

tirar ('to throw away') in regions of America (particularly Chile, Col, Mex, Cuba) where (as in Spanish argot) it means *copular* and is usually replaced in the sense of 'to throw away' by *arrojar* or *botar*, except in areas where the taboo meaning has not seriously affected the range of its other meanings, some of them more recently acquired, as Guatamalan 'to deceive' ("Don Marcial se *tiró* a muchos en el negocio de ahorros") and 'to kill' ("Dicen que la policía se *tiró* al jefe de los conjurados," Sandoval).

traste (std. 'guitar fret,' but rather general in America and Andalusia for *trasto* 'piece of furniture, tool, rubbish,' etc.) in Chile, where it may mean *trasero* 'posterior.'

vaina ('scabbard, vagina') by speakers from many regions (Col, Pan, etc.) where it is extremely common in the sense of 'disappointment, trouble, bother' (as in the exclamation ¡qué vaina!, euphemized in Peru as ¡qué vainetilla!) or simply 'thing, gadget' as "¿Cómo es esa *vaina* [= cuestión, asunto, negocio, trabajo]?" or "¿Cuánto vale una *vaina* [= cosa] de éstas?" (Flórez, p. 234).

zurrarse ('to have a sudden call of nature'); in southern Panama it means merely *deslizarse* 'to slip, slide.'

APPENDIX II

ILLUSTRATIONS OF GESTURES

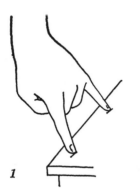

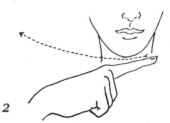

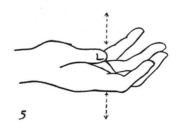

1. *cuernos.*　2. *matar.*　3. *negro.*　4. *flaco.*　5. *huevón.*

6

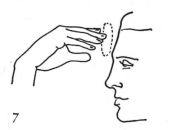

7

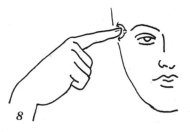

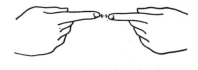

9

8

10

11

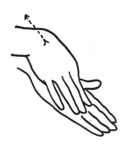

12

13

6, 7, 8. *loco.* 9. *de punta.* 10, 11, 12, 13. *rabia.*

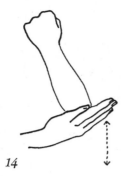

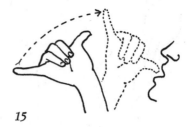

14

15

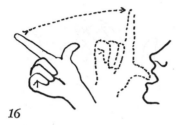

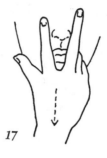

16

17

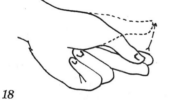

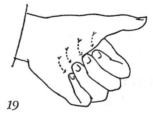

18

19

20

14. *codo.* 15, 16. *beber.* 17. *a dos velas.* 18, 19, 20. *dinero.*

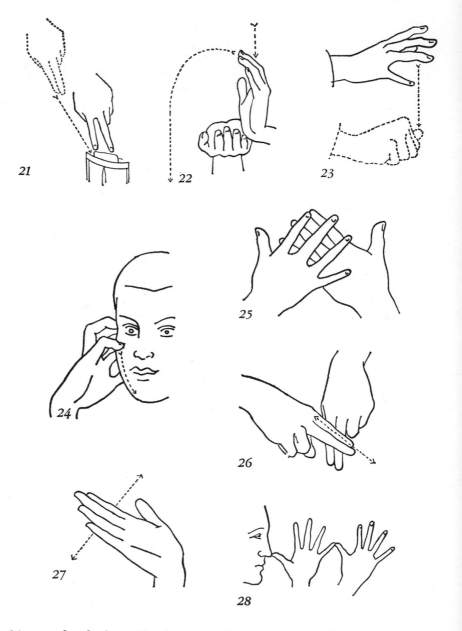

21. *tomador de dos.*   22. *clavarse el dinero.*   23, 24. *robar.*   25, 26. *cárcel.*
27. *pegar.*   28. *pito catalán.*

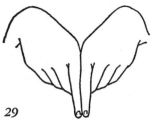

29

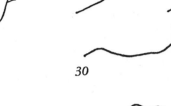

30

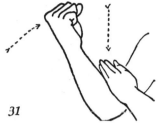

31

32

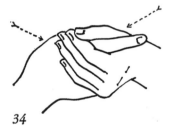

33

34

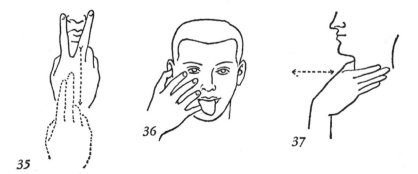

35

36

37

29, 30. *juntarse.* 31. *corte de manga.* 32, 33. *higa.* 34. *pistola.*
35. *violín.* 36. 4 *violines.* 37. *mentada.*

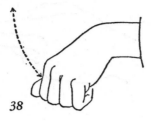

38

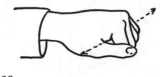

39

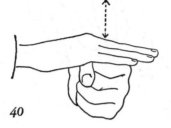

40

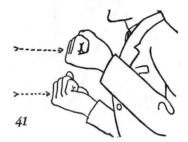

41

42

38, 39, 40, 41. *copular.*   42. *cornudo.*

BIBLIOGRAPHY

BIBLIOGRAPHY

(Works cited only once or twice are not included here if the complete title is given in the text.)

Acad = Real Academia Española, *Diccionario de la lengua española*. 17th ed. Madrid, 1947.

Acuña = Acuña, Luis Alberto. "Diccionario de bogotanismos," *Revista de Folklore* (Bogotá), No. 7 (1951), 5–187.

————. "Vocabulario campesino formado en las provincias de Vélez y Socorro," *ibid.*, No. 5 (1949), 134–143.

Aguilera = Aguilera Patiño, Luisita. *El panameño visto a través de su lenguaje.* Panamá: Ferguson & Ferguson, 1947.

Aguilera Malta, Demetrio. *Don Goya* (1933). 2d ed. Quito, Ecuador: Ediciones "Antorcha," 1938.

Alatorre, Antonio. "El idioma de los mexicanos," *Universidad de México,* X (1955), Nos. 2 and 3.

Alcalá Venceslada, Antonio. *Vocabulario andaluz.* 2d ed. Madrid: Real Academia Española, 1951.

Alvarado, Lisandro. *Glosarios del bajo español en Venezuela* (1929). Also in *Obras completas,* Vols. II and III. Caracas: Ministerio de Educación, 1954.

Álvarez, José S. See *Fray Mocho.*

Álvarez Nazario, Manuel. *El arcaísmo vulgar en el español de Puerto Rico.* Mayagüez, 1957.

AmSS = Kany, Charles E. *American-Spanish Syntax* (1945). 2d ed. Chicago: University of Chicago Press, 1951.

AmSSem = Kany, Charles E. *American-Spanish Semantics.* Berkeley and Los Angeles: University of California Press, 1960.

Anda, J. Guadalupe de. *Los bragados.* México: Compañía General Editora, 1942.

Ángulo = Ángulo Chamorro, Gustavo A. *Carne de cuartel.* México, 1940.

Arango = Arango Villegas, Rafael. *Bobadas mías.* Manizales, Colombia: Arturo Zapata, 1936.

Arguedas, Alcides. *Vida criolla: La novela de la ciudad.* Paris: Ollendorff, n.d.

Armellada, Cesáreo de. "Apuntaciones sobre el hablar de Perijá," *Boletín de la Academia Venezolana,* XV (1948), 189–200.

Arona, Juan de (Pedro Paz Soldán y Unanue). *Diccionario de peruanismos.* Lima, 1883. "Biblioteca de Cultura Peruana," No. 10. Paris, 1938.

Azuela = Azuela, Mariano. *Los de abajo* (1915). México: Ediciones Botas, 1941.

————. *Mala yerba* (1909). 3d ed. México: Ediciones Botas, 1937.

BAAL = Boletín de la Academia Argentina de Letras. Buenos Aires, 1933—.

Barrantes = Barrantes Castro, Pedro. *Cumbrera del mundo.* Lima: Perú Actual, 1935.

Barreto, Mariano. *Idioma y letras.* León, Nicaragua. Vol. I, 1902; Vol. II, 1904.

Barros Grez, Daniel. *El huérfano.* 6 vols. Santiago, Chile, 1881.

Bayo, Ciro. *Manual del lenguaje criollo de Centro y Sudamérica.* Madrid: R. C. Raggio, 1931.

BDH = Biblioteca de dialectología hispanoamericana. Buenos Aires: Instituto de Filología, 1930–1949. 7 vols.

Beinhauer = Beinhauer, Werner. *Spanischer Sprachhumor.* Bonn: L. Röhrscheid, 1932.

————. *Spanische Umgangssprache.* Bonn: Dümmlers Verlag, 1958.

————. "Das Tier in der Spanischen Bildsprache," *Hamburger Romanistische Studien,* Reihe B: *Ibero-amerikanische Studien,* XX.

Benvenutto = Benvenutto Murrieta, Pedro M. *El lenguaje peruano.* Vol. I. Lima, 1936.

Besses, Luis. *Diccionario de argot español.* Barcelona: Manuales Gallach, n.d.

BICC = Boletín del Instituto Caro y Cuervo. Bogotá, Colombia, 1945—. *Thesaurus* since 1951.

Boggs, "Términos del lenguaje popular y caló de la capital de Méjico," *Boletín de filología* (Universidad de Chile), VIII (1954–1955), 35–43.

Bonilla Amado, José. *Jerga del hampa.* 2d ed. Lima: Editorial Nuevos Rumbos, 1957.

Bonilla Ruana, J. M. See *Mosaico.*

Brown, Lawrence K. *A Thesaurus of Spanish Idioms and Everyday Language.* New York: Marcel Rodd Co., 1945.

Bulwer, John. *Chirologia, or the Naturall Language of the Hand.* London: Tho. Harper, 1644.

Cadavid, Gonzalo Uribe. *Oyendo conversar al pueblo.* Bogotá, 1953.

Calcaño, Julio. *El castellano en Venezuela.* Caracas, 1897. Reprinted, 1950, in Biblioteca Venezolana de Cultura.

Carrasquilla, Tomás. *Hace tiempos: Memorias de Eloy Gamboa.* 3 vols. Medellín, Colombia: Atlántida, 1935–1936.

Carriegos, Ramón C. *El porvenir del idioma español en la República Argentina.* Buenos Aires: El Imparcial, 1928.

Castellón, Hildebrando A. *Diccionario de nicaraguanismos.* Managua, 1939.

Castro = Castro, Juan Modesto. *Aguas estancadas.* Santiago, Chile: La Bandera, 1939.

Castro, A. = Castro, Américo. *La peculiaridad lingüística rioplatense y su sentido histórico.* Buenos Aires: Losada, 1941.

———. "Unas palabras complementarias (sobre el lenguaje de Buenos Aires)," *Nosotros,* VII (1942), 3–10.

Cerda, Gilberto, Berta Cabaza, and Julieta Farías. *Vocabulario español de Texas.* Austin, 1953. University of Texas Hispanic Studies, Vol. V.

Céspedes, Augusto. *Sangre de mestizos; relatos de la guerra del Chaco.* Santiago, Chile: Nascimento, 1936.

Chabat, Carlos G. *Diccionario de caló: El lenguaje del hampa en México.* Guadalajara, 1956.

Cornejo, Justino. *Fuera del diccionario.* Quito: Ministerio de Gobierno, 1938.

Corominas = Corominas, Juan. *Diccionario crítico etimológico de la lengua castellana.* Madrid: Gredos. Vol. I (1954), A–C; Vol. II (1955), Ch–K; Vol. III (1956), L–Re; Vol. IV (1957), Ri–Z.

———. *Indianoromanica.* Reprinted from *Revista de filología hispánica,* VI (1944), 1–35, 138–175, 209–254.

———. "Rasgos semánticos nacionales," *Anales del Instituto de Lingüística,* I (1941), 1–29. Mendoza: Universidad Nacional de Cuyo.

Corrales, Juan Apapucio (Clemente Palma). *Crónicas político-doméstico-taurinas.* Lima: Compañía de Impresiones y Publicidad, 1938.

Correa, Gustavo. *El espíritu del mal en Guatemala: Ensayo de Semántica cultural.* New Orleans, 1955. Reprinted from Middle American Research Institute, Tulane University, Publication 19, pp. 37–104.

Cuadra, José de la. *Horno.* 2d ed. Buenos Aires: Perseo, 1940.

Cuervo = Cuervo, Rufino José. *Apuntaciones críticas sobre el lenguaje bogotano.* 7th ed. Bogotá: El Gráfico, 1939.

Del Campo, Juan (Juan Manuel Rodríguez). *Aventuras de Usebio Olmos.* 2d ed. Santiago, Chile: Centro, n.d.

Dellepiane, Antonio. *El idioma del delito.* Buenos Aires: A. Moen, 1894.

Dihigo, Juan M. *Léxico cubano,* Vol. I: *Letter* A. Habana: Academia de la Historia de Cuba, 1928. Vol. II: *Letter* B. Habana: Universidad de la Habana, 1946.

Duarte = Ramos y Duarte, Féliz. *Diccionario de mejicanismos* (1895). 2d ed. México: Herrero Hnos., 1898.

Durand, Luis. *Mercedes Urízar.* Santiago, Chile: Nascimento, 1934.

Espinosa, Ciro. *La tragedia del guajiro.* Habana: Carasa y Cía., 1939.

Flachskampf, Ludwig. "Spanische Gebärdensprache," *Romanische Forschungen,* LII (1938), 205–258.

Flórez = Flórez, Luis. *Lengua española.* Bogotá, 1953. Publicaciones del Instituto Caro y Cuervo, series minor, III.

———. "Del castellano en Colombia: El habla del Chocó," *BICC,* VII (1950), 110–116.

Flórez. "El español hablado en Montería y Sincelejo," *BICC,* V (1949), 124–162.

———. *Habla y cultura popular en Antioquia.* Publicaciones del Instituto Caro y Cuervo, XIII. Bogotá, 1957.

Forgione, José D. *Lo que no debe decirse* (1935). 2d ed. Buenos Aires: Kapelusz, n.d.

Fray Mocho = Álvarez, José S. *Cuentos de Fray Mocho* (1906). Buenos Aires: Tor, n.d.

Frenk = Frenk Alatorre, Margit. "Designaciones de rasgos físicos personales en el habla de la ciudad de México," *NRFH,* VII (1953), 134–156.

Friederici, Georg. *Amerikanistisches Wörterbuch.* Hamburg: Cram, De Gruyter & Co., 1947.

Gagini, Carlos. *Diccionario de costarriqueñismos* (1892). 2d ed. San José, Costa Rica: Imprenta Nacional, 1919.

Galeana, Benita. *Benita: autobiografía.* México, 1940.

Gallegos = Gallegos, Rómulo. *Doña Bárbara* (1929). 9th ed. Barcelona: Araluce, 1934.

———. *Pobre negro* (1937). Barcelona: Araluce, 1940.

García de Diego, Vicente. *Lingüística general española.* Madrid: Instituto Miguel Cervantes, 1951.

García Icazbalceta, Joaquín. *See* Icazbalceta.

García Muñoz, Alfonso. *Estampas de mi ciudad, segunda serie.* Quito, 1938.

Garzón, Tobías. *Diccionario argentino.* Barcelona: Borrás y Mestres, 1910.

Gil Gilbert, Enrique. *Nuestro pan.* Guayaquil: Vera & Cía., 1942.

Gillet, Joseph E. *Propalladia and Other Works of Bartolomé de Torres Naharro.* 3 vols. Bryn Mawr, Pa., 1943–1951.

Gobello, José. *Lunfardía: Acotaciones al lenguaje porteño.* Buenos Aires: Argos, 1953.

Gómez Palacio. Martín. *El potro.* México: Ediciones Botas, 1940.

¡González Arrili, Bernardo. *Manganá.* Buenos Aires: Editorial Argentina, 1927.

Granada, Daniel. *Vocabulario rioplatense razonado.* Montevideo, 1890.

Grases = Grases, Pedro. "Locha, nombre de fracción monetaria en Venezuela," *BICC,* V (1949), 112–113.

———. "La idea de *alboroto* en castellano," *BICC,* VI (1950), 384–430.

Guerrero, Leoncio. *Pichamán.* Santiago, Chile: Ediciones Yunque, 1940.

Güiraldes, Ricardo. *Don Segundo Sombra* (1926). (*Obras,* Vol. VI.) Buenos Aires: Espasa-Calpe, 1937.

Guzmán Maturana, Manuel. *Don Pancho Garuya* (1933). 2d ed. Santiago, Chile: Minerva, 1935.

Guzmán Riore, Darío. *Cuentos chapines.* Guatemala: Centro, 1932.

Herrero Mayor, Avelino. *Apuntaciones lexicográficas y gramaticales.* Buenos Aires: Kapelusz y Cía, 1947.

———. *Lengua, diccionario y estilo.* Buenos Aires: Joaquín Gil, 1938.

Hidalgo, Juan. *Romances de germanía* (1609), ed. John M. Hill. Bloomington: Indiana University, 1945.

Hildebrandt, Martha. "El español en Piura," *Letras,* Universidad Nacional de San Marcos, Lima, 2d semester, 1949, pp. 256–272.

Icaza = Icaza, Jorge. *Huasipungo* (1934). 5th ed. Quito: Tipo-lito "Romero," 1937.

————. *Cholos.* Quito: SEA, 1938.

Icazbalceta = García Icazbalceta, Joaquín. *Vocabulario de mexicanismos.* México, 1899.

Inclán, Luis G. *Astucia: El jefe de los hermanos de la hoja* (1865). 2 vols. México: El Imparcial, 1908.

Iribarren, José María. *Vocabulario navarro, seguido de una colección de refranes, adagios, dichos y frases proverbiales.* Pamplona: Institución "Príncipe de Viana," 1952.

Jiménez, R. Emilio. *Del lenguaje dominicano.* Ciudad Trujillo: Montalvo, 1941. Academia Dominicana de la Lengua, Publication No. 3.

Kany, Charles E. See *AmSS* and *AmSSem.*

Kaulfers, W. V. "Curiosities of Colloquial Gesture," *Hispania,* XIV (1931), 249–264.

Kercheville, F. M. "A Preliminary Glossary of New Mexican Spanish," *University of New Mexico Bulletin,* V, No. 3 (1934), 1–69.

Kiddle, Lawrence B. "Indice de americanismos comentados por el Doctor Rudolfo Lenz en su obra *La oración y sus partes,*" Hispania, XXV (1942), 333–342.

————. *"Turkey* in New Mexican Spanish," *Romance Philology,* V (1951–1952), 190–197.

Kröll = Kröll, Heinz. "Designações portuguesas para embriaguez," *Revista portuguesa de filología,* V (1952), VI (1953–1955).

————. "Termes désignant les seins de la femme en portugais," *Orbis* (Louvain), II (1953), 19–32.

Krüger, Fritz. "Etimologías hispánicas," *Anales del Instituto de Lingüística* (Universidad Nacional de Cuyo, Mendoza, Arg.), IV (1950), 82–113.

Lafone Quevedo, Samuel A. *Tesoro de catamarqueñismos.* 3d ed. Buenos Aires: Coni, 1927.

Latorre, Mariano. *Hombres y zorros.* Santiago: Ercilla, 1937.

Lenz = Lenz, Rodolfo. *Diccionario etimolójico de las voces chilenas derivadas de lenguas indíjenas americanas.* Santiago, Chile: Cervantes, 1904–1910.

————. *La oración y sus partes.* 3d ed. Madrid, 1935. See Kiddle, L. B.

León, Aurelio de. *Barbarismos communes en México.* Part I. México: Mundial, 1936. Part II. México: Porrúa, 1937.

Lira, Jorge A. *Diccionario kkechuwa-español.* Tucumán: Universidad Nacional, 1944.

Lizondo Borda, Manuel. *Voces tucumanas derivadas del quichua.* Tucumán: Universidad de Tucumán, 1927.

Llorante Maldonado de Guevara, Antonio. *Estudio sobre el habla de la Rivera.* Salamanca. Colegio Trilingüe de la Universidad, 1947.

Lockward, Yoryi. *Acúcheme uté: Cuentos típicos dominicanos.* Puerto Plata, R.D., 1941.

López y Fuentes, Gregorio. *Campamento* (1931). 2d ed. México: Ediciones Botas, 1938.

Lynch, Benito. *El romance de un gaucho* (1930). Buenos Aires: Anaconda, 1933.

Lyra, Carmen (María Isabel Carvajal). *Los cuentos de mi tía Panchita.* San José, Costa Rica: Soley & Valverde, 1936.

Madueño, Raúl R. *Ampliación y corrección de un lexicón.* Buenos Aires: Optimus, 1958.

————. *Léxico de la borrachera.* Buenos Aires: Optimus, 1953.

————. *Más voces para un léxico.* Buenos Aires: Optimus, 1955.

Malaret = Malaret, Augusto. *Diccionario de americanismos.* 3d ed. Buenos Aires: Emecé, 1946.

————. *Los americanismos en la copla popular y en el lenguaje culto.* New York: S. F. Vanni, 1947.

————. "Los americanismos en el lenguaje literario," *Boletín de filología* (Universidad de Chile), VII (1952–1953), 1–113.

————. "Lexicón de fauna y flora," *BICC* (continuous).

————. *Semántica americana.* Cataña, Puerto Rico, 1943.

————. *Vocabulario de Puerto Rico.* San Juan, 1937.

Malbrán A., Pedro J. *Los dos quesos de Balta Marín.* Santiago, Chile: Nascimento, 1920.

Malkiel, Yakov. "Studies in Spanish and Portuguese Animal Names," Part I, *Hispanic Review,* XXIV (1956), 115–143. Part II, *ibid.,* pp. 207–231.

Martín Fierro. See Tiscornia.

Martínez, J. G. Review of Tobón Betancourt's *Colombianismos* (1953), in *Archivos Venezolanos de Folklore* (Caracas: Universidad Central), Año II–III, Vol. II, No. 3 (1953–1954), 209–218.

Mateus, Alejandro. *Riqueza de la lengua castellana y provincialismos ecuatorianos* (1918). 2d ed. Quito: Ecuatoriana, 1933.

Medina = Medina, José Toribio. *Chilenismos: Apuntes lexicográficos.* Santiago: Universo, 1928.

————. *Voces chilenas de los reinos animal y vegetal.* Santiago: Imprenta Universitaria, 1917.

Membreño, Alberto. *Hondureñismos* (1895). 3d ed. México, 1912.

Mendoza, Angélica. *Cárcel de mujeres.* Buenos Aires: Claridad, n.d.

Miragaya, Eduardo. *Diccionario de correcciones.* Buenos Aires: Ebro, 1945.

Montoya, Wenceslao. "Colombianismos," *Universidad de Antioquia,* Nos. 84–90 (1947–1949). Medellín, Colombia.

Morínigo, Marcos A. "La formación léxica regional hispanoamericana," *NRFH,* VII (1953), 234–241.

Mosaico = Bonilla Ruano, José María. *Mosaico de voces y locuciones viciosas.* Guatemala, 1939.

Navarro [Tomás], Tomás. *El español en Puerto Rico.* Río Piedras: Universidad de Puerto Rico, 1948.

NRFH. Nueva revista de filología hispánica. México, 1947—.

Nyrop, Kristoffer. *Grammaire historique de la langue française.* 6 vols. Copenhagen, 1913. Vol. IV.

Obando, Luis de. *Corrección del lenguaje.* Bogotá: Biblioteca Aldeana de Colombia, 1938.

Oroz = Oroz, Rudolfo. *El uso metafórico de nombres de animales en el lenguaje familiar y vulgar chileno.* Santiago: Imprenta Universitaria, 1932.

———. "Metáforas relativas a las partes del cuerpo humano en la lengua popular chilena," *BICC,* V (1949), 85–100.

Ortiz = Ortiz Fernández, Fernando. *Glosario de afronegrismos.* Habana: "El Siglo XX," 1924.

Ortiz, Adalberto. *Juyungo.* Buenos Aires: Americalee, 1943.

Palma, Clemente. *See* Corrales.

Patín = Patín Maceo, Manuel A. *Dominicanismos.* 2d ed. Ciudad Trujillo: Librería Dominicana, 1947.

———. "Notas gramaticales," *Revista de educación* (Ciudad Trujillo), XVII, Nos. 82–84 (1946).

Plath, Oreste. *Grafismo animalista en el hablar del pueblo chileno.* Santiago, Chile: Diario "La Tarde," 1941.

Preis, Paul. *Die Animalisierung von Gegenständen in den Metaphern der spanischen Sprache.* Tübingen, 1932.

Quevedo y Zubieta = Quevedo y Zubieta, Salvador. *México marimacho.* México: Ediciones Botas, 1933.

———. *La camada.* México, 1912.

Quintana, Carlos Alberto. *Malagüero.* Quezaltenango, Guatemala, 1937.

Rabanales = Rabanales Ortiz, Ambrosio. "Uso tropológico, en el lenguaje chileno, de nombres del reino vegetal," *Boletín de filología,* V (1947–1949), 137–243. Santiago, Chile, 1950.

———. "Recursos lingüísticos, en el español de Chile, de expresión de la afectividad," *Boletín de filología,* X (1958), 205–302.

Ramos y Duarte, Féliz. *See* Duarte.

Rendón, Francisco de P. *Cuentos y novelas.* Ed. Benigno A. Gutiérrez. Medellín, Colombia: Bedout, 1954.

Restrepo = Restrepo, Roberto. *Apuntaciones idiomáticas y correcciones de lenguaje.* Bogotá: Cromos, 1943.

Restrepo, P. Félix. *Diseño de semántica general: El alma de las palabras.* 3d ed. Bogotá: Librería Voluntad, 1946.

Revollo, Pedro María. *Costeñismos colombianos.* Barranquilla: Mejoras, 1942.

Reyles, Carlos. *El gaucho Florido.* Buenos Aires: Espasa-Calpe, 1939.

RFE = *Revista de filología española.* Madrid, 1914—.

Riegler, Richard. "Das Tier im Spiegel der Sprache," *Neusprachliche Abhandlungen,* ed. Klöpper-Rostock, Heft 15–16. Dresden and Leipsig, 1907.

Rivas Larrauri, Carlos. *Del arrabal* (1931). México: Cicerón, 1937.

Rivera, L. M. *Origen y significación de algunas frases.* Guadalajara, 1922.

Robelo, Cecilio A. *Diccionario de aztequismos.* México: Fuente Cultural, 1940.

Rod, Elgin. *El hampa.* México: Elgin Book, 1955.

Rodríguez Herrera, Esteban. "El plebeyismo en Cuba," *Boletín de filología* (Universidad de Chile), VIII (1954–1955), 407–437.

Rojas Gallardo, Luis. *Aventuras de Tristán Machuca.* 2d serie. Santiago, Chile: Cultura, 1935.

Román, Manuel Antonio. *Diccionario de chilenismos y de otras voces y locuciones viciosas.* 5 vols. Santiago: Imprenta de San José, 1901–1918.

Romanángel (Joaquín Moscoso G.). *Fidel Cornejo y Cía.* Santiago, Chile: Cultura, 1935.

Romera-Navarro, Miguel. *Registro de lexicografía hispánica.* Madrid: Instituto "Miguel de Cervantes," 1951. Anejo 54.

Rosenblat = Rosenblat, Ángel. *Buenas y malas palabras en el castellano de Venezuela.* Caracas and Madrid: EDIME, 1956.

————. *Lengua y cultura de Venezuela.* Caracas: Instituto de Filología "Andrés Bello," 1955.

————. "Notas de morfología dialectal," *BDH,* II (1946), 105–316.

Rubio, Darío. *Refranes, proverbios y dichos y discharachos mexicanos* (1937). 2d ed. 2 vols. México: A. P. Márquez, 1940.

Salesiano = *Vocabulario de palabras-modismos y refranes ticos por un salesiano.* Cartago, Costa Rica, 1938.

Sánchez Arévalo, Francisco. "Notas sobre el lenguaje de Río de Oro," *BICC,* VI (1950), 214–252.

Sandoval, Lisandro. *Semántica guatemalense o Diccionario de guatemaltequismos.* 2 vols. Guatemala, 1941–1942.

Santamaría = Santamaría, Francisco J. *Diccionario general de americanismos.* 3 vols. México: Pedro Robredo, 1942.

————. *Diccionario de mejicanismos.* Méjico: Porrúa, 1959.

Saubidet, Tito. *Vocabulario y refranero criollo.* Buenos Aires: Guillermo Kraft, 1943. 3d ed., 1948.

Schallman, Lázaro. *Coloquios sobre el lenguaje argentino.* Buenos Aires: El Ateneo, 1946.

Selva = Selva, Juan B. *Crecimiento del habla.* Buenos Aires: A. García Santos, 1925.

————. *Guía del buen decir.* Buenos Aires: El Ateneo, 1944.

————. "Modismos argentinos," *BAAL,* XVII (1948).

Serrano García, Pedro. *Caló delincuente.* 3d ed. Madrid: La Xilográfica, n.d.

Solá, José Vicente. *Diccionario de regionalismos de Salta.* Buenos Aires: S. de Amorrortu e hijos, 1947.

Sologuren, Javier. "Fórmulas de tratamiento en el Perú," *NRFH,* VIII (1954), 241–267.

Speratti Piñero, Emma Susana. *La elaboración artística en Tirano Banderas.* México: El Colegio de México, 1957.

Spitzer, Leo. "¡Polaina!," *Zeitscrift für romanische Philologie,* XLIV (1924), 576–589.

Spitzer, Leo, and Ernst Gamillscheg. "Beiträge zur romanischen Wortbildungslehre," *Biblioteca dell' Archivum romanum,* ser. 2, Vol. II. Genève: L. S. Olschki, 1921.

Stern, Gustaf. *Meaning and Change of Meaning with Special Reference to the English Language.* Göteborg, 1931. Göteborgs Högskolas Årsskrift, XXXVIII (1932), No. 1.

Suárez = Suárez, Victor Manuel. *El español que se habla en Yucatán.* Mérida: Díaz Massa, 1945.

Suárez, Constantino. *Vocabulario cubano.* Habana: R. Veloso, 1921.

Sundheim, Adolfo. *Vocabulario costeño o lexicografía de la región septentrional de la república de Colombia.* Paris: Librería Cervantes, 1922.

Taracena, Alfonso. *Los abrasados.* México: Ediciones Botas, 1937.

Tascón, Leonardo. *Diccionario de provincialismos y barbarismos del Valle del Cauca.* Bogotá: Santafé, 1935.

Thesaurus. See *BICC.*

Tiscornia, I = Tiscornia, Eleuterio F. *"Martín Fierro" comentado y anotado. Texto, notas y vocabulario.* Buenos Aires, 1925. Tiscornia, II = *La lengua de "Martín Fierro,"* in *BDH,* Vol. III (1930).

Tobón Betancourt, P. Julio. *Colombianismos y otras voces de uso general.* 2d ed. Bogotá: Imprenta Nacional, 1953.

Toro y Gisbert, Miguel de. *Americanismos.* París: Sociedad de Ediciones Literarios y Artísticos [1912].

Torres Arjona, Rafael. *Correntada.* San Salvador: Arce, 1934–1935.

Toscano Mateus, Humberto. *El español en el Ecuador.* Madrid, 1953. Anejo 61.

Tovar = Tovar y R[amírez], Enrique D. "Identidades y diferencias en el habla de peruanos y portorriqueños," *Boletín de la Academia Chilena,* VIII (1943), 29–157.

———. "Hacia el gran diccionario de la lengua española," *BAAL,* Vols. IX (1941) and X (1942).

———. "La labor de un quicheatra centroamericano," *BAAL,* XV (1946), 57–153.

Ugarte, Miguel Ángel. *Arequipeñismos.* Arequipa, Peru, 1942.

Uribe Uribe, Rafael. *Diccionario abreviado de galicismos, provincialismos y correcciones del lenguaje.* Medellín, Colombia, 1887.

Valle = Valle, Alfonso. *Diccionario del habla nicaragüense.* Managua, La Nueva Prensa, 1948.

Vargas Ugarte, Rubén. *Glosario de peruanismos.* Lima, Peru: San Marcos, 1953.

Velasco Valdés, Miguel. *Vocabulario popular mexicano.* México: Olimpo, 1957.

Vicuña Cifuentes, Julio. *Coa.* Santiago, Chile: Imprenta Universitaria, 1910.

Vidal = Vidal de Battini, Berta Elena. *El habla rural de San Luis.* Part I, in *BDH,* Vol. VII (1949).

————. "El léxico de los yerbateros," *NRFH,* VII (1953), 190–208.

————. "Voces marinas en el habla rural de San Luis," *Filología* (Buenos Aires), I (1949), 105–150.

Wagner = Wagner, Max Leopold. "Über den verblümten Ausdruck im Spanischen," *Zeitschrift für romanische Philologie,* XLIX (1929), 1–26.

————. "Apuntaciones sobre el caló bogotano," *BICC,* VI (1950), 181–213.

————. "Ein mexikanish-amerikanischer Argot: Das Pachuco," *Romanistisches Jahrbuch,* VI (1953–1954), 237–266.

————. "Mexikanisches Rotwelsch," *Zeitschrift für romanische Philologie,* XXXIX (1918), 513–550.

Wartburg, Walter von. *Problemas y métodos de la lingüística.* Tr. by Dámaso Alonso and Emilio Lorenzo. Madrid: *RFE,* 1951.

Yrarrázaval Larrain, José Miguel. *Chilenismos.* Santiago, Chile, 1945.